FREE EXPRESSION AND DEMOCRACY

Free Expression and Democracy takes on the assumption that limits on free expression will lead to authoritarianism or at least a weakening of democracy. That hypothesis is tested by an examination of issues involving expression and their treatment in countries included on *The Economist*'s list of fully functioning democracies. Generally speaking, other countries allow prohibitions on hate speech, limits on third-party spending on elections, and the protection of children from media influences seen as harmful. Many ban Holocaust denial and the desecration of national symbols. Yet, these other countries all remain democratic and most of those considered rank more highly than the United States on the democracy index. The book argues that while there may be other cultural values that call for more expansive protection of expression, that protection need not reach the level present in the United States in order to protect the democratic nature of a country.

Kevin W. Saunders holds his Ph.D. from the University of Miami and J.D. from the University of Michigan. He clerked at the US Court of Appeals for the DC Circuit for Judge Kenneth Starr. He taught at the Universities of Arkansas and Oklahoma, and as visiting James Madison Chair at Drake University, before moving to Michigan State University, where he holds the Charles Clarke Chair in Constitutional Law. He is the author of three earlier books: *Violence as Obscenity* (1996), *Saving Our Children from the First Amendment* (2006), and *Degradation: What the History of Obscenity Tells Us about Hate Speech* (2011).

Free Expression and Democracy

A COMPARATIVE ANALYSIS

KEVIN W. SAUNDERS
Michigan State University

CAMBRIDGE
UNIVERSITY PRESS

CAMBRIDGE
UNIVERSITY PRESS

University Printing House, Cambridge CB2 8BS, United Kingdom

One Liberty Plaza, 20th Floor, New York, NY 10006, USA

477 Williamstown Road, Port Melbourne, VIC 3207, Australia

4843/24, 2nd Floor, Ansari Road, Daryaganj, Delhi - 110002, India

79 Anson Road, #06-04/06, Singapore 079906

Cambridge University Press is part of the University of Cambridge.

It furthers the University's mission by disseminating knowledge in the pursuit of education, learning, and research at the highest international levels of excellence.

www.cambridge.org
Information on this title: www.cambridge.org/9781107171978

10.1017/9781316771129

First published 2017

Printed in the United States of America by Sheridan Books, Inc.

A catalogue record for this publication is available from the British Library.

ISBN 978-1-107-17197-8 Hardback
ISBN 978-1-316-62308-4 Paperback

To my wife, Mary E. Scott, and the next generation, our daughter, Molly J. Saunders-Scott, and son-in-law, David M.K. Knapp.

Contents

Acknowledgments

There are a number of professional colleagues who are due thanks for a variety of contributions, from providing citations to case law, to helping me understand cases not available in English or even cases that are available in English, to reading and commenting on sections of the manuscript. They include Eric Barendt, University College London; Bjørnar Borvik, University of Bergen; Luis Grau, Universidad Carlos III de Madrid; Koji Higashikawa, University of Kanazawa; and Russell Weaver, University of Louisville. More generally, those who attended several of the annual sessions of the Free Expression Discussion Forum provided valuable feedback to my contributions to the forum, and I learned a great deal from their contributions. Three unnamed referees for Cambridge University Press also made valuable suggestions.

I have also learned from my students in courses on comparative free expression. Seeing and understanding the differing reactions on issues of free speech provided insights on cultural and political differences. In addition to my students at Michigan State University, I would like to thank participating students from courses at the University of Białystok in Poland, Vytautas Magnus University in Lithuania, and Yeditepe University in Turkey, and the faculties of those universities for the opportunities to teach there.

Valuable help on research and cite checking was provided by the librarians and student assistants at Michigan State University's John F. Schaefer Law Library. Thanks also to those at Cambridge University Press involved in the production of the volume. The financial support of the Michigan State University College of Law, in the form of summer research grants and a sabbatical, was also appreciated.

Lastly, some of the material covered here received earlier treatments in other works. The material in Chapter 12 on children and expression follows themes similar to those originally expressed in Kevin W. Saunders, *A Comparative Look at Children and Free Expression*, 22 TRANSNAT'L L. &

CONTEMP. PROB. 455 (2013). Chapter 13's discussion on the tension between free expression and the rights of defendants in criminal trials was also addressed in Kevin W. Saunders, A *Comparative View of Media Coverage of Criminal Trials* in COMPARATIVE PERSPECTIVES ON THE FUNDAMENTAL FREEDOM EXPRESSION 347 (András Koltay, ed. 2015).

1

The Protection of Free Expression in a Democracy

Any advocate for democracy must also be an advocate for free expression; the latter is essential to the former. But the scope of that necessary right of free expression may not be clear. The view in the United States seems to be that any restrictions on expression, perhaps except those that are historically justified, will lead to totalitarianism or at least a non-democratic form of government. This leads to protection for forms of speech that most of the rest of the world sees as undeserving of protection and perhaps even as destructive.[1]

This book will examine a number of topics in free expression in a number of democratic countries. Seeing how these issues are treated differently from country to country should call into question the belief that democracies must not accept limitations on expression or that, when there is an exception or limitation, it can have only one form. There are clear differences in expression law, and the existence of those differences should open to discussion the dimensions of the freedoms of speech and the press.

THE IMPORTANCE OF FREE EXPRESSION TO DEMOCRACY

It should be clear why free expression is essential to democracy. Without the ability to receive the political views of others, the citizen is unable to come to an informed view as to the direction in which government should proceed. He or she would be simply incapable of casting an intelligent vote. One who

[1] As an example, most countries, even democratic countries, place limits on hate speech; the United States refuses to do so. *See* Chapter 4 for a discussion of hate speech. This has led to the migration of Internet hate sites from those other countries to the United States. As a result, to the consternation of other democracies, the United States is the source of much of the world's hate speech. *See* Russell Working, *Illegal Abroad, Hate Websites Thrive Here: 1st Amendment Lets Fringe Groups Use U.S. Sites to Spread Their Message Around the World*, Chi. Trib., Nov. 13, 2007 at A1, 2007 WLNR 22413864.

already has a firm political position is also, without the free expression to convey that position, unable to convince others to follow the path advocated.

It was the role of speech in self-government that the philosopher Alexander Meiklejohn argued was behind the provision in the First Amendment to the Constitution of the United States that "Congress shall make no law ... abridging the freedom of speech, or of the press ..." In his book *Free Speech and Its Relation to Self-Government*, he wrote:

> It is that mutilation of the thinking process of the community against which the First Amendment to the Constitution is directed. The principle of freedom of speech springs from the necessities of the program of self-government. It is not a Law of Nature or of Reason in the abstract. It is a deduction from the basic American agreement that public issues shall be decided by universal suffrage.[2]

Meiklejohn's view of self-government, with the New England town meeting as its model, assumed far greater participation than is currently the practice in American society. But there are less participatory views of the First Amendment that still place public participation in the political process at its core. Professor Vincent Blasi found central the role that "free speech, a free press, and free assembly can serve in checking the abuse of power by public officials."[3] While perhaps less regular in the role it plays, it is still clear that this "checking value" is important because of its furtherance of the ability of the governed to impact government. It, too, in that sense, finds its justification in self-government.

While the role of free expression in self-government is clear, it is perhaps less clear just how much free expression is required. It would seem that, to the degree that the freedom of expression is justified by democracy and self-government, what must be protected is political speech. Speech that is other than political might be regulated without being destructive of democracy.

OTHER JUSTIFICATIONS FOR FREE EXPRESSION AND THE CENTRALITY OF POLITICAL SPEECH

There are other values that are arguably furthered by free expression, and those values should be examined. If, for example, another value turned out to be more important than democracy, then the fact that democracies differed in

[2] Alexander Meiklejohn, Free Speech and Its Relation to Self-Government 25 (1948).

[3] Vincent Blasi, The *Checking Value in First Amendment Theory*, 2 Amer. Bar Found. Res. J. 521, 527 (1977).

the treatment of expression might be unimportant. The real dichotomy would not be between democracies and non-democracies but between countries that recognize and those that fail to recognize the more basic value. But it may be difficult to arrive at another value more basic than democracy.

Rather than finding a value more basic than, or more important than, democracy, a value might be identified that stands alongside democracy in mandating the freedom of expression. If so, then there are reasons to criticize countries that restrict speech important to that value. It is still, however, important to recognize that restrictions impacting another value do not destroy the democratic nature of a country. And, as long as the country remains democratic, the people have the opportunity to change the law, and the protection of political speech will allow advocacy in the direction that coequal value indicates.

Turning to potential other values underlying free expression, the best source is the work of Professor Thomas Emerson.[4] Among the values he suggested was "participation in decision-making." This would clearly encompass the self-government that justifies the protection of political speech, but he argued that it encompasses more. It includes the right of the individual to participate in building the entire culture and reaches the right to express oneself with regard to religion, literature, the arts, and science.

This may not be that great a departure from the political justification. The structure of culture is, to a large degree, a political determination. If Emerson is asking only for the protection of speech relating to social and cultural structure, it is relatively easy to accept the position. If, instead, he is arguing that all expression is protected because expression is part of the culture, that may be open to debate. All acts, speech or otherwise, are part of the culture, so why is it only expression that merits protection? In any case, the more general protection of expression would seem better justified, if at all, by the other values Emerson presents.

A second justification, in fact the first Emerson presents, is "individual self-fulfillment." He posits that the purpose of society is to promote individual welfare which, in conjunction with the principle of equality, leads to the right to express beliefs and opinions. Further, "the proper end of man is the realization of his character and potentialities as a human being ... [and] every man – in the development of his own personality – has the right to form his own beliefs and opinions ... [and] the right to express these beliefs and opinions."[5]

4 Thomas I. Emerson, *Toward a General Theory of the First Amendment*, 72 YALE L.J. 877 (1963).

5 *Id.* at 879.

Again, to the degree that this right extends to political beliefs and opinions, or even to beliefs and opinions about society and social change, this value does not lead to much expansion in the scope of free expression. If, however, this right extends further, and includes the right to view or say anything, because it is the expression of character, then it is an extension.

Whether or not Emerson intended to rely on the general value of autonomy, the right to be whomever we want as manifested by what we say or what media we consume, this position has had a more recent champion in Professor Edwin Baker. Professor Baker saw individual self-fulfillment as one of the fundamental purposes, alongside self-government, behind the United States' First Amendment.[6] Professor Martin Redish went even further, arguing that self-realization or self-fulfillment is the only real value served by free expression in that the value of democracy was, itself, based in the value of self-realization.[7]

The problem with any autonomy-based argument for free expression is distinguishing expression from other acts for which autonomy-based protection might be argued. Who we are is determined not only by what we say or read but by what we do. If expression is to be protected because of autonomy, why not protect these acts as well? A response might be that autonomy justifies the acts of an individual, only when those acts do no harm to others, or at least to no others who are not consenting adults, and that expression causes no real harm to others.

The difficulty with this position is in the assumption that expression causes no harm. Members of minorities at least believe, and there would appear to be scientific evidence of dire consequences,[8] that they are harmed by racist and sexist speech. Professor Charles Lawrence says that "Psychic injury is no less an injury than being struck in the face, and it is often far more severe."[9] He also says that racist speech "produce[s] physical symptoms that temporarily disable the victim, and the perpetrators often use these words with the intention of producing this effect."[10] Professors Richard Delgado and Jean Stefancic add: "Hate speech is not merely unpleasant or offensive. It may leave physical impacts on those it visits . . . The immediate, short-term harms of hate speech include rapid breathing, headaches, raised blood pressure, dizziness,

6 *See* C. Edwin Baker, Human Liberty and Freedom of Speech 54 (1989).

7 *See* Martin H. Redish, *The Value of Free Speech*, 130 U. Pa. L. Rev. 591 (1982).

8 *See* Brian Mullen & Joshua M. Smyth, *Immigrant Suicide Rates as a Function of Ethnophaulisms: Hate Speech Predicts Death*, 66 Psychosomatic Medicine 343, 346 (2004).

9 Charles R. Lawrence III, *If He Hollers Let Him Go: Regulating Racist Speech on Campus*, 1990 Duke L.J. 431, 462.

10 *Id.* at 452–53.

rapid pulse rate, drug-taking, risk-taking behavior, and even suicide."[11] Those who are the targets of hate speech certainly see harm growing out of expression.

The question then becomes how this debate should be resolved. Perhaps the best answer is through the democratic process. If those who believe that expression can cause harm convince the polity, then expression such as hate speech might be banned, although clearly there will be line-drawing problems. Alternatively, if those who believe expression causes no harm convince others, then the democratic process is likely to lead to no restrictions on expression. As long as the debate on this issue is open, and the protection of political speech justified by participation in self-government protects that debate, then a societal answer can be reached.

Emerson also offers, as a justification for free expression, the attainment of truth. He says that free expression is the best way to advance knowledge and discover truth. This position is basically a rephrasing of that put forward by John Stuart Mill in *On Liberty*.[12] Emerson says that "discussion must be kept open no matter how certainly true an accepted opinion may seem to be . . . [, and] regardless of how false or pernicious the new opinion appears to be."[13] Even false opinions have value in leading to a deeper understanding. This approach entered the United States Supreme Court's jurisprudence in Justice Holmes' appeal to the "marketplace of ideas" in *Abrams v. United States*, where he said:

> [W]hen men have realized that time has upset many a fighting faith, they may come to believe even more than they believe the very foundations of their own conduct that the ultimate good desired is better reached by free trade in ideas – that the best test of truth is the power of the thought to get itself accepted in the competition of the market . . .[14]

This "marketplace of ideas" metaphor for free speech is powerful and extends beyond the speech that would be protected under the self-governance rationale. When the opinions protected under the marketplace rationale have

[11] Richard Delgado & Jean Stefancic, Understanding Words That Wound 13 (2004).

[12] *See generally* John Stuart Mill, On Liberty (1859). In Mill's view of the marketplace of ideas, expression, either true or false or a mix of the two, should be protected. If the position asserted is true, the application of the search-for-the-truth rationale is obvious. When the asserted position is false, it still has value; without it the received opinion would simply have the status of dogma, as an unexamined position. Where the received view is partially true and partially false, contrasting views provide the thesis/antithesis interaction that leads to the synthesis of a better developed view.

[13] Emerson, *supra* note 4, at 881–82.

[14] Abrams v. United States, 250 U.S. 616, 630 (1919)(Holmes, J., dissenting).

to do with political or social issues, the extension of the two rationales is identical. But the marketplace approach can apply to truth in any area. It is important to note, however, that it may be seen as applying only to opinion, rather than fact, a position that will be discussed later in the context of Holocaust denial.

As long as there is an open marketplace for political opinion, a democracy can remain vibrant. If that is the limit of the marketplace, a society may suffer in other ways. In a democracy, it would seem likely that the free market in ideas would be fairly broad. But as the Holocaust denial cases demonstrate,[15] there may be limits placed on some expression, without leading the country to devolve into totalitarianism.

Lastly, Emerson argues that freedom of expression fosters a balance between stability and change. If discussion is suppressed, force will be substituted for logic. "[S]uppression of expression conceals the real problems confronting a society and diverts public attention from the critical issues. It . . . hides the extent of opposition and hardens the position of all sides, . . . drives opposition underground . . . [and] makes resort to force more likely."[16]

This argument, however, speaks most strongly to the suppression of political speech. If the expression of political dissent through speech or press is not allowed, that may well lead to the violent expression of that dissent. However, as long as political speech is free, limits on other forms of expression seem less likely to lead to the same result. If a society suppresses obscene material, those who disagree may devote their energies to changing the law.

The role of expression in self-government, then, appears to be the central value justifying the freedoms of speech and of the press. Justice Douglas, in a dissent in an obscenity case, did say "There are regimes in the world where ideas 'offensive' to the majority (or at least to those who control the majority) are suppressed. There life proceeds at a monotonous pace. Most of us would find that world offensive."[17] But if political expression remains free, he and others who agree with him may work to make society fit their model.

THE SOURCES OF PROTECTION AFFORDED EXPRESSION IN DEMOCRACIES

All democracies do protect expression, but they vary not only in what is protected but also in where the basis for the protection is found. On one end of the spectrum is the explicit, and absolute sounding, protection found in

[15] *See* Chapter 5. [16] Emerson, *supra* note 4, at 884.

[17] Paris Adult Theatre I v. Slaton, 413 U.S. 49, 71 (1973)(Douglas, J., dissenting).

the First Amendment to the Constitution of the United States. There are also textual protections in other countries that are less absolute in their terms and even invite the balancing of free expression against other values. There are, finally, democracies with no explicit constitutional protection for free expression where at least political expression has still found protection.

The First Amendment to the United States Constitution

The language of the First Amendment seems absolute in its tone: "Congress shall make no law respecting an establishment of religion, or prohibiting the free exercise thereof; or abridging the freedom of speech, or of the press; or the right of the people peaceably to assemble, and to petition the Government for a redress of grievances." While the language places a disability on Congress, the amendment also applies to the other branches of the federal government. Further, the First Amendment has been applied to the states and local governments as incorporated in the Due Process Clause of the Fourteenth Amendment.

Despite the strong language, the First Amendment has never been held to protect all expression. The Supreme Court has long recognized exceptions for obscene expression[18] and fighting words.[19] While libel has been said to be unprotected, the Court has adopted rules regarding plaintiffs who are public officials or public figures; defendants are only liable if they knew the statements they made were false or were reckless with regard to falsity.[20]

Even expression that does not fit within a recognized exception may be restricted, under certain circumstances. The Court has held that speech that raises a "clear and present danger" of inciting imminent unlawful acts, and was intended to do so, may be the basis for prosecution.[21] This is so, even if there is a political dimension to the speech. The same is true of threats and intimidation.[22] In addition to the "clear and present danger" test, a restriction on expression might be justified by, as may the infringement of any United

[18] *See* Roth v. United States, 354 U.S. 476 (1957). The Court later developed the present test for obscenity in Miller v. California, 413 U.S. 15 (1973), with a slight modification in Pope v. Illinois, 481 U.S. 497 (1987). Obscenity is discussed in Chapter 11.

[19] *See* Chaplinsky v. New Hampshire, 315 U.S. 568 (1942).

[20] *See* New York Times Co. v. Sullivan, 376 U.S. 254 (1964)(public officials); Curtis Publishing Co. v. Butts, 388 U.S. 130 (1967)(public figures). Libel is discussed in Chapter 9.

[21] *See* Brandenburg v. Ohio, 395 U.S. 444 (1969). Criminal advocacy is discussed in Chapter 3.

[22] *See* Virginia v. Black, 538 U.S. 343 (2003)(allowing prosecution for burning a cross with the intent to intimidate but seeing such activity as protected political speech, when such intent is lacking). The case is discussed in Chapter 4 on hate speech.

States constitutional right, the government meeting strict scrutiny. It must show that the restriction is necessary to a compelling governmental interest.

Despite existing exceptions and the possibility of meeting strict scrutiny, adding new areas of expression to those that may be limited seems unlikely. The existence of exceptions at least seems limited to those that are historically recognized. Relatively recently, the Supreme Court refused to recognize a new exception for depictions of animal cruelty.[23] Still more recently, the Court held unconstitutional a federal statute criminalizing knowingly false claims to have been awarded certain military medals, despite arguments that there should be an exception for such knowingly false speech.[24] Its one acceptance of a new exception has addressed child pornography.[25]

The Court has also been unwilling to accept attempts to justify limitations based on strict scrutiny. In the military medals case, the Court rejected arguments that the law was necessary to compelling military interests in troop morale.[26] The Court has also rejected evidence demonstrating negative impacts of violent video games on children in striking down a statute limiting the sale and rental of such games to minors.[27]

In addition to exceptions to First Amendment protection and the possibility of meeting strict scrutiny, the Supreme Court has set out situations in which a test that is more lenient than strict scrutiny may apply. One such situation depends on the content of the expression. Commercial speech, expression that offers to provide goods or services for a price, is protected by what could be characterized as an intermediate scrutiny test. If commercial speech is neither false nor misleading, it enjoys some protection, but a weaker protection. To justify a restriction, the *Central Hudson* test requires that there be a substantial government interest, the regulation must directly advance the interest, and it may not be more extensive than necessary to promote the interest.[28] While that last clause may sound like strict scrutiny, the Court has made it clear that what is required is not the least restrictive means but a reasonable fit that is narrowly tailored to the result.[29]

[23] *See* United States v. Stevens, 559 U.S. 460 (2010).

[24] *See* United States v. Alvarez, 132 S.Ct. 2537 (2012).

[25] *See* New York v. Ferber, 458 U.S. 747 (1982). [26] Alvarez, 132 S.Ct. at 2548–50

[27] *See* Brown v. Entertainment Merchants Ass'n, 131 S.Ct. 2729 (2011). The issue of children and the media will be discussed in Chapter 12.

[28] *See* Central Hudson Gas & Elec. Corp. v. Public Serv. Comm'n, 447 U.S. 557 (1980). There are those on the Court who would provide stronger protection to commercial speech by requiring strict scrutiny. *See, e.g.*, the opinions of Justice Kennedy, joined by Justice Scalia, and Justice Thomas in Lorillard Tobacco Co. v. Reilly, 533 U.S. 525 (2001). Commercial speech is discussed in Chapter 2.

[29] *See, e.g.*, Lorillard Tobacco Co. v. Reilly, 533 U.S. 525, 556 (2001).

The First Amendment has also been seen as requiring a similar, intermediate scrutiny, test when a limit is placed on conduct that is intended to communicate. While communicative, and thus seemingly deserving of protection, the behavior may be of a variety the government may legitimately limit. The *O'Brien* test distinguishes between government regulation aimed at the message conveyed by the conduct and regulation motivated only by concerns over the conduct itself. If the regulation is aimed at message, strict scrutiny applies. If the interest is, instead, in the conduct, the limitations are justified if there is an important or substantial governmental interest and the restriction is no greater than is essential to further that interest, effectively also a narrow tailoring requirement.[30]

An intermediate scrutiny test also applies when a regulation is aimed not at a message but at the method of communication of the message. For example, regulation against amplified speech in a residential neighborhood or the posting of material on telephone poles may be justified, if the regulation is not based on content, is narrowly tailored to a significant governmental interest and leaves open ample alternative channels of communication.[31]

The United States, even if not protecting all expression and applying intermediate scrutiny in some cases, comes closer than other countries to absolute protection. While the constitutional protections of many countries invite the balancing of interests, the Supreme Court has generally refused to engage in any such balancing in its First Amendment cases. As a result, the United States stands apart from much of the rest of the democratic world in such areas as the protection of hate speech[32] and the access children are allowed to have to media that may do them harm.[33] The United States also has a more complex, categorical scheme for the protection of free expression. The use of categories, and the tests that apply to the category, rather than balancing, serves to limit judicial discretion, but it also leads to more theoretical complexity.[34]

[30] *See* United States v. O'Brien, 391 U.S. 367 (1968). Communicative conduct is discussed in Chapter 2.

[31] *See, e.g.*, Ward v. Rock Against Racism, 491 U.S. 781 (1989). Time, place, and manner regulation is discussed in Chapter 2.

[32] This issue is discussed in Chapter 4.

[33] This issue is discussed in Chapter 12.

[34] *See* Frederick A. Schauer, *Categories and the First Amendment: A Play in Three Acts*, 34 VAND. L. REV. 265, 275–76 (1981)("The development of definitional-absolutist theories was encouraged largely by the desire to narrow the area of judicial discretion. In searching for absolutism, however, theories of this type have collapsed the important distinction between coverage and protection. This distinction is important in separating the question of the category of action to which the right (if any) applies from the question of whether the right should prevail in cases of conflict with other interests, or for that matter other rights.").

Examples of Protections Containing Exceptions

There are constitutions that provide protection for free expression but explicitly call for a balancing of free expression protection against other values. Such constitutions do not require as many explicit exceptions to protection, since expression in areas that would be within exceptions in the United States can be limited through balancing. Lesser, weaker tests for categories of speech are also not required, since the lesser value of some speech or method of communication may be taken into account in balancing the speech interest against the conflicting values.

Canada

Freedom of expression is protected in Canada under the Canadian Charter of Rights and Freedoms. Section 2 of the Charter provides: "Everyone has the following fundamental freedoms: a) freedom of conscience and religion; b) freedom of thought, belief, opinion and expression, including freedom of the press and other media of communication; c) freedom of peaceful assembly; and d) freedom of association." So, Section 2(b) would seem to provide protections similar to those found in the First Amendment to the United States Constitution. There is, however, a limiting provision in the Charter. Section 1 provides: "The *Canadian Charter of Rights and Freedoms* guarantees the rights and freedoms set out in it subject only to such reasonable limits prescribed by law as can be demonstrably justified in a free and democratic society."

Section 1 seems to provide an explicit invitation to override the freedom of expression, as long as statutory limits are reasonable and justifiable in "a free and democratic society." The Canadian Supreme Court has developed a test to determine whether that standard has been met. The test was set out in the case *Regina v. Oakes*.[35] As summarized by the Canadian Supreme Court, in a later case, under *Oakes*,

> it must first be established that the impugned state action has an objective of pressing and substantial concern in a free and democratic society . . . The second feature of the *Oakes* test involves assessing the proportionality between the objective and the impugned measure. The inquiry as to proportionality attempts to guide the balancing of individual and group interests protected in s. 1, and in *Oakes* was broken down into the following three segments:

[35] [1986] 1. S.C.R. 103.

> First, the measures adopted must be carefully designed to achieve the objective in question. They must not be arbitrary, unfair or based on irrational considerations. In short, they must be rationally connected to the objective. Second, the means, even if rationally connected to the objective in this first sense, should impair "as little as possible" the right or freedom in question ... Third, there must be proportionality between the *effects* of the measures which are responsible for limiting the *Charter* right or freedom, and the objective which has been identified as of "sufficient importance."[36]

Rather than the limited categories of speech left unprotected by the First Amendment to the United States Constitution, the Canadian Charter allows for a balancing that would not be allowed in the United States. While the objective of "pressing and substantial concern" required under *Oakes* might not seem that different from the compelling governmental objective necessary to override free expression in the United States, and the requirement of impairment of the Charter right "as little as possible" and the proportionality between objective and effect on free expression might not seem that different from the "necessary to" aspect of United States law, in application it becomes clear that Section 1 allows limitations on expression that would be unconstitutional under the First Amendment.[37]

Germany

The German Basic Law, like the Canadian Charter, includes a limitations provision in its protection of free expression. Article 5(1) of the Basic Law provides:

> Every person shall have the right freely to express and disseminate his opinions in speech, writing, and pictures and to inform himself without hindrance from generally accessible sources. Freedom of the press and freedom of reporting by means of broadcasts and films shall be guaranteed. There shall be no censorship.

But Article 5(2) establishes that these rights may be limited: "These rights shall find their limits in the provisions of general laws, in provisions for the protection of young persons, and in the right to personal honor." Thus, there seems to be broad authority for statutory limitations.

[36] Regina v. Keegstra, (1990) 1 C.R. (4th) 129.

[37] As an example, Regina v. Keegstra, (1990) 1 C.R. (4th) 129 (1990), allowed prohibitions on hate speech, a position clearly in conflict with the protection offered such speech in the United States. The case will be discussed in Chapter 4.

Article 5 is interesting in that it goes on, in Article 5(3), to provide: "Art and scholarship, research and teaching shall be free. The freedom of teaching shall not release any person from allegiance to the constitution." What is most interesting here is the impact of the structure of the article. Since Article 5(3) comes after Article 5(2), the authorization of statutory limitations, the German courts have held that statutes are not capable of limiting art.[38] That does not mean that art is absolutely protected, but infringement cannot be justified based solely on the existence of a statute. Limitations on art have to be based on constitutional values. Thus, in the *Strauss Caricature Decision*,[39] the core constitutional value of human dignity, found in Article 1(1), was sufficient to justify the imposition of liability in the case of a magazine's caricature of the Prime Minister of Bavaria as a pig engaged in sexual intercourse with other pigs dressed in judicial robes.

The European Union

The European Union is, of course, not a democratic country. It is, however, a union composed primarily of fully democratic countries.[40] The protection of free expression provided by its European Convention on Human Rights would seem indicative of the views of the member countries that developed and signed on to the Convention. The Convention also serves as a check on limitations on expression by all member states, even those that might not be seen as fully functioning democracies.[41] For those reasons, the relevant provisions of the Convention are worth discussing, and cases based on those provisions will be discussed throughout.

Article 10(1) provides "Everyone has the right to freedom of expression. This right shall include freedom to hold opinions and to receive and impart information and ideas without interference by public authority and regardless of frontiers. This Article shall not prevent States from requiring the licensing of broadcasting, television or cinema enterprises." Thus, all those within the European Union enjoy the freedom of expression.

38 *See, e.g.*, the German Flag Desecration case, BVerfGE 81 (1980). The case may be found in translation at www.utexas.edu/law/academics/centers/transnational/work_new/german/case.php?id=632.

39 75 BVerfGE 369 (1987). The case may be found in translation at www.utexas.eduwww.utexas.edu/law/academics/centers/transnational/work_new/german/case.php?id=634.

40 Some of the members of the European Union are not included among the fully functioning democracies. They are, instead, seen as flawed democracies, but democracies nonetheless.

41 While the European Court of Human Rights may not be able to declare a law of a member state to be invalid, it can find conflicts with the European Convention, and member states are committed to recognizing the Court's judgments.

There are, however, limits on this freedom, as set out by Article 10(2).

> The exercise of these freedoms, since it carries with it duties and responsibilities, may be subject to such formalities, conditions, restrictions or penalties as are prescribed by law and are necessary in a democratic society, in the interests of national security, territorial integrity or public safety, for the prevention of disorder or crime, for the protection of health or morals, for the protection of the reputation or rights of others, for preventing the disclosure of information received in confidence, or for maintaining the authority and impartiality of the judiciary.

Thus, infringements on the freedom of expression may be justified by a number of reasons.

Countries without Explicit Constitutional Protections

There are countries that lack constitutional provisions protecting expression, but where these countries are democracies, their traditions, and perhaps statutes, lead to some form of protection for expression, as shown by the following examples.

The United Kingdom and the Human Rights Act

The United Kingdom does not have a singular document titled "Constitution." It may, instead, be said to have an unwritten constitution, even if that unwritten constitution includes certain written documents, such as Magna Carta. The unwritten constitution includes a recognition of the value of free expression. While British courts have always been reticent, or even unwilling, to declare an act of Parliament invalid as a violation of the constitution, with rather less deference paid to administrative actions, the courts have generally taken free-speech principles into account in statutory interpretation.[42]

A more recent addition to the law of the United Kingdom is the Human Rights Act of 1998, which effectively brings into domestic law the provisions of the European Convention on Human Rights.[43] The Act does not destroy Parliamentary supremacy but directs judges to attempt to interpret statutes in such a way as to be consistent with the European Convention.[44] If that proves

[42] For a discussion of free speech law in the United Kingdom, *see* RONALD J. KROTOSZYNSKI, JR., THE FIRST AMENDMENT IN CROSS-CULTURAL PERSPECTIVE 183–213 (2006).

[43] Human Rights Act 1998 (enacted Oct. 2, 2000). For a discussion of the act, *see* Clive Walker & Russell L. Weaver, *The United Kingdom Bill of Rights 1998: The Modernisation of Rights in the Old World*, 33 U. MICH. J.L REF. 497 (2000).

[44] *See* Human Rights Act § 3(1).

to be impossible, a court may declare the statute incompatible with the European Convention.[45] Even that does not have the impact of voiding the statute but invites Parliament to amend its work. Such an amendment may, instead, come from a Crown Minister.[46] Ronald Krotoszynski suggests that the impact of the Act is minimal: "British judges have been sensitive to free speech claims for many years. Moreover, the principal new judicial power, a mandate to render saving constructions whenever it is feasible to do so, merely ratifies the prior practice of the British courts."[47]

The example of the United Kingdom demonstrates that a country that is committed to democracy will protect the freedom of expression, even without a written constitutional mandate to do so. Courts will interpret statutes so as to be consistent with the freedom, although if Parliament is supreme, Parliament must also keep in mind the country's traditions. Of course, the area in which this is most clear will be that of political speech. Other areas, such as hate speech, may not enjoy the protection it does in the United States, and Professor Krotoszynski sees United Kingdom law regarding hate speech as similar to that in Canada and Germany.[48]

Australia

Australia does have a written constitution, but that constitution has no provision explicitly protecting expression. Indeed, there are no constitutional provisions for the protection of any individual rights. This was not simply an oversight. As was explained in *Australian Capital Television Pty. v. Commonwealth*:

> The adoption by the framers of the Constitution of the principle of responsible government was perhaps the major reason for their disinclination to incorporate ... guarantees of individual rights ... The framers of the Constitution accepted, in accordance with prevailing English thinking, that the citizen's rights were best left to the protection of the common law in association with the doctrine of parliamentary supremacy.[49]

The Court, in that case, considered the constitutionality of limits on political broadcasts that would have had the impact of providing television and radio exposure to parties that, and individuals who, were already represented or served in Parliament, while significantly limiting exposure for those not already in power. Such individuals were legally unable to purchase

[45] *See id.* at § 4. [46] *See id.* at § 10(2). [47] Krotoszynski, *supra* note 42, at 185.
[48] *See id.* at 187. [49] (1992) 177 CLR 106.

additional broadcast time. Without any individual expression right, the Court had to develop another rationale for overturning the limits.

What the Court did was to recognize an implied right to the freedom of certain forms of expression. The implication came from a constitutional provision providing for a system of representative government. The Court recognized that freedom of communication is indispensable to representative government, but this applied only to communication regarding politics and public affairs. The Chief Justice explained the scope of the communication protected:

> Freedom of communication in relation to public affairs and political discussion cannot be confined to communications between elected representatives and candidates for election on the one hand and the electorate on the other. The efficacy of representative government depends also upon free communication on such matters between all persons, groups and other bodies in the community ... [I]n a representative democracy, public participation in political discussion is a central element of the political process.[50]

So, Australia protects free expression, but only when that expression is political. Its position is in keeping with that of Meiklejohn, but it would reject, as a matter of constitutional protection, material encompassed only by the other rationales offered by Emerson.

Once material is recognized as protected political speech, the protection is not absolute. As with Canada, Germany, and the European Union, a balancing against other interests is allowed. In *Lange v. Australian Broadcasting Corp.*,[51] the High Court stated a two-part test, first determining whether there has been a breach of the implied right, and if there has, then asking whether the restriction is

> reasonably appropriate and adapted to serve a legitimate end the fulfillment of which is compatible with the maintenance of constitutionally prescribed system of representative and responsible government and the procedure prescribed ... for submitting a proposed amendment of the Constitution to the informed decision of the people.[52]

New Zealand

Like Australia, New Zealand has a written constitution with no textual provision protecting expression. Unlike Australia, however, New Zealand has a statute that protects speech. Section 14 of the New Zealand Bill of Rights Act

[50] *Id.* at 135–36 (opinion of Mason, C.J.). [51] (1997) 189 CLR 520. [52] *Id.* at 561.

of 1990 provides: "Everyone has the right to freedom of expression, including the freedom to seek, receive, and impart information and opinions of any kind in any form."[53] Since the provision is contained in a statute, rather than having the superior status of a constitutional provision, it cannot override an inconsistent statute. In fact the Bill of Rights Act itself, in Section 4, provides:

> No court shall, in relation to any enactment (whether passed or made before or after the commencement of this Bill of Rights),—(a) hold any provision of the enactment to be impliedly repealed or revoked, or to be in any way invalid or ineffective; or (b) decline to apply any provision of the enactment—by reason only that the provision is inconsistent with any provision of this Bill of Rights.[54]

There are two other provisions in the Bill of Rights Act that are necessary to understand in examining the freedom of expression in New Zealand. Section 5 provides: "Subject to section 4, the rights and freedoms contained in this Bill of Rights may be subject only to such reasonable limits prescribed by law as can be demonstrably justified in a free and democratic society."[55] And, Section 6 provides: "Wherever an enactment can be given a meaning that is consistent with the rights and freedoms contained in this Bill of Rights, that meaning shall be preferred to any other meaning."[56]

New Zealand then shares some characteristics of the United Kingdom, in that provisions are to be interpreted, when they can, so as to be consistent with rights found in the Bill of Rights Act, in the case of New Zealand, or the European Convention, in the case of the United Kingdom. It also has a similarity to the protections found in Canada, in that the source of the protection also contains a test that justifies the limitation of that protection. The interaction of these provisions will be seen in New Zealand's application of its flag-desecration statute.[57]

An example of how the New Zealand courts use even this somewhat limited protection to manage still to be protective of, at least, political speech is provided by *Hopkinson v. Police*.[58] The case grew out of a protest in which the defendant burned the New Zealand flag. He was convicted of violating New Zealand's flag-protection statute, which creates an offense when a person "within view of any public place, uses, displays, destroys, or damages the New Zealand Flag in any manner with the intention of dishonouring it."[59]

[53] New Zealand Bill of Rights Act 1990, Public Act 1990 No 109 (Aug. 28, 1990), § 14, *available at* www.legislation.govt.nz/act/public/1990/0109/latest/DLM225513.html.

[54] *Id.* at §4. [55] *Id.* at §5. [56] *Id.* at §6. [57] For further discussion, see Chapter 8.

[58] [2004] 3 NZLR 704.

[59] Flags, Emblems, and Names Protection Act 1981 § 11(1), Public Act 1981 No 47 (Oct. 15, 1981), www.legislation.govt.nz/act/public/1981/0047/latest/whole.html.

On appeal, Hopkinson argued that his actions were protected by the Bill of Rights Act.

Even with the inability to strike down the statute as a violation of the Bill of Rights Act, the Court managed to overturn the conviction. Following the instruction to interpret statutes so as, if possible, to make them consistent with the Bill of Rights Act, the Court determined that the Flag Act prohibited only those acts that "vilify" the flag, and the simple burning of the flag was not of that nature. "The Court did so without providing examples of what actions would meet the requirements of vilification, but it has been argued that the Court may have intended to limit vilification to the sorts of acts mentioned in the appellant's submission, such conduct as urinating on the ashes of the flag or knowingly blowing one's nose on it."[60]

SIMILARITIES AND DIFFERENCES

It should, once again, be clear that democracies must protect at least certain forms of expression and that central to that protection is political expression. We have also seen the various roots of that protection in constitutional provision, implication, statute, or tradition.[61] What is not yet clear are the dimensions of the protections that must be afforded such speech. Must political speech be so open as to include speech by corporations? May channels of communications be limited, so that candidates may not buy television time but instead receive a portion of free broadcast access? May anti-democratic parties be barred from participation in the political process?

While the protection of political speech is central to democracy, there are other varieties of expression that might or might not be protected. Should hate speech be protected? Obscene depictions? Libel? The intentional infliction of

[60] *See* Sigrid Bridgette Buschbacher, *Protection of Public Symbols in New Zealand and the United States of America: Flag Burning Versus Freedom of Expression*, 2 NZ POSTGRAD. L. E-J. 29 (2005), www.nzpglejournal.auckland.ac.nz/webdav/site/nzpglejournal/shared/Subscribe/Documents/2005-2/3%20Siggi's%20Final.pdf.

[61] There are also differences in the enforcement of constitutional provisions. In some systems, a statute might be declared unconstitutional only by the Constitutional Court, while in others any court may address the constitutionality of a statute. In some countries, even the highest courts are reluctant to overturn an act of the legislature, perhaps limiting themselves only to adopting interpretations consistent with constitutional provisions. In other countries, that reluctance is lacking. What is important here, however, is the result. It is the current status of free speech in these various democracies that helps in exploring the relationship between free expression and democracy.

emotional distress? The distribution of media to children? Falsehoods and denial of historical fact? Flag burning?

Any of the proffered questions may be answered yes or no and a variety of rationales offered. A political society that answers yes to any question will clearly differ in some respect to one that answers no. But will the answers mean that one society is a democracy and the other is not? That issue might best be addressed by looking to democracies to see how they handle thc issues. If some democracies protect hate speech, while others do not, and both in fact remain democracies, it would appear that the determination to protect hate speech is not essential to democracy. Similarly, if there are effective democracies that ban vicious attacks on personal honor, it would seem that such attacks are not necessary to open political debate.

The remainder of this book will be an examination of similarities and differences regarding questions of free expression in a variety of democracies. The treatment is not encyclopedic; an encyclopedic treatment would be of encyclopedic length.[62] Rather, the effort will be, on each issue, and there are certainly issues that will not be addressed, to find democracies that take different positions. If there is a failure to find such differing democracies, that may be an indication that a particular variety of expression is essential to democracy. If countries do differ, and both are democracies, that is at least an indication that the protection of a particular variety of expression is not essential to democracy.

What countries are examined can make a difference. By defining democracy broadly enough a great number of differences might be found, but the findings could be open to the criticism that countries analyzed are not true democracies. For that reason, the examination herein will be limited to countries that were listed as full democracies in the Democracy Index 2012 compiled by the Intelligence Unit of the magazine *The Economist*.[63] There are only twenty-five such countries led by the European democracies, New Zealand, Australia, and Canada with the United States at twenty-first.

This is a conservative choice, in the sense that other countries might also be democracies that could add to the consideration but are considered by *The Economist* to be flawed democracies, including Portugal, France, Slovenia,

[62] For a more encyclopedic treatment, although in one rather large volume, *see* Eric Barendt, The Freedom of Speech (2d ed. 2005).

[63] *The Economist* Intelligence Unit, *Democracy Index 2012: Democracy at a Standstill*, www.eiu.com/Handlers/WhitepaperHandler.ashx?fi=Democracy-Index-2012.pdf&mode=wp&campaignid=DemocracyIndex12 or at portoncv.gov.cv/dhub/porton.por_global.open_file?p_doc_id=1034.

Italy, and Greece. Where any of these flawed democracies are included in the analysis, there will be a reminder that the country is not a full democracy.

Perhaps, at this point, there should be a brief discussion of the methodology of *The Economist*. If it is, in some way, flawed, then so would be the list itself, and the validity of any conclusions based on comparisons would be called into question. *The Economist* claims that:

> [M]ost observers today would agree that, at a minimum, the fundamental features of democracy include government based on majority rule and the consent of the government, the existence of free and fair elections, the protection of minority rights and respect for basic human rights ... [and] equality before the law, due process and political pluralism.[64]

With that definition in mind, the Intelligence Unit developed a measure along five dimensions: "electoral process and pluralism; civil liberties; the functioning of government; political participation; and political culture."[65]

The factors seem reasonable. Without an electoral process that is fair and free with a sufficient range of political viewpoints represented, there cannot be a democracy. If government fails adequately to function, the democratic will cannot be fulfilled. If there is a lack of political participation, the government cannot legitimately claim to be ruling in the name of the people. The two factors that may require deeper explication are political culture and civil liberties.

Political culture appears to measure the commitment of the population to democracy. Factors leading to a decrease in a country's score are the percentages of the population that prefer strong leadership, bypassing parliament and elections, a preference for military rule, a preference for rule by experts or technocrats, and a belief that democracy is not good at maintaining public order.[66] Factors increasing a country's score include the proportion of the population believing that democracy benefits the economy, general popular support for democracy, and a strong tradition of church-state separation.[67]

The civil liberties score depends on a number of factors, some addressing free expression. The non-free expression questions address judicial independence, property rights and business freedom, equality under the law, religious freedom, and general perception in the society of the protection of human rights.[68] Questions more directed at expression include measures of freedom in the electronic and print media and in Internet access, the robustness of media coverage, and a general freedom of expression and protest.[69] There is

64 *Id.* at 25. 65 *Id.* at 26. 66 *See id.* at 35–36. 67 *See id.* at 36.
68 *See id.* at 37–39. 69 *See id.* at 37.

also a factor that is important to free expression, while also being important in other areas: "Extent to which government invokes new risks and threats as an excuse for curbing civil liberties."[70]

Since this analysis studies the centrality of certain aspects of free expression to democracy by examining the treatment of those aspects in a list of fully functioning democracies, it is important to consider any circularity that might result from the role freedom of expression played in placing the countries on the list. Defining democracy so as to require freedom in political expression would certainly lead to the conclusion that all democracies protect political expression, and that might be a circularity. But the protection of political speech seems to be a true hallmark of democracy.

With regard to other issues involving expression, it may be that the more expression that is protected, the higher the democracy ranking. This might be a concern in a comparison of a country that is a full democracy with a country that is a flawed democracy, where the only difference between the two is in the treatment of some variety of non-political expression. If this is considered a true concern, it would have to be factored out, and differences in the resulting set of democracies would be even larger. Furthermore, if the comparison were being drawn based on differences in scores in countries considered full democracies, it might again have to be factored out. What this study examines, however, are differences among countries that are full democracies. It would seem that these countries must protect political speech, and the interest is in seeing the dimensions of that protection and the other varieties of expression that may or may not enjoy protection.

Even limiting consideration to fully functioning democracies, not every such country can be discussed for each issue, without the book becoming unacceptably long. So, a word should be said about the selection of countries for each topic. As will be seen, the United States is discussed on each issue. This is not the simple result of a United States-centric focus. Rather, on most issues the United States' position differs from that of much of the rest of the democratic world. Failure to discuss the United States' position would leave out one of the conflicting views on the issue. On the opposite side, there are a number of countries that can serve as a counterexample to the United States. The countries chosen for each issue provide the best contrast. They are also generally, although not quite exclusively, more highly ranked than the United States. They then serve as good evidence that an alternative approach still allows a country to be equally, or more, democratic.

70 *Id.* at 39.

As will clearly be seen, there are differences among democratic countries in the protections afforded. The differences in protection regarding political speech are most important to democracy, but even here differences have not led these particular countries to be less than full democracies. Differences in the protection afforded to other varieties of expression may be important to the culture of a country, but among the countries to be examined, they have at least not led to the demise of democracy, and the democratic process is still available to effect any changes in protection that the populace may desire.

The lesson to be drawn from this endeavor is that there is no unique, democratic set of answers to free expression issues. While any democracy must protect political speech, democracies vary in the dimensions of that protection, while still remaining democracies. For non-political speech, the differences among democracies may be greater, with some rejecting protection for expression that is protected by others, and again they remain democracies. There will certainly be differences in the resulting societies, and there will be arguments for preferring one model over another, but those arguments would seem not to include the claim that the failure to protect a variety of expression not protected in some democracies excludes those countries from the community of democratic nations.

2

Varieties of Expression

Central to this chapter is a comparison of the absolutist tone of the First Amendment's protection of expression to the balancing allowed by the free expression provisions of other countries. As will be seen, some varieties of expression, under United States law, are in fact less protected; infringement may be justified under a less strict standard. Furthermore, some varieties of limitation on what is concededly important free expression may also be tested under a lesser standard. The chapter will begin with political speech, the variety of speech that must be protected in a democracy, and in particular the United States and Canada will be examined in terms of the test applied for regulation. We will then turn to other varieties of speech, both to see whether they will be included in free expression provisions and what differences, if any, may exist in the level of protection provided.

POLITICAL SPEECH

Central to democracy is the protection of political speech, but that does not necessarily mean that even such speech must be fully free. There may be restrictions on where such expression may be offered and the manner in which it is presented. Limits, or the lack of limits, based on location raise the issue of what constitutes a public forum, a place open to expression. Limits based on manner are addressed, in United States law, as time, place, and manner regulations. This subsection will concentrate on the comparison between the United States and Canada on these two issues. The United States' absolute sounding protection for the freedom of expression has required the adoption of special tests. Canada, with the balance of Section 1 of the Charter of Rights and Freedoms, simply allows these factors to be taken into account in determining whether an infringement on the free expression right in Section 2(b) is justified.

United States law recognizes that certain places have historically been available to those who wish to make their opinions known to the public. The Supreme Court in *Perry Education Assn v. Perry Local Educators' Assn*, explained the law of the public forum.

> In places which by long tradition or by government fiat have been devoted to assembly and debate, the rights of the state to limit expressive activity are sharply circumscribed. At one end of the spectrum are streets and parks which "have immemorially been held in trust for the use of the public, and, time out of mind, have been used for purposes of assembly, communicating thoughts between citizens, and discussing public questions."[1]

The government may also choose to designate an area as a public forum, and such a designated public forum need not be open to speech by all parties and on all topics. It may be a limited public forum, and as the Court said in *Good News Club v. Milford Central School*, "When the State establishes a limited public forum, the State is not required to and does not allow persons to engage in every type of speech. The State may be justified 'in reserving [its forum] for certain groups or for the discussion of certain topics.'"[2]

But not every place is a public forum, general or limited. The free expression right that importantly attaches to political speech does not give one license to speak in every venue owned by the government. Free expression does not guarantee access to the most appropriate, in the speaker's view, place for that speech; the Pentagon need not open all of its doors to those who wish to criticize military policy. Even when doors are open, speech may be prohibited. The fact that the balcony at the United States House of Representatives may be open to visits by the public does not give an individual the right to convey his or her political views to those on the floor.

Identification of what may or may not constitute a public forum is of great importance in determining when speech is protected. In United States law, the tie of the public forum to history limits the locations that are open for even political speech; identification has some complexity. *International Society for Krishna Consciousness v. Lee*[3] provides some insight. The case was a challenge by a religious group to certain regulations the Port Authority of New York promulgated for the airports under its control. One of the duties imposed on members of the religion was to go out into the public to distribute material

1 460 U.S. 37, 45 (1983) (quoting Hague v. CIO, 307 U.S. 496, 515 (1939)).

2 533 U.S. 98, 106 (2001) (quoting Rosenberger v. Rector and Visitors of Univ. of Va., 515 U.S. 819, 829 (1995)).

3 505 U.S. 672 (1992).

and solicit funds in support of the religion. The Port Authority regulations prohibited that practice.

The first issue in the analysis of whether or not this was a violation of the members' free expression rights was a consideration of whether airports are public fora. The case was well before the terrorist attacks that have tightened airport security, so the general public had more access to more areas of the airport that provided the audience for the adherent's expression. In some sense, the commercial areas of the airport are like sidewalks, but they are not sidewalks. The Court noted the relatively short history of air travel and, hence, the short history of airports. That short history prevented airports from being considered public fora. They could not have been used, immemorially, for public discourse.

The religious group argued that the correct analysis was the history of transportation nodes. Whether mass transportation has been around long enough to provide sufficient history was not considered. Instead, the Court noted that transportation nodes, such as rail terminals, were generally privately owned and their practices did not speak to the duty the government faced in allowing free expression. Furthermore, the Court said that "the relevant unit for our inquiry is an airport, not 'transportation nodes' generally."[4]

The Court did say that "[w]hen new methods of transportation develop, new methods for accommodating the transportation are also likely to be needed. And with each new step it therefore will be a new inquiry whether the transportation necessities are compatible with various kinds of expressive activity."[5] But given the Court's restricted view as to the history that can establish a traditional public forum, that new inquiry seems unlikely to lead to new fora.

The conclusion that an airport terminal is not a public forum did not end the inquiry. Government regulation of expression in a nonpublic forum must still be reasonable. Here, the last quoted language is clearly correct. Reasonableness will depend on context, and new transportation nodes may yield different results. Here, the Court noted that the Port Authority allowed leafleting and the solicitation of funds on the sidewalks outside the terminal buildings and noted that in that era a significant majority of those inside the terminal crossed the sidewalk to arrive there. The Court also noted potential interference with the rather hurried foot traffic within the terminal; the potential for fraud in a quick encounter; and the lack of likelihood that a hurried traveler, perhaps from out of town, would take the time to report attempted fraud to the authorities or

[4] *Id.* at 681. [5] *Id.*

participate in its prosecution. The ban on solicitation was, thus, reasonable. A separate majority concluded that the ban on the distribution of literature, an encounter that was quicker than solicitation and less likely to involve fraud, was not reasonable and violated the First Amendment.[6]

Canadian case law has its own airport decision. The case, *Committee for the Commonwealth of Canada v. Canada*,[7] involved a group of individuals who went to Montréal's Dorval Airport in order to inform the public of their political aims. They were told that, under regulations relevant to the airport, they could not do so. The decision is rather complex, with a number of opinions discussing issues ranging from the application of the Canadian Charter of Rights and Freedoms in an airport to whether or not the regulations actually addressed to commercial activity were broad enough to reach this sort of political speech.

Fortunately, an opinion in a later decision of the Supreme Court of Canada provides a relatively succinct summary of the positions taken in *Committee for the Commonwealth*. Justice Iacobucci delivering the judgment of the Court in *Ramsden v. Peterborough*,[8] described the viewpoints of the various justices in the prior decision.

> In *Committee for the Commonwealth of Canada* there were three separate approaches articulated as to the appropriate standard to be applied to determine whether expressive activity falling prima facie within s. 2(*b*) and occurring on public property is constitutionally protected . . .
>
> The broadest approach was taken by L'Heureux-Dubé J., who emphasized . . . that for those with scant resources, the use of public property may be the only means of engaging in expressive activity . . . Nonetheless, L'Heureux-Dubé J. recognized that certain kinds of public property must remain outside of the scope of s. 2(*b*). She held that restrictions on the time, place and manner of expressive activity must be justified under s. 1, rather than within the s. 2(*b*) analysis. She stated . . . that "some, but not all, government-owned property is constitutionally open to the public for engaging in expressive activity." She then listed the criteria for determining when public property will be considered a "public arena" and prohibitions on expressive activity thereon will not be justified under s. 1:
>
> 1. The traditional openness of such property for expressive activity.
> 2. Whether the public is ordinarily admitted to the property as of right.
> 3. The compatibility of the property's purpose with such expressive activities.

6 *See* Lee v. Int'l Soc'y for Krishna Consciousness, 505 U.S. 830 (1992).
7 [1991] 1 S.C.R. 139. 8 [1993] 2 S.C.R. 1084.

4. The impact of the availability of such property for expressive activity on the achievement of s. 2(*b*)'s purposes.
5. The symbolic significance of the property for the message being communicated ...
6. The availability of other public arenas in the vicinity for expressive activities.

The Chief Justice reviewed the interest of the individual wishing to express him- or herself, and the government's interest in ensuring effective operation of services and undertakings in accordance with their intended purpose. Lamer C.J.C. concluded as follows:

> In my opinion, the "freedom" which an individual may have to communicate in a place owned by the government must necessarily be circumscribed by the interests of the latter and of the citizens as a whole: the individual will only be free to communicate in a place owned by the state if the form of expression he uses is compatible with the principal function or intended purpose of that place.

The Chief Justice therefore held that "if the expression takes a form that contravenes or is inconsistent with the function of the place where the attempt to communicate is made, such a form of expression must be considered to fall outside the sphere of s. 2(*b*)." ...

McLachlin J. had a different approach:

> the test for the constitutional right to use government property for public expression should conform to the following criteria. It should be based on the values and interests at stake and not be confined to the characteristics of particular types of government property. Reflecting the concepts traditionally associated with free expression, it should extend constitutional protection to expression on some but not all government property. The analysis under s. 2(*b*) should focus on determining when, as a general proposition, the right to expression on government property arises. The task at this stage should be primarily definitional rather than one of balancing, and the test should be sufficiently generous to ensure that valid claims are not excluded for want of proof. Once it has been determined that the expression in question at the location in question falls within the scope of s. 2(*b*) thus defined, the further question arises of whether the government's limitation on the property's use for the expression in question is justified under s. 1. At this stage the concern should be primarily one of weighing and balancing the conflicting interest — the individual's interest in using the forum in question for his or her expressive purposes against the state's interest in limiting the expression on the particular property.

Under this approach, once the activity in question is found to be expression,

> [A] further enquiry into the purpose served by the expression in question must be made before it can be found that s. 2(*b*) applies. In a case where

> the restriction involves a state-owned property, that examination will focus on whether the forum's relationship with the particular expressive activity invokes any of the values and principles underlying the guarantee. The effect of that inquiry is to screen out many potential claims to the use of government property as the forum for public expression.[9]

As for the issue in *Ramsden*, the Court concluded that an absolute ban on placing posters on public property was a violation of Section 2(b) of the Charter, under any of the three approaches taken in *Committee for the Commonwealth*. It was also an infringement that could not be justified under Section 1. While avoiding litter and aesthetic blight may be pressing and substantial concerns to which the ban was rationally related, a total ban lacked proportionality and the prohibition could not pass muster under the *Oakes* test.[10]

Returning to the decision in *Committee for the Commonwealth*, the Court concluded that the ban on the Committee's activities was a violation of Section 2(b) that could not be justified under Section 1, with some members of the Court believing that the regulation didn't apply, so that the enforcement by authorities was not justified by law, and others concluding that the regulation was a violation of the Charter.[11] The most interesting aspects of the various opinions, for purposes here, are the comparisons in several opinions between United States and Canadian law on the issue of public fora.

Chief Justice Lamer, joined by Justice Sopinka, looking to United States law said that "public forum doctrine can be criticized for over-emphasizing the nature of the place at the expense of the real interests involved . . . It would be preferable to disregard the nominalist approach developed by the American courts and instead to balance the interests underlying the public forum doctrine."[12] The Chief Justice noted that the United States Constitution had no provision similar to Section 1 of the Canadian Charter and that there was, since such a balancing provision was not present, the need to develop a doctrine such as public forum analysis to "reconcile[] the individual's interest in expressing himself in a place which is itself highly propitious to such expression and of the government's interest in being able to manage effectively the premises that it owns."[13]

9 *Id.* at ¶¶ 24–30 (citations omitted). 10 The *Oakes* test is discussed in Chapter 1.

11 For further discussion of Committee for the Commonwealth of Canada v. Canada, see Richard Moon, *Out of Place: Comment on* Committee for the Commonwealth of Canada v. Canada, 35 McGill L.J. 204 (1993).

12 [1991] 1 S.C.R. 139 at ¶ 8–9. 13 *Id.* at ¶ 9.

Justice L'Heureux-Dubé noted that the lack of a provision like Section 1 prevented United States courts from balancing and forced the reliance on categorization, quoting an article in the *Canadian Bar Review*. "While the Americans must do their balancing in the context of the definition of the right, Canadians can take advantage of the existence of section 1. A priori exclusions of whole categories of free expression are not necessary in Canada."[14] Providing a comparison in her own words, she went on to say:

> Unlike the American system whereby delineated tests are required for the various "types" of expression, our s. 1 is flexible enough to accommodate all these types, the result depending on what objectives are put forward by the government, and what means are selected to advance these objectives. This enables us to construct a contextual rather than a categorical approach, focusing not only on the scope of the right, but also on the setting in which the freedom of expression claim is made.[15]

The flexibility provided by Canadian free expression law also frees the determination of public fora from history. Again according to Justice L'Heureux-Dubé:

> The list of sites traditionally associated with public expression is not static. As means of locomotion progress, people shall begin to gather in areas heretofore unknown. Hence the "traditional" component of the public arena analysis must appreciate the "type" of place historically associated with public discussion, and should not be restricted to the actual places themselves.[16]

Even in a public forum, there may be restrictions. The fact that the streets and sidewalks may be public fora does not mean that a community must tolerate highly amplified speech from such a location in a residential neighborhood in the middle of the night. United States law tolerates time, place, and manner restrictions on expression. One case recognizing the acceptability of such limits is *Ward v. Rock Against Racism*.[17] Rock Against Racism was an organization that presented a series of rock music concerts at the band shell in New York City's Central Park. The organization's message was, as the name would indicate, anti-racist. There had been some noise complaints involving the band shell, and the city decided that the best way to address those complaints would be for the city itself to provide high-quality sound equipment and an experienced technician for all performances.

[14] *Id.* at ¶ 87 (quoting A. Wayne MacKay, *Freedom of Expression: Is it All Just Talk?*, 68 CAN. BAR REV. 713, 730 (1989)).

[15] *Id.* at ¶121. [16] *Id.* at ¶154. [17] 491 U.S. 781 (1989).

While not all music venues are necessarily public fora, use of the band shell seemed to be open to all, and the Court proceeded as though it were a public forum. The Court said that, even in a public forum, government may impose reasonable time, place, or manner restrictions. Such restrictions are valid "provided the restrictions 'are justified without reference to the content of the regulated speech, that they are narrowly tailored to serve a significant governmental interest, and that they leave open ample alternative channels for communication of the information.'"[18]

Applying the test to the case at hand, since the rule applied to all uses of the band shell, it was not content dependent. The Court also found the regulation narrowly tailored to the city's significant interest in protecting neighbors and other users of Central Park from unwanted noise. Narrow tailoring was established by the fact that other measures to address the noise problem had not been successful. With regard to alternate channels the Court said that the regulation limited only amplification, with no impact on quantity or content, and that they were alternative venues.

Justice L'Heureux-Dubé, in *Committee for the Commonwealth*, also addressed time, place, and manner regulations. She quoted the holding of an Ontario court.

> Mere regulation as to time and place ... cannot be considered an infringement of freedom of expression, unless there is evidence that such regulation in intent or effect adversely impacts upon content or adversely interferes with production, availability and use determines who can be involved in these.[19]

She went on to say:

> Under the aforementioned circumstances "mere regulation" may survive a Charter challenge, yet such survival, in my view, will hinge on the determination under s. 1. Even when the regulation is content-neutral, both on its face and in its application, it will be up to the government to prove what constitutes reasonable time, place, and manner limitations.[20]

She did note that the criteria employed in time, place, and manner regulation in the United States are "remarkably similar" to what is required by Section 1.[21]

What the comparison between the United States and Canada demonstrates is that absolutist language, if it is not actually to be absolute protection,

[18] *Id.* at 791 (quoting Clark v. Community for Creative Non-Violence, 468 U.S. 288, 293 (1984)).
[19] [1991] 1 S.C.R. 139 at ¶ 112 (quoting R. v. Videoflicks, 48 O.R. (2d) 395, 431 (C.A. 1984)).
[20] *Id.* at ¶ 113. [21] *See id.* at ¶ 116.

requires the adoption of special tests to address different varieties of, or contexts for, expression. Canada, along with other jurisdictions that invite the balancing of free expression rights against other important values, can simply take the variety and context into account in that balancing. Balancing may be seen to exist in the free expression jurisprudence of the United States, but it is a category-based balancing. Rather than balancing interests in a particular situation, United States law accepts that some categories of speech, or of the regulation of speech, do not have to meet the strictest standards. But once one of the categorical tests is recognized, it is applied to all speech in the category. A balancing regime, on the other hand, balances particular instances or varieties of expression against other interests, without the need for special category-based tests.

LITERATURE AND FILM

The 1940s saw a debate between two United States free expression scholars over the scope of expression to be afforded protection under the First Amendment. Zechariah Chafee, a law professor, had taken the general position that the First Amendment protects not only societal interests but also individual autonomy.[22] The philosopher Alexander Meiklejohn disagreed, arguing that it was only societal interest, specifically the interest in self-government, that is protected by the First Amendment.[23] He would not have left autonomy interests completely unprotected; they would, like other forms of liberty, be protected by the Due Process Clauses of the Fifth and Fourteenth Amendments. Meiklejohn's concern was that a First Amendment stretched to include the protection of autonomy would be too weak to provide the strength he felt necessary for the protection of self-government. It was, at least initially, unclear where that left literature. For his part, Chafee pointed to an example of a novel that dealt with race relations, as making a contribution to political concerns.[24] He saw public aspects in a wide variety of forms of expression.

A decade later, another law professor, Harry Kalven, again questioned whether Meiklejohn's emphasis on self-government would withhold protection from literature, saying "people do not need novels or dramas or paintings or poems because they will be called upon to vote. Art and belle-lettres do not

[22] *See generally*, ZECHARIAH CHAFEE, JR., FREE SPEECH IN THE UNITED STATES (1941).

[23] *See generally*, ALEXANDER MEIKLEJOHN, FREE SPEECH AND ITS RELATION TO SELF-GOVERNMENT (1948).

[24] *See* Zechariah Chafee, Jr., *Book Review*, 62 HARV. L. REV. 891, 900 (1949) (reviewing Meiklejohn's book).

deal in such ideas-at least not good art or belle-lettres."[25] Meiklejohn directly addressed Kalven's reading of his earlier work, seeing it is a misinterpretation.

> I believe ... that the people do need novels and dramas and paintings and poems, "because they will be called upon to vote." The primary social fact which blocks and hinders the success of our experiment in self-government is that our citizens are not educated for self-government. We are terrified by ideas, rather than challenged and stimulated by them.[26]

Thus, literature is protected because it does play a role in self-governance; it is a form of political speech.

Whether Meikeljohn's affirmation of the role of literature represents a clarification or a recognition, the United States Supreme Court had already, in *Winters v. New York*,[27] recognized the need to include literary entertainment within the protection of the First Amendment. The materials involved may not have been anything close to great literature, given that the statute at issue addressed publications "principally made up of criminal news, police reports, or accounts of criminal deeds, or pictures, or stories of deeds of bloodshed, lust or crime ..."[28] Nonetheless, the Court rejected the claim that the First Amendment did not apply.

> We do not accede to [the] suggestion that the constitutional protection for a free press applies only to the exposition of ideas. The line between the informing and the entertaining is too elusive for the protection of that basic right. Everyone is familiar with instances of propaganda through fiction. What is one man's amusement teaches another's doctrine. Though we can see nothing of any possible value to society in these magazines, they are as much entitled to the protection of free speech as the best of literature.[29]

The Court, in addition to concluding that this sort of writing must be treated as literature, clearly concluded that literary entertainment is protected by the First Amendment.

The later view of Meiklejohn and that of the Supreme Court seem correct. At least some literature is more than simple entertainment. Setting aside the question of whether the autonomy interests should protect even what is purely entertainment, at least some literature is educational and even political. This conclusion would also have to extend to film. Clearly, a motion picture can make a political point. As such, even limiting the core value of free expression to democracy justifies protecting the medium.

[25] Harry Kalven, Jr., *Metaphysics of the Law of Obscenity*, 1960 SUP. CT. REV. 1, 16.

[26] Alexander Meiklejohn, *The First Amendment is an Absolute*, 1961 SUP. CT. REV. 245, 263.

[27] 333 U.S. 507 (1948). [28] *Id.* at 508. [29] *Id.* at 510.

The definitional issue is really only of great import in the United States. There the central issue is whether a particular work is protected by the First Amendment. Category matters, and the conclusion that literature fits within the protected category is important. In countries where freedom of expression may be balanced against other considerations and values, definition is less important. Such a balancing regime can simply accept that literature and film are protected and then determine whether other values justify the denial of protection in a particular case.

COMMUNICATIVE CONDUCT

In addition to the pure speech of an orator standing on a soapbox in the park and the free press of a newspaper or leaflet, people express themselves in a great variety of ways. If a group of picketers march back and forth in front of a business carrying signs, the signs may be akin to pure speech or press, but there may also be a message in the activity of picketing. Indeed, the marching itself, with no signs, may convey some sort of message. Under some circumstances, even standing silently might be communicative. What is required in the United States for conduct to be communicative is "[a]n intent to convey a particularized message . . . and . . . the likelihood . . . that the message would be understood by those who viewed it."[30]

Communicative conduct, as a form of communication, would seem to merit protection. But government may have an interest in preventing certain conduct, whether or not it is intended to communicate. Certainly, the authorities need not tolerate bank robbery, even if the robber intends it as a statement asserting the illegitimacy of private property. Some communicative conduct must be allowed, while the government must be allowed to restrict some conduct. Here, too, the United States courts have had to adopt a special test.

The United States test for limits on communicative conduct is presented in *United States v. O'Brien*.[31] The case grew out of an anti-war demonstration on the steps of the South Boston Courthouse. O'Brien and three others burned their Selective Service registration certificates. They thereby violated a law prohibiting the destruction of such certificates, as well as a law that required all those subject to the draft to carry their certificates. O'Brien said that, although he knew doing so was a violation of federal law, he burned the certificate in protest of actions by the United States.

[30] Spence v. Washington, 418 U.S. 405, 410–11 (1974).

[31] 391 U.S. 367 (1968).

O'Brien claimed that, because of the political nature of his conduct, he could not be punished for this chosen form of communication. The Supreme Court rejected that conclusion.

> [E]ven on the assumption that the alleged communicative element in O'Brien's conduct is sufficient to bring into play the First Amendment, it does not necessarily follow that the destruction of a registration certificate is constitutionally protected activity ... [W]hen "speech" and "nonspeech" elements are combined in the same course of conduct, a sufficiently important governmental interest in regulating the nonspeech elements can justify incidental limitations on First Amendment freedoms.[32]

The Court went on to state a test for restrictions on communicative conduct.

> [A] government regulation is sufficiently justified if it is within the constitutional power of the Government; if it furthers an important or substantial governmental interest; if the governmental interest is unrelated to the suppression of free expression; and if the incidental restriction on alleged First Amendment freedoms is no greater than is essential to the furtherance of that interest.[33]

Applying the test to the action and government interests at issue, the Court found no violation of free expression rights, seeing the government's interest as aimed at maintaining an army rather than suppressing protest.

Canada takes a very broad view as to what constitutes expression and, here too, no special test is required. In *Dolphin Delivery v. R.W.D.S.U., Local 580*,[34] the Supreme Court of Canada considered whether or not secondary picketing by a labor union was protected by Section 2(b). The Court recognized that labor picketers convey a message that attempts to persuade people not to do business with the targeted company. That is expression, and while action may accompany the expression, action does not necessarily remove expression from the protection of the Charter. There are, however, actions that, despite communicative intent, are unprotected, threats or acts of violence or the destruction of property.[35]

The Canadian Supreme Court reiterated that position in *Irwin Toy v. Québec*.[36] An opinion for three justices, written by Chief Justice Dickson, said:

> [I]f the activity conveys or attempts to convey meaning, it has expressive content and *prima facie* falls within the scope of the guarantee ... The

[32] *Id.* at 376. [33] *Id.* at 377. [34] [1986] 2 S.C.R. 573.

[35] *See id.* at ¶ 27. The Court, despite the nonviolent communicative nature of the picketing, held that the issuance of an injunction against such picketing in a civil action did not constitute a violation of the Charter.

[36] [1989] 1 S.C.R. 927.

> content of expression can be conveyed through an infinite variety of forms of expression: for example, the written or spoken word, the arts, and even physical gestures or acts. While the guarantee of free expression protects all content of expression, certainly violence as a form of expression receives no such protection.[37]

That, of course, would not be the end of the analysis. Nor, however, is any special test required. As with any infringement of the freedom of expression, the question becomes whether or not it can be justified under Section 1, as a "reasonable limit[] prescribed by law as can be demonstrably justified in a free and democratic society." As will be seen, the restriction at issue in *Irwin Toy* met that test.[38]

Australia has its own case recognizing conduct as expression. In *Levy v. Victoria*,[39] an individual sought to protest duck hunting by entering an area reserved for the activity and retrieving dead and injured ducks in order to display them on television. The protester challenged his conviction for entering the area without a hunting license. The High Court recognized that political speech is not limited to classic verbal or printed expression and could include this sort of conduct, even though the protester eventually lost his case, when the Court found the balance to favor the restriction.

While perhaps not setting the analysis out in as much detail, a number of other countries must be seen as protecting communicative conduct. Any country that protects the burning of the flag is protecting communicative conduct; indeed, any country whose courts feel the need to explain why flag burning is unacceptable may be seen as establishing an exception to the general principle that conduct can be protected expression.[40] For example, the New Zealand High Court, in *Hopkinson v. Police*,[41] considered a conviction growing out of the burning of the national flag as part of a political protest. The issue for the Court was whether the prohibition on the destruction of the flag of New Zealand violated Section 14 of the New Zealand Bill of Right Act of 1990, which provided: "Everyone has the right to freedom of expression, including the freedom to seek, receive, and impart information

[37] *Id.* at ¶¶ 42–43. Justices Beetz and McIntyre, who dissented from the final holding that the advertising limits at issue in Irwin Toy were justified under Section 1 of the Charter, did not disagree that Section 2(b) had this broad extension.

[38] *See infra* notes 94–98 and accompanying text.

[39] (1997) 189 CLR 579. The case is discussed in GEORGE WILLIAM, HUMAN RIGHTS UNDER THE AUSTRALIAN CONSTITUTION 192–93(2002).

[40] The desecration of national symbols is discussed in Chapter 8.

[41] [2004] 3 NZLR 704 (H.C.).

and opinions of any kind in any form."[42] The Court managed to protect the flag burner by interpreting the statute at issue narrowly. While the case will be later discussed in more depth,[43] what is important here is that the need to consider whether or not the act was protected indicates that this conduct constituted expression for purposes of the Bill of Rights Act.

Eric Barendt states as a general proposition that "courts are prepared to hold that forms of conduct, intended by the actors to communicate opinions and so understood by others, are covered by [free expression] provisions,"[44] providing as examples wearing badges and uniforms or making gestures. He goes on to say that "in some circumstances, views can only be expressed effectively to the public by engaging in a course of conduct. Politicians, celebrities, writers, and intellectuals can disseminate their ideas in print and on the broadcasting media, but for most people marching in the streets, wearing badges, and engaging in other activities are the best means of communication."[45]

ART

Edward Eberle provides an analysis of the various expressive dimensions of art.[46] With regard to United States law, Professor Eberle notes that the Supreme Court has found particular manifestations of art to be protected, without providing a general analysis.[47] He then undertakes to provide that general analysis, arguing that there are at least three reasons why art is special and is entitled to protection.

> First, art is special because it partakes of the creative process central and unique to human existence. Second, art provides an avenue to dimensions of human life less accessible by ordinary rational or cognitive processes. Art is a portal to nonrational, non-cognitive, non-discursive dimensions to human life, offering a fuller conception of the human person. Third, art functions as a private sphere of freedom not subject or susceptible, on the whole, to the normal rules of society.[48]

The values he finds would certainly justify protection under an autonomy-based theory. The admittedly creative nature of the expression would also seem to require protection under the broad standards in Canada.

[42] New Zealand Bill of Rights Act 1990, Public Act 1990 No 109 (Aug. 28, 1990), § 14, www.legislation.govt.nz/act/public/1990/0109/latest/DLM225513.html.

[43] The case will be discussed in more detail in Chapter 8.

[44] Eric Barendt, Freedom of Speech 78 (2d ed. 2005). [45] *Id.*

[46] *See* Edward J. Eberle, *Art as Speech*, 11 U. Pa. J.L. & Soc. Change (2007–2008).

[47] *See id.* at 1. [48] *Id.* at 6.

What is perhaps less convincing would be an argument from these features to a conclusion that it must be protected in all democracies. That conclusion would be justified, at least in those instances, by examples of art that convey a political message. There clearly are such examples. Eberle points to an example commonly cited, Pablo Picasso's *Guernica*, a painting depicting the horrors of war through a depiction of the bombing of a Basque village during the Spanish Civil War, and one less cited, the paintings of Felix Nussbaum depicting the despair and hopelessness of European Jews during the Nazi era.[49] Art, when it serves as political expression, must be protected in a democracy. And, as with other forms of expression the best approach may be to protect art more generally, subject to any exceptions and justifications.

The European Court of Human Rights, in *Müller v. Switzerland*,[50] an obscenity case based on the display of oil paintings, discussed the protected status of art. If art were not protected, there would be no need to determine whether a restriction based on its obscenity could be justified under Article 10 (2). The Court, however, concluded that Article 10 applied.

> Admittedly, Article 10 does not specify that freedom of artistic expression ... comes within its ambit, but neither, on the other hand, does it distinguish between the various forms of expression ... [I]t includes freedom of artistic expression-notably within freedom to receive and impart information and ideas-which affords the opportunity to take part in the public exchange of cultural, political and social information and ideas of all kinds.[51]

A particularly interesting approach is found in German law. In the *Mephisto* decision,[52] the German Constitutional Court noted that Article 5 (3) of the Basic Law declares that art, science, research, and teaching are free. The Court then provided a definition for art.

> The field of "art" must be determined by the distinctive structural features of the artistic enterprise. The essence of artistic endeavour lies in the free creative process whereby the artist, in his chosen communicative medium, gives immediate perceptible form to what he has felt, learnt, or experienced. Artistic activity involves both the conscious and the unconscious, in a manner not rationally separable. Intuition, imagination, and knowledge of the artist all play a part in artistic creation; it is not so much

49 *See id.* at 8.
50 (1991) 13 E.H.R.R. 212. The Court's obscenity analysis is discussed in Chapter 11.
51 *Id.* at ¶ 27.
52 BVerfGE 30, 173 (1971), available in translation at www.utexas.edu/law/academics/centers/transnational/work_new/german/case.php?id=1478.

communication as expression, indeed the most immediate expression of the artist's individuality.[53]

After setting out this definition, the Court discussed limitations placed on artistic freedom. Article 5 (1) protects the freedom of opinion, but Article 5 (2) allows statutory limitations on that freedom. In Article 5(3), art received different treatment.

> Art having its special nature and rules, its guarantee by Art. 5 III, 1 GG is absolute. The clear terms of that provision foredoom any attempt to limit it, whether by narrowing the idea of art in the light of one's value-judgments or by extending or invoking the limitations applicable to other constitutional provisions ... Art. 5 II GG which limits basic rights under Art. 5 I is inapplicable here. The different guarantees in Art. 5 GG are systematically separated, and this shows that the limitations in Art. 5 II are inapplicable to matters covered by Art. 5 III, since Art. 5 III is a lex specialis in relation to Art. 5 I. Nor is it acceptable to sever parts of a narrative work of art, call them expressions of opinion under Art. 5 I and then apply to them the limitations laid down in Art. 5.[54]

Thus, the German Court answers the question of whether art merits the protection of other aspects of expression by concluding that it merits greater protection, protection that cannot be overridden by statute. That does not mean that there can be no limits on art, but the limits must be found not simply in statutes but must find their basis in constitutional values.

MUSIC

Ward v. Rock Against Racism, a time, place and manner case, did involve musical performances, so it is unsurprising that the United States Supreme Court had something to say about music as protected speech.

> Music is one of the oldest forms of human expression. From Plato's discourse in *The Republic* to the totalitarian state in our own times, rulers have known its capacity to appeal to the intellect and to the emotions, and have used musical compositions to serve the needs of the state. The Constitution prohibits any like attempts in our own legal order. Music, as a form of expression and communication, is protected under the First Amendment.[55]

There are not a significant number of attempts to limit the distribution of music, and what attempts there are seem motivated by lyrics rather than music

[53] *Id.* Part III (1). [54] *Id.* Part III (4). [55] 491 U.S. at 790.

itself. For example, there were attempts to limit the distribution of record albums by the rap group 2 Live Crew, but the basis was a belief that the group's lyrics were obscene.[56] The objections were not to the beat or whatever melody may have been present. And, in the German *National Anthem* case, the concern was not over alteration of a musical score but over changes to the lyrics of the anthem.[57]

If music is seen to include lyrics, it is undeniable that music may, at least at times, convey a political message. The protest songs of the United States civil rights movement and the anti-war movement were clearly political and clearly had their impacts. Whether this should be seen as an argument that music should be protected or, instead, that the poetry that often accompanies music should be protected, it should be clear that those songs should be protected. Just as courts are reluctant to try to distinguish between great and poor literature, it would seem that protection should extend to lyrics generally. That, of course, does not mean that specific lyrics, either because they fit within an exception under United States law or are balanced by other values in the law of other countries, cannot be banned.

There are situations in which a musical score itself could be seen as political. Consider the scene from the film *Casablanca*, in which German officers' singing of the German national anthem is met with an impromptu rendition of *La Marseillaise* by the largely French clientele of Rick's. The World War II–era singing was clearly political, but of course, it was the lyrics that were sung. Suppose that instead of the customers singing, Sam, the piano player, had played the melody. That, too, would seem political, although here the political nature of the music itself would be the result of the lyrics by which it is normally accompanied. This demonstrates the difficulty in separating the two for purposes of looking at free expression protection.

There could certainly be instances in which it is a melody itself, with no connection to lyrics, that has a political purpose. During the Soviet occupation of Eastern Europe, the playing of a non-Russian ethnic melody might have had a political dimension. The same might have been true of the playing of an Irish reel, during the British occupation of Ireland. Music, with or without lyrics, would seem to be the sort of expression that, at least in certain

[56] For material on the attempts, *see* Brian O Gallagher & David P. Gaertner, *2 Live Crew and Judge Gonzales Too-2 Live Crew and the Miller Obscenity Test*, 18 J. Legis. 105 (1991).

[57] *See* BVerfGE 81, 298 (1990). The case may be found in translation at www.utexas.edu/law/academics/centers/transnational/work_new/german/case.php?id=631. The case is discussed in Chapter 8.

cases, should be protected. Again, probably the best approach is to protect music generally, absent an exception or justification.

DANCE

Dance presents an interesting issue. It may be protected in some contexts but not in others. The United States Court of Appeals for the Fourth Circuit drew a distinction between dance as a stage performance and dance as an activity. *Willis v. Town of Marshall*[58] concerned a town that held regular Friday night concerts at its community center. While the primary focus of the events was on music, with local music groups being allowed to sign up for playing time, there was an area off to the side of the stage and audience seating area where people danced to the music. Rebecca Willis enjoyed attending the concerts and dancing. Her dancing, however, raised concerns. According to the town, "Willis danced in a sexually provocative manner– gyrating and simulating sexual intercourse with her partner while 'hunched' on the floor."[59] That led to complaints and, after a talk with a town committee member failed to change her behavior, her being banned from attending the concerts.

Willis brought suit alleging, among other things, a violation of her free expression rights under the First Amendment. The court recognized that a stage performance consisting of dance, such as a ballet, would be protected by the First Amendment. It distinguished that situation from dancing on the dance floor. In the court's view, Willis was not engaging in communicative conduct. She was participating in an activity. The court seemed to see dancing as being more akin to playing basketball or engaging in a boxing match, both activities that are not expressive. It seems an odd parallel in this case, since the reason for banning Willis would seem to have been the erotic expression to be found in her dancing.

In other contexts, the distinction would seem more reasonable. Most people attending and participating in a dance may well be doing so solely because they enjoy the activity and with no intent to convey a message. However, some participants may also arguably be conveying a message that they possess a degree of grace or some other characteristic. The *Willis* court did draw support from a Supreme Court case, *Dallas v. Strangin*.[60] That case involved an ordinance that limited admission to certain dance halls to those between fourteen and eighteen years of age. The ordinance was challenged as a

[58] 426 F.3d 251 (4th Cir. 2005). [59] *Id.* at 254. [60] 490 U.S. 19 (1989).

violation of the First Amendment's freedom of association, but the Court rejected the claim. According to the *Willis* court, that constituted a rejection of the claim that there was expressive activity involved, since the presence of such expression would have justified a claim of expressive association.

Whether or not Willis's dancing should have been seen as expressive activity, there are clearly cases in which dance, not on the stage but on the dance floor, could be seen as expressive or even political. Those on the dance floor engaged in a national or culturally relevant dance may be making a political or cultural point. Consider, again, the scene from *Casablanca*. If the patrons, instead of singing, had danced a gavotte, that would seem equally political.

For the most part, there is little reason for governments to try to suppress dance. There may be dance performances, such as ballets or interpretive dances, that make a political point that upsets the government. If that is the motivation for suppression, it is an attack on the political speech that is essential to the maintenance of democracy and cannot be allowed in a democratic state. More likely, as was the case in *Willis*, there is some sort of moral objection. There are dance cases based on such concerns that arise in the context of nude dancing as entertainment.

The United States cases in this area are additionally interesting as an example of the lengths to which the courts have had to go to deny the protection of the First Amendment to such performances, in spite of the seemingly absolute language of the Amendment. The method employed is known as the "secondary effects" doctrine.

The secondary effects doctrine finds its genesis in *Young v. American Mini Theatres*.[61] The case presented a First Amendment argument that a Detroit ordinance that prohibited operating "adult" movie theaters, bookstores, or the like within 1,000 feet of each other or within 500 feet of a residential area was unconstitutional. The other establishments included within the ambit of the ordinance were those that presented material with an emphasis on the depiction of "specified sexual activities" or "specified anatomical areas." The theaters affected were, hence, defined based on the expression they chose to convey. And, the impact did not require that the material be legally obscene, only that it have the required emphasis.

It might be thought that treating free expression differently on that basis, seemingly a content-based distinction, should be a violation of the First Amendment. Yet, the Court found the ordinance constitutional. The key to this result was the conclusion that the ordinance was not intended to restrict

[61] 427 U.S. 50 (1976).

the material exhibited but to combat the *secondary* effects of adult entertainment districts. Where there is a concentration of such establishments, the city believed that those with a penchant for crime are joined together. Separating adult uses was intended to limit that secondary effect.

The Court saw the ordinance as a sort of zoning law. It recognized that the impact was based on content but indicated that the content was, in fact, not of great value.

> [F]ew of us would march our sons and daughters off to war to preserve the citizen's right to see "Specified Sexual Activities" exhibited in the theaters of our choice. Even though the First Amendment protects communication in this area from total suppression, we hold that the State may legitimately use the content of these materials as the basis for placing them in a different classification from other motion pictures.[62]

The Court's analysis may be seen as strained. While concluding that restricting material using a definition based on content was not a content-based restriction, if the aim of the ordinance was to reduce the secondary effects, it also took the time to belittle the material involved.

The Detroit ordinance did not act as a total ban on the exhibition of this sort of protected material. A later case had that practical effect. *Renton v. Playtime Theatres*[63] applied the same reasoning to an ordinance that prohibited adult motion picture theaters within 1,000 feet of a residential area, church, park, or school. The only areas that remained available were well developed, and operating a movie theater was not economically feasible. The Court was untroubled by the effective elimination of this variety of protected entertainment from the city, seeing the First Amendment as not requiring an economically favorable result.

It was against that background that the Court considered the constitutionality of prohibitions on nude dancing. There were actually two cases on the issue, *Barnes v. Glenn Theatre*[64] and *Erie v. Pap's A.M.*[65] Both upheld anti-nudity ordinances when challenged by adult entertainment venues offering nude dancing. The second case, as the last word even though lacking a majority opinion on the issue, better speaks to the thinking of the Court. The *Erie* plurality of four justices said that, while simply being in a state of nudity was not expressive conduct, nude dancing is expressive, "although . . . it falls only within the outer ambit of the First Amendment's protection."[66] Here too, the value in such expression was minimized.

62 *Id.* at 70–71. 63 475 U.S. 41 (1986). 64 501 U.S. 560 (1991). 65 529 U.S. 277 (2000).
66 *Id.* at 289.

Since nude dancing is conduct, even if seen as communicative conduct, the plurality applied the *O'Brien* test. The most important factor in that test is whether the restriction is aimed at the conduct addressed or the message conveyed by that conduct. The conclusion was that the ordinance was purely an anti-nudity ordinance and was not aimed at the erotic message conveyed by nude dancing. The plurality was not swayed by the fact that the city had not enforced its ordinance against a dramatic, non-erotic performance that involved nudity, accepting the city's claim that there had been no complaint and that it had not realized that there was nudity. It was also noted that the dancers were free to convey an erotic message; they could just not be nude in so doing.

O'Brien also requires an important governmental purpose, and the plurality was willing to find that in the city's attempt to combat harmful secondary effects. "In trying to control the secondary effects of nude dancing, the ordinance seeks to deter crime and the other deleterious effects caused by the presence of such an establishment in the neighborhood."[67] The ban was also seen as furthering the governmental interest, even if requiring dancers to wear pasties and G-strings did not eliminate, or even greatly reduce, secondary effects. With regard to the requirement that the impact on expression be limited, the plurality had already noted that the dancers could still convey their erotic message, even if not while in the nude.

A concurrence in the judgment by Justice Scalia, joined by Justice Thomas, agreed that the ordinance was aimed at nudity, as conduct, rather than at expression. According to the concurrence, that was sufficient to hold the ordinance constitutional.

> [E]ven if one hypothesizes that the city's object was to suppress only nude dancing, that would not establish an intent to suppress what (if anything) nude dancing communicates. I do not feel the need … to identify some "secondary effects" associated with nude dancing that the city could properly seek to eliminate.[68]

Indeed, Justice Scalia was skeptical over the impact of minimal clothing on any such secondary effects.[69]

Justice Souter, in a partial concurrence and partial dissent, disagreed with the plurality's analysis of the issues discussed here. A separate opinion by Justice Stevens, joined by Justice Ginsburg, noted the expansion of the secondary effects doctrine. While earlier use of the doctrine had justified zoning of adult entertainment districts, here secondary effects were seen as

67 *Id.* at 293. 68 *Id.* at 310 (Scalia, J., concurring). 69 *See id.*

justifying the total suppression of one form of adult entertainment. "If one assumes that the same erotic messages conveyed by nude dancers as by those wearing minimal costumes, one means of expressing that messages is banned. If one assumes that the message is different, one of those messages is banned. In either event the ordinance is a total ban."[70]

Given the German position that creative endeavors constitute art protected by Article 5(3) of the Basic Law, it would seem likely that nude dancing to convey an erotic message would be protected. As art, limitations would have to be justified by constitutional values. There is a relevant German case that, while not addressing a restriction on nude dancing, did distinguish such dancing from the situation the court was addressing. The *Peep Show Decision*[71] concerned an application for a license to conduct a peep show in which the nude body of a woman would be shown to spectators sitting in single-seat booths around the stage.[72] The license was denied, and the denial was appealed to the Federal Administrative Tribunal. The court held that the license should have been refused, because the display would have violated morality. The morality of the issue, however, had to do with the respect and protection due to human dignity, under Article 1 of the German Basic Law. It also made no difference that the woman who would be performing would be doing so voluntarily.

The court drew a distinction between this sort of display and the sort of dance at issue in the United States cases.

> The mere display of the naked female body does not violate human dignity, so that, at least as regards a violation of human dignity, no objections exist in principle against the usual striptease performances . . . Peep shows are fundamentally different from striptease performances. The actions of a woman performing a striptease in front of an audience she can see are in line with the traditional stage and dance show and leave the personal individuality of the performer intact . . . In a peep show, however, the woman is placed in a degrading position, she is treated like an object . . .[73]

It would seem that the distinction is between the simple stage display of nudity and the situation in which the performer conveys a message to the viewer.

[70] *Id.* at 319 (Stevens, J., dissenting) (citation omitted). [71] BVerfGE 64, 274 (1981).

[72] Discussions of the case may be found in a number of places, including SABINE MICHALOWSKI & LORNA WOODS, GERMAN CONSTITUTIONAL LAW: THE PROTECTION OF CIVIL LIBERTIES 104–7 (1999); Shayana Kadidal, *Obscenity in the Age of Mechanical Reproduction*, 44 AM. J. COMP. L. 353, 353–55 (1996). The viewer would place coins in a slot, and that would cause a window flap to open to provide a view of the woman. *See id.* at 355.

[73] The translation is from MICHALOWSKI & WOODS, *supra* note 72, at 105.

In other countries in which the constitution allows other interests to be balanced against free expression, nude dancing might well be recognized as expression, even if limitations are allowed. As seen, Canadian law recognizes anything, other than an act of violence, that attempts to convey a meaning as expression for purposes of Section 2(b) of the Charter. Dance performances would seem to qualify.

The issue was addressed by the Saskatchewan Court of Appeal in *Saskatchewan Ltd. v. Saskatchewan.*[74] The issue there was the legitimacy of provincial alcohol regulations that prohibited nude dancing in bars. Before turning to the regulation itself, the court had to consider the status of such performances as expression, concluding that they do qualify. The lead opinion stated: "Several dancers testified … they were expressing a fantasy, or an erotic idea or emotion. They said they were attempting to connect with the audience and attempting to portray a sexual message."[75] The opinion also quoted from an earlier opinion in a case before the same court and involving the same parties:

> [I]t is difficult to conceive of entertainment consisting of "a strip tease performance" not falling within the scope of the term "expression." Neither the Authority nor the Attorney General, however, was prepared to concede the point, submitting that such activity is purely physical and, as such, devoid of meaning. With respect, this is simply not so. Were it so, there would be no material distinction, for example, between persons removing their clothing in preparation for going to bed and in the performance of the striptease act; the one would be as expressively empty as the other.[76]

Nonetheless, the court concluded that the prohibition on nude entertainment where alcohol is sold could stand. Since nude dancing was otherwise allowed in the province, the restriction was aimed at the physical consequences of mixing alcohol and nudity.[77] Furthermore, "the granting of constitutional protection to this type of activity which can only be classified as a marketing tool to sell alcohol, would trivialize and demean the rights guaranteed by the Charter."[78]

There is contrary law in an earlier Ontario case. In *Regina v. Zikman,*[79] the appellant had been convicted of being nude in a public place, as a result of her nude dancing in a tavern. The lead, single justice, opinion concluded that the Charter did not apply, but it seemed to take a very weak view of Charter protections. "Dancing is clearly a mode of expression, but it is hardly necessary

[74] [2001] 4 W.W.R. 603. [75] *Id.* at ¶ 19.

[76] *Id.* at ¶ 20 (quoting Saskatchewan Ltd. v. Saskatchewan, [1998] 7 W.W.R. 209, 259–60 (Sask. C.A.)(opinion of Cameron J.A.)).

[77] *See id.* at ¶ 29. [78] *Id.* at ¶ 31. [79] 1 C.C.R. (2d) 221 (1990).

to say that the appellant had a *Charter* protected right to dance, or even to dance in the nude. She could do whatever she wished, provided it was not prohibited by law."[80] This would seem to have the logical form "the Charter protects expression, dancing is expression, but dancing is not protected," not one of the classic syllogistic forms.

The Saskatchewan opinion seems more reasonable, given the broad view of expression provided by the Canadian Supreme Court in *Irwin Toy*. It is also consistent with other Canadian cases allowing restrictions on nude dance, where alcohol is sold,[81] or where audience participation turns the dance into an indecent public act.[82]

COMMERCIAL SPEECH

Commercial speech, the offer to provide goods or services for compensation, presents an interesting issue. It is expression that seems unrelated to democracy, yet it is widely protected in the democratic countries. A seeming major exception is found in Australia, where the implied freedom of expression reaches only political speech. Chief Justice Mason, with Justices Toohey and Gaudron, in *Theophanous v. Herald & Weekly Times*,[83] suggested that commercial speech was not protected, and a commentator on Australian expression law finds no later cases, at least as of the 2,000, clearly taking a contrary position.[84]

The fairly widespread protection afforded to commercial speech does not mean that democratic countries do not attempt to place any limitations on such expression. It is common for governments to place limits on advertising where the products or services advertised concern health or professional services.[85] There are also attempts to limit advertising where products may be unhealthy.[86] Lastly, there may be a need to shield a particularly susceptible

[80] *Id.* at ¶ 6 (opinion of Finlayson, J.A.).

[81] In Rio Hotel v. New Brunswick, [1987] 2 S.C.R. 59, the Supreme Court of Canada recognized the provincial right to control nude dancing in places where alcohol is sold, as an aspect of its licensing authority.

[82] *See* Regina v. Ludacka, 105 CCC (3d) 565 (Ont. 1996). [83] (1994) 182 CLR 104.

[84] *See* Michael Chesterman, Freedom of Speech in Australian Law: A Delicate Plant 46 (2000).

[85] *See infra* notes 89–91, 99–115 and accompanying text.

[86] For a comparative analysis of restrictions on commercial speech based on health concerns, *see, e.g.*, Micah I Berman, *Commercial Speech Law and Tobacco Marketing: A Comparative Discussion of the United States and Canada*, 39 Am. J. of Law & Med. 218 (2013); J. Steven Rich, *Commercial Speech in the Law of the European Union: Lessons for the United States*, 51 Fed. Comm. L.J. 263 (1998).

population, such as children.[87] Nonetheless, with the exception of Australia, commercial speech does receive some protection, even if with a less stringent test in the United States or with a greater likelihood of other interests balancing the infringement on commercial expression in other countries.

The Supreme Court of the United States concluded in *Virginia State Board of Pharmacy v. Virginia Citizens Consumer Council*,[88] that commercial speech enjoys at least some protection. It declared unconstitutional a Virginia rule of professional conduct that prohibited pharmacists from advertising the prices at which they would sell prescription drugs. The Court rejected claims by the state that it was trying to protect the professional status and competence of pharmacists and the relationship between patients and pharmacists and saw the regulation as being aimed at keeping consumers ignorant, at least with regard to prices. The Court did accept that there could be some limitations, specifically recognizing prohibitions on false and misleading advertising. "The First Amendment . . . does not prohibit the State from ensuring that the stream of commercial information flows cleanly as well as freely."[89] Commercial speech is clearly less protected, under this stipulation, than, for example, political speech, since the state cannot assure that the stream runs cleanly in that area.

As has been the case for testing varieties of regulation of speech, in United States law there is also the need for a special test for this less protected variety of speech. That test is found in *Central Hudson Gas & Electric v. Public Service Commission*.[90]

> In commercial speech cases . . . a four-part analysis has developed. At the outset, we must determine whether the expression is protected by the First Amendment. For commercial speech to come within that provision, it at least must concern lawful activity and not be misleading. Next, we asked whether the asserted governmental interest is substantial. If both inquiries yield positive answers, we must determine whether the regulation directly advances the governmental interest asserted and whether it is not more extensive than is necessary to serve that interest.[91]

Lorillard Tobacco v. Reilley[92] provides an example of the application of the *Central Hudson* test in the context of the regulation of an unhealthy product and the need to protect a vulnerable population. The Attorney General of

[87] For comparative analysis of commercial speech and vulnerable groups, *see, e.g.*, David Darwin, *Advertising Obesity: Can the U.S. Follow the Lead of the UK in Limiting Television Marketing of Unhealthy Food to Children?*, 42 Vand. J. Transnat'l L. 317 (2009).

[88] 425 U.S. 748 (1976). [89] *Id.* at 771–72. [90] 447 U.S. 557 (1980). [91] *Id.* at 566.

[92] 533 U.S. 525 (2001).

Massachusetts, being authorized to regulate misleading advertising, concluded that tobacco advertising accessible to children fell into that category. He adopted regulations barring outdoor advertising of tobacco products within 1,000 feet of a school or playground. Within retail establishments, advertisements visible from the street were also barred in the same areas, and advertisements not visible from the street had to be a minimum of five feet above the floor.

The Supreme Court struck down the regulations.[93] The products involved were lawful for adults, and the advertising was seen as not misleading. The Court did accept the government's interest in preventing youth consumption of the products as substantial. The Court also accepted that limits on outdoor advertising directly advanced the interest. The outdoor advertising regulation could not, however, meet the fourth prong of the test. The fact that almost the entirety of all the major metropolitan areas in Massachusetts were within 1,000 feet of a school or playground, and thus that there was a greatly lessened ability to reach adult consumers, meant that the regulation was not sufficiently tailored. The indoor regulation requiring that advertisements be at least five feet above the floor failed the third prong. Given that children can see advertisements at that height meant there was no direct advancement of the government interest. The result shows that commercial speech in the United States does receive a significant level of protection. Even with an unhealthy product and a vulnerable population, at least these regulations could not stand.

In the Canadian case *Irwin Toy*, the three Justice opinion by Chief Justice Dickson concluded, given the broad view expressed as to what costumes expression, that "there is no sound basis on which commercial expression can be excluded from the protection of s. 2(b) of the *Charter*."[94] The law at issue was a provision of the Québec *Consumer Protection Act* that prohibited television advertisements directed at children under thirteen.[95] While such commercial speech may be protected under the Charter, Section 1 may justify infringement. In considering the limitation, the Court found a pressing and substantial concern, "the protection of a group which is particularly vulnerable to the techniques of seduction and manipulation abundant in advertising."[96] The ban on such advertising would contribute to the goal of protecting that group. The

[93] The regulations addressed all tobacco products, including cigarettes, cigars, and smokeless tobacco. The commercial speech analysis in the case actually addressed all but cigarettes, since the Court concluded that federal law regarding the advertising of cigarettes preempted state regulation. It does seem clear that had there not been this preemption, the same analysis would have applied to cigarettes.

[94] *Id.* at ¶ 46. [95] R.S.Q., c. P-40.1, §§ 248–49. [96] [1989] 1 S.C.R. 927 at ¶ 72.

Court also seemed to minimize the value of the speech involved, saying "television advertising directed to young children is *per se* manipulative. Such advertising aims to promote products by convincing those who will always believe."[97] Furthermore, the impact was minimized and there was proportionality, in that "[a]dvertisers are always free to direct their message at parents and other adults."[98]

There are Canadian cases that conclude that at least some limitations on commercial speech do violate the Charter. *Rocket v. Royal College of Dental Surgeons*[99] involved discipline imposed on two dentists for violating a prohibition on advertising. Interestingly, the advertisement at issue was not placed by the two dentists. It was instead an ad for Holiday Inns. The ad talked about the dentists' innovative delivery of services in shopping malls and other convenient locations and the rapid growth of their business. It concluded by saying that, when they travel on business, they stay at Holiday Inns.

Since the prohibition on advertising infringed on expression, and was intended to do so, it was a violation of Section 2(b). So, the question became whether or not the infringement could be justified under Section 1. The Canadian Supreme Court applied the *Oakes* analysis. The Court was willing to accept that the regulation's objective was sufficiently important saying that "it is essential to accord to professional societies the power to regulate the methods by which their members advertise."[100] Furthermore, the Court said that the regulations further the objective of promoting professionalism and limiting misleading advertising.[101] The difficulty for the regulation was over proportionality. It could not be seen as a minimal impairment, given the breadth of its application, prohibiting all advertising even of dentists' hours and languages spoken. Such a limitation did not further the objective, so the effect on expression was disproportionate.[102]

Since the European Union also employs a balancing test, there is again no need for a special test for commercial speech. In fact, in an early case, the European Court of Human Rights analyzed an advertising restriction, without determining the status of commercial speech as protected expression. *Barthold v. Germany*[103] grew out of proceedings against a veterinarian for violating standards that forbade advertising and publicity. The veterinarian published critical comments regarding the availability of after hours emergency veterinary services. In so doing he had discussed his own practice and his availability. The Court decided that penalties imposed against the veterinarian could be analyzed in terms of Article 10, without

[97] *Id.* [98] *Id.* at ¶ 90. [99] [1990] 2 S.C.R. 232. [100] *Id.* at ¶ 41. [101] *Id.* at ¶ 42.
[102] *See id.* at ¶¶ 43–44. [103] (1985) 7 E.H.R.R. 383.

actually deciding that commercial speech comes within its purview. On the assumption that it did, the Court examined the aim of the regulation, said to be the protection of the rights of others and not allowing the acquisition of a commercial advantage over colleagues adhering to the rules, and found it legitimate. The Court held, however, that the act went beyond what was necessary in a democratic society. Any publicity obtained through the publication of the article was "altogether secondary having regard to the principal content of the article and to the nature of the issue being put to the public at large."[104] The impact on an issue of public concern was not proportionate to the aim.

In a later case, *Casado Coca v. Spain*,[105] the European Court did consider the issue of whether or not commercial speech came within the scope of Article 10. In that regard, the Court said: "Article 10 guarantees freedom of expression to 'everyone'. No distinction is made in it according to whether the type or aim pursued is profit-making making or not . . ."[106] That was, of course, not the end of the issue, since the Court still had to decide whether restrictions on advertising by attorneys could be justified under Article 10(2). The Court found a legitimate aim.

> The Court does not have any reason to doubt that the Bar rules complained of were designed to protect the interests of the public while ensuring respect for members of the Bar. In this connection, the special nature of the profession practiced by members of the Bar must be considered; in their capacity as officers of the court they benefit from an exclusive right of audience and immunity from legal process in respect of their oral presentation of cases in court, but the conduct must be discrete, honest and dignified. The restrictions on advertising were traditionally justified by reference to these special features.[107]

The Court said that the Member States were in a better position than the Court in determining the proper balance between the rights of the public to receive information and the administration of justice and maintaining the dignity of the bar.[108] The States, as in other areas of the regulation of expression, enjoyed a margin of appreciation. Having noted that the advertising ban was not absolute, allowing notice to the public when a practice was being established or when the membership, address or phone number changed,[109] the Court concluded that the ban was within the margin of appreciation.

[104] *Id.* at 58. [105] (1994) 18 E.H.R.R. 1. [106] *Id.* at ¶ 35. [107] *Id.* at ¶ 46.
[108] *See id.* at ¶ 55. [109] *See id.* at ¶ 52.

In Japan, the Moxa Advertising Case, *Ono v. Japan*,[110] addressed restrictions on advertising among the practitioners of certain purportedly therapeutic methods. A practitioner of acupuncture, moxa cautery, massage, and judo therapy challenged the complete ban on all advertising of these methods, other than simply providing a name and address. The Supreme Court found the restrictions justified.

> There is concern about inviting ... loss of opportunity to receive the proper medical treatment at the proper time. Prohibiting the advertisement of other than the prescribed matters in order to prevent such ill effects before hand must be approved as a measure unavoidable for the maintenance of the public welfare from the standpoint of the nation's health and hygiene.[111]

Perhaps more importantly, the Court also said "restrictions on advertising such as the above do not *ipso facto* impair freedom of thought and freedom of conscience."[112] This might be taken as indicating a broader exclusion of commercial speech from protection. A commentator on Japanese law notes a variety of restrictions on commercial speech aimed both at the protection of consumers and unfair competition.[113] The types of restrictions mentioned include prohibitions on false, misleading, or exaggerated advertising, the advertising of illegal conduct, and prohibitions on advertising certain medical treatments.[114] Other than the last category, the restriction seems similar to those allowed in the United States, and even restrictions in the last category might be able to meet the *Central Hudson* test. Referring to *Ono*, the commentator says "[t]he Court gave almost no protection to commercial speech ... Commercial speech can be restricted ... if the Diet found it capable of bringing about some kind of danger to the public health and safety."[115] Again, it is not clear how different this is from United States law.

Professor Barendt, as part of an extensive discussion of commercial speech,[116] raises some questions as to why it should be protected. In a section titled "Should Commercial Speech be Covered by Free Speech Clauses?"[117] he examines the arguments offered by Justice Blackmun in *Virginia State Board of Pharmacy*, consumer interest, societal interest in consumer information, public interest, and the role of such information in the free market,

[110] 5 Keishū 2 at 347 (1961). The case may be found in translation at HIROSHI ITOH & LAWRENCE WARD BEER, THE CONSTITUTIONAL CASE LAW OF JAPAN: SELECTED SUPREME COURT DECISIONS, 1961–70, 217 (1978).

[111] *Id.* at 219 [112] *Id.*

[113] *See* Shigenori Matsui, *Freedom of Expression in Japan*, 38 OSAKA UNIV. L. REV. 13 (1991).

[114] *Id.* at 28–29, [115] *Id.* at 29–30. [116] *See* BARENDT, *supra* note 44, at 392–416.

[117] *See id.* at 399–401.

and seems to find them lacking. Neither does he find justification in later opinions or scholarship.

> The Supreme Court has considered the case for commercial speech coverage in many subsequent cases, but has not significantly added to the arguments it deployed in *Virginia Pharmacy*. Courts in other jurisdictions have contributed little to the theoretical debate. The Supreme Court of Canada, for instance, has generally been content to say that advertising falls within the scope of "expression" for the purposes of section 2(b) of the Charter. It conveys meaning. There is no reason to *exclude* it from its coverage. The academic literature, particularly in the United States, is vast, but it either refines, rather than adds significantly to, the case made by Blackmun J. for coverage of commercial speech, or is very critical of it.[118]

Professor Barendt makes a good point. The arguments from free speech theory seem lacking. Certainly, such speech does not touch on the concerns surrounding the maintenance of democracy. Yet, there is a significant degree of uniformity in providing protection, even if differences exist in the details and tests employed. Perhaps the best explanation for the widespread protection democratic countries provide commercial speech is found not in democracy but in a belief in the free market. The United States Supreme Court said, in *Virginia State Board of Pharmacy*:

> So long as we preserve a predominantly free enterprise economy, the allocation of our resources in large measure will be made through numerous private economic decisions. It is a matter of public interest that those decisions, in the aggregate, be intelligent and well-informed. To this end, the free flow of commercial information is indispensable.[119]

That may well be true, but it does not speak to democracy. A democratic country could clearly deny protection to commercial speech, as does Australia, and not fall out of the community of democracies.

CONCLUSIONS

As the various sections demonstrate, there is a wide variety, perhaps an almost inexhaustible number, of ways to express oneself. There are a variety of approaches to the issue of how different methods of expression on different subject matters should be treated. Because of the absolute sounding nature of the protection of free expression in the United States, special categories and

[118] *Id.* at 401 (footnote omitted). [119] 425 U.S. at 765.

tests based on the place and the nature of the expression have been required. The Supreme Court has recognized that not all forms of expression on all subject matters and in all places need to be treated the same. But because the language of the First Amendment has an absolutist tone, the Court has had to struggle with expression in its various manifestations.

Countries, and the European Union, where the relevant provisions protecting expression are accompanied by provisions expressly allowing a balancing of free expression values against competing fundamental values or, indeed, of factors such as the nature of the property or of the type of expression involved, have not required the adoption of special tests. The balancing called for in the free expression provision simply takes those factors into account.

In most cases, the results may well be similar. Indeed, for expression that is important to the maintenance of a democracy, particularly for political speech, the results would have to be similar. The differences may be most significant in learning and applying law. The approach of the United States requires an understanding of a number of categories and tests, but once the category and test are identified, the application may be simple. In a balancing regime, there is less need to learn to identify categories and differing tests, but each application of the law may require more analysis in balancing the interests involved.

3

Incitement of Crime

There are varieties of speech that are commonly suppressed, even in fully functioning democracies. One important such variety is the incitement of crime.[1] Soliciting another to commit an ordinary crime does not further any of the values, with the possible exception of self-fulfillment, that underlie the freedom of expression. Criminal behavior is not a part of the democratic process, so punishing the advocacy of crime would not seem odd.

On the other hand, limitations on speech critical of the government raise a more difficult issue. The right to criticize the government is a necessary aspect of democracy, yet even democratic governments need not leave themselves open to violent overthrow. Classic sedition statutes that prohibit expression that brings the government into contempt are of the former variety that must be open. Orders to a group engaged in violent overthrow are the latter and may be suppressed.

There are many cases in between. Where there is political motivation for the advocacy of crime, there is a need for democracies to determine how closely such political speech must come to actually inciting crime, before it may be prosecuted. It would seem that the United States, with its strongly worded freedom of expression, might have the most difficulty with this issue. Democracies with balancing provisions attached to the freedom of expression,

[1] Another area in which speech can be punished, under United States law, is the true threat, expression that intentionally and reasonably places a person in fear. This is so even in the context of political contention. A case out of the United States Court of Appeals for the Ninth Circuit allowed civil liability in a suit brought by abortion providers against anti-abortion activists. Planned Parenthood of the Columbia/Willamette, Inc. v. American Coalition of Life Activists, 290 F.3d 1058 (9th Cir. 2002), grew out of a series of actions including a wanted poster for those involved in providing abortions and a website in which there was indication of those on the list of such providers who had been killed or wounded. *See also* Elonis v. United States, 135 S.Ct. 2001 (2015)(requiring an intent for threats in an internet posting).

especially where the provision provides for restrictions necessary to the maintenance of public order, might have less difficulty. Lastly, a country that protects only political speech might see any speech touching on incitement as being other than political and, thus, subject to limitation.

THE UNITED STATES AND "ABSOLUTIST" PROTECTIONS

There is a long history of the suppression of speech in the United States, when the speech is thought potentially to lead to criminal behavior, even when the speech has a political aspect. The earliest important cases were in the era of World War I.[2] Those cases include *Debs v. United States*,[3] a case in which the defendant, the leader of the Socialist Party and that party's regular candidate for president, was convicted of causing and inciting and attempting to cause and incite refusal of duty in the military and obstructing or attempting to obstruct recruitment and enlistment. The charges were based on a speech Debs gave on socialism that included, at least implied, sentiments that individuals should not submit to the military draft. Since refusal to submit to the draft would be illegal, Debs' speech could be seen as inciting unlawful activity. But the fact that the government could convict a political leader for what was also political speech might provide justification for a general unwillingness to allow the government to restrict speech.

The Cold War fears over communism led to another series of cases. In fact, the concern over the advocacy by the Communists of illegal conduct, including the overthrow of the government by violence, began prior to the Cold War. In the 1927 case *Whitney v. California*,[4] a conviction was upheld against an individual who had helped organize the Communist Labor Party of California, an organization seen as advocating such activity. During what is within the Cold War era, there were still further cases. For example, in *Dennis v. United States*,[5] the Supreme Court affirmed convictions based on organizing the Communist Party and advocating and teaching the duty of overthrowing the government. While none of the defendants had the political status of Debs, the speech involved did have a political aspect to it, and looking back at such convictions may have contributed to a general mistrust of government regulation of speech.

The Supreme Court's analysis of when advocacy can be prosecuted evolved from that era, and the modern test, in the United States, regarding the

[2] There was, also, the Sedition Act in the early days of the Republic, but it was short lived.
[3] 249 U.S. 211 (1919). [4] 274 U.S. 357 (1927). [5] 341 U.S. 494 (1951).

suppression of such speech is found in *Brandenburg v. Ohio*.[6] That case grew out of a rally of the Ku Klux Klan. A local leader invited a reporter and cameraman from a Cincinnati television station to attend a rally held on a local farm, with only members of the Klan and the television station personnel present. Film of the rally was later shown on television and provided some of the basis for the prosecution of the Klan leader. The film showed twelve individuals, wearing Klan regalia and some carrying firearms, burning a cross. The film also showed Brandenburg speaking to the group. In the speech, he said:

> This is an organizers' meeting. We have had quite a few members here today which are-we have hundreds, hundreds of members throughout the State of Ohio. I can quote from a newspaper clipping ... The Klan has more members in the State of Ohio than does any other organization. We're not a revengent organization but if our President, our Congress, our Supreme Court, continues to suppress the white, Caucasian race, it's possible that there might have to be some revengeance taken.[7]

This appeared to the state to be the advocacy of violence, but it also, in a real sense, had a political content, advocating action by the federal government. Brandenburg was charged under Ohio's Criminal Syndicalism Act. The Act was quite broad. As described by the Court:

> The Act punishes persons who "advocate or teach the duty, necessity, or propriety" of violence "as a means of accomplishing industrial or political reform"; or who publish or circulate or display any book or paper containing such advocacy; or who "justify" the commission of violent acts "with intent to exemplify, spread or advocate the propriety of the doctrines of criminal syndicalism"; or who "voluntarily assemble" with a group formed "to teach or advocate the doctrines of criminal syndicalism."[8]

This prohibition was too broad for the Court. The Court said that "the constitutional guarantees of free speech and free press do not permit a State to forbid or proscribe advocacy of the use of force or of law violation except where such advocacy is directed to inciting or producing imminent lawless action and is likely to produce such action."[9] Teaching, in the abstract, the morality of resorting to force to accomplish change falls short of leading to imminent lawless action.[10]

It deserves mention that the requirement that the advocacy be "directed to inciting or producing imminent lawless action" would indicate an intent

[6] 395 U.S. 444 (1969). [7] *Id.* at 446. [8] *Id.* at 448. [9] *Id.* at 447.
[10] *See id.* at 448.

requirement. Speech that happens to lead to such action, without intent that it occur, as in the case of a crime committed by an individual inspired by a crime drama, does not fit within the *Brandenburg* definition. It is also clear that the Court was serious about the requirements of imminence. In *Hess v. Indiana*,[11] the Court found unconstitutional a conviction based on speech that called for later action. During an antiwar demonstration on the campus of Indiana University, a street had become blocked and the Sheriff's office attempted to clear it. Hess was reported to have said "We'll take the fucking street later [or again]." The Court said that the exhortation could be seen as counseling present moderation, and that at worst "it amounted to nothing more than advocacy of illegal action at some indefinite future time."[12] Such advocacy of future action did not meet the *Brandenburg* test.

The *Brandenburg* test, also known as the "clear and present danger" test, may be seen as a specific form of the usual United States requirement that the infringement of constitutional rights must be justified under strict scrutiny. The infringement must be necessary to, or narrowly tailored to, a compelling governmental interest. The prevention of illegal activity is a compelling interest, and the likelihood and imminence of the harm makes the suppression of the speech necessary to that interest. If the harm is not imminent, then not only is more speech the best remedy for bad speech, it is a less restrictive alternative than suppression. The existence of this specific form of strict scrutiny does not mean that the government is barred from relying on other compelling interests to which a limitation is necessary.[13]

There are United States cases in which liability for expression, either civil or criminal, has been found, even with a lack of imminence. Perhaps the most interesting is a case decided by the United States Court of Appeals for the Fourth Circuit. *Rice v. Paladin Enterprises*[14] was a wrongful death suit growing out of a multiple murder. The person who had committed the murders had purchased a book, published by Paladin, titled *Hit Man: A Technical Manual for Independent Contractors*. The book was a step-by-step, how-to guide with instructions on finding clients, selecting weapons and locations, carrying out the contracted murder, getting away, and destroying the evidence. The person committing the murders followed the instructions to the letter, even if the instructions on escaping and avoiding conviction were unavailing.

[11] 414 U.S. 105 (1973). [12] *Id.* at 108.

[13] For example, in Burson v. Freeman, 504 U.S. 191 (1992), the Court allowed limitations on electioneering within 100 feet of the entrances of polling places as necessary to protect free and fair elections.

[14] 128 F.3d 233 (4th Cir. 1997).

The suit was based on a claim of accessory liability on the part of the publishers. The book had clearly been of assistance to the person committing the crime, but liability also required the intent that the crime be committed. Such an intent might, theoretically, have been found in the book's exhortations regarding becoming a real man by engaging in professional murder and separating oneself from the "herd of pathetic sheep" that makes up the rest of society. But such an argument was not necessary; the publishers admitted an intent that the book's purchasers follow the instructions and engage in contract murder. Their position was that, even with such an intent, the book was protected by the First Amendment. The admission was unwise, and the Fourth Circuit allowed the suit to proceed.

There are other United States cases in which instructional materials, together with intent, have been sufficient for even criminal liability. As an example, *United States v. Barnett*[15] involved the manufacture of the illegal drug phencyclidine. The Drug Enforcement Administration (DEA) arrested an individual who was attempting to manufacture the drug. The DEA found instructional material, produced by Barnett, that the attempted manufacturer had used in his efforts. Agents determined the source of the materials, ordered additional instructional manuals, and then arrested Barnett. He was convicted of aiding and abetting a violation of drug laws.

Barnett claimed the First Amendment right to disseminate materials, but the court said that the First Amendment "does not provide a defense to a criminal charge simply because the actor uses words to carry out his illegal purpose."[16] The court noted, in support of that proposition, that a threatening note, used to induce a teller to hand over the money in a bank robbery, or a forged check can both be the basis for criminal liability, even though both are forms of expression. The court seemed untroubled by the fact that the case at hand involved a more widely disseminated publication, in comparison to a targeted threat or inducement to part with money.

The difficulty with *Rice* and *Barnett*, in terms of the *Brandenburg* test, is the lack of imminence. There still has to be intent that the expression lead to an unlawful act, but the *Brandenburg* requirement that the harm, the unlawful act, be imminent seems not to have been present at the time of publication. It is true that the instructional nature of the material means that the expression is continuously available, and there may be imminence at the point at which it is read. Perhaps, the better distinction is that in the *Brandenburg* line of cases the expression is stopped before the unlawful act occurs. In such a case, it

[15] 667 F.2d 835 (9th Cir. 1982). [16] *Id.* at 842.

must be shown that the harm would have quickly ensued, so that the only way to stop it was to interrupt and punish the expression. In *Rice* and *Barnett*, the crimes actually did occur, and instruction, combined with intent, was sufficient for liability.

The Japanese Constitution sets out its guarantee of expression in similar, seemingly absolute, terms. Article 21 provides: "Freedom of assembly and association as well as speech, press, and all other forms of expression are guaranteed. No censorship shall be maintained."[17] Given the similarity in the nature of the guarantees, it would not be surprising if Japan took a position similar to that of the United States with regard to limits on even inciting political speech. However, the Japanese Court has made it clear that expression rights must be exercised responsibly and must give way to the public welfare.[18]

A Japanese case raising the particular issue of incitement, *Japan v. Kanemoto*,[19] grew out of the distribution of printed material supporting insurrection. While initially convicted, the Nagoya High Court overturned the conviction, seeing the political expression involved as presenting an abstract, rather than concrete, danger and concluding that, while the "'clear and present danger' rule ... is not the sole, absolute, or universal principle to be followed, [it] should be recognized as one criterion for regulating freedom of expression in such cases."[20] Indeed, concerns over the impact of such laws on political speech were written into the law addressing subversive activities. The law states: "Because it has an important relation to the fundamental rights of the people, this law must be applied only within the narrowest possible limits necessary for the preservation of public safety and must not be interpreted to extend beyond this in the slightest degree."[21] With this caveat, the law provided for imprisonment of any person "who publicly posts, distributes, or prints any document or drawing that has proclaimed the propriety or the necessity of the performance of such crime."[22]

When the case reached the Japanese Supreme Court, the Court dismissed the appeal. The Court added that the potentially subversive acts of expression must be carried out with the intent to incite insurrection.

[17] Shigenori Matsui, *Freedom of Expression in Japan*, 38 Osaka Univ. L. Rev. 13 (1991).

[18] *See id.* at 14–15.

[19] Hanrei Jihō, No. 396, 19 (1965). The case is available in translation in Hiroshi Itoh & Lawrence Ward Beer, The Constitutional Case Law of Japan: Selected Supreme Court Decisions, 1961–70 242 (1978).

[20] *See id.* at 242 (editor's note).

[21] *See id.* at 242 (translating Subversive Activities Prevention Law (Law 240 of 1952), Article 2).

[22] *See id.* (translating Subversive Activities Prevention Law (Law 240 of 1952) Article 38, 2 (2)).

> The intent of the court below is that caution should be exercised in judging the presence or absence of that motive, since it is not permissible to interpret lightly the question of motive, particularly in light of the legal intent of Article 2 of the same law which establishes a prohibition on its broad interpretation and confines application of this law to the minimum measures necessary for the preservation of public safety.[23]

While the clear and present danger rule may play a role, and intent is required, Shigenori Matsui, a commentator on Japanese law indicates that the test falls short of requiring the demonstration of a clear and present danger.[24] There are statutes addressing advocacy for the violent overthrow of the government, illegal strikes and tax evasion.[25] The commentator's analysis of the *Emergency Food Supply Order Case*[26] is that "if the speech fell within prescribed advocacy, it then did not matter whether the speech was direct incitement or indirect or abstract advocacy of doctrine. Nor it matted [sic] what danger the speech had created or whether the danger was imminent."[27] More directly, the commentator points to another case in which "the Court quite summarily rejected the argument that the Government could not prohibit subversive speech unless there was clear and present danger."[28]

BALANCING PROVISIONS AND THE EUROPEAN UNION

The protection of free expression in Germany, provided by Article 5, has recognized limits on expression. Article 5(2) provides: "These rights shall find their limits in the provisions of general laws, in provisions for the protection of young persons, and in the right to personal honor." Limitations in "provisions of general laws" seem very broad, and the German Penal Code contains a number of provisions directed at the sorts of acts discussed in the previous section. Section 30 (1) generally prohibits attempting to incite the commission of a felony, and Section 89 prohibits interfering with the activities of the German armed forces.[29] Section 89 includes punishment for anyone who "intentionally lends support to efforts directed against the existence or security of the Federal Republic of Germany, or its constitutional principles ..."[30] There is also a provision directed at threatening mob violence or "stir[ring] up

[23] *Id.* at 243. [24] *See* Matsui, *supra* note 17, at 22–23. [25] *See id.* at 22.

[26] Keishu vol. 3, no. 6 at 839 (cited in Shigenori Matsui, *supra* note 17, at 23). [27] *Id.*

[28] *Id.*

[29] The German Penal Code may be found in translation at JOSEPH J. DARBY, THE PENAL CODE OF THE FEDERAL REPUBLIC OF GERMANY (1987).

[30] *Id.* at § 89.

a mob of people in order to promote their willingness to take such action."[31] Further, there is a ban on the distribution, display or presentation of any writings "which are capable of serving as instructional guidance for the commission of [certain major crimes]" or providing such guidance at a public meeting.[32] As a commentator points out, with regard to instructional guidance, explicit encouragement is not required.[33]

The same commentator, University of Freiburg law professor Albin Eser, reports the threatened use of the German incitement provisions in a political context, the prosecution in 1987 of opponents to the German census.[34] Seeing the census as an invasion of privacy, opponents had engaged in a media and poster campaign asking persons who received census forms to remove the reference number from the forms. That would have made the census useless for at least some purposes. In the view of the authorities, the campaign was incitement to damage property, the census forms.

Another chapter in the same book containing the essay by Professor Eser compiles a number of statutes from other European countries.[35] Under Austrian law, using the media in order to call for disobedience to the law or the commission of a crime may lead to imprisonment.[36] Swiss law also punishes any public call for the commission of a felony or violent misdemeanor.[37] The law of the Netherlands makes it a crime to incite others to commit offenses or acts of violence against the authorities or to publicly disseminate material containing such incitement.[38] Swedish law bans the public incitement of people to commit criminal acts or evade civic duties or disobey public authorities.[39] Greece has similar provisions prohibiting plotting against public order; there are bans on inciting disobedience to statutes or lawful orders of authorities and causing people to disturb the peace by inciting disharmony.[40]

31 *Id.* at § 125. 32 *See id.* at 130(a)(2).

33 *See* Albin Eser, *The Law of Incitement and the Use of Speech to Incite Others to Commit Criminal Act: German Law in* Comparative Perspective in Freedom of Speech and Incitement Against Democracy 119, 124 (David Kretzmer & Francine Kershmen Hazan, eds., 2000).

34 *See id.* at 138–39.

35 *See* Mordechai Kremnitzer & Khaled Ghanayim, *Incitement, Not Sedition in* Freedom of Speech and Incitement Against Democracy, *supra* note 33, at 147, 201–7.

36 *See id.* at 201 (providing a translation of Articles 281 & 282 of the Austrian criminal code).

37 *See id.* (providing a translation of Article 259 of the Swiss criminal code).

38 *See id.* at 202 (providing a translation of Articles 131–33 of the criminal code of the Netherlands).

39 *See id.* at 203 (providing a translation of chapter 16, Article 5 of the Swedish criminal code).

40 *See id.* at 204 (providing a translation of Articles 183, 184, & 192 of the Greek criminal code).

The same chapter also notes the existence of statutes addressing the approval of criminal activity. Under German law, it is illegal to reward or to distribute writings approving of certain wrongful acts or to express such approval at a meeting.[41] Austria seeks to support a "general feeling of lawfulness," by placing a ban on approving or condoning the commission of certain offenses.[42] Greek law bans praising a committed felony.[43]

Given the concerns of Spain over terrorist activities by Basque separatists, it is not surprising that that country not only has, but has been willing to enforce, prohibitions on inciting or even endorsing terrorism. A 2013 case[44] indicates that something less than direct incitement may be sufficient for criminal liability. Individuals were charged with praising terrorism for shouting expressions of support for the ETA at a rally. They received sentences of one year in prison. Neither the Constitutional Court nor the appellants seemed troubled by the law itself. Rather, the conviction was contested, and reversed, based only on the use by the government of an unidentified witness.

Spain has, however, recognized limits in the enforcement of the prohibition on advocating terrorism. In a case pitting criminal advocacy of terrorism against the freedom of the press, a newspaper editor was charged based on the publication of statements issued by a terrorist organization.[45] The Court recognized that the prosecution interfered with the right of a journalist to inform and of the public to receive information and excluded the prosecution of a journalist who simply forwards information, rather than providing his or her own advocacy.

In another Spanish case, *Castells v. Spain*, the Spanish courts upheld a conviction based on a more classic sedition statute, and it took the European Court of Human Rights to overturn the conviction.[46] Castells was a member of the Spanish Senate and of the Herri Batasuna Party, a party advocating Basque separatism that would later become a banned political party.[47] He had written an article that was highly critical of the government. It noted a series of murders in the region, as well as less serious crimes, that remained unsolved. He suggested that this was the result of the unwillingness of the government he described as right wing to try to bring the perpetrators to justice. He further said that the fascist associations he thought to be guilty of the crimes were guaranteed immunity and, indeed, were associated with the government.

41 *See id.* at 205–6 (discussing Article 140 of the German criminal code).
42 *Id.* at 206–7 (discussing Article 282 of the Austrian criminal code).
43 *See id.* at 207 (providing a translation for Article 185 of the Greek criminal code).
44 S.T.C. 75/2013, Apr. 8, 2013 (Spain).
45 S.T.C. 159/1986, Dec. 16, 1986 (Spain).
46 App. No. 11798/85, 14 Eur. H.R. Rep. 445 (1992).
47 *See* Chapter 6 for a discussion of bans on political parties including Batasuna.

He was charged under Article 161 of the Criminal Code, which addresses "[t]hose who seriously insult, falsely accuse or threaten ... the Government ..." and provides for a penalty of between six years and a day and twelve years imprisonment.[48] He was, however, eventually convicted of a violation of Article 162, which provides that, when the insult or threat is not serious, a prison sentence of between six months and a day and six years is applicable.[49] He received a sentence of one year, and when his appeals within the Spanish court system were exhausted, he appealed to the European Court of Human Rights.

Given the authorization for limitations on free expression in the European Convention on Human Rights, it would appear that the protection of expression can be limited by concerns over crime in these incitement cases. Article 10(2) specifically mentions restrictions to protect public safety and the prevention of disorder or crime:

> The exercise of these freedoms, since it carries with it duties and responsibilities, may be subject to such formalities, conditions, restrictions or penalties as are prescribed by law and are necessary in a democratic society, in the interests of national security, territorial integrity or public safety, for the prevention of disorder or crime, for the protection of health or morals, for the protection of the reputation or rights of others, for preventing the disclosure of information received in confidence, or for maintaining the authority and impartiality of the judiciary.

At least some limits on incitement would then seem authorized in the provisions included above and might not be a violation of the Convention.

The limitations on Castells were, however, found to be violative of Article 10. The European Court was willing to find the aim of the Spanish government legitimate. Spain had argued that the security of the state could be threatened by an article that discredited its democratic institutions. The Court concluded that the government's aim was the "prevention of disorder," an aim specifically accepted by Article 10(2). The restriction must, however, also be necessary to the aim, and that is where the conviction was found to be flawed.

The Court found the appellant's freedom of expression to be even more protected than usual.

> While freedom of expression is important for everybody, it is especially so for an elected representative of the people. He represents his electorate, draws attention to their preoccupations and defends their interests. Accordingly, interferences with the freedom of expression of an opposition member of

[48] *See* App. No. 11798/85, 14 Eur. H.R. Rep. 445 at ¶ 20. [49] *See id.*

parliament, like the applicant, call for the closest scrutiny on the part of the Court.[50]

This is so, the Court said, even when an opinion is expressed in a place other than parliament.

The Court also recognized the centrality of speech critical of the government to democracy.

> The limits of permissible criticism are wider with regard to the Government than in relation to a private citizen, or even a politician. In a democratic system the actions or omissions of the Government must be subject to close scrutiny not only of the legislative and judicial authorities but also of the press and public opinion. Furthermore, the dominant position which the Government occupies makes it necessary for it to display restraint in resorting to criminal proceedings, particularly where other means are available for replying to the unjustified attacks and criticisms of its adversaries or the media.[51]

It is seemingly important to note that the article in question contained no direct incitement. Nor did it praise the criminal acts of separatists or terrorists. Instead, it criticized criminal acts, even if it also alleged that those acts were at least protected, if not encouraged, by the government.

The action against Castells seemed based in the sedition law of an earlier era, a variety of law that would seem inconsistent with democracy. Even with regard to these more classic sedition actions, the Court was unwilling to impose a complete ban. Immediately following the language quoted above, the Court said: "Nevertheless it remains open to the competent State authorities to adopt, in their capacity as guarantors of public order, measures, even of a criminal law nature, intended to react appropriately and without excess to defamatory accusations devoid of foundation or formulated in bad faith."[52] Here, Castells had not been allowed to demonstrate either the truth of his allegations or his good faith. The implication is that, with sufficiently serious seditious language that is false and offered in bad faith, the lack of direct incitement may not bar criminal prosecution.

A European Commission of Human Rights case from the United Kingdom presents an example of a case that is more clearly incitement. *Arrowsmith v. United Kingdom*[53] grew out of a conviction under the United Kingdom's Incitement to Disaffection Act of 1934. The defendant, a pacifist and an advocate of the British withdrawal from Northern Ireland, had distributed leaflets at an Army center housing soldiers who would soon be posted to Northern Ireland. The leaflets took the position that what was happening in

[50] *Id.* at ¶ 42. [51] *Id.* at ¶ 46. [52] *Id.*
[53] App. No. 7050/75, 3 Eur. Ct. H.R. Rep. 218 (1978).

Northern Ireland was wrong and provided information about quitting the Armed Forces, including seeking asylum in Sweden, seeking a compassionate discharge, or simply refusing to serve in Northern Ireland, admitting that this last option would lead to court-martial and imprisonment.

The conviction was challenged before the European Commission as a violation of, among other rights, the free expression provision of the European Convention. With regard to the Article 10 claim, the United Kingdom responded that the statute was aimed at the protection of national security, the prevention of disorder, and the protection of the rights of others. The Commission agreed that desertion would be a threat to national security and that the aim of the statute fit within Article 10(2).

The Commission said that the applicant had gone beyond simply stating political opinion in distributing the leaflets, which "were to be understood, or could have been interpreted by soldiers, as an encouragement for incitement to disaffection."[54]

> It is important to draw the line between the expression of political opinions as to the situation in Northern Ireland including the use of the Army on the one hand and this case on the other. The applicant was not convicted for statements showing her discontent with British policy in Northern Ireland. She was convicted because in the leaflets distributed she encouraged individual soldiers to disaffection indicating specific means of assistance.[55]

Thus, the prosecution and conviction served the aim of protecting national security and preventing disorder within the Army.

Turning to the issue of whether the restriction on expression was necessary in a democratic society, the applicant argued for the adoption of the "clear and present danger" test under United States law. The Commission responded that the word "necessary," in the European standard, implies a "'pressing social need' which may include the clear and present danger test and must be assessed in light of the circumstances of a given case."[56] The implication would seem to be that the justification in Article 10(2) is broader than that under United States law.[57] While prosecution for this sort of

[54] *Id.* at 232. [55] *Id.* [56] *Id.* at 233.

[57] Professor Barendt agrees that, had the Commission accepted the invitation to adopt the *Brandenburg* test, the result would have been favorable to the applicant. *See* ERIC BARENDT, FREEDOM OF SPEECH 167 (2d ed. 2005).

András Koltay notes that, with the exception of a dissenting opinion, "the possibility of applying the clear and present danger test has not been suggested in the judgments of the Strasbourg court." András Koltay, *The Clear and Present Danger Doctrine in Hungarian Eight Speech Laws and the Jurisprudence of the European Court of Human Rights in* FREE SPEECH, DEFAMATION, AND CRIMINAL LAW: THE GLOBAL PAPERS SERIES, VOLUME II ___, ___ (Russell

leafleting would not have been unconstitutional in an earlier era, it would seem unlikely to survive the *Brandenburg* test.[58]

The European Court of Human Rights has considered other cases in which language that came closer to incitement was involved and has not always found limitations based on the interest in the prevention of crime and public disorder to be acceptable. The Court, in a number of cases out of Turkey, has found violations of Article 10. For example, in *Şener v. Turkey*,[59] the Court considered the case of the editor and owner of a weekly newspaper whose publication had been seized on the grounds that it contained separatist propaganda. The editor was also sentenced to six months in prison and a fine, although the sentence was suspended on condition of no further violation. The Court provided a translation of the objectionable article. According to the translation, the article claimed that there was an ongoing genocide of an unprecedented scale in Kurdistan and that, instead of taking a stand, people are simply groaning. Further, again according to the translation, "we forget that in our own words a dirty war can only end in defeat . . . that the only way to oppose the war is to wage a just war."[60]

Even the reference to Kurdistan was objectionable, since it carried the implication that the residents of the region were Kurdish citizens. According to Turkish courts, the article contained propaganda against the indivisibility of

L. Weaver & Steven J. Friedland, eds., in press)). The result, at least as applied to the use of hate speech, is that "[i[n the area between clear incitement to violence that does not fall under the protection of the freedom of speech, and those offending and outrageous opinions that clearly do, the states have wide leeway in sanctioning or permitting hate speech." *Id.* at ___.

58 One of the earlier cases from the United States, Schenck v. United States, 249 U.S. 47 (1919), also involved leafleting and the Army. The defendant had distributed leaflets at a military induction center declaring that military conscription violated the Thirteenth Amendment's proscription against involuntary servitude and telling those about to be inducted that they should assert their rights. The Supreme Court held that the conviction for attempting to obstruct the recruiting and enlistment service was not inconsistent with the First Amendment. Another case decided in the same year, Abrams v. United States, 250 U.S. 616 (1919), was also based on antiwar publications. There were a number of counts, two of which sounded in more classical sedition language, addressing "disloyal, scurrilous and abusive language about the form of government of the United States" and language "intended to bring the form of government of the United States into contempt, scorn, contumely and disrepute." *Id.* at 617. There was also a count based on inciting, provoking, and encouraging resistance to the war efforts against Germany. The Court said that any First Amendment argument was negated by *Schenck*. Justice Holmes, in a dissent joined by Justice Brandeis, said that "nobody can suppose that the surreptitious publishing of a silly leaflet buy an unknown man, without more, would present any immediate danger that its opinions would hinder the success of the government . . .", *id.* at 628 (Holmes, J., dissenting). It is the Holmes position that is more consonant with the later development of United States law.

59 App. No. 26680/95, Eur. Ct. H.R. (2000).

60 *Id.* at ¶ 7.

Turkey, in violation of Section 8 of the Prevention of Terrorism Act 1991, which made it an offense to so undermine the integrity of Turkey or the indivisibility of the nation, in writing or at a meeting.[61] The conviction was challenged before the European Court as a violation of Article 10.

In considering whether this infringement was justified, the Court accepted as legitimate the aim of the statute.

> The Court considers that, having regard to the sensitivity of the security situation in southeast Turkey and to the need for the authorities to be alert to acts capable of fueling additional violence, the measures taken against the applicant can be said to have been in furtherance of certain of the areas mentioned by the Government, namely the protection of national security and public safety. This is certainly true where, as with the situation in southeast Turkey at the time of the circumstances of this case, the separatist movement had recourse to methods which relied on the use of violence.[62]

The Court then turned to an assessment of whether the restriction was necessary in a democratic society. That was seen as an issue of proportionality.

> [T]he dominant position which a government occupies makes it necessary for it to display restraint in resorting to criminal proceedings, particularly where other means are available for replying to the unjustified attacks and criticisms of its adversaries. Nevertheless, it certainly remains open to the competent State authorities to adopt, in their capacity as guarantors of public order, measures, even of a criminal-law nature, intended to react appropriately and without excess to such remarks. Finally, where such remarks incite people to violence, the State authorities enjoy a wider margin of appreciation when examining the need for an interference with freedom of expression.[63]

Referencing the duties and responsibilities that accompany the exercise of the freedom of expression, the Court said that "[p]articular caution is called for when consideration is being given to the publication of views which contain incitement to violence against the State lest the media become a vehicle for the dissemination of hate speech and the promotion of violence."[64] Nonetheless the government could not restrict the public right to be informed of such views.[65]

While the Court said that certain of the phrases in the article might seem aggressive in tone, the article did not constitute incitement. It was, instead, "an intellectual analysis of the Kurdish problem which calls for an end to the armed conflict."[66] Further, the Court said that the conviction had been based

[61] *See id.* at ¶ 18 (citing Law no. 3713 of Apr. 12, 1991). [62] *Id.* at ¶ 35. [63] *Id.* at ¶ 40.
[64] *Id.* at ¶ 42. [65] *See id.* [66] *Id.* at ¶ 45.

not on incitement but on the reference to southeast Turkey as Kurdistan and a suggestion that the residents of that region were being oppressed.[67] The conviction went against the public's right to know, was disproportionate, and was not necessary in a democratic society.[68]

Even with the conviction overturned, it is clear that the European Court does accept the possibility that the prevention of crime or disorder will justify a limit on free expression. A case from Ireland, however, provides an interesting limit. Abortion is not freely available in Ireland. In fact, the Irish Constitution contains a provision, Article 40, stating: "The State acknowledges the right to life of the unborn and, with due regard to the equal right to life of the mother, guarantees in its laws to respect, and, as far as practicable, by its laws to defend and vindicate that right." The constitutional provision is backed up by statutory prohibitions on abortion.[69]

There is also a provision more relevant to the subject of this chapter.

> It shall not be lawful for any person, otherwise than under and in accordance with a permit in writing granted to him under this section
>
> (a) to print or publish or cause to procure to be printed or published, or
> (b) to sell or expose, offer or keep for sale or
> (c) to distribute, offer or keep for distribution,
>
> any book or periodical publication ... which advocates or which might reasonably be supposed to advocate the procurement of abortion or miscarriage or any method, treatment or appliance to be used for the purpose of such procurement.[70]

Since abortion is a crime, under Irish law, the proscription on expression might seem justified under Article 10(2). It seems aimed at the prevention of

67 *See id.*

68 *See id.* at ¶ 47. This is not the only case in the European Court to take such a position with regard to Turkey's Prevention of Terrorism Act. Just one other example is provided by Ceylan v. Turkey, App. No. 23556/94, 30 Eur. H.R. Rep. 73 (1999). There, suppression of a trade union leader, who expressed an identity of interests between workers and the Kurdish people, was overturned on similar grounds. The government's aims were legitimate, but the eight months in prison was disproportionate to the legitimate aim.

69 Section 58 of the Offenses Against the Person Act 1861 provides: "Every woman, being with child, who, with intent to procure her own miscarriage, shall unlawfully administer to herself any poison or other noxious thing or shall unlawfully use any instrument or other means whatsoever with the like intent ... shall be guilty of a felony ..." Section 59 makes it a misdemeanor to supply the means to inducing a miscarriage.

70 Censorship of Publications Act 1929, §16, as amended by §12 of the Health (Family Planning) Act 1979.

crime by limiting advocacy for, and perhaps instruction in, the commission of that crime.

Open Door and Dublin Well Woman v. Ireland,[71] a case based on a violation of this ban on publications, reached the European Court of Human Rights. Open Door Counseling and Dublin Well Woman Centre both counsel pregnant women. As a part of their "non-directive" counseling, they included information regarding the availability of abortion in Great Britain and contact information for medical clinics located there. Both organizations were enjoined by the Irish courts from further offering such advice, based on the conclusion that counseling Irish women to go abroad to obtain an abortion was unlawful according to the Article 40 and the Offenses against the Person Act. According to the Supreme Court of Ireland,

> The performing of an abortion on a pregnant woman terminates the unborn life which she is carrying. Within the terms of Article 40.3.3(o) it is a direct destruction of the constitutionally guaranteed right to life of that unborn child.
>
> It must follow from this that there could not be an implied and unenumerated constitutional right to information about the availability of the service of abortion outside the State which, if availed of, with have the direct consequence of destroying the expressly guarantee constitutional right to life of the unborn.[72]

Abortion was criminal in Ireland, as both a matter of criminal and constitutional law, and the Irish courts saw it as acceptable to prevent the occurrence of that crime by limiting expression regarding availability of abortion, even outside of Ireland.

When the European Court considered the claim that the injunction was a violation of Article 10, it had to determine the aim of the statute. It rejected the position that the law was aimed at the prevention of crime, because providing or obtaining an abortion outside of Ireland is not a criminal violation.[73] The Court did note Ireland's "profound moral values concerning the nature of life which were reflected in the stance of the majority of the Irish people against abortion as expressed in the 1983 referendum."[74] So, instead of an injunction aimed at the prevention of crime, the Court said the restriction had the aim, which the court saw as legitimate, of protecting morals.

That distinction may have been dispositive. In the Court's analysis of whether or not the restriction was necessary in a democratic society, the Court

[71] App. No. 14234/88, 15 Eur. H.R. Rep. 244 (1992).

[72] *Id*. at ¶ 19 (quoting the opinion of the Irish Supreme Court). [73] *See id*. at ¶ 63. [74] *Id*.

said that the limit on expression was disproportionate to the government's aim. And, that conclusion rested heavily on Irish abortion law.

> While the relevant restriction . . . is limited to the provision of information, it is recalled that it is not a criminal offense under Irish law for a pregnant woman to travel abroad in order to have an abortion. Furthermore, the injunction limited the freedom to receive and impart information with respect to services which are lawful in other Convention countries and may be crucial to a woman's health and well-being. Limitations on information concerning activities which, notwithstanding their moral implications, have been and continue to be tolerated by national authorities, call for careful scrutiny by the Convention institutions as to their conformity with the tenants of a democratic society.[75]

There is at least the implication that it was the fact that no crime would be committed in Ireland that led to the conclusion that the injunction was disproportionate and, hence, a violation of Article 10.[76]

AUSTRALIA

Australia provides an example in which the government was allowed to act to prevent publication in a situation in which the imminence of an unlawful act was lacking. Furthermore, the instructional publication was not shown to have led to an actual crime. The case, *Brown v. Classification Review Board*,[77] involved an issue of *Rabalais*, the newspaper of the La Trobe University Student Representative Council. The edition at issue contained an article titled "The Art of Shoplifting." It was refused classification, which meant that it could not be distributed, because it "instruct[ed] in matters of crime."[78]

75 *Id.* at ¶ 72.

76 There is a case from the United States that is, at least somewhat, similar. Bigelow v. Virginia, 421 U.S. 809 (1975), involved the editor of a Virginia newspaper convicted for violating a statute banning, encouraging, or prompting the procuring of an abortion. The newspaper, circulated around the campus of the University of Virginia, contained an advertisement regarding abortion availability in New York. The circulation and conviction occurred prior to the United States Supreme Court's ruling in Roe v. Wade, 410 U.S. 113 (1970), legalizing abortion. The appeal was, however, decided after *Roe*. The case is actually remembered for the conclusion that commercial speech, and this case did involve an advertisement instead of the counseling in *Open Door*, is not without any First Amendment protection. Nonetheless, the publication was with regard to a procedure that would be criminal in the state of circulation but regarding a service that was not criminal where it would be performed and is, in that regard, similar.

77 82 F.C.R. 225 (1998).

78 *Id.* at 227. The same article led to a refusal of classification of a publication of the Royal Melbourne Institute of Technology Students Union. *See id.* at 227–28.

That decision was appealed, eventually reaching the Federal Court of Australia.

The article was not devoid of content with, at least some, political dimension. It began with a criticism of capitalism and suggested limits as to the targets of shoplifting. It cautioned readers not to steal from anyone who might be a "comrade" and particularly against stealing from corner stores, as those stores were likely run by individuals similar to the reader. There was also an argument that proscriptions against theft were themselves part of the capitalist ideology that the article criticized. There were also other articles in *Rabelais* that were clearly of a political nature.

Other than these potentially political positions, the article was largely a step-by-step guide to shoplifting. In that regard, it was similar to *Hitman*, although in the United States case liability was based on the actual commission of a crime, while here the material at issue did not contribute to any actual crime, since it was not published. There were sections in the article dedicated to preparations, including bringing a bag that would not be used to carry the purloined objects but would likely be the focus of any search by store security, identifying security blind spots, and exiting the store. It was also suggested the stolen goods might later be returned or exchanged.

Justice French examined international agreements to which Australia was a party with explicit provisions for the freedom of expression, but he rejected their application, since they do not become part of Australian domestic law without being given effect by statute. He was then left with the Commonwealth's common-law treatment of expression and the implied constitutional freedom of political discourse. In that regard, he said that the article might still be banned.

> There is much to be said for the conclusion that "The Art of Shoplifting" falls outside the scope of political discussion. But, inelegant, awkward and unconvincing as its attempt to justify its practical message about shoplifting by reference to the evils of capitalism, it is arguable that in some aspects it would fall within a broad understanding of political discussion. That characterisation, however, will not invalidate the effective operation upon it of a law which is enacted for a legitimate end, is compatible with representative and responsible government and is reasonably appropriate and adapted to achieving that end.[79]

Taking all that into account, the Classification Board's decision and the statute authorizing the action met those criteria.

[79] *Id*. at 238.

The appellants had offered an argument suggesting an approach that would be more in line with that in the United States. The argument was that the publication could not be said to "instruct in matters of crime," unless there was evident intent to bring about the crime and the likely effect of publication would be the commission of the crime. Justice French rejected the analysis, saying "[i]t is difficult to see how a rule requiring assessment of the likely effect of a publication in bringing about the commission of a crime would work in practice."[80]

Justice Heerey agreed that the appeal should be dismissed. He found intent that the instructions be followed in that part of the article that gave advice on what to do when caught. Thus, the article provided instruction along with encouragement or exhortation. He also concluded that the article was not within the scope of Australia's protection of political speech. He specifically rejected any analysis that might be used in the United States or Canada: "In the United States and Canada, the Constitutional protection of speech is not conditioned on its subject matter or purpose, or the occasion of its exercise. In Australia by contrast, the freedom springs from, and is concerned to protect, the system of representative and responsible government."[81]

The appellant had argued that various writers have advocated theft as a way of reallocating resources, as the expression of political dissent, or as a central theme of Anarchist theory. The Justice was unimpressed, noting that the Australian freedom of political communication assumes the rule of law and saying that "advocacy of lawbreaking falls outside this protection and is antithetical to it."[82] Turning again to United States law, Justice Heerey said

> United States decisions like *Brandenburg* ... and the line of cases which follow it are not applicable to the implied freedom under the Australian Constitution. There is no Constitutional protection for speech which is "mere advocacy" or abstract teaching of the necessity or propriety of criminal or violent conduct. The reason is simple. Such conduct is not part of the system of representative and responsible government or the political and democratic process.[83]

Lastly, Justice Sundberg also rejected the suggested requirements that the statutory prohibition on promoting and inciting crime required both the intent to bring about the crime and that the crime be the likely consequence of the article.[84] What was required was providing instruction and encouragement. Turning to the freedom of expression, he quoted the decision by the High Court:

[80] *Id.* at 240. [81] *Id.* at 243. [82] *Id.* at 246. [83] *Id.* [84] *See id.* at 257–58.

> The freedom of communication ... operates as a restriction on legislative power. However, the freedom will not invalidate a law enacted to satisfy some other legitimate end if the law satisfies two conditions. The first condition is that the object of the law is compatible with the maintenance of the constitutionally prescribed system of representative and responsible government or the procedure for submitting a proposed amendment to the Constitution to the informed decision of the people which the Constitution prescribes. The second is that the law is reasonably appropriate and adopted to achieving that legitimate object or end.[85]

In his view, while the article may have opened with some political matter, "its true character is not political because it is overwhelmingly a manual about how successfully to steal."[86] The article had no relationship to free and informed choice by the electorate and the restriction was justified by the legitimate end of protecting the community.[87]

CONCLUSIONS

When it comes to sedition and the solicitation of criminal acts, all governments seem to see the need to protect themselves. The totalitarian state will have no reluctance in suppressing such expression, but as this chapter shows, democratic countries also impose limits. The difference is in the recognition by democratic countries that political speech must be protected, even if there is some danger to the state.

The differences among the democratic countries is with regard to how close the expression must come to causing criminality, before it can be suppressed. The answer to that question, in the various countries, seems to be correlated with the nature of its free expression guarantee. The strong, absolute sounding, protection in the United States' First Amendment seems the most protective. Only the clear and present danger of imminent lawless action can justify suppression. In countries that regularly allow free expression to be balanced against other concerns, it appears that suppression can be justified on a somewhat lesser showing. Australia, with its protection extending only to political speech, will not tolerate the solicitation of crime, even if the motive may be political.

[85] *Id.* at 257–58 (quoting Lange v. Illustrating Broadcasting Corporation, (1997) 189 CLR 520, 561–62).
[86] *Id.* at 258. [87] *Id.*

4

Hate Speech

The treatment of hate speech demonstrates a deep divide between the approach taken in the United States and that taken in most of the rest of the world. In an evocatively titled paper, "Wild-West Cowboys versus Cheese-Eating Surrender Monkeys: Some Problems in Comparative Approaches to Hate Speech," Eric Heinze of the University of London contrasts the wild-west approach of Americans compared to Europeans "who cheerfully sacrifice liberty for any paltry measure of security, or even for sheer decorum."[1]

Similarly, Michel Rosenfeld points to "a big divide between the United States and other Western democracies," when it comes to hate speech.[2] He notes that constitutional protection is given to such speech in the United States, "while under international human rights covenants and in other Western democracies, such as Canada, Germany, and the United Kingdom, it is largely prohibited and subjected to criminal sanctions."[3] Alexander Tsesis adds, as a "non-exhaustive list" of countries banning hate speech, Australia, Austria, Belgium, Brazil, Cyprus, Denmark, France, India, Ireland, Israel, Italy, Sweden, and Switzerland,[4] most of which are fully functioning democracies.

Professor Tsesis finds the impetus in establishing hate speech laws in the belief that such speech incites violence and is harmful to human dignity.[5]

[1] Eric Heinze, *Wild-West Cowboys versus Cheese-Eating Surrender Monkeys: Some Problems in Comparative Approaches to Hate Speech in* Extreme Speech and Democracy 182, 183 (Ivan Hare & James Weinstein, eds., 2009).

[2] Michel Rosenfeld, *Hate Speech in Constitutional Jurisprudence: A Comparative Analysis*, 24 Cardozo L. Rev. 1523, 1523 (2003).

[3] *Id.*

[4] Alexander Tsesis, *Dignity and Speech: The Regulation of Hate Speech in a Democracy*, 44 Wake Forest L. Rev. 497, 521 (2009).

[5] *See id.*

Indeed, the genesis of hate speech regulation appears to have been the result of the Nazi treatment of Jews in World War II. Professor Tsesis points to the verbal and written attacks on the Jewish population in pre-war Germany, as an example of "how hate groups rely on destructive messages to develop ideologically grounded organizational infrastructure."[6] His examination of history leads him to conclude: "The historical evidence that hate speech is critical to the perpetration of violence is overwhelming. Expressions meant to incite harm are not merely self-expressive ... They can influence some of the most destructive behavior."[7] John Knechtle adds: "To ignore or deny the relationship between hate speech and threat or incitement to violence is to not know history, including recent history."[8]

Where there is actual incitement to violence, the law of the United States and that of much of the rest of the world converge, with disagreement only on the degree of the level of incitement necessary to justify limits. Where the incitement is not so clear is where the differences arise. Many countries are willing to forbid hate speech without clear incitement, because of a perceived lack of value in such speech, the harm it does to the dignity of target populations, or out of a commitment to multiculturalism. That view is not shared in the law of the United States.

In an earlier era, the United States and the rest of the world might have had little impact on each other in this regard. Hate materials might be available in the United States, with minimal impact on efforts by other countries to shield their citizens from such influences. But in the Internet age the unwillingness or inability of the United States to regulate hate speech has resulted in making such speech more available in countries in which it is banned. Professor Rosenfeld notes the availability of California-generated Neo-Nazi propaganda in Canada and Germany, where such groups have established a more significant foothold,[9] and Professor Knechtle notes more generally that "the United States is becoming a hub for Internet hate speech."[10]

6 *Id.* at 505.

7 *Id.* at 516. He adds, as examples of hate speech leading to violence against its target groups, the slavery era in the United States, Spain's expulsion of its Jewish population during the Inquisition, tribal clashes in Kenya, and genocide in Rwanda and Darfur, Sudan. *See id.* at 507–10

8 John C. Knechtle, *When To Regulate Hate Speech*, 110 PA. ST. L. REV. 539, 546 (2006). He adds ethnic cleansing in Bosnia to the historical examples. *See id.* at 546–47.

9 *See* Rosenfeld, *supra* note 2, at 1524.

10 Knechtle, *supra* note 8, at 540. *See also* Christopher D. Van Blarcum, *Internet Hate Speech: The European Framework and the Emerging American Haven*, 62 WASH. & LEE L. REV. 781 (2005); Peter J. Breckheimer II, *A Haven for Hate: The Foreign and Domestic Implications of Protecting Internet Hate Speech under the First Amendment*, 75 S. CAL. L. REV. 1493 (2002).

After examining the limits imposed by a number of fully functioning democracies, United States law will be considered. Special attention will then be paid to Canada. While the United States seems to feel that there is no need to justify free expression in this area, and most of the rest of the world takes the need to regulate almost as a given, the Supreme Court of Canada provides a reasoned consideration. Whether one agrees with the Canadian Court or not, examining the Court's balancing of values provides valuable insight. Lastly, the problems that inhere in any hate speech limitations, particularly issues in line drawing, will be examined.

THE REGULATION OF HATE SPEECH IN THE WORLD BEYOND THE UNITED STATES

The sheer number of countries with hate speech prohibitions makes it impossible, in the context of this effort, to present them all individually.[11] The individual countries discussed have been selected to present a history of, or to raise particular issues with regard to, hate speech regulation.

Generally, the attitude of most democracies toward hate speech is reflected in a United Nations Convention opened for signature in 1966. The International Convention on the Elimination of All Forms of Racial Discrimination (known as CERD) provides in Article 4:

> States Parties condemn all propaganda and all organizations which are based on ideas or theories of superiority of one race or group of persons of one colour or ethnic origin, or which attempt to justify or promote racial hatred and discrimination in any form, and undertake to adopt immediate and positive measures designed to eradicate all incitement to, or acts of, such discrimination and, to this end, with due regard for the principles embodied in the Universal Declaration of Human Rights and the rights expressly set forth in article 5 of this Convention, *inter alia*:
>
> (a) Shall declare an offense punishable by law all dissemination of ideas based on racial superiority or hatred, incitement to racial discrimination, as well as all acts of violence or incitement to such acts against any race or group of persons of another colour or ethnic origin, and also the provision of any assistance to racist activities, including the financing thereof;
> (b) Shall declare it illegal and prohibit organizations, and also organized and all other propaganda activities, which promote and incite racial discrimination, and shall recognize the participation in such organizations or activities as an offence punishable by law;

[11] For discussion of hate speech in a number of other countries, *see* Tsesis, *supra* note 4, at 497.

(c) Shall not permit public authorities or public institutions, national or local, to promote or incite racial discrimination.[12]

With regard to the European Union, the European Convention on Human Rights, in Article 10(1) provides "Everyone has the right to freedom of expression. This right shall include freedom to hold opinions and to receive and impart information and ideas without interference by public authority and regardless of frontiers . . ." Beyond the provision in Article 10(2), allowing for limits based on the prevention of disorder or crime, the protection of morality, and the protection of the rights of others, Article 17 might be read so as to exclude hate speech, entirely, from the protections of Article 10. Article 17 provides: "Nothing in this Convention may be interpreted as implying for any State, group or person any right to engage in any activity or perform any act aimed at the destruction of any of the rights and freedoms set forth herein or at their limitation to a greater extent than is provided for in the Convention." Thus, Article 10 is trumped by Article 17. "The purpose of the latter provision is to withhold the benefit of the Convention's guarantees from those who wish to use them to further an objective contrary to the values protected by the Convention."[13]

Germany

Turning to a brief consideration of individual countries,[14] Germany is seen as a particularly strong supporter of codes banning hate speech,[15]

[12] International Convention on the Elimination of All Forms of Racial Discrimination, Article 4, *opened for signature* Mar. 7, 1966, 660 U.N.T.S. 195 (entered into force Mar. 12, 1969). Article 5 contains rights to the freedoms of thought, conscience, religion, opinion and expression, and peaceful assembly and association. The Convention is not in conflict with the International Covenant on Civil and Political Rights, International Covenant on Civil and Political Rights, *opened for signature* Dec. 16, 1966, 999 U.N.T.S 171, S. Exec. Doc. E, 95-2 (1978) (entered into force Mar. 23, 1976). While the Covenant protects the freedom of expression, Article 20, provides: "any advocacy of national, racial or religious hatred that constitutes incitement to discrimination, hostility or violence shall be prohibited by law." *Id.* at Article 20, § 2.

[13] Mario Oetheimer, *Protecting Freedom of Expression: The Challenge of Hate Speech in the European Court of Human Rights Case Law*, 17 Cardozo J. Int'l & Comp. L. 427, 429–30 (2009). Article 14 of the Convention further provides: "The enjoyment of the rights and freedoms set forth in this Convention shall be secured without discrimination on any ground such as sex, race, colour, language, religion, political or other opinion, national or social origin, association with a national minority, property, birth or other status."

[14] For sources containing more in-depth analyses of hate speech in the countries discussed, *see infra*, notes 15–61.

[15] German law regarding hate speech is discussed in Edward J. Eberle, *Human Dignity, Privacy, and Personality in German and American Constitutional Law*, 1997 Utah L. Rev. 963; Ronald J. Krotoszynski, A *Comparative Perspective on the First Amendment: Free Speech, Militant*

seemingly in reaction to its own history of Nazi atrocities against the Jewish population.[16] A summary, while a decade old, seems to capture the German concern over hate speech.

> Germany has sought to curb hate speech with a broad array of legal tools. These include criminal and civil laws that protect against insults, defamation and other forms of verbal assault, such as attacks against the person's honor or integrity, damage to reputation, and disparaging the memory of the dead ... Under current law, criminal liability can be imposed for incitement to hatred, or for attacks on human dignity against individuals or groups determined by nationality, race, religion, or ethnic origin. Some of these provisions require showing a threat to public peace, while others do not.[17]

Germany does, as already seen, have a free expression provision in Article 5 (1) of its Basic Law. Article 5(2) does provide an invitation to balance free expression rights against other interests, providing: "These rights shall find their limits in the provisions of general laws, in provisions for the protection of young persons, and in the right to personal honor."[18] While the protection of personal honor might, itself, provide an adequate justification for prohibiting hate speech, an even stronger justification is provided in Article 1(1) of the Basic Law. That Article provides: "Human dignity shall be inviolable. To respect and protect it shall be the duty of all state authority."[19] Position in the Basic Law makes a difference; the Basic Law establishes a hierarchy. According to Ronald Krotoszynski,

> free speech simply is not the most important constitutional value in the German legal order; instead, pursuant to the first clause of the Basic Law, human dignity holds this position. Article 1 of the Basic Law "is both 'the supreme constitutional principle' and a fundamental right." Accordingly,

Democracy, and the Primacy of Dignity as a Preferred Constitutional Value in Germany, 78 TULANE L. REV. 1549 (2004); Michel Rosenfeld, *supra* note 2, at 1548–54.

[16] *See* Knechtle, *supra* note 8, at 553. *See also id.* at 551 ("In Germany, which hosts some of the most expansive hate speech codes, the jurisprudential history was largely predicated upon equal rights due to the treatment of the Jews during the Holocaust."), The Nazi era has also been seen as leading Germany to adopt a "militant democracy," which may lead to a more limited view of free expression. "[T]he German justification from democracy does not encompass extremist anti-democratic speech, including hate speech advocating denial of democratic constitutional rights to its targets." Rosenfeld, *supra* note 2, at 1549.

[17] Rosenfeld, *supra* note 2, at 1551 (footnotes omitted).

[18] Grundgesetz [GG][Basic Law], *translation at* www.gesetze-im-internet.de.englisch.gg/index.html.

[19] Additionally, Article 2(1) of the Basic Law provides: "Every person shall have the right to free development of his personality insofar as he does not violate the rights of others or offend against the constitutional order or the moral law." This development of personality would, seemingly, be limited by being the subject of hate speech.

when cases present facts in which human dignity and free speech collide, free speech usually must give way.[20]

The United Kingdom

Discussions of hate speech law in the United Kingdom may be found in a variety of places.[21] The sources commonly find the first hate speech prosecution to have been thc 1732 case *Regina v. Osborne*.[22] The expression at issue was a newspaper's claim that a group of Jewish immigrants had killed a woman and her child, because the child's father was a Christian. Since the story led to the beating of some of the Jews who were named, the case might be seen as involving the promotion of violence, rather than hate speech more generally.

After a series of statutes that required the likelihood of a breach of the peace, a 1976 statute was directed at expression with, perhaps, a less inciting nature. The Race Relations Act addressed language that was threatening, abusive, or insulting and was likely to stir up hatred against any racial group.[23] The Public Order Act of 1986 went on to ban the expression of

[20] Krotoszynski, *supra* note 15, at 1553–54 (quoting Ernst Benda, *The Protection of Human Dignity (Article 1 of the Basic Law)*, 53 S.M.U. L Rev. 443, 444 (2000)). Professor Krotoszynski expresses concern that this protection of dignity does not reach prohibiting a sign in a bar stating "no Turks allowed." *See* Ronald J. Krotoszynski, Jr., The First Amendment in Cross-Cultural Perspective 135 (2006). An explanation, perhaps unsatisfactory to an American reader, is that German hate speech law grows out of German insult law and that, under that law, the sign may not be an insult.

> The mere rejection of another person is not an insult. For this reason, with regard to expressions of hostility to ethnic non-Germans . . ., it is a question of interpretation whether there has also been an intent to express the view that the targeted person is of lesser value . . . The same is true for refusals to admit certain groups of persons to bars, etc., which qualify as an insult only if they are to be understood as meaning that the owner of the establishment regards the targeted persons as unworthy of being served . . . In general, such refusals to admit are permissible only where they are made with a view to the needs of other clients, who otherwise threatened to stay away.

James Q. Whitman, *Enforcing Civility and Respect: Three Societies*, 109 Yale L.J. 1279, 1303–04 (2000) (quoting Schönke-Schröder Strafgesetzbuch §185, at 1385–86 (Theodor Lenckner et al. eds., 25th ed. 1999) (F.R.G.)) (ellipses added by Whitman). Professor Whitman does note that, while the slight might not constitute hate speech, it may be impermissible discrimination. *Id.* at 1304 n.65.

[21] *See, e.g.*, Stanley Halpin, *Racial Hate Speech: A Comparative Analysis of the Impact of International Human Rights Law upon the Law of the United Kingdom and the United States*, 94 Marq. L. Rev. 463, 466–74 (2010); Rosenfeld, *supra* note 2, at 1544–47.

[22] (1732)25 Eng. Rep. 584 (Ch.) 584. *See* Halpin, *supra* note 21, at 467; Rosenfeld, *supra* note 2, at 1545.

[23] *See* Halpin, *supra* note 21, at 471.

racial hatred against any "group of persons ... defined by reference to colour, race, nationality (including citizenship) or ethnic or national origins."[24] The 1986 Act "made hate speech punishable if it amounted to harassment of a target group or individual."[25]

The 1986 Act does not include religion-based groups within the groups protected. Indeed, religion would not really define, in most cases, a group against which racial hatred could be expressed. Islam, for example, has believers who, while sharing a religion, have ethnicities that range from Moroccans, through Arabs, Somalis, and Indonesians.

The United Kingdom, in the Racial and Religious Hatred Act of 2006, did add protection for religious groups, amending the Public Order Act to include "stirring up hatred against persons on religious grounds."[26] The Act is careful in setting out limitations on its application.

> Nothing in this Part shall be read or given effect in a way which prohibits or restricts discussion, criticism or expressions of antipathy, dislike, ridicule, insult or abuse of particular religions or the beliefs or practices of their adherents, or of any other belief system or the beliefs or practices of its adherents, or proselytizing or urging adherents of a different religion or belief system to cease practicing their religion or belief system.[27]

It would appear that the United Kingdom recognizes a difference between attacking individuals because of their membership in a religious group and attacking the beliefs of the group itself.

If hate speech prohibitions are to include religious hate speech, the distinction drawn by the United Kingdom seems important. While religious belief may be psychologically core for an individual, it is not core in the same sense as those properties, such as ethnicity and sex, that are based in genetics. Religious belief may be thought of as a matter of choice, even if adherents could not conceive of making a different choice. Thus, protection against religiously-based hate speech might not be thought to be as essential as protection against the expression of racial hatred.

However, if protection is to be granted against religious hate speech, the distinction drawn in the 2006 Act seems important. To attack a group of individuals identified by religious belief, in the manner in which racial and ethnic groups are sometimes denigrated, shares some of the characteristics of racist speech. Depending upon the particular nature of the speech, it may

[24] Public Order Act, 1986, § 17. [25] Rosenfeld, *supra* note 2, at 1547.
[26] Racial and Religious Hatred Act 2006, 1. [27] *Id.* at § 291.

assert the inferiority of such individuals, and that may be seen as being as objectionable as racist speech.

On the other hand, the right to disagree with the religious belief deserves protection. Religious beliefs may have impact in the physical world and in society. Democratic debate about the nature of society and addressing issues of the physical world would be stifled if the assertion of a religious belief ended the debate. Those on the other side of the debate must be allowed to call the belief or its application into question. Furthermore, proselytization seems to require the questioning of the religious beliefs of those targeted for conversion. To prohibit such questioning would hinder or bar the development of new religions or the growth of any established religion other than through its members giving birth.

Denmark

Denmark provides an example of a country attempting to apply its hate speech laws against a person who was not himself espousing racist positions and of the review of hate speech convictions by the European Court of Human Rights. *Jersild v. Denmark*[28] grew out of a television interview on the program *Sunday News Magazine* broadcast on Danish television. The interview was with a group of young people known as the "Greenjackets." In the course of the interview, the Greenjackets, among other racist comments, said there are physical similarities between gorillas and Africans, as all well as "all other foreign workers . . ., Turks, Yugoslavs, and whatever they are called."[29] The three youths were convicted of violating Article 266(b) of the Danish Pedal Code, which provides: "Any person who, publicly or with the intention of disseminating it to a wide circle . . . of people, makes a statement, or other communication, threatening, insulting or degrading a group of persons on account of their race, colour, national or ethnic origin or belief shall be liable to a fine or to . . . a term not exceeding two years."[30]

The conviction of the three youths was not appealed, but Jersild was not one of the youths. He was the interviewer, and he and the head of the news section of Danmarks Radio were convicted under a general provision of the Danish Criminal Code for aiding and abetting the violation by the youths. Their convictions seem to raise no problem under Danish law and were upheld by the highest national court. It was that case that made its way to the European Court. The Court overturned the conviction, but in doing so,

[28] Jersild v. Denmark, 298 Eur. Ct. H.R. (ser. A)(1994). [29] *Id.* at 5–6. [30] *Id.* at 12.

did explain the relationship between hate speech prohibitions and Article 10 (1), the free expression provision, of the European Convention on Human Rights.

The Court recognized that Denmark had ratified CERD and was required to criminalize the dissemination of ideas based on hatred or theories of racial superiority. Furthermore, Article 10 of the European Convention, in Section 2, allows limitations on expression, when they are prescribed by law and are "necessary in a democratic society" for a variety of purposes, including the protection of the "reputation or rights of others." The Court accepted that Article 10 had to be interpreted so as to be compatible with obligations under CERD.[31] That might be sufficient to support the conviction of the Greenjackets, but the Court held that the conviction of the news people involved violated their free expression rights. The Court noted the finding by the European Commission of Human Rights that, "taken in the context of the broadcast as a whole, the offending remarks had the effect of ridiculing their authors rather than promoting their racist views."[32] As a result, the interference with the expression of the news people was not necessary in a democratic society and was disproportionate in the effort to protect "the reputation or rights of others."[33]

Spain, France, and the Internet

A consideration of Spain and France doesn't add much to the variety of laws in European countries banning hate speech, but it does illustrate responses to the problem of Internet hate speech. Residents of a country with a ban on hate speech may still be affected by such speech originating in other countries. If a website hosted in the United States contains hate speech, as allowed by United States law, that material may be accessible in countries where such material is illegal.

It might be thought that the global accessibility of the Internet, coupled with the inability of European countries to obtain jurisdiction over United States content providers, would indicate an inability to enforce any meaningful restrictions. That, however, is not completely true. Spain requires that Internet service providers (ISP) operating within its borders block websites that violate Spanish law regarding hate speech.[34] Nonetheless, this may not be completely successful, since ISPs would have to know that a site contains hate speech, before taking steps.

[31] *Id.* at 18. [32] *Id.* at 16. [33] *Id.* at 21. [34] *See* Van Blarcum, *supra* note 10, at 824.

France has gone a step further, bringing an action in French courts against a United States content provider.[35] The target of the French action was Yahoo! a United States company operating the website www.yahoo.com. Yahoo! also has a French subsidiary, Yahoo! France with its own French website. Part of the Yahoo website is an auction service, and among the items available for sale at the time of the action were approximately 1000 items related to the Third Reich and the Nazis. The sale and possession of such goods is illegal under a French law known as the Loi Gayssot.[36]

The legal action arose through a private suit brought by several organizations dedicated to combating racism and anti-Semitism.[37] The French court ruled against Yahoo! and directed that the company deny French residents access to the material. Yahoo! agreed to remove the material from its French website but said it would not impose the same limits on its main website. It also said that it was unable to direct residents of France away from the main website to the French site. Despite Yahoo's protestations, the French court ordered the company to comply, imposed significant daily fines for failure to do so, and said the penalties had to be assessed against Yahoo!, not the French subsidiary.

The Yahoo! case also gave rise to an action in United States courts also.[38] Yahoo! sought a declaratory judgment in federal district court that any judgment by the French court could not be assessed against the company through the courts of the United States. The District Court said that France could enforce its laws within its territory, but it concluded that any penalties assessed could not be enforced in the United States. On appeal, the United States

[35] Germany has also taken action against an individual posting hate speech in the United States, making it available to residents of Germany, but only after obtaining physical jurisdiction over the individual. Van Blarcum discusses the case of Frederick Toben, a German immigrant to Australia with a website on an American server, who denied the occurrence of the Holocaust. *Id.* at 803–4. While on a visit to Germany, he was arrested and convicted of violating German law through, among other activities, his foreign website. The German High Court allowed the conviction, saying "German authorities may take legal action against foreigners who upload content that is illegal in Germany – even though the Websites may be located elsewhere." *Id.* at 804.

[36] The law, Loi 90-615 du 13 Juillet 1990, tendant à réprime tout acte raciste, anti-sémite ou xénophobe [Law No. 90-615 of Jul. 13, 1990 to suppress all racist, antisemitic or xenophobic acts], JOURNAL OFFICIEL DE LA RÉPUBLIQUE FRANÇAISE [J.O.][OFFICIAL GAZETTE OF FRANCE], Jul. 14, 1990, 8333, is discussed in Lycombe Eko, *New Medium, Old Free Speech Regimes: The Historical and Ideological Foundations of French & American Regulation of Bias-Motivated Speech and Symbolic Expression on the Internet*, 28 LOY. L. A. INT'L & COMP. L. REV. 69, 101–2 (2006).

[37] For a discussion of the case, *see* Eko, *supra* note 36, at 71–82.

[38] *See* Yahoo! Inc. v. La Ligue Contre le Racisme Et L' Anti-Semitisme, 169 F. Supp. 2d 1181 (N.D. Cal. 2001), *dismissed en banc*, 433 F.3d 1199 (9th Cir.).

Court of Appeals for the Ninth Circuit, en banc, dismissed the case over issues of jurisdiction over the defendants and the lack of ripeness, although there was a group of judges that would have held that any enforcement of the French judgment would be in violation of the First Amendment.[39] It would certainly seem that any United States court reaching the substance, would shield a United States defendant from enforcement of a foreign judgment resulting from its provision of hate speech. Nonetheless, the French case indicates the seriousness of the concerns other countries have over hate speech and their willingness, wherever they may be able, to take action.

Australia

Australia provides an example from another part of the world and presents an interesting example of the problem presented by drawing lines. The Racial Discrimination Act of 1975 was passed to meet the nation's obligations under CERD. It addresses a variety of forms of discrimination but also includes a section prohibiting offensive behavior based on racial hatred.[40] The Act, in Section 18C, provides:

> It is unlawful for a person to do an act, otherwise than in private, if:
>
> (a) the act is reasonably likely, in all the circumstances, to offend, insult, humiliate or intimidate another person or group of people; and
> (b) the act is done because of the race, colour or national or ethnic origin of the other person or some or all of the people in the group.[41]

Interestingly, actions under the Commonwealth statute are civil; however, there are a number of statutes at the State/Territorial level that allow for either civil or criminal remedies or for only criminal remedies.[42]

The Commonwealth statute also contains exceptions:

> Section 18C does not render unlawful anything said or done reasonably and in good faith:
>
> (a) in the performance, exhibition or distribution of an artistic work; or

[39] *See* Yahoo! Inc. v. La Ligue Contre le Racisme Et L' Antisemitisme, 433 F.3d 1199 (9th Cir. 2006) (en banc). Eko argues that the dismissal resulted from a failure completely to understand the ruling of the French court. *See* Eko, *supra* note 36, at 76–78.

[40] Racial Discrimination Act 1975 Cth, pt. IIA.d.18C, available at www.comlaw.gov.au/Details/C2013C00013.

[41] *Id.* at d.18C, sub-div 1.

[42] *See* Michael Chestermen, Freedom of Speech in Australian Law 197 (2000).

(b) in the course of any statement, publication, discussion or debate made or held for any genuine academic, artistic or scientific purpose or any other genuine purpose in the public interest; or
(c) in making or publishing:
  (i) a fair and accurate report of any event or matter of public interest; or
  (ii) a fair comment on any event or matter of public interest if the comment is an expression of a genuine belief held by the person making the comment.[43]

There does appear to be some form of intent required. It might not be required that one intends to offend, insult, humiliate, or intimidate, since the standard there seems to be reasonableness. The act, however, has to be done because of the race, color, or national or ethnic origin of the offended group or individual. Thus, intentional targeting seems to be required.

Turning to the exceptions to the statute, the Federal Court of Australia, in *Toben v. Jones*,[44] looked at the defendant's claim of having made statements that were seen as anti-Semitic as part of an academic publication made in good faith. The Court indicated that good faith required minimization of the offensive impact. "In the context of knowing that Australian Jewish people would be offended by the challenge which the appellant sought to make, a reasonable person acting in good faith would have made every effort to express the challenge and his views with as much restraint as was consistent with the communication of those views."[45]

This requirement of, perhaps false, restraint has led Judith Bannister to argue that the law may discriminate between sophisticated and unsophisticated racists.[46]

> [I]n many cases, the Australian racial vilification laws favor certain voices over others. Privileged speakers, who conform to judicial interpretations of reasonableness, are exempted; those who use inflammatory or intemperate language are silenced. These laws restrict the form of expression rather than the racist message itself. Thus, it is not so much what you say, but how you say it.[47]

[43] Racial Discrimination Act, *supra* note 40, at d.18D.

[44] (2003) 129 FCR 515. The case will also be discussed in Chapter 5.

[45] *Id.* at ¶44 (opinion of Carr, J.). The other two judges on the panel, in their own opinions, agreed that there was a lack of good faith. *See id.* at ¶78 (opinion of Kiefel, J.) ("there was no proof of the appellant's good-faith"); *id.* at ¶159 (opinion of Allsop, J.) ("I agree entirely with the reasons of Carr J that the contents of the Document, taken as a whole, do not establish that the publication was done reasonably and in good faith.").

[46] *See* Judith Banister, *It's Not What You Say but the Way that You Say It: Australian Hate Speech Law and the Exemption of 'Reasonable' Expression*, 36 FLA. ST. U. L. REV. 23, 33 (2008).

[47] *Id.* at 25.

It appears that this was recognized by the legislative committee considering the exemptions in that they felt that the exceptions were necessary accommodations of the freedom of expression.[48] Dr. Bannister notes that, "when it comes to comedy and artistic work, the courts allow a margin of tolerance that is not necessarily extended to speakers in other contexts."[49]

The argument with regard to comedy is based in, and justified by, the case *Kelly-Country v. Beers & Anor.*[50] This civil action was brought by an Aboriginal activist against a comedian who performs under the name "King Billy Cokebottle." The comedian is not an Aborigine, but in his act he portrays an Aborigine. The complaint alleged a violation of the Racial Discrimination Act, in that: "The respondent portrays Aboriginal persons as rude, stupid, unable to pronounce longer words, unable to speak English properly, dirty, ill educated, always drunk (or at least always drinking), and always swearing."[51] He appeared in black make-up on his face and arms, with a white beard and a "white or ceremonial ochre stripe" on his nose and cheeks.[52] The complainant also took issue with the name "King Billy Cokebottle," saying that it "holds Aboriginal people generally up to ridicule and suggest the Aboriginal people are somehow simple or less intelligent than other members of the community because of their names."[53]

The court, the Federal Magistrates Court of Australia, noted first that the statute requires that the content of the performance be reasonably likely, under the circumstances, to offend, insult, humiliate, or intimidate. Since the test is objective, the intent of Cokebottle was irrelevant.[54] The fact that the complainant is an "activist" and, in the court's view, possibly unduly susceptible also made his subjective reaction irrelevant.[55] The court, however, did take into account the social disadvantages of Aborigines in Australian society and concluded that a reasonable Aborigine might be more likely to take offense, compared to, for example, a New Zealander. The relevant standard was the "reasonable person with the racial, ethnic or relevant attributes of the complainant."[56] Keeping that in mind, the court said that "a joke about a historically oppressed minority group, which is told by a member of a racially dominant majority, may objectively be more likely to lead to offence."[57] The court also took into account the circumstances, particularly the fact that the respondent is a stand-up comedian. "By comedic convention, stand up

48 *See id.* 49 *Id.* at 34.
50 [2004] FMCA 336 (May 21, 2004), www.austlii.edu.au/au/cases/cth/FMCA/2004/336.html.
51 *Id.* at ¶5. 52 *Id.* at ¶30. 53 *Id.* at ¶31. 54 *Id.* at ¶85. 55 *Id.* at ¶87.
56 *Id.* at ¶90. 57 *Id.* at ¶92.

comedians make vulgar jokes, which are often regarded as being in poor taste ... Humour to be effective must often sting and insult."[58]

There is also a requirement that the offensive speech be because of the race or ethnicity of the targets. The respondent had claimed that his purpose was simply to make a living from his abilities to mimic Aboriginal people. In the court's view,

> the racial identity of King Billy Cokebottle although a necessary vehicle for these purposes was largely incidental to them. As I have already indicated, many of King Billy Cokebottle's jokes work regardless of the ethnicity of either King Billy Cokebottle himself or the other characters which he describes. Take away King Billy Cokebottle's ethnicity and he remains a risque stand-up comedian.[59]

Hence, the court was unwilling to conclude that he performed his act "because of Aboriginal people."[60]

Turning to the Act's exceptions, the court concluded that the performances came within the statutory exception for artistic works. But for an artistic work to be excepted, it still must be done or performed reasonably and in good faith. "Reasonably" indicates an objective test, and the court, drawing guidance from *Toben v. Jones*, said that it is necessary to examine the degree of potential harm.

> In the particular context of this case, I bear in mind that Mr Beers was appearing as the character of King Billy Cokebottle, who in many ways is a grotesque caricature. As such, the character has more license than a politician or social commentator to express views. In the context of a stand-up comedy performance, the offence implicit in much of Mr Beers' material does not appear to me to be out of proportion. I do not believe that there is a high degree of gratuitous insult, given that the comedic convention of stand-up is to give offence or make jokes at the expense of some member or members of the community.[61]

While reasonableness is objective, good faith is subjective. Here the respondent's motives were relevant. The court noted evidence of his long association with Aborigines and his claimed affection for them. Also noted was the fact that King Billy Cokebottle, in many jokes, had the last laugh. "I accept that Mr Beers has not set out in his act to gratuitously and unnecessarily offend people, beyond the conventions of the comedic milieu in which he sets himself."[62] Thus, he was entitled to the exception. Thus, Dr. Bannister seems

[58] *Id.* at ¶93. [59] *Id.* at ¶109. [60] *Id.* at ¶110. [61] *Id.* at ¶127. [62] *Id.* at ¶133.

correct in her assertion that racist jokes told on stage may well be treated differently than the same racist jokes told elsewhere and may well be correct that sophisticated racism is protected, while unsophisticated racism is not allowed.

HATE SPEECH AND UNITED STATES LAW

While the United States is said not to allow the regulation of hate speech, there is one relatively early United States case in which, what was effectively, a hate speech statute was held by the Supreme Court to be constitutional. *Beauharnais v. Illinois*[63] grew out of a conviction for violating a provision of the Illinois criminal code prohibiting the dissemination of material which "portrays depravity, criminality, unchastity, or lack of virtue of a class of citizens, of any race, color, creed or religion which ... exposes the citizens of any race, color, creed or religion to contempt, derision, or obloquy or which is productive of breach of the peace or riots."[64] Beauharnais had distributed a leaflet

> setting forth a petition calling on the Mayor and City Council of Chicago "to halt the further encroachment, harassment and invasion of white people, their property, neighborhoods and persons, by the Negro * * *." Below was a call for "One million self respecting white people in Chicago to unite * * *." with the statement added that "If persuasion and the need to prevent the white race from becoming mongrelized by the negro will not unite us, then the aggressions * * * rapes, robberies, knives, guns and marijuana of the negro, surely will."[65]

The Supreme Court rejected Beauharnais' First Amendment challenge. The Court noted that restrictions on libel "have never been thought to raise any Constitutional problem."[66] The Court said that it would be libelous to charge an individual with being a rapist, a robber, a carrier of weapons, or user of marijuana, and "if an utterance directed at an individual may be the object of criminal sanctions, we cannot deny to a State power to punish the same utterance directed at a defined group ..."[67] Interestingly, the Court added: "Resort to epithets or personal abuse is not in any proper sense communication of information or opinion safeguarded by the Constitution, and its punishment as a criminal act would raise no question under that

[63] 343 U.S. 250 (1952). [64] *Id.* at 251, quoting Ill.Rev.Stat.1949, c. 38, s 471. [65] *Id.* at 252.
[66] *Id.* at 256. [67] *Id.* at 258.

instrument."[68] This statement would seem similar to the treatment of hate speech in other countries.

Professor Rosenfeld suggests that the timing of the case, the early 1950s, may be evidence that it was influenced by the events in Nazi Germany.[69] The Court did make reference to the then past three decades but also noted that Illinois did not have to look beyond its own borders to find a history of racial strife and tension.[70] In many of the incidents cited, the Court said, utterances such as that at issue had played a role.[71] So, while the Court may have been influenced by the harm growing out of hate speech, it did not have to look to Germany and could find sufficient justification at home. Thus, in the decades following World War II the United States seemed aimed along the same trajectory as European countries. The United States Supreme Court recognized the harm that can grow out of hate speech, saw it as lacking value as communication, and was willing to allow its regulation.

That early coherence to the European approach was, however, soon to change. While *Beauharnais* has never been formally overruled, it seems clear from the later cases that it can no longer be considered good law. The first of those later cases is *Collin v. Smith*,[72] a case before the United States Court of Appeals for the Seventh Circuit, which the Supreme Court chose not to review. The case involved a proposed march by the National Socialist Party of America, a group described by its leader as a Nazi party, through the village of Skokie, Illinois. Skokie had a large, in fact majority, Jewish population, including several thousand survivors of the Holocaust.[73] The planned march was to involve thirty to fifty participants, wearing uniforms that included swastikas and carrying signs with legends such as "White Free Speech," "Free Speech for the White Man," and "Free Speech for White America."[74]

In anticipation of the march, the Village of Skokie enacted three ordinances. The first required permits for parades and public assemblies; the second prohibited the "dissemination of any materials within the Village of Skokie which promotes and incites hatred against persons by reason of their race, national origin, or religion, and is intended to do so."[75] The third prohibited public demonstrations by political parties while wearing military-style uniforms. The Nazi group's application for a permit was denied, as a perceived violation of the third ordinance.

68 *Id.* at 257 (quoting Cantwell v. Connecticut, 310 U.S. 296, 309–10 (1940)).
69 Rosenfeld, *supra* note 2, at 1525. 70 343 U.S. at 258–59. 71 *Id.* at 259.
72 578 F.2d 1197 (7th Cir.), *cert. denied*, 439 U.S. 916 (1978)). 73 *See id.* at 1199 n.2.
74 *Id.* at 1200. 75 *Id.* at 1199 (quoting Village Ordinance No. 77-5-N-995).

The Seventh Circuit held that the denial of the permit was a violation of the First Amendment. Interestingly, the court seemed to feel the need, almost, to apologize for its conclusions. It said that the personal views of its judges found the group's beliefs and goals repugnant but that it was unable to resolve the case on that basis. "Ideological tyranny, no matter how worthy its motivation, is forbidden as much to appointed judges as to elected legislators."[76] Further, "our task here is to decide whether the First Amendment protects the activity in which appellees wished to engage, not to render moral judgment on their views or tactics."[77] Having set out its task, the court held the proposed activities to be within the ambit of the First Amendment and said that "[l]egislating against the content of First Amendment activity ... launches the government on a slippery and precarious path."[78]

When it came to a consideration of *Beauharnais*, the court found that the earlier decision was based in the tendency of the utterances there to cause violence and disorder. It also suggested that, given later opinions by the Supreme Court, the case might no longer pass constitutional muster. Skokie had argued that, even without a fear of violence, *Beauharnais* allowed limits on racial or religious hatred. The court rejected that interpretation, saying that even if that was a reasonable interpretation at the time, later cases run counter.

Skokie also asserted that it had the right to prevent the psychic trauma the march would bring on its Jewish population and Holocaust survivors. The court said that "[i]t would be grossly insensitive to deny, as we do not, that the proposed demonstration would seriously disturb, emotionally and mentally, at least some and probably many of the Village's residents."[79] But, the court cited to a number of cases noting that the First Amendment protects speech that invites dispute and brings about unrest, not distinguishing between uncomfortable political positions and racist invective.

The court next considered the rights of audiences not to be confronted with offensive speech within their own homes or in a captive audience situation, in which one cannot avoid exposure. It was, of course, clear that the march did not intrude into individual's homes. With regard to captive audiences, the court also failed to see an issue. "Village residents may, if they wish, simply avoid the Village Hall for thirty minutes on a Sunday afternoon, which no doubt would be the normal course of conduct in a day when the Village Hall was not open ..."[80] Lastly, the court raised the issue of line drawing, suggesting that the ordinance might be applied to dissemination of "The Merchant of Venice" or a discussion of reverse racial discrimination.[81]

[76] *Id.* at 1200. [77] *Id.* at 1201. [78] *Id.* at 1202. [79] *Id.* at 1206. [80] *Id.* at 1207.
[81] *See id.*

The Skokie case was brought to the Supreme Court twice, once seeking a stay,[82] and then petitioning for a writ of certiorari.[83] The stay and writ were both denied but in both instances there was a dissent. In the first, Justices Blackmun and Rehnquist noted a conflict with *Beauharnais*. In the second, Justices Blackmun and White argued that the Court should hear the case, because "this is litigation that rests upon critical, disturbing, and emotional facts, and the issues cut down to the very heart of the First Amendment."[84] The case raised the conflict between the establishment of a limitation on speech that might lead to future repression and "a potentially explosive and dangerous situation, inflamed by unforgettable recollections of traumatic experiences in the second world conflict."[85] The dissent from the denial of certiorari said that the speech might be protected but added that

> when citizens assert, not casually, but with deep conviction, that the proposed demonstration is scheduled at a place and in a manner that is taunting and overwhelmingly offensive to the citizens of that place, that assertion, uncomfortable though it may be for judges, deserves to be examined. It might just fall into the same category of one's "right" to cry "fire" in a crowded theater, for "the character of every act depends upon the circumstances in which it is done."[86]

The Skokie case involved one of the most virulent symbols of hate, while the most recent Supreme Court case involves the other, the burning of a cross. *Virginia v. Black*[87] was a consolidation of two cases both of which charged violations of Virginia law making it unlawful "for any person or persons, with the intent of intimidating any person or group of persons, to burn or cause to be burned, a cross on the property of another, a highway or other public place."[88] One of the cases involved a rally of the Ku Klux Klan, in a field visible from a public highway with the permission of the field's owner, at which a cross was burned. The other involved an attempted burning of a cross in the yard of an African–American family.

The Supreme Court was willing to allow a ban on cross burning with the intent to intimidate. "True threats," threats that are meant to intimidate and that a reasonable target would find intimidating, are unprotected by the First Amendment. If there is an intent to intimidate, it would certainly seem likely, given the historic relationship between cross burning and Klan violence, that the target of the action would reasonably feel in fear. The problem with the

[82] Smith v. Collin, 436 U.S. 953 (1978). [83] Smith v. Collin, 439 U.S. 916 (1978). [84] *Id.*
[85] *Id.* at 918. [86] *Id.* at 919 (quoting Schenck v. United States, 249 U.S. 47, 52 (1919)).
[87] 538 U.S. 343 (2003). [88] *Id.* at 348 (quoting Va. Code Ann. § 18.2–423 (1996)).

convictions was that the Virginia law included a provision that any cross burning is *prima facie* evidence of an attempt to intimidate.[89] While the prohibition could stand, the Court found the presumption of intent unconstitutional.

The Court was willing to recognize burning a cross as "a particularly virulent form of intimidation,"[90] but it was not willing to allow it to be banned simply because it is also a particularly virulent expression of hate. The most interesting part of the opinion in this regard was that of a four-justice plurality. The plurality said that the presumption of intent to intimidate created an unacceptable risk of suppressing ideas. "The act of burning a cross may mean that a person is engaging in constitutionally proscribable intimidation. But the same act may mean only that the person is engaged in core political speech . . . [S]ometimes the cross burning is a statement of ideology, a symbol of group solidarity."[91] It may be true that not all cross burnings involve the threat of direct physical violence, as when no one in the usual target group is present, but it would seem at least almost always to be an expression of hatred. But it is clear that the Court will not allow even the most extreme statements or symbols of hatred to be suppressed. The Court sees no clear line between hate speech and political speech, and the need to protect political speech leads to protection for hate speech.

THE CANADIAN VIEW

Among the best analyses of hate speech is that provided by the Canadian Supreme Court in *Regina v. Keegstra*.[92] While the United States seems simply to assume that the values behind free expression outweigh any concerns regarding the effect of hate speech on its targets, and European countries, after the experience with the Nazis, seem to assume the opposite conclusion, the Canadian Court examined of the balance between the two. Whatever one may think of the Court's conclusion, and indeed the Court was closely divided, the analysis is enlightening.

This careful balancing was necessitated by the Canadian constitutional scheme. While Section 2(b) of the Canadian Charter of Rights and Freedoms provides a guarantee of free expression, stating "Everyone has the following fundamental freedoms: . . . freedom of thought, belief, opinion and expression, including freedom of the press and other media of communication . . .," the Charter itself calls for balancing. Section 1 provides: "The *Canadian*

[89] *See id.* [90] *Id.* at 363. [91] *Id.* at 365–66. [92] [1990] 3 S.C.R. 697.

Charter of Rights and Freedoms guarantees the rights and freedoms set out in it subject only to such reasonable limits prescribed by law as can be demonstrably justified in a free and democratic society."

The Supreme Court of Canada, in *Regina v. Oakes*,[93] had set out the analysis for determining when a violation of Section 2 can be justified under Section 1. First, there must be a government objective of pressing and substantial concern. If so, a court must balance the impact of the limitation on the objective against its impact on the freedom or right. In that balance, it is required that the measure be carefully designed to achieve the objective, that there be as little impairment as possible with the right or freedom, and that there be a proportionality between the effect on the right or freedom and the objective.

Keegstra involved a high school teacher who had communicated anti-Semitic comments to his students.

> Mr. Keegstra's teachings attributed various evil qualities to Jews. He thus described Jews to his pupils as "treacherous," "subversive," "sadistic," "money-loving," "power-hungry" and "child killers." He taught his classes that Jewish people seek to destroy Christianity and are responsible for depressions, anarchy, chaos, wars and revolution. According to Mr. Keegstra, Jews "created the Holocaust to gain sympathy" and, in contrast to the open and honest Christians, were said to be deceptive, secretive and inherently evil.[94]

Students were expected to reflect those teachings in his class and on exams. As a result of his expression he found himself convicted of a violation of Section 319(2) of the Criminal Code of Canada. That section provides penalties, including imprisonment, for "[e]very one who, by communicating statements, other than in private conversation, wilfully promotes hatred against any identifiable group."[95]

The majority opinion, written by Chief Justice Dickson, looked for a pressing and substantial concern and easily found one present. The Court found sufficient hate propaganda in Canada to warrant concern. It does real harm to members of the target group, including emotional damage and psychological and social consequences.

> The derision, hostility and abuse encouraged by hate propaganda … have a severely negative impact on the individual's sense of self-worth and acceptance. This impact may cause target group members to take drastic measures in reaction, perhaps avoiding activities which bring them into contact with

[93] [1986] 1 S.C.R. 103. [94] 1 C.R. (4th) at ¶3.

[95] *Id.* at ¶8 (quoting § 319(2)). Section 319 does allow defenses based on truth, good faith expression of religious opinion, and statements made in the public interest. *See id.*

> non-group members or adopting attitudes and postures directed towards blending in with the majority. Such consequences bear heavily in a nation that prides itself on tolerance and the fostering of human dignity through, among other things, respect for the many racial, religious and cultural groups in our society.[96]

Hate propaganda was also seen to have a second harmful effect in its influence on society, through its potential ability to attract individuals to its causes and create discord.[97] The Court also concluded that the limitations at issue further the objective.[98]

The most interesting aspect of the opinion was an analysis of the values underlying free expression and the impact of limitations on those values. This analysis served to examine whether the limit impaired, as little as possible, the right to free expression and whether the effect on the freedom was proportional to the objective. The analysis examined the values espoused by Thomas Emerson discussed in Chapter 1, although the possibility of driving dissent underground was not discussed.

With regard to the role of free expression in ensuring the attainment of truth and the common good, the Court found hate speech to be lacking in value.

> [T]he argument from truth does not provide convincing support for the protection of hate propaganda … [T]he state should not be the sole arbiter of truth, but neither should we overplay the view that rationality will overcome all falsehoods in the unregulated marketplace of ideas. There is very little chance that statements intended to promote hatred against an identifiable group are true, or that their vision of society will lead to a better world.[99]

Hate speech was seen as lacking any role in the public debate leading to truth or a better society.

As to autonomy, or the self-fulfillment of the speaker, the Court recognized that the prohibition limited the speaker's abilities in that regard. However, the Court also found that hate speech itself limited the autonomy of its targets. Because "autonomy stems in large part from one's ability to articulate and nurture an identity derived from membership in a cultural or religious group," hate speech harms autonomy interests.

96 *Id.* at ¶65. 97 *See id.* at ¶66.

98 *Id.* at ¶102. There was dissent on this issue suggesting that the limits could promote the ends of hate-mongers by increasing the media attention they receive, raising public suspicion that their hate speech might have an element of truth, and arguing that the existence of hate propaganda laws did not stop the hate speech of Germany in the 1920s and 1930s, but the majority rejected these contentions. *See id.* at ¶322.

99 *Id.* at ¶92.

Lastly, turning to the role of free expression in democracy, the Court recognized the impact of the limitation on the participation of hate-mongering individuals. It also recognized that democracy will involve, at times, strong language and that hate propaganda might be considered political expression. But that was not adequate to require the protection of such speech.

> [E]xpression can work to undermine our commitment to democracy where employed to propagate ideas anathemic to democratic values. Hate propaganda works in just such a way, arguing as it does for a society in which the democratic process is subverted and individuals are denied respect and dignity simply because of racial or religious characteristics. This brand of expressive activity is thus wholly inimical to the democratic aspirations of the free expression guarantee.[100]

Hate speech is seen as simply lacking sufficient relevance to the values justifying free expression to merit protection in light of the harm that it does. Again, one can disagree with the conclusion, as does a significant bloc of the Court. But the serious consideration given to the issue of why free expression is valued separates the decision of the Canadian Court from the seemingly, almost presumed conclusions of the United States courts in one direction and the rest of the world the opposite direction.

It is interesting to note how broad the Canadian hate speech statute is, prohibiting "promot[ing] hatred against any identifiable group." The Court's analysis speaks most clearly to hate propaganda directed at groups defined by race, ethnicity, or religion, but the statute is not so limited. Professor Krotoszynski questions why there was no prosecution of Québec separatists, who blamed ethnic minorities for their loss in an independence plebiscite and expressed concern over the impact that immigrants might have on the ethnic identity of Québec.[101] This would seem to be an "identifiable group," which might be within the scope of the statute, and Krotoszynski suggests that the failure to prosecute was motivated by the objective of keeping Québec in the Federation.[102] Perhaps an alternative argument is that the speech was simply too close to political, and immigrants were not excoriated over their ethnicity but recognized as having different political interests.

Professor Krotoszynski also expresses concern over the lack of prosecution of a Liberal Member of Parliament for his nationally broadcast statement, "Damn Americans! I hate those bastards."[103] Again, Americans

[100] *Id.* at ¶95. [101] *See* Krotoszynski, *supra* note 20, at 83–84. [102] *See id.* at 85.
[103] *Id.* at 88 (endnote omitted).

would seem to be an identifiable group and, thus, would appear to be covered by the statute. Here, too, the failure to prosecute might be a recognition that the speech is likely to be political, rather than the expression of racial or ethnic hatred. Canadian concerns over the United States are more likely to be motivated by the political positions of the United States and the possibility of economic and cultural dominance. This is a far cry from expressing hatred with regard to core characteristics of individuals or ethnicity, particularly when directed at a group without a real shared ethnicity.

Well after Professor Krotoszynski wrote, the Canadian Supreme Court did attempt to clarify the kind of speech that may be subjected to hate speech prosecution.[104] In *Whatcott v. Saskatchewan Human Rights Tribunal*,[105] the Court considered the case of an individual who had been charged, under the Saskatchewan Human Rights Code, with promoting hatred against individuals of same-sex orientation. The individual argued that any findings against him were in violation of his Charter rights to free expression and, because his actions were religiously motivated, freedom of religion.

The Court concluded that, while some of the flyers that Whatcott had distributed were protected, others were not. In doing so, the Court added some clarity to the sort of speech that may be limited, consistent with Charter rights. The Court found that the statutory prohibition on "any representation that 'ridicules, belittles or otherwise affronts the dignity of' any person or class of persons on the basis of a prohibited ground is not a reasonable limit."[106] But, the statutory prohibition on "any representation 'that exposes or tends to expose to hatred' any person or class of persons on the basis of a prohibited ground is a reasonable limit and demonstrably justified in a free and democratic society."[107]

Looking to the Court's earlier opinion in *Canada v. Taylor*,[108] the *Whatcott* Court found there a meaning to be attached to "hatred." "'Hatred' involves detestation, extreme ill-will and the failure to find any redeeming qualities in the target of the expression."[109] Thus, "the term hatred in the context of human rights legislation includes a component of

[104] There was, actually, a companion case to *Keegstra* that did address the sorts of speech that might be limited. *See* Canada v. Taylor, [1990] 3 S.C.R. 892. But the later case, while drawing guidance from *Taylor*, was, perhaps, somewhat more limited in the sort of expression that could be characterized as hateful.

[105] 2013 CarswellSask 74, 2013 SCC 11. [106] *Id.* at ¶206. [107] *Id.* [108] [1990] 3 S.C.R. 892.

[109] 2013 CarswellSask 74 at ¶40.

looking down on or denying the worth of another."[110] The comments about which Krotoszynski complained may simply not be seen as reaching this level.

CONCERNS OVER LINE-DRAWING

Criticism over decisions in Canada as to when, and when not, to prosecute indicates the real concerns with limits on hate speech. The United States Supreme Court plurality in *Black* insisted on the "intent to intimidate" element as a way to distinguish true threats from political speech. That was certainly one way to draw a line. European courts may be less protective of hate, but there still should be concerns over the drawing of lines between the expression of hate and the expression of political views.

If there are to be limits on hate speech, lines must be carefully drawn. Not all speech that is offensive can be barred. Clearly, in a democracy, political speech must be protected, and some may be offended by some political positions. The target of hate speech limitations cannot even be all speech that offends because of the race, ethnicity, etc. of the audience. A minority person may be offended by an attack on affirmative action, and the offense might be tied to that person's minority status coupled with a belief that members of his or her group deserve protection. The debate is, however, political and must be protected.

One approach to line-drawing would be to recognize the invalidity of, at least some forms of, the *argumentum ad hominem*, the argument directed to the person rather than the position.[111] Such an argument is recognized as an informal fallacy. Ignoring the argument and attacking the speaker does not refute the argument. Thus, the *ad hominem* may be thought not to be a real contribution to any political debate.

There are, however, two varieties of *ad hominem*, the circumstantial and the abusive. For example, in a debate over race-based affirmative action, one party noting that the other would, of course, take the pro position, because he or she is a minority, or take the anti-position, because he or she is white, is circumstantial, rather than abusive. While it may still be an *ad hominem*, it should not be considered racist. The only claim made is that the conclusion offered is based on self-interest, while not defeating the conclusion that would seem relevant.

[110] *Id.* at ¶43.

[111] For a discussion of the *ad hominem* in legal argumentation, *see* Kevin W. Saunders, *Informal Fallacies in Legal Argumentation*, 44 S.C.L. Rev. 343, 345–49 (1993).

It is the abusive *ad hominem* that may constitute hate speech. The abusive variety, instead of merely suggesting self-interest, would argue that the position taken cannot be right, because there is some basic flaw in the population group of which the speaker is a member. That claim is not only irrelevant to the conclusion; it constitutes hate speech.

It is argued elsewhere that the true test of hate speech has three elements.[112] First, the speech must appeal to a degrading view of the targeted group. It should be a claim that members of the group are somehow less fully human than other groups. This part of the definition was adapted from an examination of the history of obscenity and the conclusion that sexual images are suppressed in eras in which they are seen as moving the status of humanity away from God or the gods and toward the animals.[113] Hate speech does not so move all of humanity, but it does assert that the members of the targeted group are not only lesser than God or the gods but lesser than the rest of humanity and closer to the animals. That is the sense in which hate speech is truly degrading. If the statute addressing hate speech is criminal, it would also seem that there should be an intent requirement to avoid criminal liability attaching based on a comment that the speaker did not intend to be, or even realize was, degrading.[114] If a civil statute, for example, simply calling for an apology, the now educated speaker who did not have intent would presumably be willing to apologize for the unintended offence.

It was also argued that intent alone should not be sufficient. There should actually be an offensiveness under the standards of the local community. Lastly, material with serious literary, artistic, political or scientific value should be protected. This protection, at least with regard to politics, seems necessary in a democratic society. The protection of material with serious literary or artistic value may be less central, but there is a line-drawing problem in separating literature and art from the political. Lastly, if material is serious science, it seems unlikely to have been intended to degrade in the sense suggested, but in case it does, there may be good reason to protect it.

112 *See* Kevin W. Saunders, Degradation: What the History of Obscenity Tells Us about Hate Speech (2011). The test developed was based on the test for obscenity established in *Miller v. California*, 413 U.S. 15 (1973).

113 That served to explain the acceptance of pornography in the Greek and Roman eras. Where depictions of humanity involved in sexual activity did not separate man from the sexually active gods, and the rejection of pornography in Christianity, where sex did move humans away from a non-sexually active God toward the animals.

114 An example would be the use of the phrase "to gyp." It is degrading to persons of Romany extraction, or Gypsies, but may well be used by persons having no understanding of its origin.

The Canadian Court, then, largely got it right, when it said that hate speech involves "detestation, extreme ill-will and the failure to find any redeeming qualities in the target of the expression,"[115] and that "hatred in the context of human rights legislation includes a component of looking down on or denying the worth of another."[116] If lines are drawn as carefully as those adopted by the Canadian court, it appears that bans on hate speech can be imposed, without a nation losing its democratic nature.

[115] 2013 CarswellSask 74 at ¶40. [116] *Id.* at ¶43.

5

Holocaust Denial and Other False Assertions of Fact

It is sometimes said that "there is no such thing as a false idea."[1] Thomas Emerson, in his examination of the values that underlie free expression, included the attainment of truth and took the position that free expression is the best way to advance knowledge and to discover truth.[2] Justice Holmes also placed great value in the "marketplace of ideas." He wrote: "when men have realized that time has upset many fighting faiths, they may come to believe even more than they believe the very foundations of their own conduct that the ultimate good desired is better reached by free trade in ideas – that the best test of truth is the power of the thought to get itself accepted in the competition of the market."[3]

Properly understood, these statements would seem correct. But that proper understanding requires that a distinction is drawn between expressions of opinion and assertions of fact. While opinions may be neither true nor false, assertions of fact are. The assertion either comports with reality, or it doesn't, even if we sometimes do not know which the case is.

The Court that asserted that "there is no such thing as a false idea" seemed to recognize the distinction. The opinion went on to say that "there is no constitutional value in false statements of fact. Neither the intentional lie nor the careless error materially advances society's interest in 'uninhibited, robust, and wide-open' debate on public issues."[4]

1 Gertz v. Robert Welch, Inc., 418 U.S. 323, 339 (1974). The opinion goes on to distinguish between statements of opinion and assertions of fact. *See id.* at 339–40.

2 Thomas I. Emerson, *Toward a General Theory of the First Amendment*, 72 YALE L.J. 877 (1963).

3 Abrams v. United States, 250 U.S. 616, 630 (1919) (Holmes, J., dissenting).

4 418 U.S. at 340. The Court was examining the law of defamation and false factual assertions made regarding the plaintiff. While recognizing the lack of value in false statements, the Court also recognized the need to provide breathing space, in order to avoid silencing people who

Professor Emerson was less explicit in his recognition of the distinction. He did however say, "discussion must be kept open no matter how certainly true an accepted opinion may seem to be … [, and] regardless of how false or pernicious the new opinion appears to be."[5] So, his application of this principle may be seen as confined to opinion and not to include false assertions of fact.

Justice Holmes also seems to have had the distinction in mind. Just prior to the language quoted, he talked about the inclination to limit the expression of opinion.

> Persecution for the expression of opinions seems to me perfectly logical. If you have no doubt of your premises or your power and want a certain result with all your heart you naturally express your wishes in law and sweep away all opposition. To allow opposition by speech seems to indicate that you think the speech impotent, as when a man says that he has squared the circle, or that you do not care whole heartedly for the result, or that you doubt either your power or your premises.[6]

Since the lead-in to his discussion of the marketplace of ideas involved opinion, his willingness to rely on that marketplace may not have stretched to the assertion of fact.

This distinction between fact and opinion is important. There are no true and no false opinions. There are simply individuals' assertions of values. If people disagree on matters of public concern, the best test may be provided by the competition of the market, as Holmes said, even if it is not the "best test of truth." It is, instead, the best test of opinion in that it sways more of those who hear it than does its opposing view. If more people come to accept the position, then it becomes the prevailing opinion.

With regard to assertions of fact, even everyone believing the assertion does not make it true. It is true if it comports with reality and false otherwise. The truth of the statement is not determined by counting those who believe and those who disbelieve.

The issue of false assertions of fact, other than in the context of defamation, has come up most regularly in the context of Holocaust denial. This chapter will look to the treatment of such utterances in a number of countries. It will then turn to the consideration of a more general Canadian prohibition on disseminating false news. Lastly, a very specific prohibition from the United States will be considered.

might not be absolutely sure of their assertions. The tests adopted by the United States Supreme Court in this area are discussed in Chapter 9.

5 Emerson, *supra* note 2, at 881–82.

6 250 U.S. at 630.

GERMANY'S *AUSCHWITZ LIE* CASE

The *Auschwitz Lie* case,[7] decided by the German Constitutional Court, arose out of a planned lecture by the revisionist historian David Irving at the invitation of the National Democratic Party (NPD). The NPD was told that the lecture could occur only on the condition that nothing would be said that called into question the persecution of Jews under the Third Reich. Such comments would have to be prevented, if necessary, even by interrupting or bringing the meeting to an end. Donald Kommers, in his analysis of the case, explains that a provision of the Public Assembly Act allowed meetings to be prohibited where there was a likelihood that things said there would constitute criminal violations and that Holocaust denial would constitute violations regarding criminal insult, criminal agitation, and denigrating the memory of the dead.[8]

The NPD challenged the conditions as a violation of the first sentence of Article 5(1) of the German Basic Law. That sentence provides: "Every person shall have the right freely to express and disseminate his opinions in speech, writing, and pictures, and to inform himself without hindrance from generally accessible sources."[9] The claim was that the organization was being denied the right to express and disseminate its opinions.

The Court noted that Article 5 protects opinion and went on to examine what constitutes opinion. The Court said that opinions "are characterised by the subjective relationship of the individual to the content of his statement."[10] Opinions take a position or make a judgment and cannot be proved to be true or false. If the statement is an opinion, it is protected independent of "whether [it] is well founded or unfounded, emotional or rational, valuable or worthless, dangerous or harmless."[11] It also doesn't lose its protection through sharp or hurtful formulation, although as the Court noted, Article 5(2) may provide limits.[12]

7 BVerfGE90, 241–55 (1994). The case may be found in translation at www.utexas.edu/law/academics/centers/transnational/work_new/german/case.php?id=621. It may also be found at DECISIONS OF THE BUNDESVERFASSUNGSGERICHT, VOLUME 2/PART II: FREEDOM OF SPEECH 620 (1998) [hereinafter DECISIONS OF THE BUNDESVERFASSUNGSGERICHT].

8 DONALD P. KOMMERS, THE CONSTITUTIONAL JURISPRUDENCE OF THE FEDERAL REPUBLIC OF GERMANY 383 (2d ed. 1997).

9 The German Basic Law may be found in translation at Basic Law for the Federal Republic of Germany (Grundgesetz, GG), (Federal Ministry of the Interior trans., 1999) [hereinafter German Basic Law], http://germanlawarchive.iuscomp.org/?p=212.

10 BVerfGE90, 241–5 at II.1 (from the University of Texas School of Law translation indicated, *supra* note 7).

11 *Id.*

12 Article 5(2), speaking of the rights in Article 5(1), provides: "These rights shall find their limits in the provisions of general laws, in provisions for the protection of young persons, and in the right to personal honor." Thus, there seems to be broad authority for statutory limitations. *See* GERMAN BASIC LAW, *supra* note 9.

In contrast to opinion, assertions of fact posit a relationship between the statement and reality; unlike opinions, they may be examined for falsity.[13] While statements of purported fact may not come within the scope of Article 5 (1), the Court recognized that the interplay between fact and opinion might require the protection of factual assertion. Since opinion is usually based on beliefs regarding facts, the statements of those facts is protected "insofar as they are the prerequisite for the formation of opinions."[14]

While the Court recognized the difficulty of separating opinion from underlying assertion of fact, it said,

> the protection of assertions of fact ends at the point where these ceased to contribute anything to the formation of opinion ... From this point of view, incorrect information is not an interest worthy of protection ... [A]n assertion of fact known or proved to be untrue is not covered by the protection of freedom of opinion.[15]

With regard to Holocaust denial, the Court asserted that any claim that there had been no persecution of Jews by the Third Reich has been "proved to be untrue according to innumerable eye witness reports and documents, the verdicts of courts in numerous criminal proceedings, and the findings of history."[16] Such a denial, in contrast to the denial of German guilt for the onset of World War II,[17] did not enjoy the protection of Article 5(1).

While that would be enough to resolve the issues, the Court considered whether, if the comments did have the protection of Article 5(1), they could still be limited. That issue turned on whether the "insult "of such speech impacted the personal honor protected by Article 5(2), which with regard to the rights in Article 5(1), provides: "These rights shall find their limits in the provisions of general laws, in provisions for the protection of young persons, and in the right to personal honor." In that regard, the Court found Holocaust denial to constitute an attack on the respect and human dignity of

[13] BVerfGE90, 241–5 at II.1. [14] *Id.*

[15] *Id.* The Court did recognize that the requirements of truth must not be so stringent as to chill permissible statements. *See id.*

[16] *Id.* at II.2.

[17] In another case, Historical Falsification Case (Truth for Germany Case), BVerGE 90, 1 (1994), the Court considered a book that claimed that Germany was not at fault for the war. That would seem to be a matter of opinion, and even if guilt were taken to mean causation, the Court said the conclusions regarding causation involve interpretation of complex historical facts. Since the book was primarily opinion, placement on a list of books that were harmful to youth was a violation of the author's rights under Article 5(1). The case may be found in DECISIONS OF THE BUNDESVERFASSUNGSGERICHT, *supra* note 7, at 570.

contemporary German Jews.[18] It, like other forms of hate speech, could be prohibited.

There have also been criminal convictions in Germany for Holocaust denial. Fredrick Toben was convicted of inciting racial hatred, insulting the memory of the dead, and denying genocide, as a result of Holocaust denial claims sent by him from Australia to recipients in Germany.[19] He was sentenced to ten months of imprisonment.

A, perhaps, better known case and one certainly resulting in a lengthier term of imprisonment was that of Ernst Zundel.[20] Zundel was a longtime resident of Canada,[21] but his applications for Canadian citizenship had been rejected. After it had become known that he'd published a short book titled *The Hitler We Loved & Why*, he began to have trouble with Canadian authorities. In 2005, a federal court concluded that he was a national security threat, because he was closely associated with violent white supremacist groups. It was that conclusion, rather than just his hatemongering, that led to his deportation to Germany. The German extradition request was based on the accessibility in Germany of his Canadian website. Once Germany gained jurisdiction, Zundel was convicted of Holocaust denial and inciting racial hatred and sentenced to five years.

OTHER EUROPEAN CASES

Germany is not the only European country that prohibits Holocaust denial. Such claims are also barred in Austria, Belgium, the Czech Republic, France, Germany, Lithuania, Poland, Slovakia, and Switzerland.[22] More broadly, Stephen Gey maintains that Holocaust denial is a crime in virtually every other Western democracy, except the United States.[23] The European Union,

[18] *See id.*

[19] *See German Court Sentences Australian Holocaust Skeptic*, 18(4) J. HIST. REV. 2 (Jul./Aug. 1999), www.ihr.org/jhr/v18/v18n4p-2_Toben.html.

[20] For accounts of the Zundel case, *see* Victor Homola, *Holocaust Denier Gets 5 Years*, NEW YORK TIMES (Feb. 16, 2007), www.nytimes.com/2007/02/16/world/europe/16briefs-holocaustdenier.html?_r=0; Mark Bonokoski, *Zundel Released from German Jail*, TORONTO SUN (Mar. 1, 2010), www.torontosun.com/news/columnists/mark_bonokoski/2010/03/01/13074806.html.

[21] Other aspects of Zundel's interactions with Canadian law are discussed *infra*, notes 45–61, and accompanying text.

[22] Russell L Weaver, Nicolas Delpierre, & Laurence Boissier, *Holocaust Denial and Governmentally Declared 'Truth': French and American Perspectives*, 41 TEX. TECH L. REV. 495, 496 (2009).

[23] Steven G. Gey, *The First Amendment and the Dissemination of Socially Worthless Untruths*, 36 FLA. ST. L. REV. 1, 2 (2008).

itself, also criminalizes Holocaust denial in a provision barring inciting racial hatred or violence by denying or trivializing genocide, war crimes, or crimes against humanity.[24]

One of the better-known European cases is an Austrian case again involving David Irving.[25] He had given an interview and a speech in Austria, in 1989, in which he had denied the occurrence of the Holocaust. After a period of absence from the country, he was arrested in 2005 on the then sixteen-year-old warrant. Despite the fact that he said he had later changed his mind and agreed that the Holocaust had occurred, he was sentenced to three years in prison.

Russell Weaver, Nicolas Delpierre, and Laurence Boissier provide insight into French Holocaust denial law by analyzing a number of cases,[26] including that of Robert Faurisson, a case at least as well known as the Austrian Irving case. French Holocaust denial charges are brought under the Gayssot law,[27] which

> prohibits individuals from denying the existence of the Holocaust as well as from challenging the findings of the Nuremberg International Military Tribunal ... It also prohibits statements that express doubt about the existence of the Holocaust, that minimize gas chambers in an outrageous manner (e.g., speaking of "alleged" gas chambers, the "'presumed' holocaust," or "the rumour" about Auschwitz), or refer to gas chambers as a historic lie or "myth."[28]

The Faurisson case arose out of an interview in a monthly paper in which the defendant claimed that the Nazis had not used gas chambers to exterminate Jews in concentration camps.[29] It was said that this "myth" of the gas chambers had been promulgated by the victors in World War II and later adopted by the French government. Faurisson was convicted of "contesting crimes against humanity" and was fined.[30] Faurisson then sought the assistance of the United Nations Human Rights Committee, but the Committee found no violation of his free expression rights under the International Covenant on Civil and Political Rights.[31]

24 *See* Weaver et al., *supra* note 22, at 496.

25 A source for the facts presented is Peter R. Teachout, *Making "Holocaust Denial" A Crime: Reflections on European Anti-Negationist Laws from the Perspective of U.S. Constitutional Experience*, 30 Vermont L. Rev. 655, 656 (2006).

26 Weaver et al., *supra* note 22.

27 The citation for the Loi Gayssot is Law No. 90-615 of Jul. 13, 1990, Article 9, Journal Officiel de la Replublique Francaise [J.O.], Jul. 14, 1990, 8333.

28 Weaver et al., *supra* note 22, at 497. 29 *Id.* at 498–99. 30 *Id.* at 499.

31 *Id.* (citing U.N. CCPR, 58th Sess., Commc'n No. 550/1993, available at www.unhchr.ch/tbs/doc.nsf/0/4c47b59ea48f7343802566f 200352fea?).

Weaver, Delpierre, and Boissier go on to discuss a number of other French cases involving Holocaust denial. The case of Pierre Marais involved a defendant who denied the use of particular chemicals but was convicted, and his conviction was held by the European Commission of Human Rights not to be in violation of free expression rights under the European Convention.[32] The case of Bruno Gollnisch, discussed in some detail,[33] involved a Member of the European Parliament, who contested only the number of people killed in the gas chambers but received a suspended three months, sentence and was fined. In a case involving Roger Garaudy, a former member of the French National Assembly, there was a conviction for Holocaust denial, based on a book he had written, and he was fined. [34] Lastly, a number of charges brought against Jean-Marie Le Pen, the president of the National Front, involving various forms of Holocaust denial are discussed.[35]

AUSTRALIA

The main Australian case involving Holocaust denial, *Toben v. Jones*,[36] had as its defendant Fredrick Toben, an individual who was also convicted in Germany, as a result of material he had sent from Australia to German recipients.[37] While the expression at issue did constitute Holocaust denial, the prosecution was brought under the Racial Discrimination Act of 1975. That act makes it "unlawful for a person to do an act, otherwise than in private, if: (a) the act is reasonably likely, in all the circumstances, to offend, insult, humiliate or intimidate another person or group of people; and (b) the act is done because of the race, colour or national or ethnic origin of the other person or of some or all of the people in the group."[38]

The basis for the charges was the defendant's Internet publication, on the website of the Adelaide Institute, of what the Human Rights and Equal Opportunity Commission found to be racial vilification of the Jewish people. Included on the website were photographs with descriptions: "Entering the alleged gas chamber," "The four alleged gas-induction holes do not exist!," and "No holes – no Holocaust!"[39] In an interesting combination of statements, the website went on to say:

32 *See id.* 33 *See id.* at 499–503. 34 The case is discussed *id.* at 504.
35 *See id.* at 504–6. 36 (2003) 129 FCR 515 (Austl.).
37 *See supra* note 19 and accompanying text.
38 *Racial Discrimination Act* 1975, s 18C(1) (Austl.). A discussion of the Act in the context of hate speech may be found in Chapter 4.
39 129 FCR at 520.

> We are not "Holocaust deniers." We proudly proclaim that to date there is no evidence that millions of people were killed in homicidal gas chambers. That is good news all round. Why would anyone find this offensive? We are celebrating the living who were thought dead. How can this be an offence—unless it offends those who have their snout in the trough which Jewish academic, Dr. Frank Knopfelmacher called, "The Holocaust racket."[40]

The combination would seem to be equivalent to the statement: "We are not Holocaust deniers, but the Holocaust never occurred."

The website also said that the Institute, additionally, focuses on the Jewish–Bolshevik Holocaust. Based on material found in a novel, the Institute said that the novel's author "has revealed a basic historical fact, viz, that Lenin's henchman, Trotsky (Bronstein) and Stalin's henchman, Kaganovich, were Jewish mass murderers. This historical fact clearly shows the Jews were not always victims in history, but also murderers."[41]

Justice Carr, in his opinion, said that the defendant and the Institute had not confined themselves to dispassionate investigation of the Holocaust. The references to the Jewish–Bolshevik Holocaust and the seeming reference to Jews as critics of the position of the Institute and who were "intellectual midgets but materialistic giants," having "their snout in the trough [of] the Holocaust racket,"[42] led Justice Carr to believe that the comments were made because of the ethnic origin of the target group. While an academic publication would have made the effort to express its conclusions with restraint, the appellant was "deliberately provocative and inflammatory."[43]

Justice Kiefel agreed that the publication had been undertaken because of the ethnic origin of the Jewish people and that it lacked the good faith that would be required under an exemption to the statute. Justice Allsop also expressed his general agreement, concluding that the document was "designed and intended, amongst other things, to smear, hurt, offend, insult and humiliate Jews," and found no evidence of good faith.[44]

CANADA AND FALSE NEWS

As with the Australian case, a Canadian case involving the dissemination of false news, involved an individual who was also to be convicted in Germany.[45] *Regina v. Zundel*,[46] however, was brought under a statute that was not limited to Holocaust denial. The statute involved was the false news provision of the Canadian Criminal Code. The provision provided: "Every one who wilfully

[40] *Id.* at 522. [41] *Id.* at 521. [42] *Id.* at 527. [43] *Id.* at 527. [44] *Id.* at 555.
[45] *See supra* notes 20–21 and accompanying text. [46] (1992) 2 S.C.R. 731 (Can.).

publishes a statement, tale or news that he knows is false and that causes or is likely to cause injury or mischief to a public interest is guilty of an indictable offense and liable to imprisonment for a term not exceeding two years."[47]

The "false news" at the heart of this case was a booklet titled *Did Six Million Really Die?* As the title of the book suggests, the premise was that the Holocaust was a myth circulated by a worldwide Jewish conspiracy. It would appear that the Court would have accepted a conviction based on the dissemination of hate, as in *Regina v. Keegstra*.[48] If that had been the approach taken by the prosecution, the result in Canada would have been much the same as that in Australia. Holocaust denial would have led to a criminal conviction not under a statute aimed specifically at such denial, but as a form of hate speech.

Since the prosecution was, instead, for the dissemination of false news, the Court had to consider whether such a statute was consistent with Section 2(b), the free expression provision, of the Canadian Charter of Rights and Freedoms. The Court saw no question but that the statute was an infringement of free expression. It rejected the claim that a deliberate lie is not a legitimate form of expression, which like violent acts, even if expressive, should not be protected by Section 2(b). Rather, the Court concluded, deliberate lies may have value, providing examples of clear falsifications serving useful social purposes:

> A person fighting cruelty against animals may knowingly cite false statistics in pursuit of his or her beliefs and with the purpose of communicating a more fundamental message, e.g., "cruelty to animals is increasing and must be stopped." A doctor, in order to persuade people to be inoculated against a burgeoning epidemic, may exaggerate the number or geographical location of persons potentially infected with the virus. An artist, for artistic purposes, may make a statement that a particular society considers both an assertion of fact and a manifestly deliberate lie; consider the case of Salman Rushdie's Satanic Verses . . ., viewed by many Muslim societies as perpetrating deliberate lies against the Prophet.[49]

Having concluded that lies are expression, the Court also found it clear that the statute was an intentional limitation on such expression.

The difficult issue was whether the infringement could be justified under Section 1 of the Charter, which allows "reasonable limits prescribed by law as can be demonstrably justified in a free and democratic society." Application of Section 1 required an examination under the *Oakes* test.[50] The first issue in

[47] *Id.* at ¶1 (citing Criminal Code § 181, S. C. 1985, c. C-46.

[48] (1990) 3 S.C.R. 697 (Can.). *Keegstra* is discussed in Chapter 4.

[49] 2 S.C.R. at 754–55.

[50] The *Oakes* test, established in the case *Regina v. Oakes*, (1986) 1 S.C.R. 103 (Can.), was introduced in Chapter 1.

that test is whether or not there is an overriding public objective. The Court said that what must be examined is the intention of Parliament when the section was enacted or amended.

The problem in analyzing that intention was, first, in identifying it. The Court said that the relevant section could be traced back to an English statute enacted in 1275. That statute provided "'that from henceforth none be so hardy to tell or publish any false News or Tales, whereby discord, or occasion of discord or slander may grow between the King and his People, or the Great Men of the Realm.'"[51] Its continued presence in Canadian law seemed to the Court to be an oversight; it had been abolished in England in 1887 but carried over to the Canadian criminal code in 1892.[52] Furthermore, the shift from protecting the King and the Great Men to protecting minorities was seen as more than a shift in focus but a redefinition that could not be allowed.[53]

If no objective could be discerned, there would not be any overriding public objective. With no such objective, the statute could not be said to advance that objective. Furthermore, the proportionality required between the impact of the statute on free speech and the furtherance of the objective could not be met. The impact on expression, assuming as the Court did that falsehoods may have value, cannot be outweighed by the non-existent objective.

It seems clear that, even if the Court had been able to discern a purpose, it most likely still would have declared the statute unconstitutional. The Court did suggest that if the statute were aimed at Holocaust denial, the speech at which the actual prosecution was aimed, that would be "a much more finely tailored provision to which different considerations might well apply."[54] That would, seemingly, also be consistent with the Court's position in *Keegstra*.

Nonetheless, even if "different considerations" might apply, it's not clear that the Court would uphold even such a "finely tailored provision." The Court expressed concern over the ability to identify falsity at trial, even, or particularly, as to historical issues.

> The question of falsity of the statement is often a matter of debate, particularly where historical facts are at issue. (Historians have written extensively on the difficulty of ascertaining what actually occurred in the past, given the difficulty of verification in the selective and sometimes revisionist versions different witnesses and historians may accord to the same events.)[55]

[51] *Id.* at 744 (quoting Statute of Westminster, 1275 (U.K.), 3 Edw. 1, c. 34). [52] *See id.* at 745.

[53] *See id.* at 761–62. [54] *Id.* at 767.

[55] *Id.* at 747–48. The Court also expressed concern over the ability to determine the defendant's knowledge of falsity and whether the public interest was or was not injured, or likely to be injured. *Id.*

Even accepting that it may not be difficult to determine the falsity of Holocaust denial, not all such cases could be resolved with such ease. "[P]articularly where complex social and historical facts are involved, it may prove exceedingly difficult."[56]

Even such settled issues as the occurrence of the Holocaust might, in the Court's view, cause problems. The problem is "in the assumption that we can identify the essence of the communication and determine that it is false with sufficient accuracy to make falsity a fair criterion for denial of constitutional protection."[57] The Court said that meaning was something to be found in the interactive process between the listener and the speaker and that "a statement that is true on one level for one person may be false on another level for a different person."[58] Even for the expression at issue, the meaning might have been the assertion that the Nazis did not purposely exterminate Jews, but alternatively, the meaning may have been "that the public should not be quick to adopt 'accepted' versions of history, truth, etc., or that one should rigorously analyze common characterizations of past events."[59]

The Canadian Court was also not willing to accept, with the same ease as the German Constitutional Court, the distinction between fact and opinion. "The reality is that when the matter is one on which the majority of the public has settled views, opinions may, for practical purposes, be treated as an expression of a 'false fact'."[60] Specifically, with regard to the statute at issue, the court said:

> The phrase "statement, tale or news," while it may not extend to the realm of true opinion (wherever the line is to be drawn, itself a question of great difficulty), obviously encompasses a broad range of historical and social speech, going well beyond what is patent or provable to the senses as a matter of "pure fact".[61]

Thus, even if the Court were willing to conclude that there is no value in false statements of fact, the possibility of bleeding over to the prosecution of opinion would have a seriously negative impact on protected expression.

[56] *Id.* at 757. [57] *Id.* at 756. [58] *Id.* [59] *Id.* at 757.

[60] *Id.* at 749. These "settled views" would also have an impact on the jury's analysis of the defendant's subjective knowledge of falsity. If everyone knows that the statement is false, the jury would be likely to conclude that the defendant knew it was false. *Id.* at 749–50.

[61] *Id.* at 768. The Court pointed to a prosecution of an American settler in which the false statements of facts were found in posters stating "Americans not wanted in Canada. Investigate before buying lands and taking homesteads in this country." *Id.*

THE UNITED STATES AND THE STOLEN VALOR ACT

Given the view in the United States that there are no false ideas and faith in the marketplace of ideas, it is not surprising that there is nothing like a "false news" provision in United States law. Given the unwillingness to allow the prosecution of hate speech, it also seems extremely unlikely that any Holocaust denial statute would stand up to constitutional scrutiny.

There are provisions under United States law that do criminalize knowingly false statements. It is a crime knowingly to make false statements to officials of the United States government.[62] It is also a crime falsely to represent oneself as speaking as a government official.[63] There are also perjury laws, prohibiting making knowingly false statements while under oath, at both the federal and state levels. Furthermore, fraud, intentional misstatement about a past or present fact to obtain a benefit, is criminalized at both levels. But these are not general provisions against lying; they are specifically directed at harms done to law enforcement, the courts, and the government or at a form of property crime. None seem to be viewed as raising constitutional issues.

There was a 2012 case before the United States Supreme Court that addressed lies in another context, without the requirement of the showing of this sort of harm. *United States v. Alvarez*[64] concerned an individual who, as a new member of a water district board, introduced himself as a retired Marine with twenty-five years of service and as having been awarded the Congressional Medal of Honor. The claim to have been awarded the Congressional Medal of Honor, unlike his claim of military service or to have played for the Detroit Read Wings or to have been married to a Mexican starlet, placed him in violation of United States law.

The Stolen Valor Act of 2005 provided: "Whoever falsely represents himself or herself, verbally or in writing, to have been awarded any decoration or medal authorized by Congress for the Armed Forces of the United States ... shall be fined ..., imprisoned not more than six months, or both."[65] When the medal involved is the Congressional Medal of Honor, the maximum term of imprisonment increases to one year.[66] Since Alvarez seems to have been engaged in pure puffery, rather than in an attempt to gain employment, financial benefits or any privileges due such medal winners, the Act seems to have been the only statute violated.

62 *See* 18 U.S.C. §1001. 63 *See id.* at §912. 64 132 S.Ct. 2537 (2012).
65 Pub. L. No. 109–437, 12 Stat. 3266 (2006) (current text at 18 U.S.C. §704(b)).
66 *See* 18 U.S.C. §704(c).

Alvarez was convicted, after having pleaded guilty while reserving his right to appeal based on the First Amendment's freedom of speech. It was that issue that ended up before the Supreme Court, where the statute was declared unconstitutional. A four-justice plurality began by noting that the Court has rejected the principle of ad hoc balancing of the costs and benefits of free expression against other concerns. "Instead, content-based restrictions on speech have been permitted, as a general matter, only when confined to the few 'historic and traditional categories [of expression] long familiar to the bar',"[67] listing criminal advocacy, obscenity, fighting words, child pornography, fraud, and true threats as the clearest examples.[68] A general exception from protection for false statements is not among those categories.

The government had contended that false statements are of no value and cited to a variety of cases in support of that claim. But, the plurality noted, the cases all involved "defamation, fraud, or some other legally cognizable harm associated with a false statement, such as an invasion of privacy or the costs of vexatious litigation."[69] In those situations, false statements could lead to liability, but the plurality said the cases do not establish any general rule withholding protection for false statements, where no independent harm is done. "Our prior decisions have not confronted a measure, like the Stolen Valor Act, that targets falsity and nothing more."[70] Furthermore, the plurality saw the government as attempting to turn established principle on its head.

> It seeks to convert a rule that limits liability even in defamation cases where the law permits recovery for tortious wrongs into a rule that expands liability in a different, far greater realm of discourse and expression. That inverts the rationale for the exception. The requirements of a knowing falsehood or reckless disregard for truth as the condition for recovery in certain defamation cases exist to allow more speech, not less. A rule designed to tolerate certain speech ought not blossom to become a rationale for a rule restricting it.[71]

While the Court recognized that there may be as yet unidentified or undiscussed categories of historically unprotected speech, the plurality said that the government had not offered any convincing arguments that false statements are such a category.[72]

Under United States law, infringement of a constitutional right is not automatically invalid. The government still has the opportunity to show that

67 132 S.Ct. at 2544 (citations omitted). 68 *See id.* 69 *Id.* at 2545. 70 *Id.* 71 *Id.*
72 *See id.* at 2547–48.

the limitation is necessary, or narrowly tailored, to a compelling interest. The government attempted to do so by pointing to the role that medals play in military service, recognizing heroism and sacrifice, as well as fostering morale and esprit de corps.

Military preparedness may be a compelling interest, but the plurality had difficulty with the necessity aspect of the test. There were concerns that false claims would demean the awards and diminish the honor they confirm, might be offensive to those actually awarded such medals and might be taken as an insult, but that was not enough. In particular, the plurality said that the government had not shown that counter speech would not adequately serve its interests and pointed to the ridicule that Alvarez himself had received. Appealing to the general rule that the remedy for bad speech, or in this case false speech, is good speech, or in this case true speech, the plurality suggested that there were less restrictive means to further the government's interests. In particular, a government database of, at least, winners of the Congressional Medal of Honor, would provide that true speech and make false claims, if not less likely, at least, more easily discoverable.

Since the lead opinion was a four-justice plurality, a concurrence was required to declare the act unconstitutional. A concurrence by two justices agreed that the act was unconstitutional but rejected strict categorical analysis. The concurrence suggested an intermediate scrutiny approach, such as that involved in the protection of commercial speech[73] or the regulation of speech where the government is acting as an employer. Even under that weaker test for justifying infringement, the concurrence demanded that there be no less burdensome way to further the government's interest. Interpreting the statute to require knowledge of falsity would be one such step, but the concurrence also said that a publicly available registry of military awards could protect the integrity of awards against false claims.

It should be noted that Congress amended the act in the Stolen Valor Act of 2013. The Act, as amended, brings the prohibition on false claims with regard to military awards in line with other statutes aimed at the fraudulent obtaining of benefits. The Act now provides:

> Whoever, with intent to obtain money, property, or other tangible benefit, fraudulently holds oneself out to be a recipient of a decoration or medal described in subsection (c)(2) or (d) shall be fined under this title, imprisoned not more than one year, or both.[74]

[73] Commercial speech was discussed in Chapter 2.

[74] Pub. L. 113–12, 127 Stat. 448 (2013).

Lastly, it is worth mentioning that other fully functioning democracies do have laws similar to that rejected in *Alvarez*. In the United Kingdom, the Army Act of 1995 provides

> Any person who, in the United Kingdom or in any colony,—
>
> (a) without authority uses or wears any military decoration, or any badge, wound stripe or emblem supplied or authorised by the Defence Council, or
> (b) uses or wears any decoration, badge, wound stripe, or emblem so nearly resembling any military decoration, or any such badge, stripe or emblem as aforesaid, as to be calculated to deceive, or
> (c) falsely represents himself to be a person who is or has been entitled to use or wear any such decoration, badge, stripe or emblem as is mentioned in paragraph (a) of this subsection,
>
> shall be guilty of an offence against this section.[75]

Australia has similar legislation. The Defence Act of 2003 provides: "A person is guilty of an offence if: (a) the person wears a service decoration; and (b) the person is not the person on whom the decoration was conferred . . ."[76] There is an exception to allow a family member of a deceased recipient of the service decoration to wear the decoration, as long as he or she doesn't claim to be the actual recipient. There are also exceptions for dramatic performances and films.

Similarly, the Canadian Criminal Code provides:

> Every one who without lawful authority, the proof of which lies on him,
>
> (a) wears a uniform of the Canadian Forces or any other naval, army or air force or a uniform that is so similar to the uniform of any of those forces that it is likely to be mistaken therefor,
> (b) wears a distinctive mark relating to wounds received or service performed in war, or a military medal, ribbon, badge, chevron or any decoration or order that is awarded for war services, or any imitation thereof, or any mark or device or thing that is likely to be mistaken for any such mark, medal, ribbon, badge, chevron, decoration or order, . . .
>
> is guilty of an offence punishable on summary conviction.[77]

[75] Army Act 1995, § 197 (1), www.legislation.gov.uk/ukpga/Eliz2/3–4/18/section/197.
[76] Defence Act 2003, Section 80B(1), www.austlii.edu.au/au/legis/cth/consol_act/da190356/s80b.html.
[77] R.S.C., 1985, c. C-46 Section 419, http://laws-lois.justice.gc.ca/eng/acts/C-46/page-206.html.

THE IMPACT OF PROSECUTING LIES

The attorneys for Alvarez, the defendant in the Stolen Valor Act case, expressed a dim view of humanity's capacity for veracity. The brief for Alvarez posited: "Everyone lies … We lie all the time … [H]uman beings are constantly forced to choose the persona we present to the world, and our choices nearly always involve intentional omissions and misrepresentations, if not outright deception."[78] While that statement seems overly broad, it is certainly true that people do lie with some regularity. The lies may not reach the level of Holocaust denial or false claims to military awards; they may be as simple as false claims to have enjoyed a dinner party to avoid hurting the host's feelings.

So, why prosecute some lies and not others? The emphasis seems clearly to depend on the importance of the lie. Despite the German Court's more general statements about distinctions between fact and opinion, with the protection of the Basic Law reserved for opinion, it was not just any potential willful misstatement of fact that was to be prohibited at the scheduled meeting. It was Holocaust denial. Such denial, in the German view, would constitute criminal insult, criminal agitation, and denigration of the memory of the dead.[79] That sort of impact, in a country in which the first provision of the constitution protects personal dignity, was unacceptable.[80]

Other European cases have also focused on Holocaust denial, with some based on laws specifically aimed at such denial.[81] Here, too, it is not just any lie that is the basis for prosecution. Most European countries are strongly concerned with hate speech,[82] and it is certainly not a conceptual stretch to see Holocaust denial as a form of hate speech. To deny the occurrence of the events that constitute the Holocaust can be taken as an attempt to express contempt for the Jews. Any claims to a conspiracy to gain sympathy through false claims with regard to the Third Reich's treatment of the Jews could similarly be seen as hate speech.

Australia's treatment of Holocaust denial, at least in the context of the *Toben* case,[83] was clear in its treatment of such denial as hate speech. The

78 132 S.Ct. at 2563 (Alito, J., dissenting) (quoting Brief for the Respondent, 10, 39).

79 *See supra*, note 8, and accompanying text.

80 The German Basic Law provides in Article 1, "Human dignity shall be inviolable. To respect and protect it shall be the duty of all state authority." A translation of the German Basic Law may be found at http://germanlawarchive.juscomp.org/?9=212.

81 *See supra*, notes 26–35, and accompanying text.

82 Hate speech is discussed in Chapter 4.

83 *See supra*, notes 36–44, and accompanying text.

conviction was obtained, not under a statute specifically aimed at Holocaust denial, but under the Racial Discrimination Act, which addressed all actions likely to offend, insult, humiliate, or intimidate on the basis of race, color, or national or ethnic origin. Holocaust denial was simply one form of doing so.

Canada's prosecution of a Holocaust denier was not under a statute directed at hate speech; the statute addressed all knowingly false reports of news that were likely to have a negative impact on the public interest.[84] While the Canadian Court found such a prosecution to be in violation of the *Canadian Charter of Rights and Freedoms*, it seems that the Court would have accepted the prosecution for violating a statute aimed at hate speech. The more general statute, the Court said, could have been applied to more valuable speech.

The European cases prosecuting Holocaust denial were all aimed at lies that have great importance. Holocaust denial is a lie that is a form of hate speech, and the European countries that prosecute Holocaust denial more generally prosecute hate speech. Canada allows the prosecution of hate speech, but the case there was brought under the statute that could reach lies that were not as important and even, as the Court noted, lies that had positive impact.

The Stolen Valor Act case and the statutes existing in other countries barring false claims of having been awarded military decorations also address only lies that are seen as important. Reserving the honor to be found in a military medal for those who have actually been awarded the medal is important to military morale and the willingness to serve and sacrifice. This importance was not dismissed in *Alvarez*, but the criminal prohibition was not seen as necessary to the government interest. The stronger protection offered by the First Amendment, in comparison to speech protections in other countries, would not allow limits on even this seemingly important lie. In countries more willing to restrict, at least nonpolitical, speech the statutes protecting military awards are more likely to stand up to challenge.

While it would seem to be only lies implicating important interests that will be prosecuted anywhere, there remains the issue of the impact of even such limited prosecutions on important free-speech interests. The most important impact may be the chilling effect that the threat of such prosecutions can have. Rather than risk accidentally asserting a false position, even if limited to areas of importance such as Holocaust denial and military commendations, people may decide to say nothing.

[84] *See supra*, notes 46–61, and accompanying text.

Requiring that the statement be made with knowledge of its falsity might be seen to protect the unwary. Despite the examples offered by the Canadian Court, it may not be the case that citation to false statistics or location of disease outbreaks is valuable. Rational consideration of the treatment of animals or the wisdom of inoculation would seem to require knowledge of actual facts rather than false claims. Those who are mistaken should be protected, but those who intentionally mislead are not contributing to the attainment of the truth, whether or not they should be subject to criminal liability.

Perhaps, more serious concern is that raised by the Canadian Court regarding proving the knowledge of falsity. There is the possibility that a jury will conclude that the speaker must have known that the statement was false, because everyone knows that it's false. That is, of course, different from actual, subjective knowledge of falsity, and the possibility of someone being charged based on a statement that he or she actually believed to be true but was false is of concern. Perhaps, with regard to Holocaust denial, everyone really does know that it's false, and given the general anti-Semitic tenor of the writings of those charged, it would seem that the denials were, in fact, intentional misstatements. Nonetheless, there is always the possibility that someone who truly believes that the Holocaust did not occur could be charged with denial.

The Canadian Court also raised concerns over the meaning of a statement. While it seems extremely unlikely that the Zundel's denial of the Holocaust was really intended as a statement that one should not accept, uncritically, the conclusions of historians, it is true that a statement may admit of more than one meaning. If prosecutions are to be allowed, it must be clear that the defendant's intent was to convey a meaning that was, in fact, false, as well as requiring that the defendant knew that it was false.

Lastly, the concern over the ability to distinguish between statements of fact and statements of opinion is valid. Consider, as an example, one who denies the existence of climate change or global warming, or perhaps, only humanity's role in that change. If that change, and its causes, are taken as firmly established, the asserted position may be seen as a false statement. Requiring that there be knowing falsity helps, but if the proposition is sufficiently generally accepted, there is reasonable concern that the fact finder will reach the conclusion that the defendant knew the statement was false because everyone knows it is false.

More fundamentally, there may be a question as to whether causes of this variety can really be matters of fact. Annual average temperatures are matters of fact. Whether this constitutes climate change and global warming or merely a cyclical phenomenon is more a matter of opinion. The same may be said of the role of humanity. That may seem needlessly skeptical, but assertions regarding climate change are accepted, because they are the best explanations for the observations. That is true of scientific theories generally; they are accepted as the best explanations of observations. But "best" must generally be taken as indicating opinion.

In conclusion, there may well be no value in false statements of asserted facts. But there are legitimate concerns over the impact prosecuting lies will have on the willingness to speak out and the protection that should be given to opinion. If lies are to be prosecuted, it would seem that the prosecution should be limited to areas where the statements are of great importance, that the statements be clearly factual, and that the speaker must actually have known of the falsity. Prosecution of Holocaust denial might be justified, because everyone really does know that the Holocaust occurred and especially where the speaker has additionally expressed hateful views in other ways. Prosecution for stolen valor clearly involves a statement of fact, and there seems little likelihood that, unless an explanation is offered, the speaker did not recognize that falsity. There would seem to be little chilling effect or impact on opinion resulting from such a prosecution.

6

Political Party Bans

Political parties are necessary to the preservation of democracy, at least in large states. They involve freedom of association but are important to free expression. Political speech, the protection of which is essential to democracy, is less likely to be effective if it is only the individual who can speak. Swaying voters in a large state requires a concerted effort, and it is a party that provides the platform for such efforts. Samuel Isaacharoff recognizes the significance of this role of political parties and the problems inherent in barring the participation of a political party in the electoral process. "The removal of certain political views from the electoral arena limits the choices that are permitted to the citizenry and thus calls into question the legitimacy of the entire democratic enterprise."[1]

The European Commission for Democracy through Law (the Venice Commission) notes the relationship between Article 11 of the European Convention on Human Rights, which provides for freedom of association, and Article 10, which protects free expression. Citing case law from the European Court of Human Rights (ECtHR), the Commission said that the protection of expression is one of the objectives of the freedom of assembly and association.[2] Furthermore, this applies even more strongly to political parties because of their essential role in the functioning of democracy and political pluralism.[3]

Professor Isaacaroff, however, also notes the existence of anti-democratic groups using the electoral arena for propaganda purposes and to rally support,

1 Samuel Isaacaroff, *Fragile Democracies*, 120 Harv. L. Rev. 1405, 1406 (2007).

2 European Commission for Democracy through Law (Venice Commission), *Guidelines on Prohibition and Dissolution of Political Polities and Analogous Measures* (Council of Europe Dec. 10–11, 1999) at III.I.4.

3 *Id.*

and he notes that "[v]irtually all democratic countries respond by restricting the participation of groups or political parties deemed to be beyond the range of tolerable conduct or viewpoints."[4] The Venice Commission also recognized that most constitutions establish mechanisms to protect democracy; in numerous states there is the constitutional or statutory authority to ban political parties that threaten the existence of the state or its independence.[5]

There are a number of ways to restrict the participation of a political party. One is a ban on, or the dissolution of, a party. The affected political party would lose its ability to nominate candidates for election or to participate in government in any other way. While this would seem to be the most drastic measure, there are other measures that may be equally as effective. A party may be denied the ability to reach the voter through limits on, for example, the use of the broadcast media. While this may not be quite as effective in the Internet era, it has been used in the past to limit the ability of Sinn Féin to disseminate its views. Another approach is not to act directly against the political party but to prosecute the leadership of that party for their actions or expression. Eliminating the party's leadership may be as effective as banning a party in terms of limiting its ability to appeal to the populace.

What follows is not a complete catalog of actions taken against political parties. It is, rather, a sampling of the actions of a number of countries that have limited the participation of particular political groups. It is followed by a discussion of the circumstances under which such limits seem to be imposed.

GERMANY

The earliest case, in Germany's democratic era, involving a party ban is the 1952 *Socialist Reich Party Case*.[6] The case was decided under German law, in particular Article 21 of the German Basic Law. Article 21(1) provides all

[4] Isaacaroff, *supra* note 1, at 1406.

[5] Venice Commission, *supra* note 2, at III.III.11. In addition to the countries that will be discussed *infra*, the Commission notes that the Slovakian Constitution restricts freedom of association, when necessary, to protect national security, to prevent crime, to protect the rights of others, and in furtherance of separation of parties and the state. Portugal provides a detailed listing of limitations on political parties. Switzerland and Finland, among other countries, provide for the dissolution of all associations with unlawful or immoral aims. Further, the Czech Republic bans parties that try to prevent other parties from coming to power by constitutional means, and the French Constitution requires that parties respect democracy. See Venice Commission at Appendix I.

[6] BVerfGE 2, 1 (1952). There is a well translated version of the case in Donald P. Kommers, The Constitutional Jurisprudence of the Federal Republic of Germany 218 (1997). The German text is available at www.servat.unibe.ch/dfr/bv 002001.html.

political parties the freedom to organize and mobilize the electorate. The same article, however, provides limitations. Article 21(2) provides that parties that have the aim of abolishing or impairing the "free democratic basic order" or that endanger the existence of the Federal Republic of Germany are unconstitutional. Donald Kommers says that the provision

> was designed to repair a central failing of the Weimar Republic, namely, its tolerance of extremist parties bent on destroying democracy. Recalling the conditions that led to the Hitler state, the founders resolved that the Federal Republic could never be neutral in the face of its mortal enemies … and set out to create what … would become known as a "militant democracy."[7]

A militant democracy contrasts with the procedural view of democracy.[8] A proceduralist believes that if channels of communication are kept open and all sides of a political argument are presented to the people, democracy will be retained. The militant democrat sees a danger that open debate may lead away from democracy. Democracy, in a sense, needs to be protected from itself. Certain ideas, and those who further those ideas, may be barred from the political arena. Germany, in the era leading up to the *Socialist Reich Party Case* had good reason to distrust the proceduralist view. While the Nazi party may have come to power by taking advantage of democratic processes, it was, once in power, anything but democratic. In the early 1950s, there was a strongly perceived need to bar the reemergence of the Nazis.

It was relatively easy for the German Constitutional Court to conclude that the Socialist Reich Party (SRP) was little more than a reconstitution of the Nazi party. The Court noted that most of the party's leaders had been not only Nazis but members of organizations such as the SS and that they were seeking out other former Nazis. While the Court did not criticize enlisting former National Socialists, it said that the SRP was "collecting the particularly hard-core individuals who have 'remained true to themselves,' … not in order to gain positive forces for democracy, but to preserve and propagate National Socialist ideas."[9] It was not a party of former Nazis, but of those who chose to remain Nazis. Former Nazi leaders held positions of authority, the party's

7 KOMMERS, *supra* note 6, at 218.

8 *See* Judith Wise, *Dissent and the Militant Democracy: The German Constitution and the Banning of the Free German Workers Party*, 5 U. CHI. L. SCH. ROUNDTABLE 301 (1998). *See also* SABINE MICHALOWSKI & LORNA WOODS, GERMAN CONSTITUTIONAL LAW: THE PROTECTION OF CIVIL LIBERTIES 23 (1999) ("The concept of militant democracy … means that a democratic state must defend its fundamental democratic values against anti-democratic forces and prevent these powers from abusing the democratic order by abolishing it once they become the majority.").

9 KOMMERS, *supra* note 6, at 220.

organization was similar to that of the Nazis, party governance was dictatorial, and various groups of people, including those officers who had tried to assassinate Hitler, were excluded from membership.[10]

The Court was asked to rule on the constitutionality of the SRP, that is, whether the Basic Law allowed the party to exist.[11] The Court noted that Article 21 first establishes the freedom of formation of political parties. But the same article provides the Constitutional Court the authority to decide on the constitutionality of the party and to determine the factual basis for its conclusion. The Constitutional Court "is justified in eliminating them from the political scene if, but only if, they seek to topple supreme fundamental values of the free democratic order which are embodied the Basic Law."[12] Furthermore,

> a party may be eliminated from the political process only if it rejects the supreme principles of a free democracy. If a party's internal organization does not correspond to democratic principles, [one] may generally conclude that the party seeks to impose upon the state structural principles that it has implemented within its own organization.[13]

Given the leadership, organization, and the dictatorial manner in which it was governed, the Court was willing to conclude that the SRP "seeks to impose its own organizational structure on the nation as soon as it has come into power, just as the Nazi party did. [T]hus [the SRP] seeks to eliminate the free democratic basic order."[14] The Court concluded that the SRP was unconstitutional under Article 21(2) and was to be dissolved.

While there may have been good reason to be concerned over the possibility of the Nazis returning to power through the guise of the SRP, Germany also declared the Communist Party to be unconstitutional. Michalowski and Woods find the *Communist Party Case* to be particularly problematic, saying that it is difficult to see how such a small party could be a serious threat to

[10] *See id.* at 221.

[11] In addition to the Article 21(2) provision allowing the Federal Constitutional Court to declare a party to be unconstitutional, Article 9(2) provides that associations that violate the constitutional order can be prohibited. Because of the lesser significance of associations, the executive can order their prohibition, while the more important political parties are subject to limitation only by the Federal Constitutional Court. *See* Michalowski & Woods, *supra* note 8, at 18, 20.

[12] Kommers, *supra* note 6, at 220.

[13] *Id.* Kommers inserted the "[one]" in his translation.

[14] *Id.* at 221–22 (text changes originating in Kommers). Kommers also notes the Court's reliance on its conclusions that the party was committed to the mythical ideas of German racial superiority and an indestructible Reich, its contempt for the Federal Republic, its desire for a Fuhrer acceptance state, and its anti-Semitism.

the democratic order in Germany.[15] It is, of course, true that the Russians occupied a portion of the country and surrounded what had been its capital, and the 1950s were the Cold War. But the real communist threat to Germany seemed to come from without, rather than from within.

The German government brought its Article 21 action against the Communist Party in 1951, the same year in which it brought its action against the SRP, but the Constitutional Court did not issue its opinion in the *Communist Party Case*[16] until 1956. Professor Kommers says that the delay was the result of a feeling among some of the justices that the government's action was premature and that it would be better for the Communist Party simply to fade away than to be banned.[17] He notes that the Communists received only 2.3 percent of the vote in the national elections of 1953 and that, as the German economy improved, support by 1956 had "almost vanished."[18] Further, he says that it appears to be only when it became clear that the government would not withdraw the case that the Court realized that it would have to issue an opinion.[19]

When the opinion was issued, its length of 108 pages was "the longest by far of all the court's opinions."[20] Much of the opinion was an analysis of Marxism and Leninism, although the structure, leadership, and style of the party were also examined. The examination, at a theoretical level, found a direct danger; ideologically the Party was against the existing system. But there seems to have been a lack of any criminal action. That sort of illegal activity was, however, not required. As Kommers explains the opinion, "the court rejected the contention that illegal activity or some other 'concrete undertaking' to abolish the constitutional order is necessary to deprive a party of its constitutional status."[21]

The Court, however, attempted to keep advocacy, even advocacy of overthrow of the government, protected. Again, in Kommers' explanation of the Court's opinion,

> the mere advocacy of overthrow is an insufficient basis for banning a political party. What is important . . . is whether a party has "a fixed purpose constantly and resolutely to combat the free democratic basic order" and manifests this purpose "in political action according to a fixed plan." This purpose or plan . . . can be gleaned from a party's program, its official declarations, statements of its leaders, and its educational materials.[22]

[15] MICHALOWSKI & WOODS, *supra* note 8 at 19.

[16] BVerfGE 5, 85 (1956). Kommers includes a note on the case, rather than an edited translation. *See* KOMMERS, *supra* note 6, at 222–24.

[17] KOMMERS, *supra* note 6, at 222. [18] *Id.* [19] *Id.* at 222–23. [20] *Id.* at 223. [21] *Id.*

[22] *Id.* (citations omitted).

Examining those factors, the Court concluded that the Communist Party was unconstitutional under Article 21. It was dissolved, its properties were confiscated, and it lost all of its parliamentary seats.

These cases have been, as might be expected, criticized. For example, Professors Michalowski and Woods find it "questionable whether it is possible to secure democratic order by anti-democratic means ... [A] democracy should be strong enough to allow such political parties and associations and to lead an open debate regarding the values propagated by them."[23] Judith Wise criticizes the continuing ban, writing:

> The militant democracy is designed to correct for democracy's inability to ensure its own survival. Even if the militant democracy may have been necessary in the early years, when recent mass participation in the fascist state left no democratic political culture to defend, why should Germany's more mature democracy continue to need the democracy-compromising measures of the militant democracy?[24]

Professor Wise goes on to note the rise of a fascist right in modern Germany, showing that democracy in Germany may still need protection, but she questions the form that protection should take.[25] As for banning parties, "[a] democratic state runs the risk that it will protect itself out of existence, that through its state preservation efforts, it will remain a state but cease to be democratic."[26]

It does seem clear that the Germans did, in fact, have something to worry about in the early 1950s, at least with regard to the revival of Nazism. Given the country's experience in the 1930s and 40s, it is not surprising they took the steps they did, even if the action against the Communist Party seems less justified. While perhaps there should be some time limitation for that historical justification, Germany's concern with Nazism has continued for decades beyond the SRP decision.

A case from 1990, beyond being simply an interesting and even humorous read, shows the continuing concern, as well as the inability of at least a lower court to understand how far that concern might extend. The *Nazi Symbols Case*[27] involved a small business that printed and sold T-shirts. There were two T-shirts that led to legal difficulties. The first shirt showed the upper half of the body of Adolf Hitler in a uniform with an adaptation of the swastika armband

[23] Michalowski & Woods, *supra* note 8, at 23. [24] Wise, *supra* note 8, at 330.
[25] *Id.* at 333. [26] *Id.* at 334.
[27] BVerfGE 82, 1 (1990). The case may be found in translation at www.utexas.edu/law/transnational/foreign-law-translations/german/case.php?id=630.

(instead of an actual swastika, only the cross bars were shown) standing, sideways, before a map of Europe. It also showed the German campaigns of World War II. Above the picture of Hitler was his name in Gothic letters. To his left and right were the dates 1939 and 1945. Under the picture, also in Gothic, was the phrase "European Tour." Below that was a series of dates and countries, showing the year in which Germany had invaded those countries, with the entries for England and Russia bearing the notation "Canceled." Lastly, still further down was a copyright attribution to "Third Reich Promotions 1939." The overall sense was that of a T-shirt promoting a tour by a musical group, listing the places and dates of concerts.

The second T-shirt had a black-and-white picture of Hitler, again in uniform and armband with the altered swastika. In this picture Hitler had his right arm raised in a Nazi salute. Attached to the fingers of the right hand was a yo-yo with arcs indicating rotation. To the left of the area was Hitler's name, again in Gothic, and underneath the yo-yo was the legend "European Yo-Yo Champion 1939–1945." The production of the shirts really was a small business; sales for the first shirt totaled 153 and the second three.

Despite the fact that the shirts were, if anything, critical of Nazism, rather than supportive, the individuals involved were found guilty of using the symbols of an unconstitutional organization. The concern, perhaps valid in the 1950s, that the Nazis could again come to power, which justified a ban on the use of the symbols, was applied in a situation in which the symbols were used in mockery of the Nazis.

The court that found the defendants guilty rejected the use of the pictures as satire. That court said that the depictions had to be judged based on the reasonable passerby, who would not understand that the shirts were satire and the pictures meant to ridicule or disparage. The defendants' first appeal, to the Bavarian State Supreme Court was also unavailing.

When the case reached the Federal Constitutional Court, the Court found the convictions violated Article 5(3) of the Basic Law, the provision protecting art. The Constitutional Court said that the lower courts failed to appreciate the pictures' artistic content. "From several possible interpretations the Regional Court decided on one interpretation of the pictures – which is not even likely – which from the start removes them from the area of application of art. 5(3) . . ."[28] By focusing on the passerby, the hurried observer, the lower court did not recognize the ridicule contained in the pictures. "Contrary to

[28] BVerfGE 82, 1 at ¶ II.2.

the Regional Court's opinion both pictures are open to the interpretation that Hitler and his megalomania are intended to be ridiculed by using satire."[29]

This is also not the last time satirical use of Nazi symbols has come up in Germany. When the musical comedy *The Producers* was set to open in Berlin, there were concerns about Nazi uniforms and flags. The production was clearly satirical, with regard to Nazi-ism, but the use of symbols required giving some thought to their illegality. Eventually, some changes were made, with swastikas on banners outside the theater replaced by pretzels.[30]

This recent, continuing concern over Nazi symbols, long past any real danger of Nazis again coming to power and in situations in which they were not supportive of Nazi-ism may counsel in favor of limited duration for bans on symbols and parties. On the other hand, the recent concerns, as overblown as they may be, do not negate the real concerns that motivated at least the ban on the SRP.

IRELAND, THE UNITED KINGDOM, AND THE IRA

While the Nazi era that motivated the German party ban on the SRP is well over half a century old, concerns in Ireland are of more recent vintage. There has been a long history of violence, particularly in Northern Ireland, between the Irish Republican Army (IRA) and both Protestant and government forces. While centered in Northern Ireland, the strife has spilled over into the Irish Republic and into England. The IRA is outlawed, but there is a political party known as Sinn Féin that was associated with the IRA, and that party raised concerns in both the Republic of Ireland and the United Kingdom.

The approach taken with regard to Sinn Féin was not to outlaw or dissolve the party but to limit its ability directly to reach the people. This effort largely involved restricting access to the broadcast media.[31] *The State (Lynch) v. Cooney*[32] grew out of the Irish general elections of 1982. Radio Telefis Eireann (RTE) made it a practice to provide parties broadcast time on its television and radio outlets. Sinn Féin ran just enough candidates to qualify as a small

[29] *Id.*

[30] *See* Kate Connolly, *Springtime for Hitler in Germany as Berlin Stages The Producers*, The Guardian (Apr. 27, 2009), www.theguardian.com/world/2009/apr/27/berlin-stages-producers-mel-brooks.

[31] The United Kingdom has also placed limits, reaching some members of Sinn Féin, on entering the country. For a discussion of that approach, see Clive Walker, *Constitutional Governments and Special Powers against Terrorism: Lessons from the United Kingdom's Prevention of Terrorism Acts*, 35 Colum. J. Transnat'l L. 1 (1997).

[32] [1982] IR 337 at 357.

political party and was allocated one two-minute broadcast on each of RTE's five outlets.

Sinn Féin was not, however, able to avail itself of these broadcast opportunities. Rather, the Minister for Posts and Telegraphs issued an order providing:

> Radio Telefis Eireann is hereby directed to refrain from broadcasting any matter which is - (a) a broadcast, whether purporting to be a political party broadcast or not, made by, or on behalf of, or advocating, offering or inviting support for, the organization styling itself Provisional Sinn Féin, (b) a broadcast by any person or persons representing, or purporting to represent, the said organization.[33]

It was that order that was challenged, but to no avail. Examining the legislation that allowed the Minister to issue the order, the Supreme Court of Ireland said:

> The legislation deals with, amongst other things, the control of freedom of expression and free speech within the powers granted by ... Article 40 of the Constitution. This provision enables the State, in certain instances, to control these rights and freedoms. The basis for any attempt to control must be, according to the Constitution, the overriding considerations of public order and public morality. The constitutional provision in question refers to organs of public opinion and these must be held to include television as well as radio. It places upon the State the obligation to ensure that these organs of public opinion shall not be used to undermine public order or public morality or the authority of the State. It follows that the use of such organs of opinion for the purpose of securing or advocating support for organisations which seek by violence to overthrow the State or its institutions is a use which is prohibited by the Constitution. Therefore, it is clearly the duty of the state to intervene to prevent broadcasts on radio or television which are aimed at such a result or which in any way would be likely to have the effect of promoting or inciting to crime or endangering the authority of the State.[34]

The Court also rejected, as irrelevant, the contention by Sinn Féin that the broadcast should have been allowed because it would not have contained any objectionable material and that it could have been examined before being transmitted. That did not matter, since it would still have been intended to increase support for Sinn Féin, an organization whose aims included undermining state authority. In a statement seemingly reminiscent of militant

[33] *Id.* at 5.

[34] *Id.* at 6. The constitutional provision at issue, Article 40, Section 6, subsection 1 provides that "organs of public opinion shall not be used to undermine public order or morality or the authority of the State."

democracy, the Chief Justice added "A democratic State has a clear and bounden duty to protect its citizens and its institutions from those who seek to replace law and order by force and anarchy, and the democratic process by the dictates of the few."[35]

A second case from Ireland, involving a similar order, reached the European Commission of Human Rights in 1991, as *Purcell v. Ireland*.[36] The order, issued to RTE, prohibited interviews or reports of interviews with spokespersons for a variety of organizations, including the IRA, Sinn Féin, and the Ulster Defence Association. Guidelines provided that any news or current affair programming covering meetings or press conferences with such persons use only mute film or still photographs, with any statements read by newsreaders. This time the order was challenged not by members of Sinn Féin, who would not be allowed to appear, but by a group of journalists and producers of radio and television programs. The applicants alleged, among other things, a violation of their free expression rights under Article 10 of the European Convention.

The European Commission recognized an interference with expression rights and focused on the issue of whether the interference could be justified under Article 10(2). The Commission had no difficulty determining that the infringement was prescribed by law and not too vague to be so considered. In examining the aim of the order, the Commission recognized the terrorist threat to Ireland and the involvement of organizations such as Sinn Féin. It saw the order as aimed at prohibiting the use of broadcast media to advocate support for using violence to undermine the constitutional order. The order did not make Sinn Féin an unlawful organization, although the Commission indicated that Ireland could have chosen to do so. The Commission also noted that there was no ban on reporting about Sinn Féin and its activities. It saw the aims behind the order as being legitimate.

As to necessity in a democratic society, the Commission found the issuance of the order to be justified within the margin of appreciation given to member states. The defeat of terrorism was seen as a public interest of the highest importance, and the denial to spokespersons of organizations that support terrorism of the opportunity to use the media to advocate such acts, especially where the broadcast might be seen as an indication of legitimacy of the organization, was justified. The Commission's decision was seemingly made easier by what it saw as the limited scope of the restrictions that still allowed coverage of Sinn Féin, limiting only direct appearances.

35 Id. at 9.

36 Application No. 15404/89, http://hudoc.echr.coe.int/eng#%22itemid%22:[22-[%22001-893%22]}.

The United Kingdom took a similar approach with regard to Sinn Féin, among others, and the broadcast media. A 1988 order by the Home Secretary provided:

1. I hereby require the Independent Broadcasting Authority [IBA][and the British Broadcasting Corporation (BBC)] to refrain from broadcasting any matter which consists of or includes:

   any words spoken, whether in the course of an interview or discussion or otherwise, by a person who appears or is heard on the programme in which the matter is broadcast where

   (a) the person speaking the words represents or purports to represent [Sinn Fein, Republican Sinn Fein or the Ulster Defence Association], or

   (b) the words support or solicit or invite support for such an organisation, other than any matters specified in paragraph 3 below …

3. The matter excluded from paragraph 1 above is any words spoken

   (a) in the course of proceedings in Parliament, or

   (b) by or in support of candidate at a parliamentary, European Parliamentary or local election pending the election.[37]

The Home Office later provided elaboration of the order. The elaboration provided that the order

> applies only to direct statements and not to reported speech, and that the person caught by the notice is the one whose words are reported and not the report or presenter who reports them. Thus the notice permits the showing of a film or still picture of the initiator speaking the words together with a voice-over account of them, whether in paraphrase or verbatim … [P]rogrammes involving the reconstruction of actual events, where actors use the verbatim words which had been spoken in actuality, are similarly permitted.[38]

Thus, the restriction was not so much on news coverage as on the actual appearance on the broadcast media of the persons covered, and even there certain appearances would be allowed.

[37] The Home Secretary's order may be found in Graham Zellick, *Spies, Subversives, Terrorists and the British Government: Free Speech and Other Casualties*, 31 WM. & MARY L. REV. 773, 775–76 (1990).

[38] The explanation is included in Regina v. Secretary of State for the Home Department, Ex parte Brind, [1991] 1 A.C. 696, 712. It was further explained that individuals, who are covered by the order in some situations, might not be covered in others. A member of Provisional Sinn Féin, when speaking for the party, would not be allowed to appear, but as a private individual in a completely different context, appearance might be allowed. *Id.*

The order was challenged, not by Sinn Féin or even the IBA or by the BBC, but again by a group of journalists. The case eventually reached the House of Lords as *Regina v. Secretary of State for the Home Department, Ex parte Brind.*[39] The journalists claimed that the order was unreasonable, and thus was not allowed under the administrative law of the United Kingdom, and that it violated their rights under Article 10 of the European Convention on Human Rights.

The Lords refused to find the order unreasonable. The Secretary of State had explained his rationale.

> Such appearances have caused widespread offence to viewers and listeners throughout the United Kingdom, particularly just after a terrorist outrage. The terrorists themselves draw support and sustenance from access to radio and television – from addressing their views more directly to the population at large than is possible through the press. The government have decided that the time has come to deny this easy platform to those who use it to propagate terrorism.[40]

Avoiding the legitimation of terrorism and the increase in terror, more than just offense, that the appearances could cause justified the reasonableness of the action.

As for the argument that the order violated Article 10 of the European Convention, the Lords noted that the European Convention is not a part of the law of the United Kingdom. Where there is an ambiguity in an order or statute, the assumption that the government recognized its obligations under the Convention might allow the courts to use a provision of the Convention in construing ambiguous language. Here, however, the Lords found no ambiguity in the order of the Secretary. The Lords said that any argument with regard to violation of Article 10 would have to be taken up with the European Commission of Human Rights.

The group of journalists followed up on that invitation, leading to the decision by the Commission in *Brind v. United Kingdom.*[41] The journalists fared no better before the Commission. The order was an interference with the expression right found in Article 10(1), so the question became whether it was justified under Article 10(2); whether the limitation was "prescribed by law," whether the aim behind the order was legitimate under the article, and whether it was "necessary in a democratic society" to the achievement of that aim.

39 [1991] 1 A.C. 696.

40 The statement was drawn from an address to both Houses of Parliament and is included in the opinion of Lord Donaldson of Lymington M.R., *id.* at 713.

41 Application No 18714/91, (1994) 18 E.H.R.R. CD 76.

The Commission saw the situation to be similar to that which it had handled in *Purcell*. The requirement that the limitation be proscribed by law was not perhaps as clearly met as in *Purcell*, but the Commission noted that the action taken under the authority to promulgate notices was sufficient. With regard to legitimate aims, the commission said

> the restrictions in the present refer in terms to prescribed organisations and to named organisations which, although not prohibited, are known to have connections with unlawful organisations ... [T]here is no indication in the present case that the directions were anything other than part of the measures taken to combat terrorism which were made in good faith. The Commission accepts that the aim of the restrictions is legitimate.[42]

With regard to necessity, the Commission said that what was required was a "pressing social need," and that the states have a margin of appreciation, under European supervision, as to whether a need exists. In keeping with its holding in *Purcell*, the Commission said:

> [I]n the circumstances of the present case and bearing in mind the margin of appreciation permitted to States, the limited extent of the interference with the ... applicant's rights and the importance of measures to combat terrorism, ... it cannot be said that the interference with the ... appellant's freedom of expression was disproportionate to the aim sought to be pursued.[43]

SPAIN AND THE ETA

Spain has had its own difficulties with a terrorist organization. The Eusadj Ta Askatasuna (ETA), a force fighting for an independent country for the Basque people carved out of portions of Spain and France, has long engaged in terroristic activities and is, in Spain, an outlawed organization.[44] The ETA has also been associated with political parties. In 1976, it developed its first political party, and over the following three years it produced some 82 other organizations.[45] The political groups largely coalesced into a group called Herri Batasuna.[46] That organization effectively dissolved, after the imprisonment of much of its leadership, and shortly thereafter, in 1998, it was replaced by Euskal Herritarrok, which carried on its ideological and political

[42] *Id.* [43] *Id.*

[44] For a brief history of the violence associated with the ETA, see Katherine A. Sawyer, *Rejection of Weimarian Politics or Betrayal of Democracy?: Spain's Proscription of Batasuna under the European Convention on Human Rights*, 52 AM. U. L. REV. 1531, 1536–42 (2003).

[45] *See id.* at 1538. [46] *Id.*

program.[47] That party also dissolved, not through arrests but as a result of very weak results in the 2001 elections, perhaps in response to then recent violence.[48] After the electoral defeat, it was replaced by Batasuna, a political party "inheriting a political history defined by its inextricable links to E.T.A. and the imprimatur of complicity that such a history confers."[49]

It was the Spanish government's ban on Batasuna that eventually reached the ECtHR, in 2009, as the case *Batauna v. Spain*.[50] Article 6 of the Spanish Constitution protects political parties, but with limits. The article provides:

> Political parties are the expression of political pluralism; they contribute to the formation and expression of the will of the people and are an essential instrument for political participation. Their creation and the exercise of their activities are free in so far as they respect the Constitution and the law. Their internal structure and their functioning must be democratic.[51]

Spain had also enacted, in 2002, its Law on Political Parties. Section 9 of that law provided:

1. Political parties may freely engage in their activities. In engaging in those activities, they shall respect the constitutional values expressed in democratic principles and human rights. They shall perform the functions attributed to them under the Constitution democratically and in full respect for pluralism.
2. A political party shall be declared illegal when, as a result of its activities, it infringes democratic principles, in particular when it seeks thereby to impair or to destroy the system of liberties, to hinder or to put an end to the democratic system, by repeatedly and seriously engaging in any of the conduct described below:
   (a) systematically violating fundamental freedoms and rights by promoting, justifying or excusing attacks on the life or integrity of the person, or the exclusion or persecution of an individual by reason of ideology, religion, beliefs, nationality, race, sex or sexual orientation;
   (b) fomenting, encouraging or legitimising violence to be used as a means to achieve political ends or as a means to undermine the conditions that make the exercise of democracy, pluralism and political freedoms possible;

[47] *See id.* at 1540. [48] *See id.* at 1541. [49] *Id.* at 1541.

[50] Application nos. 25803/04 and 25817/04 (2009), hudoc.echrcoe.int/eng?i=001–93475#{%22itemid%22:[%22001–93475%22]}.

[51] Institutional Law no. 6/2002 of Jun. 27, 2002 on political parties. The provision is provided in translation at *id.* at ¶50. Additionally, Article 22 protects the freedom of association. *See id.*

(c) providing assistance and political support to the actions of terrorist organisations with the aim of overthrowing the constitutional order or seriously disturbing the public peace, subjecting the public authorities, certain persons or certain groups in society or the population in general to a climate of terror, or contributing to increasing the effects of terrorist violence and the resulting fear and intimidation.

3. The conditions described in the preceding paragraph shall be deemed to have been met where there has been a repetition or an accumulation, by the political party, of one or more of the following instances of behaviour:

(a) giving express or tacit political support to terrorism by legitimising the use of terrorist actions for political ends outside peaceful and democratic channels, or by excusing them or minimising their significance and the ensuing violation of human rights; accompanying violent action with programmes and activities promoting a culture of civil conflict and confrontation associated with the actions of terrorists or those who resort to intimidation; pressuring, neutralising or socially isolating anyone opposing that violent action, by forcing them to live with a daily threat of coercion, fear, exclusion or deprivation of freedom and depriving them in particular of their freedom to express their opinions and to participate freely and democratically in public affairs . . .[52]

The law goes on to provide that alleged violations of Section 9 shall be decided by a special chamber of the Supreme Court, with appeal to the Constitutional Court.[53]

Action was brought against Batasuna and its predecessor parties in the Supreme Court, and the Court unanimously declared the parties illegal, concluding that they were part of a terrorist strategy, and ordered their dissolution.[54] Interestingly, the Court took some time to explain that the Spanish constitutional system was not that of a "militant democracy." Under Spanish law any project or objective is constitutional; it is only the means of reaching those objectives that may lead to dissolution, and even then only through serious and repeated conduct.[55] Appeals were taken to the Constitutional Court, but they were unanimously dismissed by that Court.[56]

The case before the ECtHR alleged violation of Article 11 of the European Convention on Human Rights. That article provides guarantees of freedom of

[52] *Id.* [53] *See id.* (translating §§ 10 and 11 of the Law on Political Parties).
[54] *See id.* at ¶30. [55] *See id.* at ¶31. [56] *See id.* at ¶34.

assembly and association, but with limitations. Under Article 11(2), restrictions are allowed, if they

> are prescribed by law and are necessary in a democratic society in the interests of national security or public safety, for the prevention of disorder or crime, for the protection of health or morals or for the protection of the rights and freedoms of others.

Since there was clearly a restriction, the issue for the European Court was whether the restriction could be justified under Article 11(2).

The first element for the exception, whether the limitation was prescribed by law, would seem easily met, but Batasuna raised an objection with regard to retroactivity. Some of the evidence against it included acts prior to the date of enactment of the law, but the use of that evidence seems to have been for showing a "trajectory" against which actions after the enactment of the law could be analyzed. Further, the European Court noted that the European Convention's ban on retroactive application applied only to criminal proceedings and that this dissolution was not a criminal proceeding.[57]

Turning to the aim behind the law, the Court rejected the claim by Batasuna that the government was attempting to eliminate any debate by left-wing advocates of Basque independence. The Court noted the existence of other "separatist" parties that peacefully coexist with government in Spain's other autonomous communities. The Court found no reason to reject the government's claim that it was motivated by the ties of the party to terrorism.[58]

With regard to necessity in a democratic society and the proportionality of the measure to the evil the government sought to avoid, the Court said that it takes convincing and compelling reasons to justify such a drastic measure as the dissolution of a political party.[59] Political aims and party programs are not enough, but

> a State cannot be required to wait, before intervening, until a political party had seized power and begun to take concrete steps to implement a policy incompatible with the standards of the Convention and democracy, even though the danger of that policy for democracy is sufficiently established and imminent.[60]
>
> Turning to the facts presented by the Spanish government, the Court said:
>
> The Court agrees with the grounds on which the Constitutional Court ruled that the refusal to condemn violence against a backdrop of terrorism that had been in place for more than thirty years and condemned by all the other political parties amounted to tacit support for terrorism ... [T]his

57 *See id* at. ¶59. 58 *See id.* at ¶63. 59 *See id.* at ¶¶77 & 78. 60 *Id.* at ¶81.

> factor was not the sole basis for the impugned measure ... [T]he Constitutional Court found that it was part of a series of serious and repeated acts and conduct, making it possible to conclude that there had been an accommodation with terror going against organised coexistence in the framework of a democratic State.[61]

The Court concluded that the Spanish courts had arrived at a reasonable conclusion in finding that "the actions and speeches imputable to the applicant political parties, taken together, give a clear picture of a model of society conceived and advocated by them, which is incompatible with the concept of a 'democratic society' ..."[62] Furthermore, the sanction of dissolution was proportionate, given that the parties' plans were incompatible with democracy.[63]

That was not the end of the Spanish courts' cases involving political parties thought to be involved in terrorism. A number of cases have involved parties said to be successors to Batasuna, sometimes tens of parties in the same election, leading to difficulties in the development of evidence and in the speedy resolution of disputes over political participation.[64]

THE EUROPEAN UNION

There is additional case law from the European Union (EU) regarding the dissolution of political parties and commission reports on the same topic. Recent efforts have focused primarily on Turkey. Turkey is not one of *The Economist*'s fully functioning democracies. Neither is the EU itself a democracy, even if it is composed primarily of fully functioning democracies. (Nor is Turkey a member state of the EU, but because of its interest in such membership, its cases may go before EU bodies.) Nonetheless, the resolution of the cases from Turkey contributes to the analysis of party bans under the democratic values of the EU.

A good place to begin the examination of the position of the EU is with the *Guidelines on Prohibition and Dissolution of Political Parties and Analogous Measures* developed by the European Commission for Democracy through

[61] *Id.* at ¶88. [62] *Id.* at ¶91.

[63] *See id.* at ¶93. The appellants had also raised claims under Article 10, the free expression provision, of the European Convention, but the Court determined that the analysis for that claim would be the same as the analysis given to the Article 11 complaint.

[64] *See, e.g.*, S.T.C. 138/2012, Jun. 20, 2012 (Spain); S.T.C 62/2011, May 5, 2011 (Spain); S.T.C. 44/2009, Feb. 12, 2009 (Spain); S.T.C. 110/2007, May 10, 2007 (Spain); S.T.C. 68/2005, Mar. 31, 2005 (Spain); S.T.C 99/2004, May 27, 2004 (Spain); S.T.C. 85/2003, May 8, 2003 (Spain); A.T.C. 398/2008, Dec. 22, 2008 (Spain); A.T.C. 278/2003, Jul. 25, 2003 (Spain).

Law (Venice Commission) and adopted by the Commission in 1999.[65] The Venice Commission issued the following guidelines:

1. States should recognize that everyone has the right to associate freely in political parties. This right shall include freedom to hold political opinions and to receive and impart information without interference by a public authority and regardless of frontiers. The requirement to register political parties will not in itself be considered to be in violation of this right.
2. Any limitations to the exercise of the above-mentioned fundamental human rights through the activity of political parties shall be consistent with the relevant provisions of the European Convention for the Protection of Human Rights and other international treaties, in normal times as well as in cases of public emergencies.
3. Prohibition or enforced dissolution of political parties may only be justified in the case of parties which advocate the use of violence or use violence as a political means to overthrow the democratic constitutional order, thereby undermining the rights and freedoms guaranteed by the Constitution. The fact alone that a party advocates a peaceful change of the Constitution should not be sufficient for its prohibition or dissolution.
4. A political party as a whole can not be held responsible for the individual behaviour of its members not authorised by the party within the framework of political/public and party activities.
5. The prohibition or dissolution of political parties as a particularly far-reaching measure should be used with utmost restraint. Before asking the competent judicial body to prohibit or dissolve a party, governments or other state organs should assess, having regard to the situation of the country concerned, whether the party really represents a danger to the free and democratic political order or to the rights of individuals and whether other, less radical measures could prevent the same danger.
6. Legal measures directed to the prohibition or legally enforced dissolution of political parties shall be a consequence of a judicial finding of unconstitutionality and shall be deemed as of an exceptional nature and governed by the principle of proportionality. Any such measure must be based on sufficient evidence that the party itself and not only individual members pursue political objectives using or preparing to use unconstitutional means.

[65] Venice Commission, *supra* note 2.

7. The prohibition or dissolution of a political party should be decided by the Constitutional court or other appropriate judicial body in a procedure offering all guarantees of due process, openness and a fair trial.[66]

Turkey is of particular interest, because it has tested the limits of the EU's willingness to tolerate the dissolution of political parties. Between 1968 and 2009 the Constitutional Court of Turkey banned twenty-five political parties, with half the cases being in or after the 1990s.[67] Eleven of the cases resulted in applications being filed with the ECtHR, with the government's position being upheld only in the first of the cases discussed below.[68] And, the string of cases, and the government's losing streak, did not end in 2009, as shown by the second of the cases to be discussed below.

The case in which the government was successful was *Refah Partisi (The Welfare Party) v. Turkey*.[69] The case involved a growing party, which had received 10% of the vote in 1989, 16.8% in 1991, 22% in 1995, and 35% in 1996; its growth was predicted to continue, with a projection of 38% in 1997 and possibly 67% four years later.[70] Party leaders advocated wearing Islamic head scarves in public schools and buildings, the abolition of secularism in favor of a theocratic system, and a justice system in which adherents of each religion would be bound by the rules of that religion rather than by Turkish law.[71]

The government, in its application to the Constitutional Court

> contended that Refah, by describing itself as an army engaged in jihad and by openly declaring its intention to replace the Republic's statute law by sharia, has demonstrated that its objectives were incompatible with the requirements of a democratic society. Refah's aim to establish a plurality of legal systems (in which each group would be governed by a legal system in conformity with its members' religious beliefs) constituted the first stage in the process designed to substitute a theocratic regime for the Turkish Republic.[72]

The Court dissolved the party because of its anti-secular activities.

The case then went to the ECtHR, with the party alleging a violation Article 11 of the European Convention. Since the dissolution was clearly an interference, the issue was whether or not it had been prescribed by law, was

66 *Id.* at 4–5.

67 Olgun Akbulut, *Criteria Developed by the European Court of Human Rights on the Dissolution of Political Parties*, 34 Fordham Int'l L.J. 46, 71 (2010). The article also provides a study of a number of other European cases involving the dissolution of political parties, including the European Commission on Human Rights denial of the German Communist Party's appeal of its dissolution through 2009.

68 *Id.*

69 App. Nos. 41340/98, 41342/98, 41343/98 and 41344/98, 37 Eur. H.R. Rep. 1 (2003).

70 *See id.* at ¶11.

71 *See id.* at ¶12.

72 *Id.* at ¶19.

in pursuance of one of the legitimate aims set out in Article 11, and whether it was necessary in a democratic society. The issue of whether this dissolution was prescribed by law rested on whether or not the actions were a foreseeable result of the party's leaders and members engaging in anti-secular activities, and the Court had no difficulty in so holding.[73]

Turning to the legitimacy of the government's aims, the European Court, recognizing the importance of secularism in Turkey's democratic system, concluded that the party's dissolution was in pursuit of several legitimate aims under Article 11, "protection of national security and public safety, prevention of disorder or crime and the protection of rights and freedoms of others."[74]

The Court devoted most of its discussion to necessity in a democratic society. In particular, it discussed religion in democratic societies.

> [I]n democratic societies, in which several religions coexist within one and the same population, it may be necessary to place restrictions on this freedom in order to reconcile interests of the various groups and ensure that everyone's beliefs are respected . . . The Court has frequently emphasized the State's role as the neutral and impartial organiser of the exercise of various religions, faiths and beliefs, and stated that this role is conducive to public order, religious harmony and tolerance in a democratic society. It also considers that the State's duty of neutrality and impartiality is incompatible with any power on the State's part to access the legitimacy of religious beliefs . . . and that it requires the State to ensure mutual tolerance between opposing groups . . .[75]

This led the Court to recognize that, in a country like Turkey, steps may need to be taken to ensure that religious belief is not imposed.

The Court, understanding the history of Turkey and the rising power of the party involved, to the point of eventually commanding a majority, said that

> at the time of its dissolution Refah had the real potential to seize political power without being restricted by the compromises inherent in a coalition. If Refah had proposed a programme contrary to democratic principles, its monopoly of political power would have enabled it to establish the model of society envisaged in that programme.[76]

Intervention, before the party gained a majority, was within the margin of appreciation allowed under the Convention.[77]

The Court said that a plurality of legal systems would discriminate among individuals.[78] It also took a strong stand on sharia, saying that it was incompatible with democracy, particularly with regard to its criminal law and

[73] *See id.* at ¶63. [74] *Id.* at ¶67. [75] *Id.* at ¶91. [76] *Id.* at ¶108. [77] *See id.* at ¶110.
[78] *See id.* at ¶119.

procedure, its views on the legal status of women, and its intervention in the private sphere.[79] A political party whose aims include the introduction of sharia is not in compliance with the democratic ideals of the Convention.[80] Of further concern was the use of the term "jihad" and its implication that force would be used to impose sharia.[81]

Summing up the evidence, the Court said:

> the Court finds that the acts and speeches of Refah's members and leaders . . . revealed Refah's long-term policy of setting up a regime based on sharia within the framework of a plurality of legal systems and that Refah did not exclude recourse to force in order to implement its policy and keep the system it envisioned in place. In view of the fact that these plans were incompatible with the concept of a "democratic society" and that the real opportunities Refah had to put them into practice made the danger to democracy more tangible and more immediate, the penalty imposed on the applicants by the Constitutional Court, even in the context of the restricted margin of appreciation left to Contracting States, may reasonably be considered to have met a "pressing social need."[82]

Furthermore, the interference was seen as being proportionate to the aims pursued.[83]

The relatively recent unsuccessful case was *HADEP v. Turkey*.[84] That case grew out of the dissolution of a political party said to be aligned with the PKK, an organization, designated as terrorist, fighting for a separate homeland for the Kurdish people. Along with secularity, the unity of the state is a central principle in Turkey. Thus, the party was working in violation of such a core value.

Prior to the case coming to the European Court, the Venice Commission had been asked to examine Turkish practice on the dissolution of parties. In a 2009 report, the Commission said:

> The Venice Commission concludes that, when compared to the common European practice, the situation in Turkey differs in three important respects:
>
> 1. There is a long list of substantive criteria applicable to the constitutionality of political parties . . . which go beyond the criteria recognized as legitimate by the ECtHR and the Venice Commission.
> 2. There is a procedure for initiating decisions on party prohibition or dissolution which makes this initiative more arbitrary and less subject to democratic control, than in other European countries.

[79] *See id.* at ¶123. [80] *Id.* at [81] *See id.* at ¶130. [82] *Id.* at ¶132. [83] *See id.* at ¶134.
[84] (2013) 56 E.H.R.R. 5.

3. There is a tradition for regularly applying the rules on party closure to an extent that has no parallel in any other European country, and which demonstrates that this is not in effect regarded as an extraordinary measure, but as a structural and operative part of the constitution.[85]

Given the pronouncement of the Commission, it is not surprising that the Court found the dissolution to be in violation of Article 11 of the Convention.

Despite the core constitutional value of national unity, the party's advocacy for Kurdish independence was not a ground for dissolution.

> [A] political party may campaign for a change in the law or the legal and constitutional structures of the state on two conditions: first, the means used to that end must in every respect be legal and democratic; and secondly, the change proposed must itself be compatible with fundamental democratic principles. It necessarily follows that a political party whose leaders incite to violence or put forward a policy which does not comply with one or more of the rules of democracy or which is aimed at the destruction of democracy and the flouting of the rights and freedoms recognised in a democracy cannot lay claim to the Convention's protection against the penalties imposed on those grounds.[86]

While the party's position may have been contrary to core values of the Turkish Constitution, it was not contrary to the core values of democracy to campaign, nonviolently, for a change in those constitutional values or a constitutional provision.

> [E]ven assuming that . . . HADEP advocated the right to self-determination, that would not in itself be contrary to the fundamental principles of democracy. If merely by advocating such ideals a political group were held to be supporting acts of terrorism, that would imperil the possibility of dealing with related issues in the context of democratic debate and would allow armed movements to monopolise support for the principles in question.[87]

The Court did not disavow its position in *Batasuna* but failed to find an association of HADEP to terrorist activities.

THE UNITED STATES

One might assume that a country such as the United States, with this reputation as practically absolutist on free expression, would never have experienced similar prohibitions or restrictions on political parties, but history would show

[85] *See id.* at ¶28 (quoting Venice Commission, Opinion on the Constitutional and Legal Provisions Relevant to the Prohibition of Political Parties in Turkey (2009)).

[86] *Id.* at ¶61. [87] *Id.* at ¶79.

that to be incorrect. The approach, however, was not that of the direct dissolution of a political party but was, instead, criminal actions against individuals. Certainly, criminal actions brought against those who violate the law through violence or other criminal acts may be justified, but the government's approach went further. During the early 1900s, there was strong concern over socialism that led to a number of criminal convictions based on the advocacy of what would now be seen as political positions.

The most important of the criminal cases, from the point of view of impact on a political party, was *Debs v. United States*.[88] Eugene Debs was a leader of the Socialist Party in the United States and the party's candidate for president. He was charged with a violation of the Espionage Act[89] for inciting insubordination, disloyalty, mutiny, or refusal of duty in the military. While, under some circumstances, such a charge might be reasonable, the basis here seems unacceptable.

The conviction was based on an address delivered to a state Socialist Party convention in Ohio. The United States Supreme Court described the speech:

> The main theme of the speech was Socialism, its growth, and a prophecy of its ultimate success. With that we have nothing to do, but if a part or the manifest intent of the more general utterances was to encourage those present to obstruct the recruiting service and if in passages such encouragement was directly given, the immunity of the general theme may not be enough to protect the speech. The speaker began by saying that he had just returned from a visit to the workhouse in the neighborhood where three of their most loyal comrades were paying the penalty for their devotion to the working class [individuals] convicted of aiding and abetting another in failing to register for the draft. He said that he had to be prudent and might not be able to say all that he thought, thus intimating to his hearers that they might infer that he meant more, but he did say that those persons were paying the penalty for standing erect and for seeking to pave the way to better conditions for all mankind. Later he added further eulogies and said that he was proud of them. He then expressed opposition to Prussian militarism in a way that naturally might have been thought to be intended to include the mode of proceeding in the United States.[90]

He went on to say that

> the master class has always declared the war and the subject classes has always fought the battles – that the subject class has had nothing to gain and all to lose, including their lives; that the working class, who furnished the corpses,

[88] 249 U.S. 211 (1919). [89] 40 Stat. 219, as amended by 40 Stat. 553. [90] 249 U.S. at 212–13.

> have never yet had a voice in declaring war and never yet had a voice in declaring peace.[91]

Debs was found guilty and was sentenced to ten years in prison, and his conviction was affirmed by the Supreme Court in an opinion written by Justice Holmes. While it is true that the Venice Commission's reports were based on party dissolution, rather than the criminal conviction of party leaders, the principles espoused there would seem to preclude this sort of action, were it to occur in Europe today. Indeed, it seems extremely unlikely, given the evolution of law in the United States, that a similar conviction could now be obtained.

While there are any number of other cases from the time of *Debs* through the 1950s, there are two important Supreme Court cases involving actions that were taken against leaders and members of the Communist Party in the United States. The first is *Dennis v. United States*,[92] decided in 1951. The defendants in *Dennis* were charged with

> willfully and knowingly conspiring (1) to organize as the Communist Party of the United States of America a society, group and assembly of persons who teach and advocate the overthrow and destruction of the Government of the United States by force and violence, and (2) knowingly and willfully to advocate and teach the duty and necessity of overthrowing and destroying the Government of the United States by force and violence,[93]

in violation of the Smith Act.[94]

There was no actual attempt to overthrow the government, but the defendants were leaders of a party adhering to the Marxist–Leninist doctrine that the ruling class would never allow transformation to communist government other than through violence. The conviction did require intent to overthrow, but that intent seems to have been found in Marxist–Leninist philosophy. The Court did say that "Congress did not intend to eradicate the free discussion of political theories, to destroy the traditional rights of Americans to discuss and evaluate ideas without fear of government sanction."[95] But, it appears that the advocacy of these political theories could lead to criminal charges. With regard to the lack of any actual attempt, the Court said that the law does not require that

> before the Government may act, it must wait until the putsch is about to be executed, the plans have been laid and the signal is awaited. If Government is

[91] *Id.* at 213–14. [92] 341 U.S. 494 (1951). [93] *Id.* at 497. [94] 18 U.S.C. §11 (1946).
[95] 341 U.S. at 502.

> aware that a group aiming at its overthrow is attempting to indoctrinate its members and to commit them to a course whereby they will strike when the leaders feel the circumstances permit, action by the Government is required.[96]

The likelihood of communist success in the United States seems no more real than it was in Germany at the time that it banned the Communist Party. Nonetheless, the concern during this part of the Cold War was real. As the Court explained the fear,

> the Communist Party is a highly disciplined organization, adept at infiltration into strategic positions, use of aliases, and double-meaning language; ... the Party is rigidly controlled, ... Communists, unlike other political parties, tolerate no dissension from the policy laid down by the guiding forces ...[97]

Six years later another group of Communists was back before the Supreme Court. *Yates v. United States*[98] involved the same sort of indictment; the defendants were charged with conspiracy "to advocate and teach the duty and necessity of overthrowing the Government of the United States by force and violence," and organizing the Communist Party of the United States, a group that so advocated and taught, with the intent to achieve that goal.[99] In terms of action to carry out the conspiracy, it was charged that

> defendants and their co-conspirators would (a) become members and officers of the Communist Party, with knowledge of its unlawful purposes, and assume leadership in carrying out its policies and activities; (b) cause to be organized units of the Party in California and elsewhere; (c) write and publish, in the "Daily Worker" and other Party organs, articles on the proscribed advocacy and teaching; (d) conduct schools for the indoctrination of Party members in such advocacy and teaching, and (e) recruit new Party members, particularly from among persons employed in key industries of the nation.[100]

In all, fourteen defendants were convicted and sentenced to five years, imprisonment.

This time, the Supreme Court reversed the convictions, with acquittals ordered for some and retrials for others. The Court thought that the lower court had misunderstood the word "organize" in the Smith Act to allow the conviction of individuals who had merely joined the Communist Body,

[96] *Id.* at 509. [97] *Id.* at 498. [98] 354 U.S. 298 (1957). [99] *Id.* at 300.
[100] *Id.* at 301–2.

that the trial court had excluded the issue of whether there was incitement, and that the evidence was insufficient. As the Court phrased the major question:

> We are … faced with the question of whether the Smith Act prohibits advocacy and teaching of forcible overthrow as an abstract principle, divorced from any effort to instigate action to that end, so long as such advocacy or teaching is engaged in with the evil intent. We hold that it does not.[101]

Given the Court's discussion in *Dennis*, the government and the lower courts were quite reasonably "led astray." According to the Supreme Court, "both of the lower courts here misconceived *Dennis*."[102] That raises the question of whether the lower courts were, in fact, "led astray" or whether the Court simply changed its position. That is what is implied by Justice Clark in his dissent. He said:

> The conspiracy includes the same group of defendants as in the *Dennis* case though petitioners here occupied a lower echelon in the party hierarchy. They, nevertheless, served in the same army and were engaged in the same mission. The convictions here were based upon evidence closely paralleling that produced in *Dennis* … [evidence that was] equally as strong.[103]

Perhaps, the lower courts did misconstrue the earlier case. Or perhaps those at the lower levels of the party could be treated differently. Or, perhaps, as good an explanation is the diminishing effect of the communist scare. Senator Joseph McCarthy, who had been a major instigator of the scare, had been examined, and skewered, by Edward R. Morrow, on the CBS television program *See it Now* in March of 1954.[104] In the same year, the Senate passed a resolution of censure against Senator McCarthy.[105] If the communist scare was over, the need felt to suppress the Communist Party would have lessened.[106]

[101] *Id.* at 318. [102] *Id.* at 324. [103] *Id.* at 345–46 (Clark, J., dissenting).

[104] A transcript of the program may be found at www.lib.berkeley.edu/MRC/murrowmccarthy.html.

[105] A transcript of *Senate Resolution 301: Censure of Senator Joseph McCarthy* may be found at www.ourdocuments.gov/doc.php?flash=true&doc=86&page=transcript.

[106] The rehabilitation of the Communist Party may be seen as complete in *Communist Party of Indiana v. Whitcomb*, 415 U.S. 952 (1974). There, the Supreme Court concluded that the refusal of the state of Indiana to provide a place on the ballot to the Communist Party was unconstitutional. The refusal had been based on the failure of the party to provide evidence, as required by law, of oaths by its leadership that they did not advocate the overthrow of government. The major parties had not been required to submit similar material.

PARTY BANS AND PATHOLOGICAL ERAS

Vincent Blasi, in an insightful article, wrote on the effects of pathological eras on free expression.[107] He says that pathologies are "time-bound and exceptional," and he provides a definition:

> "Pathology" . . . is a social phenomenon, characterized by a notable shift in attitudes regarding the tolerance of unorthodox ideas. What makes a period pathological is the existence of certain dynamics that radically increase the likelihood that people who hold unorthodox views will be punished for what they say or believe.[108]

In terms of impact on the constitution of a country, Professor Blasi says:

> In pathological periods, at least some of the central norms of the constitutional regime are indeed scrutinized and challenged. The core commitments that derive from those norms are viewed by many as highly burdensome and controversial. In such periods the times seem so different, so out of joint, the threats from within or without seems so unprecedented, that the Constitution itself is perceived by many persons as anachronistic, or at least rigidly, unrealistically formalistic. In times when those misgivings take hold, the central norms of the constitutional regime are in jeopardy.[109]

What Blasi then goes on to discuss is how free speech issues should be handled in normal times to provide the greatest strength for the protections of free expression in these pathological eras.

Blasi recognized that this pathological view impacted not only free expression itself but its related freedom of association and political parties.

> The freedom of association takes on a special significance during pathological periods. Such periods are characterized by a search for scapegoats, and unpopular organizations serve that social need well. In order to justify suspension of traditional levels of tolerance, would-be regulators typically must identify a threat to the values of the community that can be described as unusual in its magnitude or intensity . . . It may almost be considered a defining feature of a pathological period that the public or official attention is focused to an unusual extent on the machinations of dissident political groups.[110]

The material in this chapter demonstrates that democracies may face these pathological errors and, in those eras, ban, limit the activities of, or criminally prosecute the leaders of political parties seen as dangerous.

[107] Vincent Blasi, *The Pathological Perspective and the First Amendment*, 85 COLUM. L. REV. 449 (1985).

[108] *Id.* at 450. [109] *Id.* at 456–57. [110] *Id.* at 495–96.

Blasi recognizes the Red Scare of 1919–1920 and the McCarthy Era as pathological eras in the United States.[111] Germany experienced a similar era in the aftermath of the Nazi regime and World War II. The IRA may be seen as later bringing about a similar era in Ireland and the United Kingdom. Still later, the activities of the ETA led Spain into a similar period. Still more recently, concerns over the secularity and unity of the state have led Turkey to try to impose the restrictions on political parties seen earlier in other countries.

Blasi's concerns over pathological eras and what can be done to avoid them are important. Even if they may, at times, not be avoided, the recognition of the serious impact these eras have on free expression may reduce the frequency of their occurrence. It is also important to take to heart that, even if pathological eras are not in fact time-bound, they ought to be. Even if a country sees its situation as being so serious as to justify a limitation on either free speech or political parties, it should recognize when that situation has come to an end. Concerns over socialism and communism in the United States have waned to the point that there is no need to suppress political parties based on such ideas. German concerns over any real likelihood of successors to the Nazis, or communists, coming to power should probably have lessened to the point where the parties no longer need to be banned.[112] The IRA has become less a force in Ireland and the United Kingdom and Sinn Féin can be allowed full political participation. There may still be serious concern over the ETA in Spain, and attempts to ban political parties that are successors to Batasuna may continue. Turkey's very real concerns may well see continued attempts at suppression.

[111] *See id.* at 451.

[112] The use of Nazi symbols, while they may not lead to actual power by a successor party, may still be the expression of hate directed toward Jews and foreigners. German law allows this suppression on that basis. Hate speech is discussed in Chapter 4.

7

Political Campaign Limitations

While Chapter 6 concerned attempts to prohibit certain political parties from participating in electoral politics, the material in this chapter addresses general limitations on campaigns applicable to all parties. Even these evenhanded regulations touch at the heart of democracy. An effective democracy requires more than simply the opportunity to go to the polls. It requires the right to be informed in casting a ballot, and that requires the sort of information that usually comes through a campaign. So, limits on campaigns may strongly impact democracy. Nonetheless, many fully functioning democracies do impose such limits.

The motivations behind the limits to be addressed here are not fears aimed as much at results as they are concerns about the prevention of corruption. Most of the concern has to do with the impact of money on politics and elections. Particularly where a great deal of money is required to be competitive, there is concern that those who are elected will be in the debt of those who provided the means for their election.[1] Those with wealth will influence legislation. Even where this falls short of the quid pro quo of bribery or vote buying, money may well buy access. Those who have contributed will be able to make their positions known to representatives, while those without the means may not be heard. Even when this does not occur, there may be a public perception that it does. It weakens democracy, when the public doesn't believe that its representatives are doing its will.

There are at least two approaches to reducing this concern. One is to limit campaign spending and contributions. If the amount of money that can be spent on a campaign is reduced, those seeking election will not have to raise as

[1] It may not even take large contributions to have an impact on a representative. A representative may simply be concerned that interests with significant money to spend will, if disappointed with the representative, support a future opponent.

much money. There will not be large donors that the public may see as controlling representatives. If there are no campaign spending limits, there may instead be limits on contributions. With no large donors, there is no one to seek special favors. But for this to be effective there may also be the need to control independent spending in favor of particular candidates. Even if a potential large donor cannot give money directly to a candidate or political party, if there are no limits on independent spending, that same potential donor can simply pay for advertising favoring or opposing a particular candidate. While money has not passed directly, it would seem likely that the influence would be the same.

Another approach is to take measures to limit the costs of political campaigns. The most expensive political advertising involves broadcast media, particularly time on television. This can be limited by placing limits on such advertising, providing free broadcast time to candidates, or a combination of the two.

There are, of course, great differences in the structure of governments among democratic countries, and these differences could potentially affect the need to spend money to gain election. A country with a presidential system requires a national campaign, and the most expensive elections are likely to be for positions such as President of the United States. But it is not as though parties in countries with parliamentary systems do not conduct national campaigns. If there are legal differences in what may be spent, they are perhaps better explained as differences in whether spending money is seen as counting as expression and a perception of the need to level the playing field. In any case, it is similarity in the nature of countries as democratic, rather than differences in structure, that would seem most important. Here, too, the lesson to be learned is that there can be different rules, even in this area, among equally democratic countries.

LIMITS ON CAMPAIGN SPENDING AND CONTRIBUTIONS

The United States

The United States has seen several attempts by Congress to limit the influence of money on campaigns, only to have those efforts declared unconstitutional by the Supreme Court. There are two ways to look at what has been occurring. One is that Congress, whose members are the potential beneficiaries of contributions and independent spending, recognize the corrupting influence of money and are trying to eliminate it. The other is that the members of Congress are only protecting their seats. The only way to overcome the name recognition of a sitting member of Congress, at least when recognition is not negative, is to advertise heavily. Placing limits on contributions and independent expenditures makes that possibility less likely.

Only a brief history of efforts to control contributions will be presented here, before turning to the most recent analysis of the Supreme Court. Only *Buckley v. Valeo*[2] and *McConnell v. Federal Election Commission*[3] and a later reconsideration of an aspect of *Buckley* will be mentioned at all. A far more detailed history of efforts may be found in *McConnell*.[4]

The efforts partially struck down in *Buckley* were important. That case considered limits on campaign contributions and on independent expenditures. The Supreme Court was willing to hold the contribution limits constitutional, based on the potential for, or appearance of, corruption that larger contributions might cause. The limits on independent expenditures were declared unconstitutional as limiting the speech rights of those who wish to purchase their own advertisements.

The contribution limits in the statute at issue in *Buckley* addressed the amount that could be donated to any individual candidate and placed a limit on total contributions to candidates for federal office in any campaign cycle. That later limit on total contributions was later struck down in *McCutcheon v. Federal Election Commission*.[5] Importantly, the four-justice *McCutcheon* plurality led by Chief Justice Roberts concluded that any concerns over the appearance of corruption had to be limited to the appearance of quid pro quo corruption; the appearance that elected officials would be subject to the influence of those who contribute would not suffice. A concurrence by Justice Thomas would have reversed all the contribution restrictions of *Buckley*.

When Congress attempted to close loopholes left after *Buckley*, their efforts were again held to be only partially constitutional. The Bipartisan Campaign Reform Act (BCRA) of 2002[6] attempted to address concerns over "soft money," money used for, among other things, legislative advocacy that might mention a candidate's name without advocating the election or defeat of that candidate. The act also addressed "issue ads" that did not direct a vote for or against a candidate but may have that intent. The *McConnell* Court, in an extremely complex opinion, did allow limitations on national parties soliciting and spending soft money and certain other anti-circumvention provisions. Another anti-circumvention provision forbidding contributions by minors, a provision seemingly intended to prevent parents from circumventing their

[2] 424 U.S. 1 (1976). [3] 540 U.S. 93 (2003). [4] *See id.* at 114–33.
[5] 134 S.Ct. 1434 (2014). [6] Pub. L. 107–55, 116 Stat. 81 (2002).

own contribution limits by contributing money in the names of their children, was declared unconstitutional.

Most importantly, in terms of the next round of litigation, the *McConnell* Court left intact prohibitions on the use of general treasury funds by corporations and unions to engage in "electioneering communication" or speech expressly advocating the election or defeat of a candidate. This result was consistent with the Court's earlier direct holding, in *Austin v. Michigan Chamber of Commerce*,[7] that independent corporate expenditures in support of, or in opposition to a candidate could be banned. It was that issue that came back to the Court in perhaps the most controversial of the United States campaign cases, *Citizens United v. Federal Elections Commission*.[8] That case, because it is so recent and because of its potential impact on future campaigns, deserves to be considered in some detail.

The challenge to the ban on corporate spending was brought by Citizens United, a non-profit corporation funded largely by individuals but also through some contributions from for-profit corporations. During the Democratic primaries leading up to the 2008 presidential election, Citizens United released a film titled *Hillary: The Movie*, a 90-minute documentary about Hillary Clinton. The film was quite critical of her candidacy. The film was released in theaters and on DVD, but Citizens United, seeking greater viewership, decided to make it available through the video-on-demand service of cable systems. A cable system was willing to include the film, but only in exchange for a payment of $1.2 million. Citizens United was prepared to pay and, to promote viewership, produced two 10-second ads and one 30-second ad, also negative with regard to Senator Clinton. The ads would run on broadcast and cable television at additional expense to Citizens United.

Citizens United was concerned that the film and the ads would violate provisions of the BCRA. That act amended federal law that prohibited corporations and unions from using their general treasury funds to make contributions to candidates or to make independent expenditures expressly advocating the election or defeat of a candidate in a federal election. The amendment added a provision barring any "electioneering communication," defined as broadcast, cable, or satellite communications referring to a clearly identified candidate for federal office.[9] The ban is applied within 30 days of a primary or within 60 days of a general election. Corporations and unions were allowed, under the law, to establish Political Action Committees or PACs, but the funding for the PACs had to be from corporation stockholders or employees or

[7] 494 U.S. 652 (1990) [8] 558 U.S. 310 (2010). [9] BCRA, *supra* note 6, at § 203.

from union members, and the funds for the PAC had to be held separately from general treasury funds.

Because Citizens United intended to make the film available on cable, and to run the ads, within 30 days of a primary, it was concerned that it could be held in violation of the act and sought an injunction against enforcement, arguing that the ban on expenditure, at least as applied to the film, was unconstitutional. It also asserted that the act's disclaimer and disclosure requirements,[10] also as applied to the film and ads, were unconstitutional.

The Court saw itself as being asked to reconsider *Austin*. Doing so required a re-examination of the First Amendment issues raised there and in the present case. The Court began by noting the scope of the prohibition, setting out a parade of horribles, noting that the following would all be felonies:

> The Sierra Club runs an ad, within the crucial phase of 60 days before the general election, that exhorts the public to disapprove of a Congressman who favors logging in national forests; the National Rifle Association publishes a book urging the public to vote for the challenger because the incumbent U.S. Senator supports a handgun ban; and the American Civil Liberties Union creates a Web site telling the public to vote for a Presidential candidate in light of that candidate's defense of free speech.[11]

All, the Court said, would be classic cases of censorship. But as to whether they really do represent a parade of horribles, a four-Justice dissent pointed out that "[i]f ideologically aligned individuals wish to make unlimited expenditures through the corporate form, they may utilize an MCFL organization that has policies in place to avoid becoming a conduit for business or union interests."[12]

While the law did, as noted, allow the creation of PACs to engage in political advocacy or electioneering communication, the majority found the PAC alternative inadequate to allay First Amendment concerns over limits on the speech of corporations or unions.

> PACs are burdensome alternatives; they are expensive to administer and subject to extensive regulations. For example, every PAC must appoint a treasurer, forward donations to the treasurer promptly, keep detailed records of the identities of the persons making donations, preserve receipts for three years, and file an organization statement and report changes to this

[10] *Id.* at §§ 201, 311. [11] 558 U.S. at 337.

[12] *Id.* at 415 (Stevens, J. joined by Ginsberg, Breyer, & Sotomayor, J.J. dissenting in part and concurring in part). The label "MCFL organization" comes from Federal Election Commission v. Massachusetts Citizens for Life, 479 U.S. 238 (1980).

> information within 10 days ... PACs must file detailed monthly reports with the FEC ... PACs have to comply with these regulations just to speak. This might explain why fewer than 2,000 of the millions of corporations in this country have PACs. PACs, furthermore, must exist before they can speak. Given the onerous restrictions, a corporation may not be able to establish a PAC in time to make its views known regarding candidates and issues in a current campaign.[13]

The four-justice dissent accepted that administering a PAC may be somewhat burdensome but noted that so is complying with the other portions of the statute, disclosure, disclaimer, and reporting, that the majority left intact. Despite whatever burden may be involved, the dissent found little impact. "[N]o one has suggested that the burden is severe for a sophisticated for-profit corporation ... [, and t]he owners of a 'mom & pop' store can simply place ads in their own names, rather than the store's."[14]

The best argument the majority presented for corporate speech was based on the right of, and need for, the people to hear all points of view. If the government can repress speakers, that power may be used to suppress speech. As the Court saw it, the statute's "purpose and effect are to silence entities whose voices the Government deems to be suspect."[15]

> Premised on mistrust of governmental power, the First Amendment stands against attempts to disfavor certain subjects or viewpoints. Prohibited, too, are restrictions distinguishing among different speakers, allowing speech by some but not others. As instruments to censor, these categories are interrelated: Speech restrictions based on the identity of the speaker are all too often simply a means to control content.
>
> Quite apart from the purpose or effect of regulating content, moreover, the Government may commit a constitutional wrong when by law it identifies certain preferred speakers. By taking the right to speak from some and giving it to others, the Government deprives the disadvantaged person or class of the right to use speech to strive to establish worth, standing, and respect for the speaker's voice. The Government may not by these means deprive the public of the right and privilege to determine for itself what speech and speakers are worthy of consideration.[16]

Not content to rely on the right of the public to hear political speech, whatever its source, the Court did go on to say that, until *Austin*, the Court

[13] *Id.* at 337–38 (majority opinion).

[14] *Id* at 416 (Stevens, J. joined by Ginsberg, Breyer, & Sotomayor, J.J. dissenting in part and concurring in part).

[15] *Id.* at 339 (majority opinion).

[16] *Id.* at 340–41 (citations omitted).

had recognized that corporations enjoy the protections of the First Amendment. "The Court has ... rejected the argument that political speech of corporations or other associations should be treated differently under the First Amendment simply because such associations are not 'natural persons.'"[17] *Austin* was the sole contrary case. There, the Court relied on what was styled an antidistortion interest, "a compelling governmental interest in preventing 'the corrosive and distorting effects of immense aggregations of wealth that are accumulated with the help of the corporate form and that have little or no correlation to the public's support for the corporation's political ideas.'"[18]

Given the conflicting precedent, the Court had to choose which line to follow and chose to reject *Austin*. The Court said that the Government, while noting the antidistortion rationale, had abandoned reliance on it. This, in the Court's view, was wise.

> *Austin* sought to defend the antidistortion rationale as a means to prevent corporations from obtaining "an unfair advantage in the political marketplace" by using "resources amassed in the economic marketplace." But *Buckley* rejected the premise that the Government has an interest "in equalizing the relative ability of individuals and groups to influence the outcome of elections." *Buckley* was specific in stating that "the skyrocketing cost of political campaigns" could not sustain the governmental prohibition. The First Amendment's protections do not depend on the speaker's "financial ability to engage in public discussion." ... The rule that political speech cannot be limited based on a speaker's wealth is a necessary consequence of the premise that the First Amendment generally prohibits the suppression of political speech based on the speaker's identity.[19]

Austin had distinguished wealthy individuals from corporations on the basis of the special advantages corporations enjoy: limited liability, perpetual life, and favorable treatment of the accumulation and distribution of assets.[20] The *Citizens United* majority found this unacceptable, since the enjoyment of benefits does not justify the forfeiture of constitutional rights.[21]

In an interesting argument, but one that should have been irrelevant, the Court said that accepting the antidistortion rationale would have the dangerous, and unacceptable, consequence that Congress could ban the political

[17] *Id.* at 343 (citations omitted).

[18] *Id.* at 348 (quoting Austin at 660).

[19] *Id.* at 350 (citations omitted).

[20] *See id.* at 350–51.

[21] The Court also found it irrelevant that the public, the ultimate source of corporate funds, may not support the positions taken by the corporation's speech. "All speakers, including individuals and the media, use money amassed from the economic marketplace to fund their speech. The First Amendment protects the resulting speech, even if it was enabled by economic transactions with persons or entities who disagree with the speaker's ideas." *Id.* at 351.

speech of media corporations. Media corporations can also amass great wealth, and their views may also not match those of the public from which their wealth derives.

> Thus, under the Government's reasoning, wealthy media corporations could have their voices diminished to put them on par with other media entities ... There is simply no support for the view that the First Amendment, as originally understood, would permit the suppression of political speech by media corporations ... The First Amendment was certainly not understood to condone the suppression of political speech in society's most salient media.[22]

The application of the statute to media corporations would, indeed, present a major problem, since it would exclude such things as newspaper editorials and endorsements. The relevance problem with the argument is that, as the majority recognized, the act exempted media corporations from the ban on expenditures. Instead of following the usual approach of interpreting a statute so as to be constitutional, the majority extended a statute beyond the limits set by Congress to demonstrate its unconstitutionality.

The next offered justification for the corporate speech limits was the prevention of corruption or the appearance of corruption. That claim was an attempt to resurrect the rationale rejected in *Buckley*. The majority saw it in that light and said that, just as for individuals, the corruption, or appearance thereof, concern justifies limits on contributions, but it does not justify limits on independent expenditures.[23]

The last justification offered for the prohibition on expenditures was the interest in protecting shareholders who do not share the views of the corporation from being forced to fund the corporation's political speech. Here, too, the majority asserted that that would allow a ban on the political speech of media corporations, again despite the exemption for media corporations. Furthermore, the Court said that there was little evidence of this sort of abuse

[22] *Id.* at 352–53.

[23] The dissent found the corruption argument more compelling, noting that there is a spectrum along which corruption operates and that it includes more than the quid pro quo of bribery or vote buying. A representative may vote in favor of corporate interests in hope of some future corporate expenditure in his or her support. This is almost as damaging as vote buying, since it appears corrupt to the public. "A democracy cannot function effectively when its constituent members believe laws are being bought and sold." *Id.* at 453 (Stevens, J. joined by Ginsberg, Breyer, & Sotomayor, J.J. dissenting in part and concurring in part).
This argument is, seemingly, an attempt to refight the battle lost in *Buckley*, and it was unlikely to succeed. The only way to characterize it differently was to base that difference on the special benefits the law provides corporations and the greater ability, under those benefits, to amass wealth, a difference the majority rejected.

that could not be remedied by shareholders; the exercise of corporate democracy should provide sufficient control.[24]

The majority did uphold disclaimer and disclosure provisions, at least as applied to this case. While such requirements may be burdensome, they do not prevent speech and are subject to less than strict scrutiny. There has to be a substantial relationship to a sufficiently important interest. The Court found disclosure justified by a government interest in providing the electorate with information regarding election-related spending.[25]

The result of all these cases is an extremely high level of expenditures on campaigns in the United States. While the political parties and candidates themselves may spend a great deal of money, independent expenditures by Super PACs have reached incredible levels. The three largest spending PACs in the 2012 election were American Crossroads, at over 90 million dollars, Priorities USA Action, at almost 66.5 million, and Americans for Prosperity, at approximately 33.5 million.[26] Their funds came from donors, who do not face the limits that apply to campaign contributions to candidates. American Crossroads reportedly had one individual who donated $20.5 million of his own money and another $2 million from his company.[27] Priorities USA Action did not have any single donation at that level but did have a single $5 million donation.[28] Americans for Prosperity, while not funded entirely by the Koch brothers and their companies, is significantly funded by them, but it is not

[24] *See id.* at 361–62 (majority opinion). The majority also said that this shareholder protection justification was underinclusive and overinclusive, because it was limited to the relatively short period of time before an election, and is applied to all corporations including not-for-profit corporations and for-profit corporations with a single shareholder. *See id.* at 362.
The dissent did respond to the claim that corporate democracy should be sufficient control. Many stockholders do not know what stocks they own as part of mutual fund investments. Furthermore, once they learn that the corporation has made any expenditure with which they disagree, the expenditure has already occurred. There may also be reasons, including tax liability, why an investor may not want to sell his or her stock. *See id.* at 477 (Stevens, J. joined by Ginsberg, Breyer, & Sotomayor, J.J. dissenting in part and concurring in part).

[25] *See id.* at 366–67. The Court did say that, where a group can show the disclosure would lead to threats, harassment, reprisals, the group may be protected from disclosure. *See id.* at 367. Justice Thomas split with the majority on this issue. He argued that anonymous speech is historically protected and also noted reprisals against those backing a California proposition banning same-sex marriage. *See id.* at 480–84 (Thomas, J., dissenting in part and concurring in part).

[26] *See* Kevin Quealy & Derek Willis, *Independent Spending Totals: Elections 2012*, NY TIMES, http://elections.nytimes.com/2012/campaign-finance/independent-expenditures/total.

[27] *See* Aaron Melita, *PAC profile: American Crossroads*, CENTER FOR PUB. INTEGRITY, Jan. 31, 2012, www.publicintegrity.org/2012/01/31/8056/pac-profile-american-crossroads?gclid=CLTHqM_t-70CFckWMgodozMAdg.

[28] *See* Aaron Melita, *PAC Profile: Priorities USA Action*, CENTER FOR PUB. INTEGRITY, www.publicintegrity.org/2012/01/30/8025/pac-profile-priorities-usa-action.

required to disclose its funding.[29] These super PACs spent money in support of both major presidential campaigns, with Priorities USA Action supporting the Democratic candidate and the other two the Republican.

These large sums would seem almost certain to have an impact on the beliefs of average persons in the responsiveness of government. With campaigns dominated by large donations and expenditures, the ordinary individual may see little chance that his or her views make any difference. *The Economist*, in examining what it sees as the flaws in, and decline of, democracy in the world points to a number of factors in the United States.

> All this creates the impression that American democracy is for sale and that the rich have more power than the poor, even as lobbyists and donors insist that political expenditure is an exercise in free speech. The result is that America's image—and by extension that of democracy itself—has taken a terrible battering.[30]

Canada

Canadian election law and an opinion from the Supreme Court of Canada, provide a different approach with regard to independent expenditures on elections. The Canadian Elections Act contains a provision on third-party election advertising.[31] The act provides:

(1) A third party shall not incur election advertising expenses of a total amount of more than $150,000 [during an election period] in relation to a general election.
(2) Not more than $3000 of the total amount referred to in subsection (1) shall be incurred to promote or oppose the election of one or more candidates in a given election district, including by

[29] *See Americans for Prosperity*, FACT CHECK.ORG, Aug. 9, 2010, www.factcheck.org/2010/08/americans-for-prosperity.

[30] *What's Gone Wrong with Democracy?*, THE ECONOMIST, Mar. 1, 2014, at 2, www.economist.com/news/essays/21596796-democracy-was-most-successful-political-idea-20th-century-why-has-it-run-trouble-and-what-can-be-do. The United States Supreme Court's lack of concern over money influencing elections was further demonstrated in *Arizona Free Enterprise Club's Freedom Club PAC v. Burnett*, 131 S.Ct. 2806 (2011). That case declared unconstitutional an Arizona plan in which public subsidization of a candidate would be increased if the candidate's opponent exceeded certain expenditure limits. The Court saw this plan as a penalty on the opponent's spending for political speech, rather than simply as an enhancement of the speech of the subsidized candidate.

[31] Canada Elections Act, S.C. 2000, c. 9, § 350 (Can.), laws.justice.gc.ca/eng/acts/E-2.01/page-92.html/docCont.

(a) naming them;
(b) showing their likenesses;
(c) identifying them by their respective political affiliation; or
(d) taking a position on an issue with which they are particularly associated.

(3) The limit set out in subsection (2) only applies to an amount incurred with respect to a leader of a registered party or eligible party to the extent that it is encouraged to promote or oppose his or her election in a given electoral district . . .[32]

The Act goes on to prohibit circumvention or attempts to circumvent the limits set out.[33] It also requires third parties to identify themselves in any election advertising.[34] Third parties that spend more than five dollars must register with election officials,[35] and if the third party is a corporation or union, or any entity with a governing body, the application for registration must include a copy of the governing body's resolution authorizing the expenses.[36]

The constitutionality of the statute was challenged and reached the Supreme Court of Canada in *Harper v. Canada (Attorney General)*.[37] The Court concluded that the statute, with the exception of its anti-circumvention provision, did infringe the right to free expression under Section 2(b) of the Canadian Charter of Rights and Freedoms, so the issue became whether or not it could be saved under Section 1. Was the statute "a reasonable limit prescribed by law as can be demonstrably justified in a free and democratic society?"

There was an earlier relevant case. *Libman v. Québec (Attorney General)*[38] considered Québec's limitations on independent spending in referenda elections. The Court found the limitations there unjustified but endorsed several principles. The most important of the principles was stated by the *Harper* Court:

> If the principle of fairness in the political sphere is to be preserved, it cannot be presumed that all persons have the same financial resources to communicate with the electorate. To ensure a right of equal participation in democratic government, laws limiting spending are needed to preserve the equality of democratic rights and ensure that one person's exercise of the freedom to spend does not hinder the communication opportunities of others. Owing to the competitive nature of elections, such spending limits are necessary to prevent the most affluent from monopolizing election discourse and consequently depriving their opponents of a reasonable opportunity to speak and be heard . . .[39]

The *Harper* Court said that this principle is consistent with the egalitarian model that Parliament had adopted and was essential to Canadian democracy.

[32] *Id.* [33] *See id.* § 351. [34] *See id.* § 352. [35] *See id.* § 353. [36] *See id.* § 353(5).
[37] [2004] 1 S.C.R. 827 (Can.). [38] [1997] 3 S.C.R. 569 (Can.). [39] [2004]1 S.C.R. at ¶ 61.

The egalitarian model seeks to establish a level playing field, where voters are better informed because no one's voice overwhelms others.[40]

The Court pointed to a number of experts who concluded that electoral fairness may be undermined, if third parties are allowed to spend without limits.

> First, it can lead to the dominance of the political discourse by the wealthy. Second, it may allow candidates and political parties to circumvent their own spending limits through the creation of third parties. Third, unlimited third-party spending can have an unfair effect on the outcome of an election. Fourth, the absence of limits on third party advertising expenses can erode the confidence of the Canadian electorate who perceive the electoral process as being dominated by the wealthy.[41]

The Court recognized that what was at stake was political expression, lying at the core of the expression protected by the Charter. But it also recognized that third parties with significant financial resources may be able to manipulate political discourse.[42] Spending limits balance political discourse and allow for more meaningful participation, enhancing the Charter right to vote.[43]

Turning to the *Oakes* analysis,[44] the Court said that the limits had been clearly prescribed by law, and it concluded that they address a pressing and substantial concern, promoting equality in political discourse, protecting the integrity of the financing limits placed on candidates and parties, and ensuring voter confidence in the electoral process.[45] The Court also found no difficulty in establishing a rational connection between the limitations and the substantial concern it had already accepted.[46]

With regard to proportionality, the weighing of the deleterious effects against the salutary effects of the limits, the Court found several salutary effects, effects that matched the objectives. The deleterious effect was limited to not allowing third parties to spend unlimited funds to engage in political expression, although third parties could still engage in informational speech. The balance, the Court said, justified upholding the limitations.[47]

[40] *Id.* at ¶ 62. [41] *Id.* at ¶ 79 (citations omitted). [42] *Id.* at ¶ 85. [43] *Id.* at ¶ 86.

[44] The *Oakes* test is discussed in Chapter 1. [45] 1 S.C.R. at ¶¶ 92, 101–3.

[46] *Id.* at ¶¶ 104–18.

[47] There was a two-justice dissent that felt the infringement to be serious and the benefits illusory. In the dissent's view the dangers were wholly hypothetical. And, seemingly assuming that ordinary citizens have significant assets, the dissent said that the law "effectively denies the right of the ordinary citizen to give meaningful and effective expression to her political views during a federal election campaign." *Id.* at ¶ 1 (opinion of McLachlin, C.J.C., joined by Major, J., dissenting in part).

The United Kingdom

A case from the United Kingdom reversed a conviction for third-party independent campaign spending, but it did so in a way that did not call into question limits on supporting a candidate. An older 1952 case, *Regina v. Tronoh Mines Ltd.*,[48] grew out of an ad placed by the company, criticizing Labour Party dividend limitations. The ad read: "[A] Socialist Party cannot hope to make a success of administering the Capitalist system because it does not believe in it … The coming general election will give us all the opportunity of saving the country from being reduced, through the policies of the Socialist government, to a bankrupt Welfare State."[49]

Charges, based on the ad, were brought under the Representation of the People Act of 1949:

> Section 63(1) of [the Act] prohibits the incurring of expenses with a view to promoting or procuring the election of a candidate at an election, by any person other than the candidate, his agent or those authorized by his agent "on account (*a*) of holding public meetings … or (*b*) of issuing advertisements …, or (c) of otherwise presenting to the electors the candidate or his views or the extent or nature of his backing, or disparaging another candidate …"[50]

The court concluded that there was no basis for submitting the case to the jury. In the view of the court, the statute required that the advertisement back a particular candidate. The advertisement in question, critical of the Labour Party generally, could not be found by a reasonable jury to have been addressed to a particular candidate. It is true, of course, that a court of the United Kingdom would have employed the approach of interpreting a statute so as not to be in violation of the tradition of free expression. That occurred here, but there seems to be no indication in the opinion that the court saw any difficulty with the statute that required a limiting interpretation.

There is also an independent expenditures case from the United Kingdom decided by the European Court of Human Rights. *Bowman v. United Kingdom*[51] resulted from the distribution of 1.5 million leaflets by an antiabortion group, outlining the positions of candidates standing for election. The director of the organization was charged under a statute that prohibited the expenditure of more than £5.00 on publications or other communications directed toward or against the election of a candidate, during an election. The

48 (1951) 35 Cr. App. R. 196 (1952). 49 *Id.* at 198–99.

50 *Id.* at 197 (quoting Representation of the People Act, 1949, § 63 (1)) (ellipses in original).

51 App. No. 24893/94, 26 Eur. H.R. Rep. 1 (1998).

statute prohibited incurring such expenses to promote the election of a candidate, other than by the candidate or the candidate's campaign. Even though she was acquitted, the European Court heard her claim that the statute violated Article 10 of the European Convention, because of the effect that the statute would have on any future speech.

The Court first concluded that the limitation on spending did restrict Ms. Bowman's expression rights and then turned to consider whether or not the restriction was necessary in a democratic society. The Court recognized the acceptability of the goal of the statute.

> Free elections and free expression . . . may come into conflict and it may be considered necessary, in the period preceding or during an election, to place certain restrictions of a type which would not usually be acceptable, on freedom of expression, in order to secure the "free expression of the opinion of the people in the choice of the legislature."[52]

In striking the balance between the two rights, the court noted that the member states do have a margin of appreciation but concluded that the £5.00 limit was too low.

> [The limit acted] as a total barrier to Mrs Bowman's publishing information with a view to influencing the voters of Halifax in favour of an anti-abortion candidate. [The Court] is not satisfied that it was necessary thus to limit her expenditures to £5.00 in order to achieve the legitimate aim of securing equality between candidates, particularly in view of the fact that there were no restrictions placed upon the freedom of the press to support or oppose the election of any particular candidate or upon political parties and their supporters to advertise at national or regional level, provided that such advertisements were not intended to promote or prejudice the electoral prospects of any particular candidate in any particular constituency.[53]

Third party expenditure limits are allowed under European law, but the limits must not be too low.

Other Spending and Contribution Limits

In France, donations from individuals, but not legal entities, to candidates are allowed.[54] Funding for the election of candidates is also provided by political parties, which are themselves funded by private donations and government

[52] *Id.* at ¶41. [53] *Id.* at ¶47.

[54] *See* Michael Pinto-Duschinsky & Alexander Postnikov, Int'l Found. for Election Sys., Campaign Finance Foreign Countries: Legal Regulation and Political Practices (A Comparative Legal Survey and Analysis 7 (1999).

subsidy.[55] While there is no limit in France on the amount a candidate may contribute to his own campaign, there are ceilings on expenditures.[56] There are also limits on contributions, with individuals limited to a total of €4600 and total cash contributions are not to exceed 20 percent of the ceiling on expenditures.[57]

Spain has also placed a yearly limit on donations by individuals or groups to political parties with the overall total not to exceed 5 percent of the government subsidization of campaign funding.[58] Germany appears to allow contributions by corporations to candidates but to prohibit contributions by unions.[59]

BROADCAST LIMITATIONS

Advertising on the broadcast media is likely to be the greatest expense a candidate will incur. Thus, another way to control corruption is to limit the use of those media. If the need for money is reduced, there will be less need to raise funds, and without the need for large contributions, influence and potential corruption are lessened. If the limits extend to independent expenditures, the similar concerns such expenditures raise are similarly reduced.

There may be an additional reason to limit advertisements on the broadcast media. Time is money, and any lengthy advertisements are prohibitively expensive. Thus, candidates are left with very short times to make their points. They cannot do so in a way adequately to explain their positions to the voters. It takes too long to make a positive point. Negative claims, on the other hand, seem particularly suited to these short spots. This, plus the fact that they seem to work, may be the reason that political advertising in the United States has turned so negative. When engaged in by both parties, the impression is that there is no one deserving of election, and voter turnout may suffer.

It is inconceivable that these rationales would suffice to justify broadcast limitations in the United States. Candidates have free expression rights that will be very difficult to limit. While those rights could be partially preserved by combining limits on ads with, perhaps longer blocks of, free broadcast time,

[55] *See id.*

[56] See Nicole Atwill, *Campaign Finance: France*. L. LIBR. CONGRESS, www.LOC.gov/lore/help/campaign-finance/France.php.

[57] *See id.* [58] *See* PINTO-DUSCHINSKY & POSTNIKOV, *supra* note 54, at 9.

[59] *See* Nicole Atwill, *Campaign Finance: Comparative Summary*, L. LIBR. CONGRESS, www.loc.gov/law/help/campaign-finance/comparative-summary.php#private.

the candidates and parties would also seem to have rights to determine the formats of the messages they wish to present. Broadcasters also have their own expression rights.[60] Strict scrutiny would be required, and the principle that the remedy for bad speech is good speech would seem apt.

There are, however, statutes and cases in and from other fully functioning democracies that allow limitations. While primarily directed at the use of broadcast media, other media may be affected.

Australia

The major case in election law from the High Court of Australia speaks to limitations on and the allocation of broadcast time for electioneering. The case, *Australian Capital Television Proprietary. v. Commonwealth*,[61] is that in which the implied protection of political speech, under the Australian Constitution, was recognized.[62] Beyond that, the issue had to do with the Broadcasting Act of 1942.[63] A provision of the act, added by the Political Broadcasts and Political Disclosures Act of 1991,[64] established a regulatory regime to govern the broadcasting, on both radio and television, of political advertisements.

Part IIID of the Broadcasting Act prohibited, with some exceptions including news and current affairs broadcasts and talkback radio, the broadcast of certain political material. On the other hand, the act imposed an obligation on broadcasters to provide free time to political parties, persons or groups designated by the Australian Broadcasting Tribunal to be used for election broadcasts. The act also established the criteria to determine the grant of free time by the Tribunal.

The prohibitions barred broadcasting, during an election, of material on behalf of the government other than announcements and advertisements regarding government business unconnected to politics. Specifically prohibited were political advertisements on behalf of the government. Further,

60 There was an era in which broadcast licensees, because of their use of the broadcast spectrum, a scarce public resource, were held to have the responsibility to provide fair news coverage. *See, e.g.*, Red Lion Broad. Co. v. Fed. Commc'n Comm'n, 395 U.S. 367 (1969). The responsibility was encoded in Federal Communications Commission (FCC) regulations upheld, in that case, by the Supreme Court. *Red Lion* might seem to be precedent in favor of any rule that required the provision of free time to candidates. However, the FCC later changed its rules, and there are certainly more news outlets than they were in the 1960s, so any precedential impact would seem weak.

61 177 C.L.R. 106 (1992).

62 This aspect of the Court's holding is discussed in Chapter 1.

63 Broadcasting Act 1942 (Cth)(Austl.), www.austlii.edu.au/au/legis/cth/num_act/aba1942330194227 4/.

64 Political Broadcasts and Political Disclosures Act 1991 (Cth)(Austl.), www.comlaw.gov.au/Details/C2004A04278.

broadcasters were barred from airing political advertisements on behalf of persons other than the government. "Political advertisements" were defined to include matter intended or likely to affect voting, or

> material containing an express or implicit reference to, or comment on, any of the following: (a) the election or referendum concerned; (b) a candidate or group of candidates in that election; (c) an issue submitted or otherwise before electors in that election; (d) the government, the opposition, or a previous government or opposition, of the Commonwealth; (e) a member of the Parliament of the Commonwealth; (f) a political party, or a branch or division of a political party.[65]

So, parties and candidates, insofar as broadcast campaigning, were left to the allocation of free time by the Tribunal, as controlled by regulations.

> The Tribunal is required to grant a period of free time to each political party that: "(a) was represented by one or more members in the relevant Parliament or legislature immediately before the end of the last sittings ... held before the election; and (b) is contesting the election with at least the prescribed number of candidates." ... So far as is practicable, ... the amount of free time granted to each party should bear the same proportion to the total free time period as the number of formal first preference votes obtained by that party or its candidates at the last election ... bears to the total number of such votes obtained by all of the political parties ...
>
> In cases not provided for ... , the Tribunal is required to consider applications for the grant of free time. Subject to being satisfied that an applicant is a candidate for a Senate election and was a member of the Senate immediately before the end of the last sittings of the Senate before the election and is not a member of a party to whom a grant of time has been made ..., the Tribunal must grant the applicant free time ... not less than five per cent and not more than ten per cent of the total time in respect of the election. If the Tribunal is required to grant free time to two or more applicants ..., the time must be divided equally between or among them. Otherwise, the Tribunal has a discretion to grant free time to political parties and independent candidates on an application determined in accordance with the regulations.[66]

The statute was held to violate the implied right to freedom of political expression but it was not for the reasons it would have been in the United States. There was no reliance on the right of broadcasters to air ads of their choosing. Nor was the invalidation of the scheme based on the ban on

[65] 177 C.L.R. at 125–26 (opinion of Mason, C.J.) (quoting § 95B(6) of the Act).
[66] *Id.* at 126–27 (opinion of Mason, C.J.) (quoting § 95H(1) of the Act).

advertising by parties and candidates. The government had explained the rationale for that ban.

> The Commonwealth's ... principal purpose ... is to safeguard the integrity of the political system by reducing, if not eliminating, pressure on political parties and candidates to raise substantial sums of money in order to engage in political campaigning on television and radio, a pressure which renders them vulnerable to corruption and to undue influence by those who donate to political campaign funds.[67]

Not all of the justices addressed the issue directly, but the Chief Justice was willing to accept that rationale:

> I am prepared to assume that the purpose of Pt IIID is to safeguard the integrity of the political process by reducing pressure on parties and candidates to raise substantial sums of money, thus lessening the risk of corruption and undue influence. I am prepared also to assume that other purposes of Pt IIID are to terminate (a) the advantage enjoyed by wealthy persons and groups in gaining access to use of the airwaves; and (b) the "trivializing" of political debate resulting from very brief political advertisements. Moreover, I am prepared to accept that the need to raise substantial funds in order to conduct a campaign for election to political office does generate a risk of corruption and undue influence, that in such a campaign the rich have an advantage over the poor and that brief political advertisements may "trivialize" political debate.
>
> Given the existence of these shortcomings or possible shortcomings in the political process, it may well be that some restrictions on the broadcasting of political advertisements and messages could be justified.[68]

And, Justice Brennan agreed.

> The financial dependence of a political party on those whose interests can be served by the favours of government could cynically turn public debate into a cloak for bartering away the public interest. If Pt IIID tangibly minimizes the risk of political corruption, the restrictions it imposes on political advertising are clearly proportionate to that object of the law. Whether Pt IIID would tangibly minimize the risk of corruption was a political assessment. It was for the Parliament to make that assessment; it is for the Court to say whether the assessment could be reasonably made ...
>
> The principal advertisements affected by Pt IIID are television advertisements. It is not necessary to determine finally the contribution made by television advertising to the mass of information needed or desired by electors to form their political judgments, but it is impossible to conclude that the

[67] *Id.* at 129 (opinion of Mason, C.J.). [68] *Id.* at 144–45.

> Parliament could not reasonably make an adverse assessment of the information value of television advertising. Television advertising is brief; its brevity tends to trivialize the subject; it cannot deal in any depth with the complex issues of government. Its appeal is therefore directed more to the emotions than to the intellect . . .
>
> It was open to the Parliament to make a low assessment of the contribution made by electronic advertising to the formation of political judgments. It was open to the Parliament to conclude, as the experience of the majority of liberal democracies has demonstrated, that representative government can survive and flourish without paid political advertising on the electronic media during election periods.[69]

Justice Dawson took a similar view with regard to the value of political advertising on television.[70] Justice McHugh, on the other hand, stated disagreement on this issue.[71]

The statutory scheme was declared unconstitutional, not because of the limits on political advertisements, but because the allocation scheme created an uneven playing field. Those in power received more time than those who were not already in the legislature or were in the minority. The political parties that were represented in the preceding Parliament or legislature would receive 90 percent of the free time. And, the allocation rules favored the party or parties making up the government, since they likely received more first preference votes in the preceding election. As for individual candidates, a sitting senator seeking re-election gets preferential treatment over his or her opponent, an entitlement to free time as opposed to a discretionary grant.

[69] *Id.* at 159–61 (opinion of Brennan, J.).

[70] *See id.* at 189 (opinion of Dawson, J.).

> The object of the prohibition of political advertising was . . . to enhance rather than impair the democratic process. In any event, it must be remembered . . . that television advertising (which is of far greater significance than radio advertising) leads to the packaging of information into thirty or even fifteen second messages concerned with image rather than content. Of course, upon the assumption that political advertising imparts information which is capable of assisting in the making of an informed choice in an election, the prohibition clearly denies some information to electors. But the provision of information in the press and by other means is unimpeded. Even the electronic media have an undiminished capacity to present news reports, current affairs programs, editorial comment, and talkback radio programs all relating to political issues . . .
>
> In these circumstances, I am unable to conclude that the prohibition of political advertising which the legislation in question effects is incompatible with the constitutional requirement that an elector be able to make an informed choice in an election.

[71] *See id.* at 238 (opinion of McHugh, J.)("If the electoral process has been, or is likely to be, corrupted by the cost of television and radio advertising, means less drastic than the provisions of Pt IIID are available to eradicate the evil.").

Furthermore, there was no provision allowing participation by non-candidates or parties not putting candidates up for election, even though their ads also could not be aired. Trade associations, unions, social welfare groups, and farmers' organizations were all impacted. As the Chief Justice said,

> The consequence is that freedom of speech or expression on electronic media in relation to public affairs and the political process is severely restricted by a regulatory regime which evidently favours the established political parties and their candidates without securing compensating advantages or benefits for others who wish to participate in the electoral process or in the political debate which is an integral part of that process.[72]

Justices Deane and Toohey, in a joint opinion, expressed similar objections.

> When one turns to examine the difficult provisions of the Act dealing with the allocation of the remaining ten per cent of free time, it is apparent they are heavily weighted in favour of any other political parties or existing independent senators. It is at least possible that an independent candidate who was not a member of the previous Parliament or legislature would be unsuccessful in any application for free time ... [T]he overall effect of the provisions of Pt IIID is that all individual members of the community who are not "a candidate ... in the election" and all groups and organizations which are not "a political party [which] ... has endorsed one or more candidates" are excluded altogether from the allocation of free time ... Pt IIID of the Act distorts the freedom of political communication which underlies representative government and denies to the represented the opportunity of participating in the political debate by way of what is commonly seen as the most effective means of political communication.[73]

Justices Gaudron and McHugh also joined in the decision to declare the provisions unconstitutional. Justice Gaudron said "Even allowing that the persons who ... are shut out from radio and television broadcasts may avail themselves of the print media ..., the ban ... is a serious curtailment of their freedom of political discourse."[74] And, Justice McHugh failed to find a compelling justification in potential, or even existing, corruption and undue influence in the political process. Even if the costs of television advertising led to this impact, there had to be, in his view, less drastic means to ameliorate the problem.

Summing up the positions of the Justices, it appears that the High Court of Australia would have allowed the creation of a level playing field, by reducing

[72] *Id.* at 132 (opinion of Mason, C.J.).
[73] *Id.* at 172–74 (opinion of Deane and Toohey, J.J.).
[74] *Id.* at 221 (opinion of Gaudron, J.).

the heavy expense of broadcast advertising and the advantage that would have been enjoyed by wealthy participants or those with greater party treasuries.[75] The Court would have allowed the Parliament to make the judgment that brief broadcast advertisements were not the best way to inform the public, particularly in light of the competitive advantage it gave to those with means. What the Court would not allow was the creation of a new advantaged class, those already in power.

The United Kingdom

There is a case from the United Kingdom involving broadcast bans, but the challenge was not to the general validity of bans but the application of the law to the particular entity facing the ban. In *Regina v. Radio Authority*,[76] the Court of Appeal considered the application of Section 92 of the Broadcast Act of 1990[77] to Amnesty International British Section. The statutory section at issue prohibits any licensed service from including in its broadcasts "any advertisement which is inserted by or on behalf of any body whose objects are wholly or mainly of a political nature, (ii) any advertisement which is directed towards any political end."[78]

The Broadcast Authority, which regulates independent radio, concluded that the statute precluded advertising by Amnesty International, finding the organization to be mainly political. The Broadcast Authority's jurisdiction extended only to radio, but there was a similar provision directed toward television, and there was evidence that the Independent Television Commission took the same position with regard to the relevant statutory section and Amnesty International.

Amnesty International challenged the ruling of the Authority but did not argue that the ban on advertising by political organizations was a violation of the principle of free expression. Rather, the contention was that Amnesty International is not a mainly political body, so the statute should not apply. That became the focus of the opinions issued by the members of the court.

The ads at issue involved Amnesty International's campaign to bring to the people of the United Kingdom the plight of people in Rwanda and Burundi. The Radio Authority, drawing what might seem odd lines, concluded that

[75] This conclusion requires the votes of the justices who found no implied right to freedom of political speech. For these justices, with no right to be violated, the limitations could not be unconstitutional.

[76] R. v. Radio Authority Ex parte Bull, [1998] Q.B. 294.

[77] Broadcast Act 1990 (Eng.), www.legislation.gov.uk/ukpga/1990/42/section/166.

[78] *Id.* at § 92.

some of the goals of the campaign were not political, including putting an end to extrajudicial executions and disappearances and abolishing torture, while some were, including freeing all prisoners of conscience, ensuring prompt trials for political prisoners, and abolishing the death penalty. An overall examination of the campaign and the organization generally led the Radio Authority to conclude "we are unable to satisfy ourselves that the objects of Amnesty International cannot be said to be 'mainly of a political nature.' We conclude, therefore, that advertising by the organization may not be accepted."[79]

What may be most remarkable here is the scope of the prohibition. The advertisements at issue were not campaign ads. They were issue ads not even by inference advocating the election or defeat of any candidate or party. They focused solely on human rights, but the Authority took the position that a campaign for at least some human rights could be seen as political.

The Court did not question the statutory limits but focused solely on the application of it to Amnesty International. The issues were whether or not the Authority properly understood the definition of a mainly political organization and whether Amnesty international fit that definition. Amnesty International argued that promoting the observance of human rights is not political, because such rights are fundamental in international law and are recognized by the Charter of the United Nations. Lord Woolf, in his opinion, responded:

> The problem with this submission is that it makes no allowance for the fact that regrettably the laws and policies of many countries do not match the standards set by the United Nations Charter. To campaign to change those laws and policies so that they do comply with the Charter is political even though it is also commendable . . . [T]o promote education on human rights, if it is an objective in itself it is a non-political objective. On the other hand if awareness of human rights in a particular country is promoted with the objective of bringing pressure to bear upon a government so that it will change its policy, the activity becomes political.[80]

While the members of the Court might not have taken the same position as the Authority, they were unwilling to declare it void. The onus was on Amnesty International to show that it was not political, and the organization had failed to do so with such clarity that the Authority could be said to have misapplied the law. The Authority is a regulatory body made up of lay members charged to "do all that they can to secure that the rules . . . are

79 3 Q.B. at 301 (quoting a letter from the Radio Authority to Amnesty International).
80 *Id.* at 307–8 (opinion of Woolf, M.R.).

complied with."[81] "This rather unusual statutory provision does not create an absolute obligation but instead places an obligation to do its best."[82] The Authority was only required to act reasonably, and the Court could not find that it had failed to do so.

What would seem a harsh result was mitigated by the fact that Amnesty International could file another application. Given a new application, perhaps with better evidence, and the direction provided by the Court, the ads might be approved. But again, what is of greatest note is the extent of the ban on political advertising. It reaches far beyond campaigning for an elective position. It includes what would be considered pure issue advertisements taking political positions on issues of great public concern. It carries to a new level the concern that brief presentations on the broadcast media are not the best, or perhaps even an adequate, way to debate these issues.

New Zealand

New Zealand regulates election broadcasts through the Broadcasting Act of 1989.[83] Part 6, addressing parliamentary elections, prohibits election programs. Election programs are defined as those that encourage or persuade, or appear to do so, voters to vote for, or not to vote for a political party or candidate. The Act goes on to prohibit paid election programs.

(1) Except as provided in subsections (2) and (2A), no broadcaster shall permit the broadcasting, within or outside of election period, of an election programme.
(2) Nothing in subsection (1) applies in respect of
  (a) an opening address or closing address that is broadcast
    (i) for a political party or group of related political parties; and
    (ii) by TVNZ or RNZ during time allocated to that political party or group of related political parties . . .; or
  (b) an election programme broadcast for a political party or group of related political parties and paid for with money allocated to that political party or group of related political parties . . .; or
  (c) an election program—
    (i) broadcast for a fee or other consideration; and
    (ii) relating solely to 1 named constituency candidate at an election; and

[81] *Id.* at 303–4. [82] *Id.* at 309.
[83] Broadcasting Act 1989 (N.Z.), www.legislation.govt.nz/act/public/1989/0025/31.0/whole.html#DLM157416.

(iii) used or appearing to be used to promote or procure the election of the candidate; and
(iv) broadcast by the candidate or with the candidate's authority within the election period; or
(d) any advertisement placed by the Electoral Commission, a Registrar of Electors, a Returning Officer or other official . . .; or
(e) any non-partisan advertisement broadcast, as a community service, by the broadcaster.[84]

The Act also provides that TV New Zealand and Radio New Zealand will provide free time for broadcasting opening and closing addresses of political parties.[85] The Electoral Commission will also allocate money to the parties to use in the cost of production and broadcasting of electoral programs.[86] When parties or candidates buy broadcasting time, broadcasters must treat the parties equally and the candidates equally.[87]

Norway

Norway bans political ads on both television and radio.[88] There is a case from the European Court of Human Rights holding that a particular application of the statute violated Article 10 of the European Convention. *TV Vest AS and Rogaland Pensjonistparti v. Norway*[89] was an appeal of a fine imposed against a television broadcasting company for its broadcast of three paid advertisements explaining the views of, and soliciting votes for, the Pensioners Party. The Pensioners Party was a small party that had obtained only 1.3 percent of the votes, nationally, in recent local elections.

When the Court tested the limitation against Article 10, it found it wanting. The Court looked to Norway's justification for the statute.

> [T]he Court notes that the rationale for the statutory prohibition of broadcasters of political advertising through television was, as stated by the Supreme Court, the assumption that allowing the use of such a form and

84 *Id.* at § 70. 85 *Id.* at § 71.
86 *Id.* at §§ 74, 74A, 74B. The allocations are based on the numbers of all persons who voted for the party, the number of members of Parliament, relationships between political parties other indications of public support, and the need to provide fair opportunities for the parties to convey their policies to the public. *Id.* at § 75(2).
87 *Id.* at § 79B.
88 *See* Nick Thompson, *International Campaign Finances: How Do Countries Compare*, CNN World (Mar. 5, 2012), www.cnn.com/2012/01/24/world/global-campaign-finance/.
89 App. No. 21132/05 Eur. Ct. H.R. (2009), http://hudoc.echr.coe.int/eng?I=001–90235.

> medium of expression was likely to reduce the quality of political debate generally. In this way complex issues might easily be distorted and groups that were financially powerful would get greater opportunities for marketing their opinions than those that were not . . . Moreover, the prohibition had contributed to limiting election campaign costs, to reducing participants' donor dependence and ensuring a level playing field in elections. That was aimed at supporting the integrity of democratic processes, to obtain a fair framework for political and public debate and to avoid that those who were well endowed obtained an undesirable advantage to the possibility of using the most potent and pervasive medium.[90]

The Court found the justifications relevant but also concluded that they were not sufficient to justify the particular interference.

> [T]here is nothing to suggest that the Pensioners Party fell within the category of parties or groups that were the primary targets of the disputed prohibition, namely those which because of their relative financial strength might have obtained an unfair advantage over those less endowed by being able to spend most on broadcast advertising. On the contrary, while the Pensioners Party belongs to a category which the ban in principle was intended to protect, the Court . . . is not persuaded that the ban had the desired effect. In contrast to the major political parties, which were given a large amount of attention in the edited television coverage, the Pensioners Party was hardly mentioned. Therefore, paid advertising on television became the only way for the Pensioners Party to get its message across to the public through that type of medium.[91]

It was unacceptable that the statute put the Pensioners Party at such a disadvantage. The Court also noted that there was no contention that the specific advertising in any way lowered the quality of political debate. As a result there was a lack of proportionality between what the Court considered a legitimate aim and the means imposed.

Switzerland

Swiss law also prohibits political advertising to prevent powerful groups from gaining a competitive advantage. An application of that law to prohibit broadcasting commercials by an animal protection association campaigning against animal experimentation and battery cage farming was found to be in violation of Article 10 in *Verein Gegen Tierfabriken Schweiz v. Switzerland*.[92]

[90] *Id.* at ¶70. [91] *Id* at ¶72–73. [92] App. No. 32272/02, 52 Eur. H.R. Rep. 364 (2009).

There, the European Court held that Switzerland's blanket prohibition was disproportionate to its legitimate aims. The Court said that

> there is little scope under art. 10(2) of the Convention for restrictions on political speech or, as in this case, on debate of questions of public interest ... Moreover, the TV commercial concerned battery pig-farming. Accordingly, as it related to consumer health and to animal and environmental protection, it was undeniably in the public interest.[93]

The Court did not accept that the grounds offered to support the prohibition of political advertising justified the particular interference. The fact that those seeing the broadcast might find it unpleasant also could not justify the prohibition. "[F]reedom of expression is applicable not only to 'information' or 'ideas' that are favourably received or regarded as inoffensive or as a matter of indifference, but also to those that offend, shock or disturb."[94]

Japan

In Japan, political speech is said to be "most rigorously curtailed."[95] The Public Offices Election Act "prohibits door-to-door canvassing ... It places an almost total ban on distribution of pamphlets as well as on posting of written documents. Moreover it places severe limits on public meetings and gatherings. Because of these restrictions, the almost only permissible method of election campaign in Japan is limited to repeatedly announcing the names of candidates on sound-trucks."[96] Japanese campaigns are also limited to designated campaign periods out of concern that "wanton spending and campaign work might cause imbalance among candidates because of the unequal spending capacities, thus bringing about corruption of election."[97]

CONCLUSION

Even where political campaigns, activities that are at the heart of democracy, are involved, there is great variation among equally democratic countries. The differences, once again, come down to a belief in unbridled free expression compared to a belief that there are other values that must be balanced against free expression. The unbridled side leads to unlimited independent spending in support of candidates or issues, although even the United States allows

93 *Id.* at ¶92. 94 *Id.* at ¶96.

95 Shigenori Matsui, *Freedom of Expression in Japan*, 38 OSAKA UNIV. L. REV. 13, 23 (1991).

96 *Id.* at 24. 97 *Id.*

limits on contributions to candidates. Further, the unbridled side of the debate would not allow limits on the form campaigns may take. Limits on the ability of candidates to purchase broadcast time are not acceptable.

The side that favors balance is concerned that the wealthy not be allowed to dominate the election process. Not only would campaign contributions be limited, but independent expenditures in support of a candidate or party might also face limits. Limits on campaign broadcasts, either because of the costs they entail or because of the unsuitability of, usually short, election ads as a method to present issues and positions with any depth, are allowed. Instead, information is provided to voters through free broadcast time, usually in larger blocks of time and allocated not based on wealth but on some other measure.

Once again, either approach would seem consistent with democracy. Which approach a country takes may be an indication of the nature of the democracy in that country, but neither approach prevents a country from being a fully functioning democracy.

8

The Desecration of National Symbols and *Lèse Majesté*

There are two well-known lines of cases involving the desecration of national symbols. In the United States, the Supreme Court has protected the right to burn the flag, as a form of protest. In Germany, the Court has recognized the right of the state to protect the national flag and national anthem, even though in the two cases to do so, convictions were overturned as disparaging neither the flag nor the anthem. In addition to those two lines of cases, there is statutory and, in some countries, case law protecting either the flag or other national symbols. In some cases, that law is of the *lèse majesté* variety, protecting the monarch or head of state against insult. After examining the law, as it has developed in the United States and in Germany, consideration will turn to other democracies. As a part of that examination, there will be a suggested explanation of the differences among the democracies.

THE UNITED STATES AND GERMANY

The United States Flag Burning Cases

Texas v. Johnson[1] was the first of two United States Supreme Court cases protecting the right to destroy a flag as a means of political protest. The case resulted from a protest in Dallas during the 1984 Republican National Convention. Johnson and a group of others protested the policies of the Reagan administration and actions by some Dallas-based corporations. The protest ended at City Hall. There, Johnson doused an American flag

[1] 491 U.S. 397 (1989).

with kerosene and set it on fire, while protesters chanted "America, the red, white, and blue, we spit on you."[2]

Johnson was charged under a Texas statute that prohibited the desecration of venerated objects, providing: "A person commits an offense if he intentionally or knowingly desecrates ... a state or national flag."[3] The statute defined "desecrate" as to "deface, damage, or otherwise physically mistreat in a way that the actor knows will seriously offend one or more persons likely to observe or discover his action."[4] Johnson was convicted and sentenced to one year in prison and a fine of $2000. The Texas Court of Criminal Appeals found the result to be in violation of the First Amendment and overturned the conviction.[5]

When the case reached the Supreme Court, the Court agreed with the Texas Court of Criminal Appeals' conclusion that Johnson's conviction was inconsistent with the freedoms protected by the First Amendment. The Court first had to conclude that the defendant's conduct constituted expression, but since the conduct was intended to convey a particular message and it was likely that the message would be understood by those observing the conduct, it was expression for First Amendment purposes.[6]

When communicative conduct is the basis of prosecution, the constitutionality of any action is determined by a test set out in *United States v. O'Brien*.[7] As *O'Brien* recognized, the government may have an interest sufficient to allow the regulation of conduct, even when the conduct was intended to, and did, communicate a message. If the government's interest is in limiting the message itself, the attempt to suppress that message will have to meet the very difficult test applied to pure speech not mixed with conduct.[8] But, when the government's interest is in the conduct and not the message, a less strict test is used to justify the limit.[9]

Texas, hoping to be seen as interested in the conduct, rather than the message, argued that its interest was in preventing a breach of the peace. The Court, however, concluded that there was no evidence of any actual disturbance or even of the threat of a disturbance of the peace.[10] The state

[2] 491 U.S. at 399. The flag had been taken from a flagpole at one of the targeted buildings, but by a protester other than Johnson. *See id.* Johnson was not charged with receiving stolen property or any of the other illegal activities engaged in by some of the protesters.

[3] Texas Penal Code Ann. §42.09(a) (West 1989). [4] *Id.* at §42.09(b).

[5] 755 S.W.2d 92 (Tex. Crim. App. 1988). [6] *See* 491 U.S. at 404.

[7] 391 U.S. 367 (1968). [8] *See* 491 U.S. at 406.

[9] The test, known as the *O'Brien* test, asks, when the interest is not in the message but in the conduct, if there is an important or substantial governmental interest and if the restriction is not greater than is essential to further that interest. *See* 391 U.S. at 377.

[10] *See* 491 U.S. at 408.

then fell back on an interest in "preserving the flag as a symbol of nationhood and national unity."[11] The problem with that interest is that it is based in the message rather than the conduct. As the Court noted, there is nothing inherently wrong with burning a United States flag; it is the preferred method of disposing of a tattered or dirty flag.[12] The charge against Johnson was brought under a statute that required that his actions would cause serious offense.[13] Serious offense would be found only in the communicative impact of his otherwise acceptable conduct. The state's interest was, therefore, content-based,[14] and that interest would be tested under "the most exacting scrutiny."[15]

Not deterred by facing strict scrutiny, Texas argued that its interest in preserving the flag as a symbol of the nation and of national unity was sufficient to pass that test; it asserted that the flag occupies a "special place" in our nation.[16]

> According to Texas, if one physically treats the flag in a way that would tend to cast doubt on either the idea that nationhood and national unity are the flag's referents or that national unity actually exists, the message conveyed thereby is a harmful one and therefore may be prohibited.[17]

The Court rejected that claim, responding "If there is a bedrock principle underlying the First Amendment, it is that the government may not prohibit the expression of an idea simply because society finds the idea itself offensive or disagreeable."[18] There would be no exception for the flag.[19] The Court explained "We do not consecrate the flag by punishing its desecration, for in doing so we dilute the freedom that this cherished emblem represents."[20]

There were four justices who dissented. Chief Justice Rehnquist, joined in his dissent by Justices White and O'Connor, argued that the flag's unique position justifies its protection.

> The American flag, ... throughout more than 200 years of our history, has come to be the visible symbol embodying our Nation. It does not represent the views of any particular political party, and it does not represent any particular political philosophy. The flag is not simply another "idea" or "point of view" competing for recognition in the marketplace of ideas. Millions and millions of Americans regard it with an almost mystical reverence regardless of what sort of social, political, or philosophical beliefs they may have.[21]

[11] *Id.* at 407. [12] *See id.* at 411. [13] *See id.* [14] *See id.* at 411–12.
[15] *Id.* at 412 (quoting Boos v. Barry, 485 U.S. 312, 321 (1988)). [16] *See id.* at 413. [17] *Id.*
[18] *Id.* at 414. [19] *Id.* [20] *Id.* at 420. [21] *Id.* at 429 (Rehnquist, C.J., dissenting).

This role of the flag, and the fact that the statute "deprived Johnson of only one rather inarticulate symbolic form of protest" led the Chief Justice Rehnquist to conclude that the conviction was constitutional.[22]

A second dissent, one written by Justice Stevens, found similar value in the flag.

> A country's flag is a symbol of more than "nationhood and national unity." It also signifies the ideas that characterize the society that has chosen that emblem as well as the special history that has animated the growth and power of those ideas … The value of the flag as a symbol cannot be measured.[23]

There was a strong political reaction to the Court's decision. That led Congress to pass the Flag Protection Act of 1989, which, provided: "Whoever knowingly mutilates, defaces, physically defiles, burns, maintains on the floor or ground, or tramples upon any flag of the United States shall be fined … or imprisoned for not more than one year, or both."[24] The act included a provision that the act was not intended to prohibit conduct involved in disposing of a worn or soiled flag.[25]

This effort did no better at the Supreme Court than had the Texas statute. In *United States v. Eichman*, the Court rejected the government's claim that it was interested in the flag's physical integrity; the only interest the Court saw in a privately owned flag would "rest[] upon a perceived need to protect the flag's status as a symbol of our Nation and certain national ideals."[26] Moreover, the Court rejected the view that flag burning interfered with the association between the flag and the Nation.[27] The Court saw no real difference between the congressional and the Texas statutes. "[T]he Act still suffers from the same fundamental flaw: It suppresses expression out of concern for its likely communicative impact."[28]

The four justices who dissented in *Johnson* also dissented in *Eichman*, but this time there was only a single dissent written by Justice Stevens. The dissent expressed sentiments similar to those in the *Johnson* dissents and also suggested that the earlier decision had had a negative impact.

> Burning a flag is not, of course, equivalent to burning a public building. Assuming that the protester is burning his own flag, it causes no physical harm to other persons or to their property. The impact is purely symbolic, and it is apparent that some thoughtful persons believe that impact, far from

[22] *Id.* at 432. [23] *Id.* at 436–37 (Stevens, J., dissenting).
[24] 18 U. S. C. § 700(a)(1) (1988 ed. Supp. I). [25] *See id.* at (a)(2).
[26] 496 U.S. 310, 316 (1990). [27] *Id.* [28] *Id.* at 317.

> depreciating the value of the symbol, will actually enhance its meaning. I most respectfully disagree. Indeed, what makes these cases particularly difficult for me is what I regard as the damage to the symbol that has already occurred as a result of this Court's decision to place its stamp of approval on the act of flag burning.[29]

Despite the narrow victory on the side of free expression, it is clear that the United States recognizes a constitutionally protected right to burn the flag as a means of protest.

The German Flag and National Anthem Cases

The German flag desecration case was the result of the publication of a paperback book titled, in English translation, *Just Leave me in Peace*.[30] The book's content was a combination of prose and poetry expressing anti-military sentiments. That was, however, not the basis for the charges that were brought. The objections were, instead, with regard to the back cover, which consisted of a two-picture collage. The lower half of the cover was a photo of a swearing-in ceremony for the German Armed Forces, with soldiers holding a spread out German flag. The upper half was a photo of a male urinating. The photos were juxtaposed so that the man appeared to be urinating on the flag; a yellow stream of urine flowed from the top photo onto the flag in the lower and into a puddle on the ground below the flag.

The manager of the company that distributed the book was charged with violating a section of the German Criminal Code that prohibited the "Disparagement of the State and its Symbol." The section provided:

> Whosoever publicly, in a meeting or through the dissemination of writings . . .
>
> (1.) 1. Insults or maliciously maligns the Federal Republic of Germany or one of its Lands or its constitutional order; or 2. disparages the colors, flag, coat of arms or anthem of the Federal Republic of Germany, shall be punished with imprisonment for not more than three years or a fine . . .[31]

The manager was convicted and fined, and he appealed, eventually reaching the Constitutional Court.

[29] *Id.* at 323 (Stevens, J., dissenting).

[30] BVerfGE 81, 278, 1 BvR 266/86 and 913/87, Mar. 7, 1990). The case may be found in translation at https://law.utexas.edu/transnational/foreign-law-translations/german/case.php?id=632.

[31] Criminal Code (Strafgesetzbuch) §90(a). The section called for enhanced punishment of up to five years imprisonment if the act was done intentionally to support efforts against the continued existence of the country or its constitutional principles. *See id.* at §90(a)(3).

The appeal was based on a claim that the conviction violated individual rights guaranteed under the German Basic Law. The free expression provisions of the Basic Law, in Article 5, provides in Section 1 that all persons enjoy the right to free expression. Section 2, however, allows certain statutory restrictions on the Section 1 rights. Section 3 protects art, scholarship, research, and teaching. Because of the placement of the limiting provision, Section 2, after Section 1 but before Section 3, Section 2 has been held not to apply to rights protected under Section 3.[32]

Art may still be subject to limitations, but only constitutional values can justify such restrictions. The German Court decided that the back cover was art, saying that a collage is a conventional art form.[33] "The work's creator makes an original statement capable of, and requiring, interpretation through the ... relationship of the photographs to one another ... He expressed his view of the oath-taking ceremony through free, creative invention."[34] While the art also expressed opinion and was the artwork of a person other than the defendant, that did not matter.

As art, a limitation on the back cover would have to be justified through a constitutional value, and the Court found such a value in Article 22 of the Basic Law. Article 22 simply sets out the colors of the German flag, but the Court found more implied in the provision.

> [T]his basic legal provision is significant insofar as it assumes the right of the state to use such symbols to portray itself. It is the purpose of these symbols to appeal to the citizens' sense of civic responsibility ... As a free state, the Federal Republic relies rather on the identification of its citizens with the basic values represented by the flag. The values protected in this sense are represented by the state colours, stipulated in art. 22 ... They stand for the free democratic constitutional structure ... The flag serves as an important integration device through the leading state goals it embodies; its disparagement can thus impair the necessary authority of the state.[35]

While this is a clear statement of the authority of the state to protect its flag from desecration, the Court overturned the conviction. The Court said that the lower courts misinterpreted the collage. In the view of the Court, the collage was a caricature or a satirical portrayal, and the nature of such a work is to exaggerate, distort, and de-familiarize.[36] Where artwork of this sort is involved, the core statement of the art and its form must be distinguished, and the Court said that the lower court had misinterpreted the core statement.

[32] The free speech provisions of the German Basic Law are discussed in Chapter 1. The special treatment of art is discussed in Chapter 2.

[33] *See* BVerfGE 81, 278 at II. 1. a. [34] *Id.* [35] *Id.* at II, 2, b. [36] *See id.* at II, 3, aa.

> [T]he ceremony of oath to the flag ... was mere form ... The caricature expresses primarily an anti-militaristic, and only in this respect anti-state, tendency. It is directed against the governmental ceremony for swearing in of soldiers, and it thereby expresses disapproval, if not abhorrence, of the military service. The illustration did show a state symbol which is assigned a degrading treatment; however, neither statehood in general, nor the broader constitutional structure of the Federal Republic is attacked thereby.[37]

While the Court said that the state has the authority to protect the flag from desecration, the collage did not desecrate the flag.

The national anthem case was handled in much the same way.[38] The same section of the criminal code that protects the flag also protects the national anthem, so the charges were similar. The charges were based on a text appearing in the magazine *Howler*. The words of *Deutschland Uber Allos* were modified to focus on ills thought to be problems in German society. The magazine's editor was convicted and sentenced to four months in prison, and the magazines were confiscated.

On appeal, the Court found a violation of article 5(3).[39] The Court said that the substituted lyrics constitute art, because they were a form of poetry. The fact that they might be seen as poor poetry was immaterial.

> The author uses the forms of poetry in order to communicate his experiences and impressions of certain events in life which one could summarize under the title "Everyday German Life." Since a qualitative restriction of the term of art is not reconcilable with the comprehensive guarantee of liberty in art. 5 (3), first sentence GG, the "level" of the poetry does not matter in the process of constitutional classification and evaluation.[40]

Just as in the flag case, the Court found that the lower court, in trying to protect the anthem from disparagement, misinterpreted the art.

> The core-statement takes the form of a take-off of the Deutschland Song in which use of the verse's meter, phonetic approximation and defamiliarization of the original text turn that text's idealizations into exaggerated negative descriptions of our reality; they are reversed to become their exact opposite. The regional court completely neglects this conceivable core-statement of

[37] *Id.*

[38] BVerfGE 81, 298, 1 BvR 1215/87, Mar. 7, 1990. The case may be found in translation at www.utexas.edu/law/academics/centers/transnational/work_new/german/case.php?id=631.

[39] The Court also saw a problem in the statutory reference to the national anthem. It concluded that not all three verses are afforded protection. It is only the third verse that is sung at state occasions, so only that verse should be considered the national anthem. *See id.* at B, II.

[40] *Id.* at B, I, 2, a.

> the satire – the denunciation of contradictions between claim and reality. It therefore inevitably reaches the conclusion that the song was meant to disparage the anthem of the Federal Republic of Germany and this state itself, without considering whether – on the contrary – the ideals represented within the anthem and constitutional order should actually be made more effective through the drastic portrayal of reality.[41]

So, here too, the conviction was overturned, while the constitutionality of the provision protecting the flag and the national anthem was not denied.

Militant vs. Procedural Democracy

It has been argued that the difference between the United States view that burning a flag, as a means of protest, is constitutionally protected and the German position that, despite the outcomes of the cases, the flag and anthem should be protected is due to differences in the concept of democracy in the two countries. "Perhaps the United States and Germany have different concepts of democracy. While the American concept of democracy is based on the spirit of popular sovereignty, the German concept is based on the notion that the democratic state needs to defend its own foundations."[42]

Germany has what has been referred to as a "militant democracy." Judith Wise says that Germany's militant democracy is an example of a "substantive democracy," as opposed to the United States' "procedural democracy."[43]

> Procedural democrats view democracy as a set of institutional arrangements, a framework for decision-making which does not prescribe the content of the decisions ... [P]rocedural democracy rests on faith that rational discourse ensures liberty ... Proceduralists rely on free speech to counter anti-democratic speech.
>
> The substantive democrat rejects the proceduralist claim that a democracy must allow itself to become undemocratic if the majority so desires ... [S]ubstantive democrats prioritize the long-term survival of democratic form over the political rights of the anti-democratic actors.[44]

41 *Id.* at B, 3.

42 Ute Krüdewagen, *Political Symbols in Two Constitutional Orders: The Flag Desecration Decisions of the United States Supreme Court and the German Federal Constitutional Court*, 19 Ariz. J. Int'l & Comp. L. 679, 704 (2002).

43 Judith Wise, *Dissent and the Militant Democracy: The German Constitution and the Banning of the Free German Workers Party*, 5 U. Chi. L. Sch. Roundtable 301 (1998).

44 *Id.* at 305.

It is this same militant democracy that Professor Wise sees as being the theory behind Article 21, Section 2 of the German Basic Law that allows bans on anti-democratic political parties.[45] This explanation of the differences between German and United States law in this area makes sense, if the comparison is limited to those two countries. But when the examination is expanded to include other countries, it does not hold up as well.

Germany did, in a sense, give up democracy through the democratic process. A party was elected that imposed anti-democratic measures. A militant democracy approach might be a reasonable reaction to try to assure that this internal abrogation of democracy did not happen again. On the other hand, as will be shown in the next section, there are countries that also protect their national symbols that did not experience this same internal anti-democratic history. The Czech Republic, as part of Czechoslovakia, may have been non-democratic during World War II and the Cold War, but it did not give up democracy in the same way that Germany did in the 1930s. Its provisions barring disrespect for national symbols must come from a different motivation. Neither did Finland parallel the German experience. French law protecting the flag also would seem not to be motivated by militant democracy. France was invaded by Germany and the experience during the occupation was certainly non-democratic, but there is no recent trend toward anti-democratic government that would require the same protection as in Germany. Even if that had been a concern immediately after the war, it was not, as will be seen, until much later that France's flag protection law was adopted. And, New Zealand's flag protection statute, even though weakened through interpretation, was presumably not motivated by a militant democracy view, since there seemingly has never been a threat to democracy there. It may be that Spain, having its own fascist past, could have had motivation similar to that of Germany in protecting its national symbols, but even here, there may be a better explanation.

THE MEANING OF NATIONAL IDENTITY

A better understanding of the differences between the United States and Germany regarding the treatment of the national flag might be gained from, as it were, increasing the data set to include other countries. The countries that will be added to the consideration, many of the European democracies, as well as Canada, Japan, Australia, and New Zealand, are almost all included as

[45] *See id.* This issue is discussed in Chapter 6.

fully functioning democracies in the *Democracy Index 2012* of *The Economist* magazine.[46] There are, however, countries that will be considered that are not on that list, countries that are considered flawed democracies. The added countries are Portugal, France, Slovenia, and Greece, all of which were listed as full democracies in earlier versions of the *Index*.[47] Having already considered the differences between the United States and Germany, it is clear that fully functioning democracies can take different views with regard to their national symbols. The addition of other democracies serves not to establish that differences may exist but to provide additional data to try to explain the basis for those different views.

Ethnic vs. Political Identity

A distinction may be drawn between countries with and those without an ethnic identification, even if there are countries where it may not be clear into which class they fit. There are certainly countries with no ethnic identification. The United States provides an example; although Native Americans may claim an ethnic identification, for most Americans, their ethnic identification comes from their countries of ancestry. Identification with the United States is a political identification. Indeed, an American who is asked about his or her ethnicity and responds "American" is likely to be seen as making a political point having to do with either immigration or a belief that Americans ought not to be categorized by race or ethnicity.

The same would seem true of Canada, again with the exception of people of the First Nations. Combining the two countries, consider an individual, two of whose grandparents came from Ireland to the United States, with the other two coming from Canada. If asked about his ethnicity, he might well claim to be half Irish, but claiming to be of half Canadian ethnicity would seem odd. It

[46] *See* The Economist Intelligence Unit, *Democracy Index 2012: Democracy at a Standstill*, available at https://portoncv.gov.cv/dhub/porton.por_global.open_file?p_doc_id=1034http://portoncv.gov.cv/dhub'porton.por.global.open.file?pdocid=1034.

[47] *See, e.g.*, Laza Kekic, *The Economist Intelligent Unit's Index of Democracy* (2006 Index), available at www.economist.com/media/pdf /democracy_index_2007_v3.pdf. It has been suggested that the decline in democracy scores in Europe has been the result of the global financial crisis, leading to an erosion in confidence in democracy in the face of strong austerity measures and an increasing role of technocrats in government. *See* Kavitha A. Davidson, *Democracy Index 2013: Global Democracy at a Standstill, The Economist Intelligence Unit's Annual Report Shows*, THE HUFFINGTON POST (Mar. 21, 2013), www.huffingtonpost.com/2013/03/21/democracy-index-2013-economist-intelligence-unit_n_2909619.html. Since the decline in democracy scores seems unrelated to any issue regarding treatment of national symbols, it seems reasonable to continue to include the countries with the recent drop.

is more likely that the individual would look to the original ethnicity of the grandparents from Canada. The same is true of Australians and New Zealanders, again with exceptions for those with ancestry in the original populations.

On the other hand, "German," "French," and "Greek" are not only political identifiers. They are ethnic identifiers as well. They are not only a matter of political affiliation. They also represent cultural, and even genetic, identification. It may be true that "American" or "Canadian" can also be seen as cultural identifiers, but it seems weaker in countries the nonpolitical culture of which is a mixture of cultures, than in countries with a single ethnic identity and a long history of a more singular culture.

In a country for which the identification is primarily political, an attack on the flag or some other national symbol would seem more likely to be seen as political speech. Rather than aimed at the people, the ethnic population, and culture, it would be seen as indicating disagreement with the political leadership of the country. Where a country does have an ethnic identity, desecration of the flag or other national symbols may be seen as something other than political dissent. It may be seen as aimed not at government but at the people, as an attack on the nation rather than those in political power.

This distinction also finds support in the *lèse majesté* statutes. Several of the countries with ethnic identities prohibit insult to the head of state. It is important to note that these statutes protect not the head of government but the head of state. Denying people the right to criticize those in political power would certainly be inconsistent with democracy. A *lèse majesté* statute can escape that same criticism if it is not directed at criticism of government but is seen as directed at protecting the nation itself, the state, in countries in which the monarch or the president has a largely ceremonial role.

Countries where Identification is Political

The United States

The United States fits this category. It is a nation of immigrants, where ethnic identity, again with the exception of Native Americans, is with the county or countries of one's ancestors. An attack on the flag, as was the case in *Johnson*, is political in nature. It is more a complaint against the political leadership than a criticism of the American people. Where it is criticism of the people, it is most likely to be against the policies the people may be seen as having endorsed through the electoral process. Even here, it would seem best seen as political. Thus, the United States fits the model of countries with primarily political identification allowing attacks on national symbols as a means of political protest.

Australia

Australia does not have a law prohibiting burning or otherwise desecrating the flag. The Flags Act of 1953 does give the Governor-General the authority to promulgate rules "for the guidance of persons in connexion with the flying or use of flags . . ."[48] Whether or not the authority to provide guidance includes a right to impose criminal sanctions, there are no criminal prohibitions.[49] Flag burning may run afoul of other laws, such as prohibitions on the destruction of property, where the burner is not the flag's owner, or public order provisions, that would be violated if the act causes a breach of the peace.[50] There are also prohibitions on using national, state, or territorial symbols in an attempt to impersonate officials.[51]

There have been flag burnings in Australia, and they have led to calls to provide protection. One such event occurred in 2008 on Australia Day, called "Invasion Day" by the Aboriginal population.[52] Despite the fact that this clearly was a political protest, it did lead a member of Parliament to propose a flag desecration statute.[53] This was, in fact, not the first attempt to provide for the protection of the flag. The Protection of Australian Flags (Desecration of the Flag) Bill of 2003 would have criminalized "the desecration, dishonouring or destruction of the Australian National Flag" and a number of Australian ensigns.[54] The bill set out the history of such attempts dating back to 1953.[55] Still another attempt was made in 2006,[56] but neither the 2003 nor the 2006 bill was passed.

It would be an interesting issue as to whether or not such a prohibition would be constitutional in Australia. There is an implied right to freedom of political speech based in the constitutional provision for a democratic society.[57] Such an implied freedom might well protect political protests involving the desecration of the Australian flag, but this is a matter of debate. In a speech in support

48 Flags Act, 1953 §7 (Austl.).

49 *See* Caslon Analytics Note: Flag Burning, www.caslon.com/au/flagfiresnote1.htm.

50 *See id.* 51 *See id.*

52 *See PM Called on to Outlaw Flag-Burning*, ABC News (Jan. 29, 2008), www.abc.net.au/news/stories/2008-01-29/pm-called-on-to-outlaw-flag-burning/1026430.

53 *See id.*

54 *See* Jennifer Norberry, Information and Research Services, *Protection of Australian Flags (Desecration of the Flag) Bill of* 2003, Bills Digest No. 42 (2003–2004) at 15, available at www.aph.gov.au/binaries/library/pubs/bd/2003-04/04bd042.pdf (hereinafter *Protection of Australian Flags*).

55 *See id.*

56 *See* Protection of the Australian National Flag (Desecration of the Flag) Bill, 2006, www.comlaw.gov.au/Details/C2006800037.

57 *See* Australian Capital Television Pty. v. Commonwealth (1992), 177 CLR 106 (Austl.). The case is discussed in Chapter 1.

of her 2006 bill, Bronwyn Bishop argued that there was no constitutional violation, because there are alternative ways in which the political point can be made.[58] On the other hand, Prime Minister Howard concluded that flag desecration should not be made a criminal offense, because it is the expression of political opinion.[59]

Flag burning is, then, protected in Australia. This may or may not be required as a part of the protection of political speech implied under the Australian Constitution. But even if it is not protected by the constitution, Australia seems to have concluded that it is important to allow this form for the expression of political dissent, as shown by the rejection of attempts to criminalize such acts.

Canada

Canadian law contains no prohibition on flag burning or desecration, although there have been attempts to impose such bans. A 2001 bill would have provided, "Every one who, without lawful excuse, willfully burns, defaces, defiles, mutilates, tramples upon or otherwise desecrates the national flag of Canada is guilty of an offence . . .," with the penalty being a fine.[60] The bill was a private member's bill and was discussed before the Sub-Committee on Private Members' Business of the Standing Committee on Procedure and House Affairs. The sponsor was given five minutes to convince the committee that the bill should be put forward for a vote.[61] The sponsor said he had been approached by members of the Royal Canadian Legion concerned about desecration of both the Canadian and Québec flags.[62] Although he recognized the argument that the law might be seen to violate Canada's protection for free expression, he argued, "I believe that in fact this is not an expression of speech. If someone has a disagreement with our government or governments in the future, I think most Canadians would agree that defiling the flag is not an appropriate way to express that displeasure."[63]

58 *See* House of Representatives, Protection of the Australian National Flag (Desecration of the Flag) Bill 2006, First Reading, Speech 34 (Mar. 27, 2006).

59 *See Flag Burning Not Criminal, Says PM*, THE AGE.COM.AU (Jan. 27, 2006), www.theage.com .au/news/national/flag-burning-not-criminal-says-pm/2006/01/27/1138066948667.html.

60 An Act to Amend the Criminal Code (desecration of the Canadian flag), 2001 H.C. Bill [C-330].

61 *See* Canada Parliament, Edited Hansard, Committee Evidence, Sub-Committee on Private Members' Business of the Standing Committee on Procedure and House Affairs, 37th Parl., 1st Sess. (Mar. 19, 2002), www.parl.gc.ca/HousePublications/Publication.aspx?Language=E&Mode=1&Parl=37&Ses=a&DocId=138543#OOB-176920.

62 *See id.* 63 *Id.*

The sponsor also had an opportunity to request that the bill be read a second time and referred by the House of Commons to a committee. He recognized that the bill would be unsuccessful: "This is a non-votable bill and it will die, but the sentiment of the bill should not go that way."[64] In response to the sponsor's arguments in favor of the bill, a Bloc Québecois Member of Parliament offered the following.

> Quebecers, all differing in their language, culture and institutions, also differ in their sense of belonging to a nation, which causes them to define their ties to Canada quite differently than other Canadians. The Canadian flag does not resonate the same way in Québec as it does in Alberta, for example ... I understand what prompts some members ... to call for this type of legislation. However, there is no guarantee, and I am not convinced that criminalizing the desecration of the flag will bring people to respect the Canadian flag, or any of the provincial flags for that matter.[65]

Another critic of the bill expressed free expression concerns: "[T]he actions Bill C-330 would prohibit amount to little more than expression of political opinion ... If the government were to prohibit such actions against our national flag what other symbol of our nation should be so protected? Would the Maple leaf be next? Where would we draw the line?"[66]

The bill did not come to a vote, but that was not the end of the issue. In 2002, there were two more attempts to enact flag desecration laws. The first was quite similar to the earlier attempt, providing fines for damage or willful destruction.[67] The second contained the same sort of prohibitions, but added penalties of up to one year imprisonment for a first offense and up to three years for subsequent offenses.[68] The second bill also defined "national flag" to include not only the Canadian flag but provincial and territorial flags and national flags of any other country.[69] Both bills, again, private members, bills, never came to a vote, with conflicting views expressed in debate regarding the conflict between the sanctity of the flag and free expression.[70]

It is worth pointing out that, while there is not an ethnic identification with Canada, there may be a sense of ethnic identity in the province of Quebec.

64 *Id.* at 1825 (statement of Mr. Roy Bailey).
65 *Id.* at 1840 (statement of Ms. Christiane Gagnon).
66 *Id.* at 1900 (statement of Mr. Paul Harold Macklin).
67 *See* An Act to amend the Criminal Code (destruction or desecration of national flag), H.C. Bill, 2001–2002 (C-426).
68 *See* An Act to amend the Criminal Code (destruction of national flag), H.C. Bill, 2001–2002 (C-429).
69 *See id.*
70 *See* 37 Parl. Deb., H.C. (2002); EDITED HANSARD, N37 Parl. Deb. (2002) 204, 1730.

That population, while not purely so, is significantly French. That might lead to a different view of an attack on the provincial flag; it would not be solely political but might be seen as an attack on the Quebecois people. That might make it more likely that there would be a provincial statute protecting the Quebec flag. The lack of such a statute may be the result of recognition that it would be inconsistent with opposition, as expressed by the Bloc Quebecois member of Parliament, to protection of the national flag.

New Zealand

The situation in New Zealand is complicated by the status of the freedom of expression in that country.[71] There is a statute that protects the flag.

> Every person commits an offense against this Act who,–
>
> (a) without lawful authority, alters the New Zealand Flag by the placement thereon of any letter, emblem, or representation:
>
> (b) in or within view of any public place, uses, displays, destroys, or damages the New Zealand Flag in any manner with the intention of dishonouring it.[72]

There is, however, a case that raises a question with regard to the strength of the provision.

Hopkinson v. Police[73] resulted from a 2003 protest on the grounds of Parliament. The Prime Minister of Australia was visiting New Zealand, and Hopkinson burned the flag of New Zealand to protest Australia's support of the United States in Iraq. He was convicted and fined. On appeal, he claimed that the conviction violated his right to the freedom of expression under Section 14 of the New Zealand Bill of Rights Act of 1990, which provides: "Everyone has the right to freedom of expression, including the freedom to seek, receive, and impart information and opinions of any kind in any form."[74]

While the New Zealand High Court, in a single-judge decision, overturned the conviction, it seems to have left the law partially intact. The Court did not have the authority, because of Section 4 of the Bill of Rights Act, to invalidate the statute, even if it concluded that the Flags Act was in conflict with the Bill of Rights Act's protection of expression. The Court was able, however, to draw

[71] The operation of the New Zealand Bill of Rights Act is discussed in Chapter 1.

[72] Flags, Emblems, and Names Protection Act 1981 Section 11(1), Public Act 1981 No 47 (N.Z.), www.legislation.govt.nz/act/public/1981/0047/latest/whole.html.

[73] [2004] 3 NZLR 704 (H.C.).

[74] New Zealand Bill of Rights Act 1990, Public Act 1990 No 109 (Aug. 28, 1990), § 14, www.legislation.govt.nz/act/public/1990/0109/latest/DLM225513.html.

guidance from Sections 5 and 6 of the Bill of Rights Act. Section 5 provides: "Subject to section 4, the rights and freedoms contained in this Bill of Rights may be subject only to such reasonable limits prescribed by law as can be demonstrably justified in a free and democratic society."[75] And, Section 6 provides: "Wherever an enactment can be given a meaning that is consistent with the rights and freedoms contained in this Bill of Rights, that meaning shall be preferred to any other meaning."[76]

Section 5, then, provided the test for whether or not this limit on free expression could be justified; was it a "reasonable limit[] ... as can be demonstrably justified in a free and democratic society"?[77] The Court, while recognizing the importance of preserving the flag, held that the blanket limitations in the Flag Act were not rationally connected to the objective.[78] Yet, the Court still could not declare the act invalid.

What the Court did, as directed by Section 6, was provide an interpretation under which the Flags Act and the Bill of Rights Act would not conflict, at least under the facts of the case. The Court determined that the only acts barred by the Flag Act were those that "vilify" the flag, and that the defendant's actions had not done so. "That would have required some additional action on the appellant's part beyond a symbolic burning of the flag."[79] The Court did not indicate the sort of the action that would constitute vilification, but it has been suggested that the Court might have had in mind the acts mentioned in the appellant's submission, "such conduct as urinating on the ashes of the flag or knowingly blowing one's nose on it."[80]

The result in New Zealand is flag protection that is very limited in its impact. In a 2008 case, an individual discharged a cartridge into a New Zealand flag.[81] The defendant was charged only with carrying a firearm in a public place with no lawful purpose. The court noted that the prosecution did not pursue a charge under the Flags Act, because of the decision in *Hopkinson*.[82] There are also cases in which Maoris have burned the New Zealand flag, as part of protests seeking a new national flag not derived from the flag of

[75] New Zealand Bill of Rights Act 1990, Public Act 1990 No 109 (Aug. 28, 1990), § 5, www.legislation.govt.nz/act/public/1990/0109/latest/DLM225501.html.

[76] New Zealand Bill of Rights Act 1990, Public Act 1990 No 109 (Aug. 28, 1990), § 6, www.legislation.govt.nz/act/public/1990/0109/latest/DLM225502.html.

[77] *See supra* note 75. [78] *See* [2004] 3 NZLR 704 ¶¶ 50, 77. [79] *Id.* at ¶ 81–82.

[80] Sigrid Bridgette Buschbacher, *Protection of Public Symbols in New Zealand and the United States of America: Flag Burning Versus Freedom of Expression*, 2 NZ Postgrad. L. e-J 29 (2005), www.nzpglejournal.auckland.ac.nz/webdav/site/nzpglejournal/shared/Subscribe/Documents/2005-2/3%20Siggi's%20Final.pdf.

[81] *See* R. v. Iti, [2007] NZCA 119 (Apr. 4, 2007). [82] *See id.* at ¶ 63.

the United Kingdom, seemingly without even arrest.[83] Thus, while the Flags Act is still on the books, New Zealand seems to have de facto protection of flag desecration as a means of political protest, so long as it doesn't meet the level of vilification.

Belgium

It may seem odd to include Belgium as a country with political, rather than ethnic, identification. But in a sense, there is not a single Belgian ethnicity. The country has regions dominated by its Flemish and Walloon populations. This, in fact, appears to be a less than completely amicable union. In 2011, Belgium's King Albert demanded an end to political disputes between the Flemings and Walloons that had left the country without an elected government for over a year.[84] The division even led a majority of voters in Flanders to support the eventual breakup of the country.[85] So, Belgium might be seen as a federation of two peoples. An attack on the national flag may be seen not as an attack on either population but as criticism of the combined government.

In any case, it appears that there is no law prohibiting flag desecration in Belgium. At least, there was a flag burning in July 2007, and the report does not mention any prosecution.[86] There was also a claim by the organization involved that the act was not in violation of Belgian law.[87] While protection of the monarch might be seen in Article 88 of the Belgian Constitution which provides that "[t]he King's person is inviolable ...", it may not be clear just what is prohibited. A 2007 Radio Nederland report on a Netherlands conviction for insulting its queen contrasted Netherlands law with that of Belgian, saying: "According to the Belgians, laws protecting freedom of speech take priority over tackling insults to the monarchy."[88] The same article indicates that the royal family, if it "feels offended," must resort to the same justice

83 *See, e.g.*, *Protesters Burn New Zealand Flag*, TVNZ: ONE NEWS, Feb. 6, 2010), http://tvnz.co.nz/national-news/protesters-burn-new-zealand-flag-3349623.

84 *See* Bruno Waterfield, *Squabbles between Flemish and Walloons Could Bring Down EU, Warns Belgian King*, THE TELEGRAPH (Jul. 20, 2011), www.telegraph.co.uk/news/world news/Europe/Belgium/space 8650524/ Squabbles-between-Flemish-and-Walloons-Could-Bring-Down-EU-Warns-Belgian-King.html.

85 *See id.*

86 *See Les Jeunes N-VA Brûlent le Drapeau Belge*, LALIBRE, www.lalibre.be/article_print.phtml?art_id=370224) ("Le week-end du 21 juillet, alors que d'aucuns fêtaient dignement la Belgique, les jeunes partisans de la N-VA (Jong N-VA) brülaient le drapeau belge lors d'un barbecue festif.").

87 *See id.* ("[C]et acte n'est pas considéré comme un délit en Belgique.").

88 *See* Eric Hesen, *Insulting the Queen No Longer Allowed*, RADIO NEDERLAND, http://groups.yahoo.com/group/chriscrossholland/message/225.

system available to all.[89] So, while there may be some redress for insult to the monarch, it seems to be the same redress that is more widely available.

Countries where Identification is Ethnic

Germany

Germany would, of course, be a country in which national identification has an ethnic component. The country also has an immigrant population, as do many or all of the countries to be considered, and an immigrant from another country, or the immigrant's children, might eventually claim to be German in the sense of citizenship. But the label "German" may also be an indication of ethnicity. There are German people, who may even lay claim to the label, while being a citizen of another country. The same is true for the countries that follow.

Austria

Austria protects both the State and its flag and anthem from insult. As for the state itself, the Penal Code provides, "Whosoever, in a manner that the act becomes known to the general public, in a malicious way, insults and brings into contempt the Austrian Republic and its States, is liable for imprisonment for up to one year."[90] Furthermore, as to the flag and anthem,

> Whosoever, . . . in a malicious manner and at a public occasion or a function open to the public, insults, brings into contempt or belittles the flag displayed for official purposes or the national or state anthems of the Austrian Republic or its States, is liable for imprisonment of up to six months or a fine . . .[91]

The Czech Republic

Czech law protects all state symbols, and that seems to be defined so as to include the State Coat of Arms, the national flag and the national anthem.[92] "Any use of the state symbols of the Czech Republic, which would show disrespect for these symbols shall be prohibited."[93] While there was, at one

[89] *See id.*

[90] Strafgesatzbuch [StGB] [Penal Code] gazette of promulgation, abbreviation, number/year §248(1)(Austria), available in translation at Protection of Australian Flag, supra note 54, at 13 (appendix on foreign laws in a report on Australian flag desecration law).

[91] *Id.* § 248 (2).

[92] *See* Concerning the Use of the State Coat of Arms, the National Flag and Other State Symbols of the Czech Republic, Act of the Czech National Council č 68/1990 Sb.

[93] *Id.* at § 4(d).

time, law prohibiting insults directed at, among others, the President, it appears to have been amended to omit the President from its coverage.[94]

Denmark

Denmark protects the flags of other nations, but the applicable statute does not mention the Danish flag.[95] There might be the possibility of the Danish flag being protected under another statute: "Protected by the articles of this chapter are not only officials themselves . . . but also official seals or marks."[96] But, that might be a stretch, with the statute addressing primarily the unauthorized use of an official seal.

Finland

At least as of 1987, Finland protected its flag and emblems from desecration.

> Whosoever without authorization removes the flag or official emblem of Finland that has been placed in public or publicly defaces it or uses it in a disrespectful manner or publicly disgraces the flag or official emblem of Finland through a written, graphic or audio representation shall be sentenced for disgracing the flag or official emblem of Finland to a fine.[97]

France

French law in this area is of fairly recent vintage, dating from 2003 and motivated by the crowd at a football match with Algeria booing the national anthem, *La Marseillaise*.[98] The new law provides a fine or imprisonment for

[94] *See* World Press Freedom Committee, *Hiding from the People: How "Insult" Laws Restrict Public Scrutiny of Public Officials* 6 (2002), www.wpfc.org/site/docs/pdf/Publications/Hiding%20From%20The%20People-English.pdf.

[95] *See* Lars Bo Langsted, Vagn Greve & Peter Garde, Criminal Law in Denmark 88 (1998) (describing § 110(e) of the Criminal Code: "From the lower range [of penalties] openly insulting any foreign nation or State, its flag or any other recognized symbol of nationality could be mentioned . . .").

[96] *Id.* (describing § 126 of the Criminal Code). At least as of 1998, officials were also protected against insults. *See id.* (discussing §§ 119–21 of the Criminal Code). This might speak to *lèse majesté*, but it is also unclear what impact the repeal of defamation law with regard to public officials, *see World Press Freedom Committee, It's a Crime: How Insult Laws Stifle Press Freedom: A 2006 Status Report* 24 (Marilyn Greene, ed. 2006), www.wpfc.org/site/docs/pdf/It's_A_Crime.pdf [hereinafter World Press Freedom Committee, It's a Crime], would have on any such application.

[97] The Penal Code of Finland and Related Laws 58 (Matti Joutsen, trans. 1987). While the source is from 1987, at least Wikipedia reports that the acts are still prohibited. See http://en.wikipedia.org/wiki/Flag_desecration.

[98] *See Protection of Australian Flags*, *supra* note 54, at 15.

such treatment of the national anthem or the French flag or, more generally, for "offending against the dignity of the Republic."[99] In 2010, a citizen of the United Kingdom was arrested in France for blowing his nose on the French flag, before throwing the soiled flag at a police officer.[100]

There is a 2002 case from the European Court of Human Rights involving a French statute banning public insults to foreign heads of state.[101] The original conviction was based on articles insulting the King of Morocco.[102] Under the construction of French law provided by French courts, the European Court noted that the law did not forbid political criticism but "must . . . be directed at the head of State and his or her reputation, not his or her policies."[103] While the European Court recognized a legitimate aim in protecting reputation, the Court held the conviction to be a violation of the defendant's rights to free expression under Article 10 of the European Convention. While Article 10 does allow justified restrictions on expression, the justification was not allowed here, because "the offense of insulting a foreign head of State is liable to inhibit freedom of expression without meeting any 'pressing social need' capable of justifying such a restriction."[104] In 2004, France repealed its law against insulting foreign heads of state but continued to protect the French head of state from insults.[105]

Greece

There have been, and still are, provisions in the Greek Constitution and in Greek law protecting symbols of the state. The criminal code, in the days of the monarchy provided, "One who attacks the honor of the King, the Queen, the Crown Prince or one exercising the power of the King, or defames him publicly or in his presence, shall be punished by imprisonment for not less than three months."[106] That era was not one with the level of democracy present in modern Greece, as reflected in the fact that the code also prohibited insulting public, municipal, and community authorities and national party leaders,[107] a provision that is difficult to reconcile with democracy.

[99] *Id.*

[100] *See Brit for Blowing his Nose on the French Flag and Throwing It at a Policeman*, MIRROR (Feb. 20, 2010), www.mirror.co.uk/news/uk-news/brit-for-blowing-his-nose-on-the-french-flag-202718.

[101] *See* Colombani v. France, App. No. 51279/99, Eur. Ct. H.R. (2002), http://hudoc.echr.coe.int/eng?i=001-605328.

[102] *See id.* at ¶ 59. [103] *Id.* at ¶ 28. [104] Colombani, App. No. 51279/99, ¶ 69.

[105] *See* WORLD PRESS FREEDOM COMMITTEE, IT'S A CRIME, *supra* note 96, at 27.

[106] Poinokos Kodikas [P.K.] [Criminal Code], Article 168 (Greece) [hereinafter P.K.] in THE GREEK PENAL CODE 104 (Nicholas B. Lolis, trans. 1973).

[107] *See id.* at 108 (Article 181(1)).

There was also a provision that would speak more directly to the flag: "One who publicly insults or with hate or contempt removes, damages or defaces an emblem or symbol of the sovereignty of the state, the King, or indicia of the dignity of the King shall be punished by imprisonment for not more than two years."[108] The 1993 translation, presumably recognizing a change in the code, substitutes the President for the King.[109]

The Constitution of Greece provides a guarantee of free expression, but within that guarantee also provides exceptions relevant to national symbols. Article 14, Section 1 provides: "Every person may express and propagate his thoughts orally, in writing and through the press in compliance with the laws of the State."[110] But Section 3 of the same article allows the public prosecutor to seize newspapers and other publications in case of "an offence against the Christian or any other known religion [or] an insult against the person of the President of the Republic ..." The President's role as representative of the state is obvious, but there also seems to be an identification of the Greek people with the Greek Orthodox Church, which could at least partially explain the protection given religion.

Iceland

An Icelandic provision addresses disrespect toward the flag; however, the examples given all seem directed at business use. "Misuse of the flag is punishable. The use of the flag is forbidden, i.e. in firm marks, trademarks, on sales goods, packaging or in advertisements."[111] The same source reported that revisions to this provision are under consideration.[112] It is possible that Icelandic law protects foreign flags but not the flag of Iceland, but this is unclear. A 2009 newspaper article on arrests for burning the flag of NATO said that a police officer explained that "[a]lthough it is not illegal to burn all flags, it is certainly illegal to burn national flags and the NATO flag,"[113] without saying whether "national flags" includes the Icelandic flag or only the flags of other nations.[114] The same article quotes a Supreme Court advocate as

[108] *Id.* (Article 181(2)).

[109] *See Greece: Free Speech on Trial: Government Stifles Dissent on Macedonia*, 5 HELSINKI WATCH 1 (Jul. 1993), http://groups.yahoo.com/group/balkanhr/message/2605.

[110] 1975 Syntagma [SYN] [CONSTITUTION], Article 14 (Greece). Article 14 may be found in translation at www.hri.org/docs/syntagma/artcl25.html#A14.

[111] NAT Nordic Adventure Travel, Icelandic Flag, www.nat.is/travelguideeng/icelandic_flag.htm.

[112] *See id.*

[113] *Police in Iceland Arrest NATO Flag Burners*, ICELAND REVIEW ONLINE, Jan. 29, 2009, 11:36, www.icelandreview.com/icelandreview/daily_news/?cat_id=29314&ew_0_a_id=319134.

[114] There is a comment in a history of the Icelandic flag noting that, as of 1944, there was no penalty for desecrating the Icelandic flag, while there were penalties for similar treatment of the

expressing uncertainty over the status of the NATO flag but noting that "people have been arrested for flag-burning in Iceland before."[115] Unless there had been a spate of burning the flags of other nations, this might be an indication of prosecutions for burning the Icelandic flag. Iceland does protect its national anthem from performance or publication in any form other than the original and from commercial use.[116]

Ireland

Ireland does not seem to have any law prohibiting desecration of the flag. There is a publication setting out provisions for showing respect for the national flag and listing practices to avoid.[117] Those practices include defacing the flag by placing on it slogans, logos, and the like or letting the flag touch the ground, but there does not seem to be any provision for criminal penalties.

Ireland, then, may be seen as not protecting its flag, despite the fact that there is an Irish ethnicity. Perhaps the explanation here is that, while the Irish Republic considers itself to include the entire island,[118] six counties are a part of the United Kingdom. A history of strife between its politically and religiously separate populations may have resulted in a reluctance to protect state symbols.[119] Where there are separate regions, or even ethnicities, it might be expected that state symbols would be protected in an effort to foster unity.[120] But, where the regions are, in fact, legally distinct, protection may not serve that purpose.

flags of other countries, *see* Prime Minister's Office, Parliamentary Resolutions and Bills, available at page 7 of http://eng.forsaetisraduneyti.is/state-symbols/icelandic-national-flag/history, but this was as part of the debate leading up to the passage of the flag law.

115 *Id.*

116 *See* Prime Minister's Office, The Icelandic National Anthem, Feb. 1, 2003, http://eng.forsaetisraduneyti.is/state-symbols/icelandic-national-anthem/history.

117 *See* Office of the Taoiseach, An Bhratach Náisiúnta: The National Flag, www.taoiseach.gov.ie/upload/publications/1104.pdf#page=14.

118 *See* Bunreacht na hÉireann, Article 2 ("It is the entitlement and birthright of every person born in the island of Ireland, which includes its islands and seas, to be part of the Irish Nation."), www.constitution.ie/eng/Documents/Bunreacht_na_hÉireann_web.pdf.

119 The Irish Constitution states a goal of uniting all the people of Ireland in "harmony and friendship" and through peaceful means. *See id.* at Article 3 ("It is the firm will of the Irish Nation, in harmony and friendship, to unite all the people who share the territory of the island of Ireland, in all the diversity of their identities and traditions, recognising that a united Ireland shall be brought about only by peaceful means with the consent of a majority of the people, democratically expressed, in both jurisdictions in the island.")

120 This might be seen in Spain, with its population of Basques, Catalans and so on, occupying identifiable regions. The protection of the flag and the dignity of the royal family, *see infra* notes 134–37 and accompanying text, might be seen as the protection of unifying symbols.

Japan

There appears to be no prohibition on desecration of the Japanese flag. A 1987 incident in which the flag was burned is described as "stunning."[121] The protester was convicted, but the charges were based on trespass and damage to public property, rather than desecration of the flag.[122] There is also no *lèse majesté* provision, although this is seemingly a result of post-World War II revision of the law under United States guidance. A newspaper article from the time notes the abolition of *lèse majesté* and says, "Allied Headquarters is particularly gratified by this clarification of the Emperor's status . . . To accord the Emperor no special protection . . . conforms to long-established practice in the United States and the United Kingdom.'"[123] The Japanese seem to have seen the change in a different light. "The Japanese Press . . . has, like the Japanese people, been quick to emphasize that the Emperor's 'honour and dignity,' as 'the symbol of the State,' remain unimpaired by the new provisions."[124]

Thus, Japan fails to protect its flag, while the country is strongly ethnic. While this would seem contrary to expectations, the explanation may be in the source of the current Japanese Constitution. A constitution imposed by a strong free expression country such as the United States might be expected to reflect the values not of an ethnically singular country but that of a diverse country, such as the United States.

Netherlands

There does not appear to be a law against flag desecration in the Netherlands, but there are *lèse majesté* laws. Three articles of the Dutch Penal Code protect the monarch, the Consulate, the heir apparent, and the Regent against insult.[125] It does appear that European rights law has led to limited use of this law. "Criticism about the Dutch monarch or her heir-apparent that is considered 'a contribution to the public debate' enjoys protection under

[121] *See* Richard Lloyd Parry, *Okinawa Picnic Plan Brings Out the Riot Police*, THE INDEPENDENT (Mar. 31, 1996), www.independent.co.uk/news/world/okinqwa-picnic-plan-brings-out-the-riot-polics-1344984.html.

[122] *See id.*

[123] *Japanese Emperor's Status: Lèse Majesté Abolished*, THE TIMES (Dec. 2, 1947), at 3, available at http://find.galegroup.com.proxy1.cl.msu.edu/ttda/infomark.do?source=gale&prodid=TTDA&userGroupName=msu_main&tabID=T0035&docPage-article&searchTypes=AdvancedSearchForm&docid=CS51332482&type-multipage&contentSet-LTO&version=1.0.

[124] *Id.*

[125] *See Dealing with Lèse Majesté in Netherlands*, BANGKOK POST (Jan. 18, 2010), available at 2010 WLNR 1033888. The article was based on the views of the Dutch Ambassador to the Kingdom of Thailand.

European and Dutch law, and Dutch courts have applied this criterion faithfully and judiciously ... in the interest of freedom of expression in the country."[126] The law is, however, not without extension, and an individual has been charged with calling Queen Beatrix a whore.[127]

Norway

At least until 2008, Norway protected the flags and coats of arms of foreign countries, but it has not been illegal to desecrate the flag of Norway.[128] There are, however, *lèse majesté* provisions in the Norwegian Constitution and Penal Code. Article 5 of the Constitution provides: "The King's person is sacred; he cannot be censured or accused. The responsibility rests with his Council."[129] Section 101 of the Penal Code provides: "Anybody who commits an offense against the honor of the King or the Regent, shall be punished by jailing or imprisonment up to five years."[130]

Portugal

The Portuguese Penal Code provides, in translation:

> Anyone who by words, gesture, in writing or by any other means of public communication, desecrates the Republic, national flag or the national anthem the symbols or emblems of the Portuguese sovereignty, or in any other way fails to pay them their due respect, shall be punished with a prison sentence of up to 2 years ...[131]

Slovenia

Slovenian law provides that the coat of arms and national flag may not be used "in a manner that is in conflict with public order or is defamatory to the reputation of the Republic of Slovenia."[132] Slovenian law prohibiting disparagement of the Republic of Slovenia also extends to the President of the Republic but not to other parts of government.[133] Further, disparagement

[126] *Id.*

[127] *See Young Reporter Arrested for Insulting Queen*, DUTCHNEWS.NL (Aug. 1, 2007) www.dutchnews.nl/news/archives/2007/08/young_reporter_arrested_for_in.php.

[128] *Protection of Australian Flags, supra* note 54, at 19.

[129] NORWAY CONST., Article 5.

[130] THE NORWEGIAN PENAL CODE 52 (trans. Harald Schjoldager & Finn Backer, 1961).

[131] *Protection of Australian Flags, supra* note 54, at 19.

[132] Act: The Coat of Arms, Flag and Anthem, Article 7, http://ims.dz-rs.si/imis/48b1453933917d570cd2.pdf.

[133] *See* WORLD PRESS FREEDOM COMMITTEE, IT'S A CRIME, *supra* note 95, at 127 (setting out the Slovenian Criminal Code Chapter 18, Article 174).

against the Slovene people or against the Hungarian or Italian communities within Slovenia may result in fine or imprisonment.[134]

Spain

Spanish law contains a provision protecting the symbols or emblems of Spain and its Communities. Article 543 of the Penal Code provides: "Verbal or written offences or outrages, or those by action, against Spain, its Autonomous Communities or the symbols or emblems thereof, perpetrated publicly, shall be punished with the penalty of a fine for seven to twelve months."[135]

There are also two provisions of the Penal Code protecting the honor of the Royal Family. Article 490(3) provides:

> Whoever commits slander or defamation against the King or any of his ascendants or descendants, the Queen Consort or the Queen's Consort, the Regent or any member of the Regency, or the Heir to the Throne, while carrying out the duties of office or due to or on occasion thereof, shall be punished with a sentence of imprisonment of six months to two years if the slander or defamation are serious and with that of a fine of six to twelve months if not.[136]

Further, Article 491(2) provides:

> The punishment shall be imposed of a fine from six to twenty-four months upon whoever uses the image of the King or of any of his ascendants or descendants, or of the Queen Consort or the Queen's Consort, or the Regent

[134] *See id.* (setting out Article 176).

[135] Ministereo de Justicia, Criminal Code 161 (2011), www.sanchezcervera-abogados.com/en/files/2012/06/Criminal_Code_Código_Penal.pdf. There is a case decided by the Tribunal Constitucional, STC 118/1992 (Sep. 16, 1992) that declared unconstitutional another provision of the Spanish Penal Code. That provision, Article 10, párrafo 3.°, de la Ley 39/1981, de 28 de octubre, an act regulating the use of the Spanish flag and other flags and symbols, seemed intended to cast light on another provision. Article 10 provided that, with regard to Article 123 of the then Penal Code, all outrages and offenses listed will be considered to have been committed with publicity. 118/1992 at ¶ 1 ("Los ultrajes y ofensas a las banderas a que se refiere el art. 3 de esta Ley, se consideran siempre como cometidas con publicidad a los efectos de lo dispuesto en el citado art. 123 del Código Penal."). The Article 123 mentioned prohibited outrages against Spain, the conviction of its unity, and its symbols and emblems, providing for punishment of imprisonment. See 118/1992 at ¶ 1 ("Los ultrajes a la nación española o al sentimiento de su unidad, al Estado o su forma política, así como a sus símbolos y emblemas, se castigarán con la pena de prisión menor, y si tuvieren lugar con publicidad, con la de prisión mayor."). While the Court held Article 10 to be unconstitutional, it did so on grounds that have no impact on Article 123 or on Article 543. It was a lack of clarity with regard to Article 10 and its imputation of publicity to all outrages and offenses that led to its demise.

[136] *Id.* at 151.

or any member of the Regency, or Heir to the Throne, in any way that may damage the prestige of the Crown.[137]

There was a prosecution protecting the royal family in 2007, in which two cartoonists were found guilty and fined. The government had announced that it would pay Spanish couples for each new baby, and the cartoon depicted the Crown Prince and his wife having sex, with the caption, "Do you realise, if you get pregnant this will be the closest thing I've done to work in my whole life."[138] Given the humor, and the seemingly political content, the case would indicate that Spain treats seriously its protections for the Royal Family.

Sweden

Swedish law provides up to six months of imprisonment for the vilification of the Church of Sweden and other religious groups,[139] and the same penalty is applicable to insulting the flags and symbols of foreign nations,[140] but there appears to be no law protecting the Swedish flag. An article on the Swedish flag notes a 1967 prosecution for defiling the flag but maintains that the current view on the use of the flag is quite "liberal."[141] The same article suggests that there is a current problem in the adoption of the flag by right-wing and racist groups to the point where the display of the flag "has become almost suspect."[142]

Switzerland

Article 270 of the Swiss Penal Code protects against degradation and outrage of Swiss emblems of sovereignty and the coats of arms and flags of the Confederation and its cantons, but only those that have been raised by public authorities, with penalties of up to three years of imprisonment.[143] It appears that privately owned flags, and the like, are not protected. Thus, Swiss law does not prohibit attacks on its flag, except where the flag is public property.

137 *Id.*

138 *See Spain Royal Sex Cartoonists Fined*, BBC News (Nov. 13, 2007_16:16 GMT), newsvote.bbc.co.uk/mpapps/pagetools/print/news.bbc.co.uk/2/hi/europe/7092866.stm.

139 *See Comment, The Swedish Penal Code of* 1965, 1968 Duke L.J. 67, 79.

140 *See id.* at 80.

141 *See Sweden*, www.Nordic Way.com, available at www.nordicway.com/sweden_flag.htm.

142 *See id.*

143 *See* Code pénal Suisse [Pc] [Penal Code], Article 270 (Switz.) ("Celui qui, par malveillance, aura enlevé, degrade, ou aura par des actes outrage un emblem Suisse de souveraineté arbore par un autorité, notamment les armes ou le drapeau de la confederation ou d'un canton, sera puni d'une piene privative de liberté de trois ans au plus d'une peine pécuniaire.").

Switzerland may also present difficulties with regard to the consideration of ethnicity. There is certainly Swiss nationality, but the country is a confederation of cantons, with language differences in that some cantons are primarily French, some German, and some Italian. Switzerland, in terms of Swiss Nationals, is 74% German, 20% French, 4% Italian, 1% Romansh, and 1% other.[144] There may, then, not be a unifying ethnic identity as much as a political union.

United Kingdom

The United Kingdom has no prohibition on flag burning, although there have been calls by police chiefs and Scotland Yard to institute such a ban.[145] There is a *lèse majesté* provision. *Halsbury's Laws of England* says: "Contempt of the Sovereign is an offence at common law. It is triable only on indictment and punishable by fine and imprisonment at the discretion of the court."[146] But, it appears that there has been no prosecution for such contempt since 1840.[147]

The issue of a unifying ethnic identity for the United Kingdom is difficult. While outsiders may see citizens of the United Kingdom as being of the same ethnicity, the Welsh and the Scots would see themselves as ethnically different from the English. The United Kingdom is, after all, a united kingdom of England, Northern Ireland, Wales, and Scotland. While there are ethnic labels that attach to the peoples of the four constituent parts, there doesn't even appear to be a label for any united ethnicity. "Brit" might be the closest but doesn't really apply to other than the English. Thus, the United Kingdom may actually be seen as a multiply ethnic country.

CONCLUSIONS

It seems clear that there is no logical inconsistency between the maintenance of democracy and the protection of national symbols. There are fully functioning democracies that protect their flags and other symbols and their heads of state, as distinct from the heads of government. It is also not simply a matter

[144] *See TRAMsoft GmbH. Statistical Information about Switzerland*, www.about.ch/statistics/index.html.

[145] *See Flag-Burning Law Plan Criticized*, BBC News (Oct. 29, 2006), http://news.bbc.co.uk/go/pr/fr/-/2/hi/uk_news/6096810.stm; Hugh Muir, *Yard Wants Ban on Flag-Burning in Crackdown on Demos by Extremists*, The Guardian (Oct. 30, 2006), www.guardian.co.uk/uk/2006/oct/30/religion.ukcrime.

[146] Lord Mackay of Clashfern, 11(1) Halsbury's Laws of England 324 (4th ed. 2006 reissue).

[147] *Id.* at ¶ 369, n.1.

of different understandings of democracy, for example, the procedural democracy view of the United States compared to the substantive or militant democracy of Germany.

The differences among countries would seem best explained by cultural differences in how the treatment of the national symbol is understood. Where the desecration of the flag or other national symbol is seen as an attack on the people or the nation, limits may be seen as acceptable. Where the desecration is, instead, seen as aimed at those in political power, acceptance of this sort of criticism seems important to democracy.

9

Defamation

Defamation is the publication of a false statement of purported fact[1] that harms the reputation of another, libel if in writing and slander if spoken. There is a balance to be drawn between concerns about free expression and the chilling effect the potential defamation actions may have on expression and the interests of individuals in their good names. As with the other areas considered, there is a good deal of difference among democratic countries on how that balance should be drawn.

Central to the examination here will be a comparison between the United States and the United Kingdom. Not surprisingly, defamation defendants enjoy significant protection in the United States. In contrast, the United Kingdom has come to be seen as the world's libel capital and a focus for "libel tourism," forum shopping for the location best for the plaintiff.[2] The tourism aspect was the result of British courts exercising very expansive jurisdiction, even when neither the plaintiff nor the defendant had substantial connection to the United Kingdom.

[1] There is also a great deal of law regarding statements of opinion. Opinion will generally not lead to a finding of defamation. While the United States Supreme Court purported to do away with any special privilege for opinion in *Milkovich v. Lorain Journal Co.*, 497 U.S. 1 (1990), statements that are truly statements of opinion, unless they imply certain facts, are not going to be subject to the proof of falsity required for a defamation judgment under United States law. In the law of the United Kingdom, in which the plaintiff need not prove falsity, there was a common law defense of fair comment that protected opinion. The common law defense was replaced by Section 3 of the Defamation Act of 2013, a section titled "Honest opinion." There are interesting issues raised by the fact/opinion distinction, but they are beyond the scope of this effort. Instead, the material here will concentrate on false statements of purported fact.

[2] *See generally, e.g.*, Stephen Bates, *Libel Capital No More? Reforming British Defamation Law*, 34 Hastings Comm. & Ent. L.J. 233 (2012) (discussing coming changes in United Kingdom law); Lili Levi, *The Problem of Trans-National Libel*, 60 Am. J. Comp. L. 507 (2012)(examining United Kingdom law in the period leading up to the recent changes); Marlene Arnold Nicholson, *McLibel: A Case Study in English Defamation Law*, 18 Wisc. Int'l L.J. 1 (2000).

The motivation to bring suit in the United Kingdom grows out of differences in substantive law. While libel plaintiffs in the United States must prove the falsity of the statements at issue, the United Kingdom defendant must prove the truth of the statements.[3] Furthermore, there is no need for the United Kingdom plaintiff to prove actual damages; it is presumed that the defamatory publication damaged the plaintiff's reputation.[4]

The tourism issue has, at least for non-European defendants, been addressed by Section 9 of the United Kingdom's Defamation Act of 2013.[5] Section 9 provides:

(1) This section applies to an action for defamation against a person who is not domiciled—
  (a) in the United Kingdom;
  (b) in another Member State [of the European Union]; or
  (c) in a state which is for the time being a contracting party to the Lugano Convention [on jurisdiction between the EU and Denmark, Iceland, Norway, and Switzerland].

(2) A court does not have jurisdiction to hear and determine an action to which this section applies unless the court is satisfied that, of all the places in which the statement complained of has been published, England and Wales is clearly the most appropriate place in which to bring an action in respect of the statement . . .

Thus, the defendant from, for example the United States, is very unlikely to be called into a United Kingdom court based on some minimal number of copies of the publication finding their way into that country. Where there are grounds for jurisdiction, the substantive differences may still make the United Kingdom an attractive place to file suit.

The comparison will proceed primarily using the categories of plaintiff employed in United States law. Those categories are not employed in other jurisdictions but they may be seen as important in distinguishing plaintiffs for whom strong protection for reputation would harm democracy from those whose reputation may be protected with less damage.

THE GOVERNMENT

Defamation of the State has, at least in the past, constituted the crime of sedition. Eric Barendt provides an explanation of sedition that shows, at least

[3] *See, e.g.*, Stephen Bates, *supra* note 2, at 246. [4] *See, e.g.*, *id.* at 247.

[5] Defamation Act 2013, c. 26, § 9, www.legislation.gov.uk/ukpga/2013/26.

when it falls short of advocating criminal activity, just how outmoded the concept is.

> The classic definition of sedition reflects a traditional, conservative view of the correct relationship between state and society. Governments and public institutions are not to be regarded as responsible to the people, but in some mystical way, as under the doctrine of the Divine Right of Kings, are entitled to the respect of their subjects. At the very most, suggestions concerning the improvement of government may be tolerated, but not open or vehement attack.[6]

This approach is clearly antithetical to democracy, where the people, rather than some divinely instituted monarch, are sovereign. As Professor Harry Kalven puts it, "The concept of seditious libel strikes at the very heart of democracy ... [D]efamation of the government is an impossible notion for a democracy."[7]

Professor Barendt, in response to the Kalven claim, says "If this is the case, there are remarkably few free countries."[8] He notes the existence of a number of countries, including England and some Commonwealth countries and other European states in which the offense continues to exist.[9] He does, however, note that prosecutions are very rare. Indeed, in a number of jurisdictions, there are court cases recognizing the illegitimacy of this form of sedition in a democracy.

A United States Supreme Court case taking this position is *New York Times v. Sullivan*.[10] The case is best known for having established the burden that public officials must meet in order to sue for defamation.[11] The libel action was brought by the Montgomery, Alabama city commissioner having supervisory authority over the police department. It was in response to an advertisement supporting the Rev. Martin Luther King and the civil rights movement in the state. The ad was critical of the police response to demonstrations. Sullivan brought suit claiming that he had been defamed, but the ad could also be seen, even more clearly, as defamatory of the city.

While the city did not bring suit, which would have raised the issue of the status of sedition, the Court did address the issue. Although sedition had at one time been criminal, the Court saw that time as having passed.

6 Eric Barendt, Freedom of Speech 163 (2d ed. 2005).
7 Harry Kalven, Jr., *The* New York Times *Case: A Note on "The Central Meaning of the First Amendment,"* 1964 Sup. Ct. Rev. 191, 205.
8 Barendt, *supra* note 6, at 162. 9 *See id.* 10 376 U.S. 254 (1964).
11 That standard is discussed *infra*, notes 22–30, and accompanying text.

> Although the Sedition Act was never tested in this Court, the attack upon its validity has carried the day in the court of history. Fines levied in its prosecution were repaid by Act of Congress on the ground that it was unconstitutional ... Jefferson, as President, pardoned those who had been convicted and sentenced under the Act ... The invalidity of the Act has also been assumed by Justices of this Court ... These views reflect a broad consensus that the Act, because of the restraint imposed upon criticism of government and public officials, was inconsistent with the First Amendment.[12]

This is a clear recognition that punishing defamation of the government is inconsistent with democracy.

A House of Lords case from the United Kingdom, *Derbyshire County Council v. Times Newspapers*,[13] recognizes the same point. Articles had been published in *The Sunday Times* titled "Revealed: Socialist tycoon's deals with a Labour Chief," "Bizarre deals of the council leader and the media tycoon," and "Council share deals under scrutiny," questioning investments made by the Council. The issue before the Court was a libel action brought not by the Labour Chief or the "tycoon," but by the County Council. The claim was that the "council has been injured in its credit and reputation and has been brought into public scandal, odium and contempt, and has suffered loss and damage."[14] This was a complaint that clearly sounded in terms of seditious libel.

While corporate entities had been libel plaintiffs, the Court, in an opinion by Lord Keith with the concurrence of the other lords, rejected allowing such suits by governmental entities.

> There are ... features of a local authority which may be regarded as distinguishing it from other types of corporation ... The most important of these features is that it is a governmental body. Further, it is a democratically elected body ... It is of the highest public importance that a democratically elected governmental body, or indeed any governmental body, should be open to uninhibited public criticism. The threat of a civil action for defamation must inevitably have an inhibiting effect on freedom of speech.[15]

The Court noted the concerns expressed by the United States Supreme Court in *Times v. Sullivan* with regard to the chilling effect of potential defamation actions and said that the concerns were no less valid in the United Kingdom.[16] The Court concluded that:

[12] 376 U.S. at 276. [13] [1993] A.C. (HL) 534 (appeal taken from Eng.).
[14] *Id.* at 542 (quoting the filing of the plaintiff). [15] *Id.* at 547. [16] *See id.* at 548.

> [N]ot only is there no public interest favouring the right of organs of government, whether central or local, to sue for libel, but ... it is contrary to the public interest that they should have it. It is contrary to the public interest because to admit such actions would place an undesirable fetter on freedom of speech.[17]

The Court did add a point that will be seen to distinguish the law of the United Kingdom from that of the United States. The Court said:

> A publication attacking the activities of the authority will necessarily be an attack on the body of councillors which represents the controlling party, or on the executives who carry on the day-to-day management of its affairs. If the individual reputation of any of these is wrongfully impaired by the publication any of these can himself bring proceedings for defamation.[18]

Thus, while the United Kingdom government critic can defame a governmental entity without fear of facing civil damages, the critic may need to be careful not to, in the process, defame those individuals involved in the governmental action.

One might argue that there is no value in false statements that harm the reputation of government. But allowing suit or prosecution for such statements could have the impact of reducing political debate in the utterance of statements that are, in fact, true. The *Times v. Sullivan* Court recognized that "erroneous statement is inevitable in free debate, and that it must be protected if the freedoms of expression are to have the 'breathing space' that they 'need ... to survive'."[19] The Court thought even the placement of the burden of proving truth on the defendant to be unacceptable. "Under such a rule, would-be critics of official conduct may be deterred from voicing their criticism, even though ... it is in fact true, because of doubt whether it can be proved in court or fear of the expense of having to do so."[20]

If the aphorism that the remedy for bad speech is more speech is correct,[21] it will be particularly so in this instance. More speech best serves as a remedy when it reaches those who heard the bad speech. It would be difficult to think of a person or entity more capable of speech than a government, and democratically elected governments should be able to address criticism, without punishing that criticism.

17 *Id.* at 549. 18 *Id.* at 550.
19 376 U.S. at 271–72 (ellipsis in original) (quoting N.A.A.C.P. v. Button, 371 U.S. 415, 433 (1963)).
20 *Id.* at 279.
21 *See, e.g.*, Whitney v. California 274 U.S. 357, 377 (1927)(Brandeis, J., concurring)("If there be time to expose through discussion the falsehood and fallacies, to avert the evil by the process of education, the remedy to be applied is more speech, not enforced silence.").

PUBLIC OFFICIALS

The United States

Times v. Sullivan was a libel suit brought by a public official, rather than an action filed on behalf of a governmental entity. The plaintiff was a Commissioner of the city of Montgomery, Alabama. In his position, he exercised authority over the police and fire departments, as well as other units of the city government. The basis of the suit was an advertisement published in the *New York Times*, during the struggle for civil rights in the South. The full-page ad, titled "Heed Their Rising Voices," discussed the reactions of the police to the movement in Montgomery. The text of the ad appeared over the signatures of a number of prominent individuals and was officially signed at the bottom by the "Committee to Defend Martin Luther King and the Struggle for Freedom in the South."[22]

There were two paragraphs in the advertisement that were said to be libelous. The third paragraph said that:

> [A]fter students sang "My Country 'Tis of Thee," on the State Capitol steps, their leaders were expelled from school, and truckloads of police armed with shotguns and tear-gas ringed the Alabama State College Campus. When the entire student body protested to state authorities by refusing to re-register, their dining hall was padlocked in an attempt to starve them into submission.[23]

The sixth paragraph said, "Again and again the Southern violators have answered Dr. King's peaceful protests with intimidation and violence. They have bombed his home almost killing his wife and child. They have assaulted his person. They have arrested him seven times . . ."[24]

Note that nothing in either paragraph mentioned the plaintiff by name. His only connection to the claims was his supervisory authority over the police. Sullivan claimed that the paragraphs met the "of and concerning" requirement that to constitute libel of an individual, the publication must defame the individual. Because people recognized his authority, the statements would be seen as an assertion of his individual fault. The Alabama courts accepted that theory, but the Supreme Court rejected it, saying that it would "transmut[e] criticism of government, however impersonal it may seem on its face, into personal criticism, and hence potential libel, of the officials of whom the government is composed."[25]

[22] 376 U.S. at 257. [23] *Id.* at 257. [24] *Id.* at 257–58. [25] *Id.* at 292.

Alabama law did provide a defense of truth to a libel action, but the complained of material had to be true in all its particulars. In fact, there were some errors. The students had actually sung the National Anthem; while some students had been expelled, it was not because of the State Capitol demonstration; the students did reregister, although there was a one-day boycott of classes; the dining hall was never padlocked, and only students without meal cards were refused food. The police never "ringed" the campus, and Dr. King was arrested four, not seven, times.[26]

The state courts, accepting the position that the criticism was of and concerning Sullivan and that the defense of truth was not established, allowed a jury verdict of $500,000 to stand. In 1964, the Supreme Court, seeing the chilling effect of a rule requiring truth in every detail with such a significant potential penalty, concluded that political debate requires a stronger defense. The Court concluded that if a public official sues for libel, the official must prove "actual malice"; the plaintiff must prove that the statement was made "with knowledge that it was false or with reckless disregard of whether it was false or not."[27] While the *Times* might have, perhaps, been negligent in failing to check the details of the advertisement against stories in its own files, there were no indicia of knowledge or recklessness regarding any of the false claims.

The *New York Times* Court declined the opportunity to explain the extension of its holding. The Court said that it would not determine how far down the hierarchy of government one may be and still be a public official, and it declined to define what constituted official conduct.[28] It has, however, become clear that the decision covers, at least nearly, all public officials.[29] It also is clear that the scope of "official conduct" is very broad. Particularly with an elected official or a person standing for election, any issue that touches on fitness for office, which seemingly includes character issues, is covered by the *Times* standard.[30]

What the Court did in the *New York Times* case was to constitutionalize the common law of libel; that is, the Court recognized that the common law was in conflict with the freedom of expression guaranteed by the First Amendment and remedied the defect. The result is a regime in which public officials have great difficulty in recovering for harm to their reputations. They must not only prove that the defamatory statement is false but also that the defendant knew

[26] *See id.* 258–59. [27] *Id.* at 280. [28] *See* 376 U.S. at 283 n.23.

[29] *See, e.g.*, Rosenblatt v. Baer, 383 U.S. 75 (1966)(indicating that the standard could apply to the supervisor of a publicly owned ski slope).

[30] *See, e.g.*, Monitor Patriot Co. v. Roy, 401 U.S. 265 (1971)(applying the standard to a candidate who had been described as having at one time been a small time bootlegger).

that it was false or proceeded in the face of doubt or a conscious recognition that it may well be false. Furthermore, proof must be with convincing clarity.

While it may have taken some time, the courts in the United Kingdom, Australia, New Zealand, and Canada also came to recognize the need to reconcile the common law and free expression.[31] The dimensions of the protection granted to speech regarding public officials do, however, vary from that provided by the United States Supreme Court.

The United Kingdom

The United Kingdom recognition came in the 1999 House of Lords decision *Reynolds v. Times Newspapers*.[32] Reynolds was the Taoiseach of Ireland, heading up a coalition government of his own Fianna Fail Party and the Labour Party. He was, then, a public official, although not a public official of the United Kingdom. He was involved in the Northern Ireland peace process, a process that was clearly of great public interest in the United Kingdom.

The background for the allegedly defamatory article in the *Sunday Times* concerned the appointment of the President of the High Court. Reynolds favored the appointment of an individual who had been Attorney General, at a time when his office had failed to act on a Northern Ireland extradition warrant for a priest facing charges of sexual abuse of children. When the cabinet decided to forward the appointment to the President, the coalition with Labour collapsed, and Reynolds and the new President of the High Court resigned.

The *Sunday Times* article, titled "Goodbye gombeen man: Why a fib too far proved fatal for the political career of Ireland's peacemaker and Mr Fix-it," said:

> Spring [the deputy prime minister and leader of the Labour Party] was thunderstruck. Reynolds had known all along that [the Attorney General's] excuse [for his office's inaction] did not hold water, yet in the Dail on Tuesday he had backed his promotion to the High Court . . . When the Dail resumed on Wednesday afternoon, Reynolds went ahead with his volte face, to gasps of astonishment in the house, but to no avail . . . Spring rose to address a hushed house and in a masterly speech, he demolished Reynolds's

[31] For a discussion of changes in the laws of Australia, New Zealand and the United Kingdom, *see* Susanna Frederick Fischer, *Rethinking* Sullivan: *New Approaches in Australia, New Zealand and England*, 34 Geo. Wash. Int'l L. Rev. 101 (2002).

[32] [2001] 2 A.C. (HL) 127 (appeal taken from Eng.).

> reputation, exposed the lies he had been told and announced that his party would resign its cabinet posts and vote against the government.[33]

The meaning Reynolds found in the article included assertions that he had deliberately misled the Dail and the cabinet, by withholding information and lying about when he had obtained the information.[34]

The newspaper disagreed with regard to the meaning of the words in its article and also asserted the defense of common law qualified privilege, that it was justified in its assertions, and that it acted without malice. In the view of the defense, the common law qualified privilege should extend to all political speech, a position rejected by the trial judge in a trial that gave judgment for the plaintiff and damages of one pence.

The House of Lords resolved several issues that required sending the case back for new trial, but the most interesting aspect of the opinion was a discussion of the availability of qualified privilege in that retrial. Common law qualified privilege had applied in the context of communication between individuals and required communication by a person with the moral duty to do so to a person with an interest in hearing the communication.[35] The privilege might be seen as not applying well to media publication of information to the general public.

The Court concluded that there were several questions that needed to be answered in considering the application of the privilege in the media context.

> 1 Was the publisher under a legal, moral or social duty to those to whom the material was published (which in appropriate cases ... may be the general public) to publish the material in question? (We call this the duty test.)
> 2 Did those to whom the material was published (which again in appropriate cases may be the general public) have an interest to receive that material? (We call this the interest test.)
> 3 Were the nature, status and source of the material, and the circumstances of the publication, such that the publication should in the public interest be protected in the absence of proof of express malice? (We call this the circumstantial test.)[36]

Adapting the common-law test to the media, the Court said that since the task, and duty, of the media is to inform the public and further the discussion of matters of public interest, and it is in the interest of the public to be so informed at least with regard to matters of public interest, which the Court

[33] *Id.* at 141 (quoting the article). [34] *See id.* [35] *See id.* at 160–61. [36] *Id.* at 167.

distinguished from matters that may interest the public, the duty and interest tests are readily satisfied.[37] While the Court was willing to change the duty and interest aspects of qualified immunity to reflect the interests of the press and the public on issues of public concern, it remained committed to the circumstances test. Even here, however, the statement of the relevant circumstances was adapted to the media.

> [I]t is one thing to publish a statement taken from a government press release, or the report of a public company chairman, or the speech of a university vice-chancellor, and quite another to publish the statement of a political opponent, or a business competitor or a disgruntled ex-employee; it is one thing to publish a statement which the person defamed has been given the opportunity to rebut, and quite another to publish a statement without any recourse to the person defamed where such recourse was possible; it is one thing to publish a statement which has been so far as possible checked, and quite another to publish it without such verification as was possible and as the significance of the statement called for. While those who engage in public life must expect and accept that their public conduct will be the subject of close scrutiny and robust criticism, they should not in our view be taken to expect or accept that their conduct should be the subject of false and defamatory statements of fact unless the circumstances of the publication are such as to make it proper, in the public interest, to afford the publisher immunity from liability in the absence of malice.[38]

The Court, thus, developed a number of factors to be considered in determining whether there was a qualified privilege to publish, resulting in what might be seen as a reasonableness test.

It is important to note that the Court does not distinguish between public officials and other individuals. Indeed, the *Reynolds* Court cited to the Supreme Court Procedure Committee's 1991 express rejection of such a distinction, on the grounds that "it would be quite contrary to the tradition of our common law that citizens are not divided into different classes."[39] This would explain why the fact that Reynolds was a public official in Ireland, rather than the United Kingdom, did not call for a different analysis. Of course, there would seem to be no reason why the status of the plaintiff could not play a role in determining reasonableness.

[37] *See id.* at 177. [38] *Id.*

[39] *Id.* at 168 (quoting Supreme Court Procedure Committee, Report on Practice and Procedure in Defamation 164 (1991).

Section 4 of the Defamation Act of 2013 codified this analysis of reasonableness with regard to publications in the public interest, replacing what had become known as the "*Reynolds* defence" with the following:

(1) It is a defence to an action for defamation for the defendant to show that—
  (a) the statement complained of was, or formed part of, a statement on a matter of public interest; and
  (b) the defendant reasonably believed that publishing the statement complained of was in the public interest . . .

(4) In determining whether it was reasonable for the defendant to believe that publishing the statement complained of was in the public interest, the court must make such allowance for editorial judgement as it considers appropriate . . .

There is another common law defense, generally important but not central to *Reynolds*, that was also changed by the Defamation Act. The common law defense of justification was available where the statements at the basis of the action were true. Section 2 of the Act abolishes the common law defense and provides in its place a statutory protection.

(1) It is a defence to an action for defamation for the defendant to show that the imputation conveyed by the statement complained of is substantially true . . .

(3) If one or more of the imputations is not shown to be substantially true, the defence under this section does not fail if, having regard to the imputations which are shown to be substantially true, the imputations which are not shown to be substantially true do not seriously harm the claimant's reputation . . .

Note that the defense requires that the defendant establish the truth of the statement, while under United States law, the burden is on the plaintiff to prove falsity. United Kingdom law is then, in this regard, more protective of reputation at the potential expense of chilling speech, where the speaker is unsure of the ability to prove, or unwilling to undertake the expense of proving, truth.

It is worth stressing that the United Kingdom does not provide a test specifically aimed at public officials. It does, however, provide a defense for statements on matters of public interest. Certainly, many statements regarding public officials would fit that category. When they do, the law is still more plaintiff friendly than in the United States. In the United States the plaintiff must show knowledge or reckless disregard of falsity. Negligent, or unreasonable, reporting will not suffice. Not only will unreasonableness suffice in the United Kingdom, the burden of proof on the issue lies with the defendant.

Australia

The plaintiff in *Theophanous v. The Herald & Weekly Times*[40] was a member of the Australian House of Representatives and Chair of the Joint Parliamentary Standing Committee on Migration Regulations, as well as chair of his party's immigration committee. A letter to the editor, published in *The Sunday Herald* argued that he should be voted out of office because of a bias toward Greeks as immigrants, that he wished to dilute the British cultural base of Australia, so that English would become a second language, and that he engaged in idiotic antics. Theophanous sued for defamation, and the newspaper asserted defenses of truth with regard to a matter of public interest, fair comment on such a matter and qualified privilege.

A three-justice opinion of Chief Justice Mason and Justices Toohey and Gaudron rested on the implied freedom of political communication.[41] With regard to whether the implied freedom extended to matters concerning members of Parliament, their suitability for office and the performance of their duties, the plurality said "criticism of the views, performance and capacity of a member of Parliament and of the member's fitness for public office, particularly when an election is in the offing, is at the very centre of the freedom of political discussion."[42] The plurality saw the implied freedom as extending also to the political viewpoints and public conduct of all people who engage in activities that have become topics of political debate, quoting Professor Barendt as stating "'political speech' refers to all speech relevant to the development of public opinion on the whole range of issues which an intelligent citizen should think about."[43] The application of this definition to the conduct of public officials would seem to be at least approaching the breadth of the protection in the United States, although, as will be seen, the strength of the protection may be weaker.

The issue then became whether or not the implied freedom required a revision of common-law defenses against a defamation action. The plurality found that there was a conflict and adopted a reasonableness test.

> [T]he defendant should be required to establish that the circumstances were such as to make it reasonable to publish the impugned material without ascertaining whether it was true or false. The publisher should be required to show that, in the circumstances which prevailed, it acted reasonably, either by taking some steps to check the accuracy of the impugned material or by

[40] (1994) 182 CLR 104.
[41] That limited basis for the protection of free expression in Australia as discussed in Chapter 1.
[42] 182 CLR at 123. [43] *Id.* at 124 (quoting ERIC BARENDT, FREEDOM OF SPEECH 152 (1985)).

> establishing that it was otherwise justified in publishing without taking such steps or steps which were adequate.[44]

While recognizing the need to allow breathing room for political debate, the plurality said "it cannot be said to be in the public interest or conducive to the working of democratic government if anyone were at liberty to publish false and damaging defamatory matter free from any responsibility at all in relation to the accuracy of what is published."[45]

The test the plurality adopts starts out sounding like the test in the United States, except with regard to the burden of proof, but then ends up with a reasonableness requirement.

> [I]f a defendant publishes false and defamatory matter about a plaintiff, the defendant should be liable in damages unless it can establish that it was unaware of the falsity, that it did not publish recklessly (i.e., not caring whether the matter was true or false), and that the publication was reasonable in the sense described.[46]

The plurality noted that this reasonableness requirement meant that the common-law requirement of a lack of common-law malice for the assertion of a qualified privilege was no longer necessary.

Justice Brennan wrote a concurring opinion. He agreed with the need for additional protection for defamation defendants with regard to suits by members of Parliament, noting that reasons for as strong protection of reputation as provided by the common law are not valid with regard to such plaintiffs. "[H]olders of such office, particularly parliamentarians entitled to be heard in the public and privileged forum of parliamentary proceedings, are likely to have greater access, by reason of their office, to the means of communication to refute or answer an untrue or unfair statement of fact or comment."[47] The implied right required more protection for defendants, but Justice Brennan split with the plurality with regard to the test implied by that need.

> I am quite unable to accept that the freedom which the constitutional implication protects is, at least in relation to statements about the official conduct or consequent suitability for office of holders of high government office, conditioned upon the ability of the citizen or other publisher to satisfy a court of matters such as absence of recklessness or reasonableness.[48]

Given the lack of agreement on a test between the plurality and a necessary concurrence regarding the impact of the implied freedom on the common law, the case left some uncertainty.

[44] *Id.* at 137. [45] *Id.* [46] *Id.* [47] *Id.* at 182. [48] *Id.* at 188.

That uncertainty was addressed in a later case involving a public official who was, like the plaintiff in *Reynolds*, not an official of the government the defamation law of which was at issue. David Lange was a former Prime Minister of New Zealand and, at the relevant time, still a member of Parliament. Lange complained that he had been defamed on an Australian television program, that he been said to have abused his power and to be unfit for public office. In *Lange and Australian Broadcasting Corporation*,[49] the High Court of Australia had another opportunity to consider defamation and public officials.

The Court said that the common law must be adapted to the implied freedom of political communication but saw the protection of reputation as also important to good government.

> The protection of the reputations of those who take part in the government and political life of this country from false and defamatory statements is conducive to the public good. The constitutionally prescribed system of government ... would be adversely affected by ... an unqualified freedom to publish defamatory matter damaging the reputations of individuals involved in government or politics.[50]

The Court was willing to expand the qualified privilege to publications made to an audience, too wide to come within the privilege as previously understood, but added a requirement of reasonableness that was not necessary in the common-law instance of, for example, a complaint by an individual to a government minister.

The Court said that the more widely applicable qualified privilege "will be defeated if the person defamed proves that the publication was actuated by common law malice to the extent that the elements of malice are not covered under the rubric of reasonableness."[51] The plaintiff would have to prove that the publication was so motivated, but "the motive of causing political damage to the plaintiff or his or her party cannot be regarded as improper."[52]

As for reasonableness,

> [w]hether the making of a publication is reasonable must depend upon all the circumstances of the case. But, as a general rule, the defendant's conduct in publishing material giving rise to a defamatory imputation will not be reasonable unless the defendant had reasonable grounds for believing that the imputation was true, took proper steps, so far as they were reasonably open, to verify the accuracy of the material and did not believe the imputation to be untrue. Furthermore, the defendant's conduct will not be

[49] (1997) 189 CLR 520. [50] *Id.* at 568. [51] *Id.* at 574. [52] *Id.*

> reasonable unless the defendant has sought a response from the person defamed and published the response made (if any) except in cases where the seeking or publication of a response was not practicable or it was unnecessary to give the plaintiff an opportunity to respond.[53]

As in the United Kingdom, reasonableness is required, but the standard is given further definition by the provision that the failure to take certain prescribed steps may lead to a conclusion of unreasonableness.

While the test provided is not, by its own terms, limited to the defamation of public officials or involving matters of public political concern, it is worth repeating that Australian freedom of expression is limited to what is protected by the implied freedom of political communication. It is clear that the test will apply to defamation of a public official, from members of Parliament through far lower levels. It would appear also to apply, more generally, to communication on political topics, here even in regard to political issues in an important neighboring country.

New Zealand

David Lange also did not like the treatment he received in the press of his own country. An article in the magazine *North and South* was critical of his performance as a politician and in his former role as prime minister and suggested that he had selective memory in his recall of certain events. His defamation suit was considered twice by the Court of Appeal of New Zealand. The first was prior to the United Kingdom decision in *Reynolds*. When it was appealed to the Privy Council, the Council set aside the decision and remitted the case to the Court of Appeal of New Zealand for reconsideration in light of *Reynolds*.[54]

In its second incarnation, as *Lange v. Atkinson*,[55] the New Zealand Court declined the opportunity to revise its conclusions. The Court saw the situations of the press in the United Kingdom and New Zealand as quite different. "[I]t is possible to say that New Zealand has not encountered the worst excesses and irresponsibilities of the English national daily tabloids."[56] That difference, coupled with the facts that the population of New Zealand was

[53] *Id.* [54] *See* Lange v. Atkinson, [1999] NZPC 5. [55] [2000] NZCA 95.

[56] *Id.* at ¶ 34 (quoting a New Zealand journalist as saying "some British tabloids have thrown away the rulebook in their pursuit of sensational exclusives. Invasion of personal privacy, fabrication of interviews and the obtaining of information by dishonest means have become the norm in the downmarket tabloid press").

comparatively small and that daily newspapers were not nationally published, which would limit damage, led the court to adopt its own rule.

The Court required that the publisher have a genuine belief in the truth of the published statement and said that that cannot be true where there is recklessness or indifference to truth. Nonetheless, carelessness does play a role. "[W]hile carelessness will not of itself be sufficient to negate the defence, its existence may well support an assertion by the plaintiff of a lack of belief or recklessness."[57] Providing more guidance, the Court went on to say:

> What constitutes recklessness is something which must take its colour from the nature of the occasion, and the nature of the publication. If it is reckless not "to consider or care" whether a statement be true or false, ... it must be open to the view that a perfunctory level of consideration (against the substance, gravity and width of the publication) can also be reckless. It is within the concept of misusing the occasion to say that the defendant may be regarded as reckless if there has been a failure to give such responsible consideration to the truth or falsity of the statement as the jury considers should have been given in all circumstances. In essence the privilege may well be lost if the defendant takes what in all circumstances can fairly be described as a cavalier approach to the truth of the statement ... What amounts to a reckless statement must depend significantly on what is said and to whom and by whom.[58]

Professor Barendt notes that the defense in New Zealand is narrower than in Australia in that it protects only communications about politicians and candidates.[59] It is then a defense that specifically addresses public officials or those who would become public officials, rather than one that, in addressing matters of public concern generally, also applies to public officials. In summing up the rules, Professor Barendt distinguishes between rules that may be applied more mechanically against those that require the weighing of particular facts. He places the United States and New Zealand in the first camp, with England in the second; Australia he sees as a hybrid, finding a qualified privilege only in political discussion, but also requiring that the defendant show reasonableness.[60]

Canada

Hill v. Church of Scientology[61] grew out of a press conference by a barrister representing the Church of Scientology announcing a motion to commence criminal contempt proceedings against Hill, a Crown attorney. The contempt

57 *Id.* at ¶ 44. 58 *Id.* at ¶¶ 47–48. 59 *See* BARENDT, *supra* note 6, at 213.
60 *See id.* at 225–26. 61 [1995] 2 S.C.R. 1130.

allegations were based in a claim that Hill had participated in the opening of a large number of documents that he knew were sealed by court order. This was despite the fact that a member of the church had been monitoring the documents and had concluded in a report that there was no evidence that the documents had been tampered with. Indeed, when the contempt trial occurred, it was dismissed on the grounds that there was no evidence against Hill. Despite the court's ruling and the report by the church member, the Church later repeated its allegations.

Hill sued the church for defamation. The issue before the Supreme Court of Canada was whether a jury verdict in favor of Hill and the award of damages violated Section 2(b) of the Canadian Charter of Rights and Freedoms. Despite the fact that Hill was a public official, the Court adhered to the position it had adopted in *Dolphin Delivery v. R.W.D.S.U., Local* 580[62] that civil actions between private individuals or entities cannot be in violation of the Charter. While common-law defamation rules might be in conflict with Charter values, they could not violate Charter rights.

This reliance on *Dolphin Delivery* may seem to have been an expansion on this position taken there. Both parties in that case were private entities, a delivery company and a union; the only arguable government action was the issuance of an injunction against picketing. In *Hill*, the plaintiff was clearly a public official. That, in the view of the defendants, distinguished the case, but the court rejected the distinction.

> The fact that persons are employed by the government does not mean that their reputation is automatically divided into two parts, one related to their personal life and the other to their employment status. To accept the appellant's position would mean that identical defamatory comments would be subjected to two different laws, one applicable to government employees, the other to the rest of society. Government employment cannot be a basis for such a distinction. Reputation is an integral and fundamentally important aspect of every individual. It exists for everyone quite apart from employment.[63]

The Court said that the statements were directed at Hill, as an individual, not at the government and that he had sued on his own behalf.[64] No part of the government had instigated or controlled the suit, and even the fact that the Ministry of the Attorney General had funded the action did not make it governmental action.[65]

62 [1986] 2 S.C.R. 573. The case is discussed in Chapter 2. 63 [1995] 2 S.C.R. at ¶ 74.
64 *See id.* at ¶ 77. 65 *See id.*

While that resolved the issue of whether or not there had been a violation of any Charter rights, there was still the issue of whether there was a conflict between the common law of defamation and Charter values. In looking at values, the Court said:

> [D]efamatory statements are very tenuously related to the core values which underlie s. 2(b). They are inimical to the search for truth. False and injurious statement cannot enhance self-development. Nor can it ever be said that they lead to healthy participation in the affairs of the community. Indeed, they are detrimental to the advancement of these values and harmful to the interests in a free and democratic society.[66]

The Court said that extending the qualified privilege "would tend to deter sensitive and honourable men from seeking public positions of trust and responsibility, and leave them open to others who have no respect for their reputation."[67] While the Court did not extend the qualified privilege, it did later adopt a new defense that served much the same purpose.[68]

The Court specifically rejected the invitation to adopt the *New York Times* standard,[69] and it went on to add:

> The law of defamation is essentially aimed at the prohibition of the publication of injurious false statements. It is the means by which the individual may protect his or her reputation, which may well be the most distinguishing feature of his or her character, personality, and, perhaps, identity. I simply cannot see that the law of defamation is unduly restrictive or inhibiting. Surely it is not requiring too much of individuals that they ascertain the truth of the allegations they publish. The law of defamation provides for the defences of fair comment and of qualified privilege in appropriate cases. Those who publish statements should assume a reasonable level of responsibility.[70]

That still did allow the common law defenses. While the Church had, earlier, asserted justification, or the truth of its allegations, such a defense would be unsuccessful given the outcome of the contempt case, and the defense was abandoned. Since the statements asserted alleged facts, the fair comment defense was not available.

As for common law qualified privilege, the Court noted that, where it exists, it can be defeated where a statement is made with malice. That would appear to be the case with regard to the Church, since the Church had closely

[66] *Id.* ¶ 109. [67] *Id.* [68] *See infra* notes 95–97 and accompanying text.
[69] *See* [1995] 2 S.C.R. at ¶ 140. [70] *Id.*

monitored Hill for at least four years, keeping a file on him, and had designated him as an "Enemy Canada."[71]

The Court did accept that there was a qualified privilege that extends to reports on documents that relate to judicial proceedings. The barrister's comments had been with regard to an action to be filed, that is, a judicial proceeding, and the Court did not allow the fact that the actual filing did not occur until the next day to defeat the privilege. However, the conduct of the press conference was said to be "high-handed and careless," exceeding any legitimate purpose, and the privilege did not attach.[72]

The European Court of Human Rights

Given the provision in Article 10(2) of the European Convention on Human Rights that the freedom of expression provision in Article 10(1) "may be subject to such formalities, conditions, restrictions or penalties as are prescribed by law and are necessary in a democratic society ... for the protection of the reputation or rights of others ..." and the usual margin of appreciation in Article 10 cases, it is not surprising that the member states have some latitude in the application of their defamation laws. But the European Court will examine that application and, in keeping with its Article 10(2) jurisprudence, will require proportionality between the limitation and free expression values.

In *Lingens v. Austria*,[73] the Court considered a case in which a private prosecution was brought by the retiring Chancellor of Austria, Bruno Kreisky. The prosecution was brought under a criminal statute providing:

> Anyone who in such a way that it may be perceived by a third person accuses another of possessing a contemptible character or attitude or behaviour contrary to honour or morality and of such a nature as to make him contemptible or otherwise lower him in public esteem shall be liable to imprisonment not exceeding six months or a fine.[74]

The statute did provide a defense if the statement was proven true or if the defendant had sufficient reason to assume it was true.[75]

The events immediately leading to the allegedly defamatory statements began with a television interview of Simon Wiesenthal in which he accused

[71] *See id.* at ¶ 22.

[72] *See id.* at ¶ 159. Justice L'Heureux-Dubé, in her concurrence, disagreed with regard to the application of the qualified privilege to pleadings, where no judicial action had yet occurred. *See id.* at ¶ 212.

[73] App. No. 9815/82, 8 Eur. H.R. Rep. 407 (1986).

[74] *Id.* at ¶ 20 (quoting Article 111 of the Austrian Criminal Code).

[75] *See id.*

the president of the Austrian Liberal Party of having served in the SS. That led to Kreisky coming to the defense of the body president in the process of which he accused Weisenthal and his organization of being a "political mafia" and engaging in "mafia methods." Lingens' involvement came in the form of two articles published in a Vienna magazine. The first criticized Kreisky's attitude and accused him of protecting Wiesenthal's original target and other former SS members. He suggested that the criticism might be seen as opportunism, if offered by another speaker, but that it was more complex since Kreisky believed what he had said. The second criticized Kreisky's support of the party president and for being accommodating to former Nazis. He added that Kreisky's behavior was irrational, immoral, and undignified and that he lacked tact in his treatment of Nazi victims. He added that, in general, Austrians had refused to face up to their guilt and that Austrian political parties were deserving of criticism because of the presence of former Nazis as leaders.

When the case reached the European Court, the Court found no difficulty in establishing that the original action was an interference with Lingens' free expression rights, that it had been prescribed by law and had the legitimate aim of the protection of reputation. The issue was whether the interference was "necessary in a democratic society." That required proportionality. The Court had to "determine whether the interference at issue was 'proportionate to the legitimate aim pursued' and whether the reasons adduced by the Austrian courts to justify it [were] 'relevant and sufficient.'"[76]

In that analysis, the Court found the fact that Kreisky was a politician to be relevant.

> The limits of acceptable criticism are . . . wider as regards a politician as such than as regards a private individual. Unlike the latter, the former inevitably and knowingly lays himself open to close scrutiny of his every word and deed by both journalists and the public at large, and he must consequently display a greater degree of tolerance. No doubt Article 10 para. 2 . . . enables the reputation of others – that is to say, of all individuals – to be protected, and this protection extends to politicians too, even when they are not acting in their private capacity; but in such cases the requirements of such protection have to be weighed in relation to the interests of open discussion of political issues.[77]

So, while the Court did not adopt a different rule for public officials and politicians, their status as plaintiffs impacts the proportionality of any penalties imposed.

[76] *Id.* at ¶ 40 (citation omitted). [77] *Id.* at ¶ 42.

The Court noted that the comments were made in the context of a post-election political controversy. Given that it was Kreisky's statements regarding Wiesenthal that led to Lingens' reaction, the Court said that "in this struggle each used the weapons at his disposal; and these were in no way unusual in the hard-fought tussles of politics."[78] The Austrian court's imposition of a fine and order of confiscation of the magazines were disproportionate. "In the context of political debate such a sentence would be likely to deter journalists from contributing to public discussion of issues affecting the life of the community ... [It] is liable to hamper the press in performing its task as purveyor of information and public watchdog."[79]

A second case from the European Court, *Thorgeirson v. Iceland*,[80] could be seen as fitting this category. Thorgeirson published two articles, in a daily newspaper, alleging brutality by the Reykjavík police. He recounted the stories of others who claimed to be the victims of this brutality and added "there is something essentially wrong in a system where the people in charge seem to disregard all sense of justice and misinterpret their duties by allowing brutes and sadists to act out their perversions ... In my opinion the Reykjavík Chief of Police is being stubborn in refusing to relieve the accused policemen from their duties ...."[81]

At the request of the Reykjavík Police Association, the public prosecutor indicted Thorgeirson for defaming "unspecified members of the Reykjavík police."[82] The relevant criminal provision not only included defamation against public officials; it was specifically directed at such defamation.

> Whoever vituperates or otherwise insults a civil servant in words or actions or makes defamatory allegations against or about him when he is discharging his duty, on account of the discharge of his duty, shall be fined, detained or imprisoned for up to three years. An allegation, even if proven, may warrant a fine if made in an imprudent manner.[83]

The Icelandic courts concluded that the provision addressed statements against not only individuals but against limited groups of unspecified civil servants. The defendant was convicted and fined.

[78] *Id.* at ¶ 43.

[79] *Id.* at ¶ 44. The Court also recognized that Lingens' statements were value judgments protected by the freedom of opinion. It noted that the Austrian Criminal Code provided the defense of truth, but that truth is not provable in the context of opinion. *See id.* at ¶ 45–46.

[80] App. No. 13778/88, 14 Eur. H.R. Rep. 115 (1992).

[81] *Id.* at ¶ 9 (quoting paragraph 13 of the published letter to the Minister Justice).

[82] *See id.* at ¶ 13.

[83] *Id.* at ¶ 31 (quoting Article 108 of the Penal Code).

The Court said that the defendant had been reporting what was said by others with regard to police brutality but had been convicted because the lower court, in part, believed he had failed to justify what it took to be his own claims. That, the Court said, was an impossible task, since they were the statements of others. Perhaps more importantly, the Court also believed that the aim of the article had not been to damage the reputation of the police force and that the criticisms voiced did not attack any specific member, or all members, of the force.[84]

Rather than base the proportionality analysis on the role of police officers as public officials, the Court relied on the fact that the article addressed a matter of serious public concern. This may have been, at least in part, due to a distinction between an elected official, such as Kreisky, and an unelected civil servant. While using strong language, the court concluded that the language of the article could not be seen as excessive. Given the capability of the sentence to discourage discussion of matters of public concern, the interference was disproportionate.

European law does not require the categorization of United States law. The test set out in Article 10(2) is employed in all contexts. It does not really matter whether the Court looked at the issue as representing the importance of allowing criticism of public officials or as protecting the discussion of issues of public concern. Either approach would have led to the conclusion that this criminal conviction, even if leading only to a fine, was disproportionate.[85]

PUBLIC FIGURES AND MATTERS OF PUBLIC CONCERN

The United States

The United States, in a pair of consolidated cases, *Curtis Publishing Co. v. Butts* and *Associated Press v. Walker*,[86] considered the requirements necessary for a public figure to recover in a defamation case. Butts was the athletics

[84] *See id.* at ¶ 66.

[85] One commentator, examining the opinions of the European Court Human Rights, concludes that the Court has never found imprisonment to be justified in a criminal defamation action. *See* Alan Edward Shoenberger, *Connecticut Yankee Speech in Europe's Court: An Alternative Vision of Constitutional Defamation Law to* New York Times Co. v. Sullivan, 28 QUINNIPIAC L. REV. 431, 464 (2010). "While the ECHR has not rejected criminal defamation prosecutions out of hand, in practice, it has done so except for cases in which damages alone are awarded." *Id.* at 471. The criminal action, with imprisonment off the table, may not differ significantly, perhaps other than in level of stigma, from a civil action.

[86] 388 U.S. 130 (1967).

director at the University of Georgia. An article in the *Saturday Evening Post*, titled "The Story of a College Football Fix," asserted that a source had overheard, through some sort of telephonic electronic mistake, Butts providing information to the coach at the University of Alabama regarding Georgia's plays and defensive plan.

Walker was said, in an Associated Press story, to have commanded a violent crowd protesting the admission of the first African–American student to the University of Mississippi and to have led a charge against federal marshals protecting the student. Walker denied the acts, claiming to have counseled restraint and nonviolence, but he had demonstrated past interest in the federal intervention and had spoken strongly against such actions. As the Court put it, he could fairly be seen as a man of political prominence.

Neither was a public official. While Butts' position might have suggested that he was such a public official, he was actually employed by a private foundation. Walker, while having formerly commanded the United States troops involved in the desegregation of the Little Rock, Arkansas public schools, had returned to private life.

While not public officials, the plurality said that both were public figures. Butts may have attained that status by position alone and Walker by purposeful activity amounting to a thrusting of his personality into the "vortex" of an important public controversy, but both commanded sufficient continuing public interest and had sufficient access to the means of counterargument to be able "to expose through discussion the falsehood and fallacies" of the defamatory statements.[87] In a later case, the Court expanded on its analysis of what makes an individual a public figure.

> That designation may rest on either of two alternative bases. In some instances an individual may achieve such pervasive fame or notoriety that he becomes a public figure for all purposes and in all contexts. More commonly, an individual voluntarily injects himself or is drawn into a particular public controversy and thereby becomes a public figure for a limited range of issues. In either case such persons assume special prominence in the resolution of public questions.[88]

While, again, it is possible for an individual, simply through sufficient general fame, to be an all-purpose public figure, in most cases public figures and public controversies go together. A person becomes a public figure by engaging in the debate on an issue of public interest.

[87] *Id.* at 155 (citation omitted). [88] Gertz v. Welch, 418 U.S. 323, 351 (1974).

The Court has also made it clear that the public being interested does not necessarily make the matter one that is in the public interest. While people may have been interested in the allegations of the parties' sexual activities in *Time, Inc. v. Firestone*,[89] the Court concluded that the Firestone divorce did not involve a public controversy, particularly when neither party publicized those issues to influence the outcome of the divorce.

The next issue in *Butts* was the impact of designation as a public figure on the requirements necessary to recover for defamation. The plurality concluded that the First Amendment required some additional protection for defendants, when the plaintiff is a public figure. While not ruling out application of the *New York Times* standard, the plurality said that there might be other appropriate accommodations.

> We consider and would hold that a "public figure" who is not a public official may also recover damages for defamatory falsehood whose substance makes substantial danger to reputation apparent, on a showing of highly unreasonable conduct constituting an extreme departure from the standards of investigation and reporting ordinarily adhered to by responsible publishers.[90]

The plurality test, sounding in gross negligence, was only that of four justices. A fifth vote was required for the heightened protection of defendants. That vote was provided by the concurring opinion of Chief Justice Warren. His disagreement with the plurality was in the failure to apply the *New York Times* standard. Given the combination of votes, *Butts* has come to be recognizing as imposing the *Times* standard, when suit is brought by a public figure

The United Kingdom

It is important to remember that Reynolds was not a public official in the United Kingdom, nor did the *Reynolds* decision rest on his status. He would certainly have been a public figure in the United States law, especially given his role in the Northern Ireland peace process. That did not, however, lead to special protections under United Kingdom law. The English Court did conclude that the qualified privilege was available and set out circumstances that would lead to a conclusion that it was reasonable to publish the story.

There are other cases, prior to the revision of the Defamation Act that would also have been public figure cases under United States law. In *Irving v. Penguin Books*,[91] Irving, a revisionist historian and Holocaust denier, claimed

[89] 424 U.S. 448 (1976). [90] 388 U.S. at 155. [91] 2000 WL 362478 (Q.B.).

to have been libeled by a book titled *Denying the Holocaust – The Growing Assault on Truth and Memory*. He sued the publisher and author, a professor from the United States. The court set out the crux of the statements said to be defamatory. The book called Irving an apologist for Hitler and accused him of distorting and manipulating documents and data in order to exonerate Hitler. It said he was a dangerous spokesperson for Holocaust denial.

Under United States law, Irving's involvement in the debate and general recognition for the positions he had taken on the Holocaust would have made him a public figure for purposes of this sort of discussion. He would have been faced with proving the falsity of any defamatory statement and that the publication had been with *New York Times* actual malice. Under the United Kingdom law, at the time, the defense had to rest on justification; it bore the burden of establishing the truth of the statements made.

The court's opinion is extremely long, examining in detail the plaintiff's and defendants' views with regard to the truth or falsity of a significant number of statements.[92] The court concluded that most of the imputations against Irving were substantially justified; they had been proven true by the defendant. While there were some allegations that the defendant had failed to prove true and that, hence, were to be treated as false, that did not lead to liability. Given the gravity of the charges proven true, compared to those for which proof was lacking, the court said that the false statements did not materially affect the plaintiff's reputation.

A great deal of effort must have gone into the defense, in light of the great effort on the part of the trial judge. That effort, and the expense involved, would seem likely to chill this sort of speech. That would have a negative impact on the discussion of an issue of public interest.

Another case, involving a person perhaps not voluntarily entering the public fray but being thrust into it, was decided by the House of Lords in *Jameel v. Wall Street Journal Europe*.[93] The plaintiff, a Saudi Arabian businessperson, and the company of which he was president claimed to have been libeled by an article asserting that law enforcement authorities in the United States and Saudi Arabia's central bank were monitoring their bank accounts to prevent the funding of terrorism. In this post-*Reynolds* case, the publisher argued qualified privilege, but the lower courts disallowed the defense because of the failure to obtain a response to the statements prior to publication. Given

[92] A shorter summary and analysis may be found in Dennise Mulvihill, Irving v. Penguin: *Historians on Trial and the Determination of Truths under English Libel Law*, 11 Fordham Intell. Prop. Media & Ent. L.J. 217 (2000).

[93] [2007] 1 A.C. 359.

the public importance of the topic, the House of Lords refused to determine the outcome based on that fact alone and found the article to have met the test of responsible journalism.

It is important to, once again, note the 2013 revision to the Defamation Act. Section 4, titled "Publication on matter of public interest," provides:

(1) It is a defence to an action for defamation for the defendant to show that—
 (a) the statement complained of was, or formed part of, a statement on a matter of public interest; and
 (b) the defendant reasonably believed that publishing the statement complained of was in the public interest . . .

While the burden of proof for the defense is on the defendant, the revision would seem much more protective of defendants who publish statements on matters of public interest. Given the conceptual tie between public figures and matters of public interest, the revision would also be more protective when the plaintiff is a public figure.

It is worth noting that the House of Lords has also drawn a distinction between that which is in the public interest and that which interests the public. The Court, in *Reynolds*, said "the public also have an interest to receive information on matters of public interest to the community (as opposed, of course, information about matters in which the public may happen to be interested)."[94] The most recent version of the Defamation Act did abolish the *Reynolds* defense, replacing it with the public interest provision in Section 4, but this distinction between public interest and interest of the public would seem not to be the part of the *Reynolds* defense addressed by the statute, and this distinction should still stand.

Canada

The Supreme Court of Canada did recognize the need to protect comment on matters of public concern in *Grant v. Torstar*.[95] It did so while holding to the position that the Canadian Charter did not apply to interactions between private citizens. Instead, it looked to Charter values to decide whether the available common law defenses were in accord with Charter values and concluded that the defenses were inadequate.

The plaintiffs in the case were a forestry company and the company's owner. The owner wanted to expand an existing golf course, an expansion

[94] [2001] 2 A.C. at 177. [95] [2009] 3 S.C.R. 640.

that would require the purchase of government land and government approval of the plan. A newspaper article on the potential expansion included comments by some nearby residents that the process lacked integrity, because of ties between the owner and government officials. The plaintiffs sued for defamation, and after the trial court rejected the availability of qualified immunity and the jury rejected the justification and fair comment defenses, the plaintiffs were awarded close to $1.5 million.

The Supreme Court decided that Charter values required the recognition of an additional defense, a "defence of responsible communication on matters of public interest."[96] The new defense, and the Court did characterize it as new, had two essential elements; it must be on a matter of public interest and the defendant had the burden of showing the publication was responsible.

> The defence of public interest responsible communication ... will apply where: (a) the publication is on a matter of public interest, and (b) the publisher was diligent in trying to verify the allegation, having regard to the seriousness of the allegation, the public importance of the matter, the urgency of the matter, the status and reliability of the source, whether the plaintiff's side of the story was sought and accurately reported, whether the inclusion of the defamatory statement was justifiable, whether the defamatory statement's public interest lay in the fact that it was made rather than its truth (reportage), and any other relevant circumstances.[97]

Public interest was to be determined by the judge, and the factors determining the existence of the defense were to be determined by the jury. The Supreme Court, here, concluded that the defense was available; that is, the article was on a matter of public interest, but returned the case for new trial on responsible publication.

Germany

The provision protecting the freedom of opinion, Article 5(1) of the Basic Law, is followed by the limitation in Article 5(2) that "These rights shall find their limits in the provisions of general laws, in provisions for the protection of young persons, and in the right to personal honor." Given that invitation to impose limits, coupled with the protections in Articles 1 and 2 of human dignity and the free development of personality, it is not surprising that Germany employs a situational balancing approach, rather than the adoption of rules. Professor Barendt says:

[96] *Id.* at ¶ 7. [97] *Id.* at ¶126.

> German case-law makes little attempt to formulate precise rules on the basis of which free speech and reputation rights are to be balanced. No sharp line is drawn, for instance, between defamatory allegations made in the course of political speech or, more narrowly, concerning politicians on the one hand, and allegations made in public discourse generally on the other. Rather, the Constitutional Court lays down guidelines on the basis of which the ordinary civil and criminal courts are required in some circumstances to give priority to reputation or freedom of speech, and in other cases to balance in the light of particular facts.[98]

Professor Barendt adds that "[u]nder the balancing formula established by the Court in *Lüth*, lower courts must weigh the competing interest in freedom of expression and in personal reputation appropriate in light of all relevant facts in the case . . ."[99]

There is a case that, while again not adopting a special rule for public figures, does discuss the implications of thrusting oneself into the public debate. The plaintiff in the *Römerberg Speech Cases*[100] was a sculptor and art professor who had given two lectures on art criticism. The lectures themselves were quite critical of the art establishment and art critics. The defendants were broadcast journalists, one of whom said, among other things, that the plaintiff had been guided by personal resentment, was unknown as a realistic sculptor and had "quite unabashedly hauled off with hate-filled tirades and so-called revelations about the art business, delivered from the position of a blinkered schoolmaster."[101] The other added, "I listened very attentively to hear whether the art writer's tongue might not slip once to say that everything was Jew-ridden, or that the Freemasons were behind it, for that was the way the tone was."[102]

The German Court recognized the impact that a damage award could have on intellectual debate. In language sounding in chilling effect, the Court said an award "inevitably develops preventive effects by subjecting the expression of critical opinions to high financial risk; it may thus reduce willingness to exercise criticism in future, and in this way bring about adverse effects on free intellectual debate that must affect the core of the constitutional guarantees."[103] The Court said that that required protection of what might be characterized as speech on topics in the public interest.

98 Barendt, *supra* note 6, at 218. 99 *Id.* at 214 (citing Lüth, 7BVerfGE198 (1958)).

100 54 BVerfGE 129 (1980). The case may be found in translation at Decisions of the Bundesverfassungsgericht- Federal Constitutional Court-Federal Republic of Germany: Volume 2/Part I: Freedom of Speech 181 (1998). Citations are to the translated version.

101 *Id.* at 183. 102 *Id.* 103 *Id.* at 185.

The Court, without ever using the phrase "public figure," also recognized that a plaintiff, who had thrust himself into the public debate, one of the ways in which one may become a public figure under United States law, might lead to lesser protection.

> [A] person who in the public clash of opinion has given occasion for a negative value judgment must in principle put up with a sharp reaction even if it diminishes his reputation ... It is ... of decisive importance to focus on whether and to what extent the person affected by defamatory statements had in turn taken part in the process of public opinion-formation protected by Article 5(1) . . ., and thus by his own decision subjected himself to the terms of the clash of opinion and by so doing surrendered a part of his private sphere deserving protection.[104]

While not adopting a rule specifically applicable to public figures, the balance to be drawn is affected.

The European Court of Human Rights

Given the general approach of balancing the European Convention on Human Rights Article 10(1) provision protecting free expression against Article 10(2)'s acceptance of certain limitations, with a specific acceptance of "for the protection of the reputation or rights of others," it is unsurprising that the European Court would engage in that exercise in the area of defamation. Here too, with a balancing approach, there is not the need for categories. Professor Barendt says that the Court "is concerned with the character and subject matter of the defamatory material rather than the status of the libel claimant,"[105] although *Lingens* does show that status as a politician may matter.

There are European Court cases that do show that factors that would make an individual a public figure in United States law may play a role in the analysis of the Court. *Nilsen and Johnsen v. Norway*[106] grew out of a debate over police violence in the city of Bergen. An empirical study on violence had been published, claiming that there were approximately 360 incidents a year involving excessive and illegal police use of force in the years studied. That report led to strong public debate, and the Ministry of Justice appointed a Committee of Inquiry that included Anders Bratholm, a law professor, and Hans Stenberg-Nilsen, an advocate before the Supreme Court.

[104] *Id.* at 187. [105] BARENDT, *supra* note 6, at 223.
[106] App. No. 23118/93, 30 Eur. H.R. Rep. 878 (1999).

The Committee report and other later publications by the two members were not well received by the police. Arnold Nilsen, the Chairman of the Norwegian Police Association, and Gerhard Johnsen, the chairman of the Bergen Police Association, both made statements critical of Professor Bratholm. He was said to have lied, and his motives were called into question. He sued for defamation and won in the Norwegian courts.

The European Court concluded that the Norwegian decision violated Article 10. In doing so, the Court first considered the claim that the plaintiff, as an appointed expert to the Committee, should have to exhibit the greater degree of tolerance expected of a politician. Instead, the Court rested its analysis on the plaintiff's role in the debate and the impact that should have.

> The applicants were … not entirely unjustified in claiming that they were entitled to "hit back in the same way" … [G]reater weight should be attached to the plaintiff's own active involvement in a lively public discussion than was done by the national courts … In the Court's view, a degree of exaggeration should be tolerated in the context of such a heated and continuing public debate of affairs of general concern, where on both sides professional reputations were at stake.[107]

Here too, thrusting oneself into the public debate led to a lesser protection in the balance, even if not leading to a different categorization or rule.

A second Norwegian case before the European Court demonstrates the role that public interest, without a voluntary assumption of prominence by the plaintiff, may play. *Bergens Tidende v. Norway*[108] resulted from newspaper articles describing complaints by former patients of a named cosmetic surgeon with regard to the results of their procedures. The articles followed an earlier article that had described the same surgeon's practice and the benefits of cosmetic surgery. That earlier article had led to the patients' complaints to the newspaper. On the same page as one of the later, allegedly defamatory, articles, there was an additional article by another cosmetic surgeon discussing how demanding such surgery is, and suggesting that patients may have unrealistic expectations. Arguing that he had been defamed by allegations of incompetence and lack of care, the cosmetic surgeon sued for defamation and won in the national courts.

The European Court found a violation of Article 10. In doing so, it invoked public interest.

[107] *Id.* at ¶ 52.

[108] App. No. 26132/95, 31 Eur. H.R. Rep. 430 (2000).

> Although the press must not overstep certain bounds, particularly as regards the reputation rights of others . . ., its duty is nevertheless to impart - in a manner consistent with its obligations and responsibilities - information and ideas on all matters of public interest . . . [J]ournalistic freedom also covers possible recourse to a degree of exaggeration, or even provocation. In cases such as the present one, the national margin of appreciation is circumscribed by the interests of a democratic society in enabling the press to exercise its vital role of "public watchdog" by imparting information of serious public concern.[109]

The Court did say that "the safeguard afforded by Article 10 to journalists in relation to reporting on issues of general interest is subject to the proviso that they are acting in good faith in order to provide accurate and reliable information in accordance with the ethics of journalism."[110] Here, the newspaper had accurately reported the women's complaints, and the Court said that the surgeon's reputational interest was insufficient to overcome the public interest on matters of legitimate public concern.

Japan

At least as a matter of statutory law, Japan appears to come down heavily in favor of reputation, even at the expense of expression. The *Gekkan Pen Defamation Case*[111] grew out of articles critical of a Buddhist organization and its leader Daisaku Ikeda. The criminal code provision at issue provided: "A person who defames another by publicly alleging facts shall, regardless of whether such facts are true or false, be punished with imprisonment at or without force labor for not more than three years or a fine of not more than 1,000 yen."[112]

While that provision applies to true, as well as false, statements, truth may sometimes be a defense. The statute also provided:

> When the act provided for in paragraph 1 of the preceding Article is found to relate to matters of public interest and to have been done solely for the benefit of the public and, upon inquiry into the truth or falsity of the alleged facts, the truth is proved punishment shall not be imposed.[113]

[109] *Id.* at ¶ 49 (citations omitted). [110] *Id.* at ¶ 53.

[111] Gekkan Pen v. Japan, 35 Keishū 34 (1984). The Tokyo court's decision in the case on remand is reported at 1128 Hanrei Jihō 32 (1984). The remanded case is available in translation at Lawrence W. Beer & Hiroshi Itoh, The Constitutional Case Law of Japan, 1970 through 1990 637 (1996).

[112] Beer & Itoh, *supra* note 111, at 638 (providing a translation of Article 230). The current version of Article 230 provides for a fine of 500,000 yen.

[113] *Id.* (providing a translation of Article 230-2, 1).

Furthermore, the same defense applies "with regard to matters concerning a public servant or a candidate for elective public office."[114] Where truth is a defense, the burden of proof lies with the defendant.

The Supreme Court overturned the lower courts' determination that there had been defamatory allegations in the articles, because the plaintiff's status put the matters in the public interest. He was a public figure, as the leader of a religious movement with millions of members. The case was returned to the lower courts, and according to the editor's notes to the translation of the lower court case, that court found that there was a public interest motivation but that there were insufficient grounds for believing that the allegations were true.[115]

There is actually an earlier case that came out better for the libel defendant and for free expression in its balance with reputation. *Kōchi v. Japan*[116] resulted from newspaper articles alleging attempts by the plaintiff to corrupt public officials. The defendant was convicted, because of a failure to establish the truth of the allegations. The Supreme Court was not willing to rely simply on the failure to establish truth, saying, "criminal intent and a crime of defamation should not be deemed present in this case, where a party mistakenly believed his statements were true and where there was sufficient reason for this mistaken belief in light of the concrete evidence presented."[117] The Court found that there were reasonable grounds for the mistaken belief in the truth of what was alleged. This would appear to import a reasonableness defense into the statute, despite the language indicating that the defendant must prove truth.

This reasonableness defense is repeated in a case decided by the Supreme Court following the *Gekken Pen* case. The *Hoppo Journal Injunction Case*[118] involved material that attacked the dignity of a mayor running to be governor of Hokkaido. The case is discussed in Chapter 10, on attacks on personal honor,[119] but the Court also discussed the relationship between truth, reasonableness, and defamation.

> [W]hen an act constituting civil or criminal defamation is found to relate to matters of public interest, and to have been done solely for public benefit, and when the truth of the alleged facts is proved, such expression is not

[114] *Id.* (providing a translation of Article 230-2, 3). [115] *See id.* at 638.

[116] 23 Keishu 7 at 259 (1969). The case is found in translation at Hiroshi Itoh & Lawrence Beer, The Constitutional Case Law of Japan: Selected Supreme Court Decisions, 1961–1970 175 (1979).

[117] *Id.* at 177.

[118] Ona v. Igarashi, 40 Minshu 4 at 872. The case may be found in translation at Beer & Itoh, *supra* note 111, at 606.

[119] *See* Chapter 10.

> illegal. Even if the truth is not proved, when the perpetrator has sufficient grounds for mistakenly believing in the truth of the allegations, the act should not be construed as malicious or negligent.[120]

So, the reasonableness defense survives *Gekkan Pen*.

PRIVATE INDIVIDUALS

Even when the plaintiff is neither a public official nor a public figure, United States law does put some limitation on defamation suits. *Gertz v. Welch*[121] provides that there must be some degree of fault on the part of the defendant. The court said: "We hold that, so long as they do not impose liability without fault, the States may define for themselves the appropriate standard of liability for a publisher or broadcaster of defamatory falsehood injurious to a private individual."[122] Thus, the states must require that the defendant at least have been negligent, although states are free to require a higher level of culpability. The conclusion that negligence would suffice spoke only to the recovery of actual damages. The *Gertz* Court said that, for a plaintiff to recover punitive damages, the plaintiff would have to meet the *New York Times* standard.[123]

While the test for private individual defamation suits is not as protective of defendants as it is for suits brought by public figures of public officials, the defendant still enjoys more protection than in the United Kingdom. The burden of proof with regard to falsity and to negligence lies with the plaintiff, under United States law. Under United Kingdom law, the defendant, to avail itself of the justification defense, must prove truth.

The standard of fault in cases brought by private individuals in the United States does not differ as much from the reasonableness defense developing in a number of countries, but here too there are differences. Under the United Kingdom's new Defamation Act, the defense of reasonableness in the belief of the truth of what was published is only relevant when the matter is in the public interest. Much of what is said about private individuals may not be a matter of public interest, even as has been seen, when it interests the public.

DEFAMATION AND DEMOCRACY

Defamation provides another area in which law in the United States differs from that in much of the rest of the democratic world. Differences in this area have the potential to be significant with regard to the vitality of democracy.

120 Beer & Itoh, *supra* note 111, at 609.
121 418 U.S. 323 (1974).
122 *Id.* at 347 (footnote omitted).
123 *See id.* at 350.

Clearly, a country that allows legal action to be taken against someone who is critical of the government has difficulty in laying claim to the label "democratic." Even if action is brought only when the statement is false, the chilling effect of potential liability would likely be sufficient to diminish the discussion of the actions of the government that is so essential to democracy. But these sedition-like actions do not seem to occur in the democratic countries.

Differences in the treatment of public officials and of those who have become public figures by engaging in the debate on matters of public interest do exist. The United States is extremely protective of political discussion, even at the expense of the ability of public officials and public figures to protect their reputations. Other countries are more willing to protect those reputations. The issue for democracy would be the impact this willingness has on the political discussion. Most countries, including the United Kingdom, have come to recognize that there must be room for reasonably made false statements. That may well reduce the chilling effect on political discussion but at some cost. The cost is the effort necessary for the publisher to engage in the due diligence that reasonableness requires prior to publication. That is a cost that a number of countries are willing to accept. And, it is important to recognize that these countries willing to accept the cost are fully as democratic as the United States.

Where there may be the greatest difference would be with regard to those who are public figures through their general fame, rather than their engagement in the debate on matters of public interest. Under United States law, they must prove falsity and actual malice to recover in a defamation action. Under the laws of the other countries examined, simply proving the existence of a defamatory statement may be sufficient to recover damages, unless the publisher can prove truth. Even if the publisher had been reasonable, the fact that the statement is about an individual in whom the public is interested may not make the matter one of public interest, and the reasonableness defense would not be available. The cost of this difference to democracy would seem minimal. The ability to discuss the affairs of movie stars and athletes more freely, would seem a minimal contribution to democracy.

10

Attacks on Personal Honor

Protection of personal honor may extend beyond the interest protected by the law of defamation. At least in the United States, defamation requires a false statement that harms the reputation of an individual, although the label may apply more broadly in other countries.[1] An attack on dignity may be found in the expression of an opinion about an individual. The harm is not in the fact that the community may believe a statement that the target has done something evil or distasteful. It may, instead, be found in the holding up of the target to ridicule and may not require a statement that would be seen as a false assertion of fact.

In this area, too, the United States takes a position that is at odds with a number of other countries, although there are not enough cases to suggest that this is a situation of the United States' view being in opposition to that of the rest of the democratic world. The major cases have the United States refusing to protect dignity, while Germany and Japan do provide such protection.

[1] In what seems to be a one-of-a-kind case, a court in the United Kingdom allowed a defamation case to go to the jury, where the potentially defamatory statement should probably be seen as a statement of opinion. In Berkoff v. Burchill, [1997] EMLR 139 the plaintiff, Berkoff, an actor and director, brought suit against a journalist and the *Sunday Times*. In a review, the journalist wrote, "film directors, from Hitchcock to Berkoff, are notoriously hideous-looking people." *Id.* at 141. Later, she reviewed the film *Frankenstein*, where she described the creature: "The Creature is made as a vessel for Waldman's brain, and rejected in disgust when it comes out scarred and primeval. It's a very new look for the Creature – no bolts in the deck or flat-top hairdo – and I think it works; it's a lot like Stephen Berkoff, only marginally better-looking" *Id.* The Court of Appeal found no flaw in the trial court's decision to allow the case to go to the jury as a defamation action. One of the judges did note, "The law of defamation protects reputation, and reputation is not generally dependent upon physical appearance." *Id.* at 54 (opinion of Phillips, L.J.) The *sui generis* nature of this opinion may lie in the fact that the plaintiff, as an actor, could have had his business reputation injured by the review. In any event, the case seems at least close to unique in United Kingdom law.

In addition to the legal protection provided by Germany and Japan, James Whitman argues that France has an honor culture similar to that of Germany, even if it is furthered by education rather than legal sanction;[2] although he also suggests that the hate speech law of France may be an aspect of this honor culture. In Whitman's words:

> "Respect" matters over the whole landscape of law and society in Germany and France. In Germany, … it may even be a criminal offense to call someone a "jerk" or to give somebody "the finger": Germany has not only hate-speech regulation, but also civility law of a more far-reaching kind. France, for its part, is rich in widely accepted and carefully inculcated civility norms.[3]

In recognition of how great the differences in culture are between the United States, on the one hand, and Germany and France on the other, he explains the goal of his article as answering the question: "How did it come to pass that honor, a concept regarded by most Americans is almost laughable, has survived in the large industrial democracies of Continental Europe?"[4]

THE UNITED STATES

The major dignity case from the United States is *Hustler Magazine v. Falwell*.[5] Jerry Falwell was a well-known minister and conservative commentator. *Hustler Magazine* is a pornographic publication but also contains, often sexual, textual material. The suit was based on the magazine's publication of a parody based on a series of ads by Campari Liqueur. In the actual Campari ads, various celebrities were interviewed about "first times." While, on the surface, the subject was the first time the interviewee tried Campari, there was a subtext addressing first sexual experiences.

Hustler, and its publisher Larry Flint, seemingly unappreciative of subtlety, published a parody in which Jerry Falwell was supposedly interviewed. In the fake interview, "he states that his 'first time' was during a drunken incestuous rendezvous with his mother in an outhouse. The *Hustler* parody portrays respondent and his mother as drunk and immoral, and suggests that respondent is a hypocrite who preaches only when he is drunk."[6] There were indications that the "interview" was a parody. The table of contents listing for the

[2] *See generally* James Q. Whitman, *Enforcing Civility and Respect: Three Societies*, 109 Yale L.J. 1279 (2000).

[3] *Id*. at 1282.

[4] *Id*. at 1283.

[5] 485 U.S. 46 (1988).

[6] *Id*. at 48.

page said "Fiction: Ad and Personality Parody," and the bottom of the page itself said "ad parody – not to be taken seriously."[7]

Jerry Falwell did take the publication seriously, as a personal affront. He sued for invasion of privacy, libel, and intentional infliction of emotional distress. The trial court allowed the latter two issues to go to the jury, which held against the plaintiff on the defamation claim but found for him on the intentional infliction of emotional distress. With regard to the libel claim, the jury concluded that the parody would not be understood as making any factual claim that Falwell had engaged in the acts portrayed. It did, however, seem that Falwell was genuinely distressed and that the publication met the elements of intentional infliction under Virginia law, i.e., "defendant's conduct (1) is intentional or reckless; (2) offends generally accepted standards of decency or morality; (3) is causally connected with the plaintiff's emotional distress; and (4) caused emotional distress that was severe."[8]

When the case reached the United States Supreme Court, the Court saw the issue as whether or not the First Amendment limited the ability of public figures to recover damages for the intentional infliction of emotional distress. The Court, in a relatively short opinion, concluded that public figures must tolerate such abuse.

> The sort of robust political debate encouraged by the First Amendment is bound to produce speech that is critical of those who hold public office or those public figures who are "intimately involved in the resolution of important public questions or, by reason of their fame, shape events in areas of concern to society at large" ... Justice Frankfurter put it succinctly ..., when he said that "[o]ne of the prerogatives of American citizenship is the right to criticize public men and measures." Such criticism, inevitably, will not always be reasoned or moderate; public figures as well as public officials would be subject to "vehement, caustic, and sometimes unpleasantly sharp attacks."[9]

In the view of the plaintiff and of the lower courts, an outrageous utterance or publication that was intended to cause emotional distress, and did so, could lead to damages, because the interest of the state in preventing this emotional distress was superior to the speaker's interest. The Court rejected that position. Furthermore, bad motive made no difference; "many things done with motives that are less than admirable are protected by the First Amendment."[10] At least with regard to public debate about public figures, the First

7 *See id.*
8 *Id.* at 50 n.3 (citing the circuit court's citation to Womack v. Eldridge, 210 S.E.2d 145 (1974)).
9 *Id.* at 51 (citations omitted). 10 *Id.* at 53.

Amendment will not allow recovery based only on the elements for the intentional infliction of emotional distress, despite the motive.

> Were we to hold otherwise, there can be little doubt that political cartoonists and satirists would be subjected to damage awards without any showing that their work falsely defamed its subject ... The appeal of the political cartoon or caricature is often based on exploitation of unfortunate physical traits or politically embarrassing events – an exploitation often calculated to injure the feelings of the subject of the portrayal. The art of the cartoonist is often not reasoned or evenhanded, but slashing and one-sided.[11]

The Court went on to cite a long history of caustic political cartooning, from a cartoon portraying George Washington as an ass, through Thomas Nast's "graphic vendetta" against "Boss" Tweed, to Lincoln's gangliness, Teddy Roosevelt's glasses and teeth, and Franklin D. Roosevelt's jaw and cigarette holder. The Court saw the cartoons as providing an effect that could not be captured by photography and said that "[f]rom the viewpoint of history it is clear that our political discourse would have been considerably poorer without them."[12]

Limiting recovery to outrageous instances would not sufficiently protect political debate, because that standard is inherently subjective and would allow juries to find liability based on their tastes or views. Nor may speech be judged based on adverse emotional impact on its audience. The Court said that public figures and public officials could only recover for the intentional affliction of emotional distress where they could show that the publication contained a false statement that was made with knowledge that it was false or with reckless disregard as to truth or falsity. This importation of a libel standard would seem, at least almost, to eliminate the tort of intentional infliction where the plaintiff is a public figure or public official. While the emotional impact can contribute to the damage award, there can be no recovery without there also having been libel.[13]

After *Falwell*, there remained the possibility of a different rule, where the plaintiff was not a public official or public figure. That was the situation the Court faced in *Snyder v. Phelps*.[14] The case arose over events surrounding the funeral of Matthew Snyder, a United States Marine killed in Iraq. Phelps, the pastor of Westboro Baptist Church, and six church members, all related to

[11] *Id.* at 53–54. [12] *Id.* at 55.

[13] The "actual malice" standard adopted here is drawn from the libel standards set out, where public officials are involved, in New York Times Co. v. Sullivan, 376 U.S. 254 (1964), and later extended to public figures, *see* Chapter 9.

[14] 562 U.S. 443 (2011).

Phelps, informed authorities that they planned to picket the funeral. The picketers adhered to limits placed on them; they remained on public land 1000 feet from the church and separated from the church by several buildings. They were not seen from the church, and the funeral procession saw only the tops of their signs.

Most of the signs did not seem aimed at Snyder. They were critical of United States policy with regard to those of homosexual orientation and of the Catholic Church. Signs read "God Hates the USA/Thank God for 9/11," "Thank God for IEDs," "Thank God for Dead Soldiers," "Pope in Hell," "Priests Rape Boys," and "God Hates Fags."[15] Seemingly more directed at Snyder were signs reading "You're Going to Hell" and "God Hates You."[16]

The plaintiff in the suit, Matthew Snyder's father, did not see the signs, while going to, at, or coming from the funeral. He became aware of them only later that night when he saw a news broadcast covering the picketing. He sued the picketers for defamation, publicity given to private life, intentional infliction of emotional distress, and intrusion on seclusion. The trial court granted the church summary judgment with regard to the defamation and publicity given to private life claims, but the others went to trial. At trial, Snyder testified as to his emotional injuries, saying that he was unable to separate the thoughts of the events from thoughts of his son and that that made him angry and physically ill. An expert also testified that the offense had led to severe depression that exacerbated other health conditions. The jury found for Snyder, and he was awarded damages of, after reduction by the court, $2.1 million.

When the case reached the Supreme Court, the Court noted that the signs held by the picketers related to issues of interest to society. "While these messages may fall short of refined social or political commentary, the issues they highlight – the political and moral conduct of the United States and its citizens, the fate of our Nation, homosexuality in the military, and scandals involving the Catholic clergy – are matters of public import."[17] With regard to the signs that seemed more directed at Matthew Snyder himself, the Court said that the fact that the messages were related to Snyder didn't change the overall thrust and theme of the demonstration. The court concluded: "Given that Westboro's speech was at a public place on a matter of public concern, that speech is entitled to 'special protection' under the First Amendment. Such speech cannot be restricted simply because it is upsetting or arouses contempt."[18] The jury verdict violated Phelps' First Amendment rights.

[15] *Id.* at 448. [16] *Id.* [17] *Id.* at 454. [18] *Id.* at 458.

There was a dissent by Justice Alito, who began by noting that the plaintiff was not a public figure; he was a father whose son had been killed in battle and who wanted to bury that son in peace.[19] Justice Alito recognize that the church members have the right to convey their opinions but noted that they had "almost limitless opportunities to express their views:" publications, recordings, petitions, appearances on television and radio, Internet postings, and picketing in other locations.[20] Even though the expression by individuals concerning issues of public interest should be protected, "[i]t does not follow . . . that they may intentionally inflict severe emotional injury on private persons at the time of intense emotional sensitivity by launching vicious verbal attacks that make no contributions to public debate."[21]

At least one difference between the views of the majority and Justice Alito seems to lie in the fact that Justice Alito viewed the speech as aimed at Matthew Snyder. There was other material produced by the church that would bolster this belief, but the court did not consider it. The majority noted, in a footnote, that a few weeks after the funeral there was material posted to the Westboro Church's website discussing the picketing, and that that material contained "religiously oriented denunciations of the Snyders, interspersed among lengthy Bible quotations."[22] Because the website was not mentioned in the petition for certiorari, it was not considered, although the Court did note that it might raise distinct issues. Justice Breyer, in his concurring opinion, noted that the majority opinion did not say anything about the Internet postings, concluding that the Court's opinion says no more than that the First Amendment protects picketing under these particular circumstances.[23]

The two cases from the United States Supreme Court do leave open the possibility of different treatment where the plaintiff is a private individual and the speech is not on a matter of public concern. Even here, however, there would be a question of whether or not a false statement is required. The Court, in *Falwell*, seemed to reduce this sort of action to a variety of defamation by requiring proof of a false statement made with actual malice. While private plaintiffs in defamation actions do not have to demonstrate actual malice, they must still demonstrate falsity and at least negligence on the part of the defendant.[24] Perhaps, as with the public figure plaintiff, this defamation requirement would carry over. Furthermore, liability based on negligence in private plaintiff defamation suits can lead only to compensatory damages. For

[19] *Id.* at 463 (Alito, J., Dissenting). [20] *Id.* [21] *Id.* [22] *Id.* at 449 n.1.

[23] *See id.* at 461–62.

[24] For the burdens of proof involving the private-figure plaintiff, *see* Gertz v. Robert Welch, Inc., 418 U.S. 323 (1974).

punitive damages, the plaintiffs must also show actual malice. This, too, might limit the award of damages to private individuals in this sort of case.

GERMANY

Given the prominence enjoyed by the protection of dignity, as Article 1 of the German Basic Law, it is not surprising the Germany has a number of cases involving this sort of affront. The *Strauss Caricature*[25] decision is probably the best known, and one of the more colorful, opinions in this area of German law.

The case grew out of the publication of a magazine titled *Konkret*. In the magazine were several caricatures of Franz Josef Strauss, the Minister-President of Bavaria. In one of the drawings, Strauss was portrayed as a pig copulating with a pig dressed in judicial costume. A second involved pigs engaged in a variety of sexual activities. A third involved four pigs, each mounting the pig in front of it. Two of the pigs had the facial features of Strauss, and the other two were dressed in judicial costume.

The publisher of the magazine was found guilty on a charge of criminal defamation. He appealed, arguing that the conviction was in violation of his rights under Article 5(3) of the Basic Law, the provision protecting art.[26] The German Court, however, denied his claim of infringement.

The Court did conclude that the drawings were art for the purposes of protection under the Article. Such a conclusion required that the court be able to distinguish between art and non-art. Since the caricatures were said, in translation, to be "the formed outcome of free creative action in which the complainant brings his impressions, observations and experiences into direct display,"[27] they constitute artistic activity. The fact the caricatures also expressed opinion did not deprive them of their status as art.

The conclusion that the works were art led to a discussion of the nature of satire and caricature.

> Since it is of the nature of this artistic genre to work with exaggeration, distortions and alienation effects, its judicial assessment requires its

[25] BVerfGE 75, 369, 1 BvR 313/85, Jun. 3, 1987. The case may be found in translation at www.utexas.edu/law/academics/centers/transnational/work_new/german/case.php?id=634. It is also available at DECISIONS OF THE BUNDESVERFASSUNGSGERICHT, Volume 2/Part II: Freedom of Speech 420 (1998). Quotations in the text will be drawn from the University of Texas translation.

[26] The protection of art under Article 5(3) of the German basic Law is discussed in Chapter 2.

[27] BVerfGE 75, 369 at ¶2.

> divestment of "satirical garb adopted, in word and image," in order to determine its actual content. This core of statement and its dress are then separately to be checked for whether they contain an expression of contempt for the person caricatured. Account must be taken here of the fact that the criteria for assessing that dress are different and as rule less strict than for assessing the core of the statement, for alienation is intrinsic to it.[28]

The Court concluded that the lower court had performed this task correctly and adopted the view of that court that "the drawing expresses the fact that the civil party turned justice to his purposes 'in repellent fashion', and suggested the view that he 'experienced a bestial satisfaction in a justice subservient to him.'"[29]

Both levels of court saw this as the core statement, and under the United States law that would clearly be seen as political speech due the protection of the First Amendment. The German Court, however, found the depictions unprotected. In doing so it, like the United States Supreme Court in *Falwell*, considered the nature of caricature directed at public officials or public figures but was willing to place limits. "Even taking into account the fact that for caricatures exaggerations are 'structurally typical' and that persons who like the civil party are in public life are to a greater extent targets for public, including satirical, criticism, the portrayals far exceed the limits of the acceptable."[30] Particularly given the sexual nature of the depictions, the court saw the caricatures as "intended to devalue the person concerned as a person, to deprive him of his dignity as a human being."[31] That was unacceptable in "a legal system that takes the dignity of man as the highest value."[32]

Strauss is not the only German case involving dignity. In fact, there is another case involving Strauss.[33] The second Strauss case, one that was finally decided only after his death, grew out of statements to the effect that Strauss was the personification of the "coerced democrat," a person who allows himself to be converted to democracy for opportunistic reasons. The author also said that the Federal Republic of Germany yearned for a "strongman" and that Strauss was the focus and chief symbol of that yearning. The yearning for a strongman was seen as an offshoot of the Nazi Führer cult.

Strauss, upset by this characterization, obtained an injunction against the author and publisher, requiring that they not characterize Strauss as the

[28] *Id.* at ¶3. [29] *Id.* at ¶4(a). [30] *Id.* at ¶4(b). [31] *Id.* [32] *Id.*

[33] *See* Strauss-decision (coerced democrat case), BVerfGE 82, 272, 1 BvR 1165/89, Jun. 26, 1990, available in translation at www.utexas.edu/law/academics/centers/transnational/work_new/german/case.php?id=629 and at DECISIONS OF THE BUNDESVERFASSUNGSGERICHT, *supra* note 25, at 463. Citations will be to the University of Texas translation.

personification of the coerced democrat or requiring a specific disclaimer, if such a statement was made. The lower court considered a line to have been crossed and Strauss's honor to have been intentionally wounded.[34]

When the case reached the Constitutional Court, that Court found the injunction to be in violation of the author's and publisher's rights under Article 5(1) of the Basic Law. The Court found relevant the purpose of the protection of opinion:

> Contributions to debate concerning issues that are of essential importance to the public enjoy greater protection than statements that merely serve the pursuit of private interests ... Criticism expressed in overstated and polemic form must be endured particularly in public debate, especially in the political struggle of opinions, because any other result would threaten to paralyze or narrow the opinion-forming process.[35]

Also, taken in context, the Court saw the tenor of the statements as aimed at concerns over a particular school of thought in Germany, with Strauss used only as an illustration. "[T]he plaintiff was brought in only to illustrate who corresponds to the type portrayed. Within the contours of debate on the issues, even a Democratic politician must put up with the reproach contained in the characterization 'coerced democrat.'"[36] The statements made were seen as not intended as a personal affront but as a warning not to underestimate the continuing danger to the country's democratic order.[37]

Other German cases also concern statements that tied the plaintiffs to Nazism. In the *Lüth Cases*,[38] the issue was a call for a boycott of the film *Immortal Beloved*. The motivation for the called-for boycott was the fact that the film's director, Veit Harlan, had worked for the Third Reich and that his film *Jud Süss* had been instrumental in the campaign against the Jews. Lüth said that the return of Harlan "would inevitably tear open wounds barely scarred over again, and frighteningly renew loathing and mistrust, to the detriment of German reconstruction."[39] The German people were said to have a duty not only to protest but to boycott.

The Court, despite the negative comments aimed at Harlan, found the call for boycott to be protected by the free-speech provision of the Basic Law.

[34] *See* BVerfGE 82, 272 at §II.3. [35] *Id.* at §III(2)(2)(a). [36] *Id.* at §III(2)(2)(d).
[37] *See id.*
[38] BVerfGE 7, 198, 1 BvR 400/51, Jan. 15, 1958. A translation is available at DECISIONS OF THE BUNDESVERFASSUNGSGERICHT, *supra* note 25, at 1.
[39] *Id.* at part A; DECISIONS OF THE BUNDESVERFASSUNGSGERICHT, *supra* note 25, at 3.

> The complainant's statements must be seen in the context of his general political and cultural endeavors. He was moved by the concern that Harlan's re-appearance might – especially abroad – be interpreted as showing that nothing had changed in German cultural life by comparison with the National Socialist period, with Harlan now again, as then, the representative German film director. These fears concerned a very essential question for the German people: at bottom that of its moral position and its standing in the world based on it. German standing has been harmed by nothing as much as the cruel persecution of the Jews by National Socialism. There is therefore a decisive interest in having the world assured that the German people has turned away from this mental attitude and condemns it not merely for reasons of political opportunism but from insight into its contemptibility, gained from their own inner conversion.[40]

In still another case touching on Nazism, *CSU-NPD Case (Election Campaign Case)*,[41] the Court considered a statement made during an election campaign that the political party the CSU was the NPD of Europe. The lower court concluded that the statement was a factual claim asserting that the CSU was guided by the same intellectual, ideological positions that had motivated the NPD and that this was severe disparagement not protected by Article 5(1).

The Constitutional Court concluded that the statements were matters of opinion, rather than fact, and hence came within the scope of Article 5(1). Furthermore, the Court said that the lower court had not taken into account the fact that, when persons affected by the statement of opinion have taken an active part in the process of forming public opinion, they have gone outside the private sphere and submitted themselves to the clash of ideas.[42] This principle, the Court said, applies even more strongly to political parties.[43]

Any conclusion by the lower court that the statement, even if opinion, exceeded the limits placed on the right to free expression for the protection of personal honor was incorrect.

> Protection of the legal right in question can and must retreat the more [the statement is] making a contribution to the clash of ideas in a manner substantially concerning the public … [O]therwise freedom of opinion,

[40] *Id.* at part B(III)(2)(a); Decisions of the Bundesverfassungsgericht, *supra* note 25, at 10.

[41] BVerfGE 61, 1 (1982). The case is available in translation at Decisions of the Bundesverfassungsgericht, *supra* note 25, at 244.

[42] *See id.* at part B(II)(2)(b); Decisions of the Bundesverfassungsgericht, *supra* note 25, at 251.

[43] *See id.*

> the precondition for free and open political process, would be cut to the quick. This must apply to a special degree when the matter, as here, is one of debate in an election campaign, that is, a situation in which the political clash of opinions is intensified to the utmost.[44]

This criticism of one party by a representative of a competing body had to be protected.

The *Mephisto Case*[45] provides more evidence that, in German law, even the stronger protection provided for art may not prevail, when there is an injury to personal dignity.[46] The case involved a novel in which the main character was a gifted actor who gave up his political convictions and ethical principles in order to have a career in Nazi Germany. The character was based on an actual actor and director, who had been the brother-in-law of the author. After the death of the actor, his adopted son brought suit over this injury to honor and reputation.

The Court concluded that the novel is a work of art, and that has an impact on the workings of Article 5. While Article 5(2) allows the law to restrict the freedom of opinion protected by Article 5(1) in order to protect a variety of other values, the Court said that the protection of art in Article 5(3) is not limited by Article 5(2). Nonetheless, artistic freedom may be limited by constitutional values, particularly the value of human dignity protected by Article 1. The lower court had balanced Article 5(3) and Article 1 and held that the real actor's personal dignity outweighed the artistic freedom of the author. The Court was unable to reverse that conclusion.

The last of the German cases to be discussed here is the *Römerberg Speech Case*.[47] Römerberg had given lectures on art criticism and exhibition in which he strongly criticized contemporary art criticism, targeting by name several well-known art critics. It was not those targets that brought suit. Instead it was Römerberg who sued over comments on radio broadcasts. The broadcasts had, in translation, said:

> That professor ... who has remained unknown as a realistic sculptor ... unabashedly hauled off with hate-filled tirades and so-called revelations about the art business, delivered from the position of a blinkered schoolmaster ... I listened very attentively to hear whether the art writer's tongue might not

[44] *Id.* at B(III)(2)(a); Decisions of the Bundesverfassungsgericht, *supra* note 25, at 250.

[45] BVerfGE 30, 173 1 BvR 435/68, Feb. 24, 1971, available in translation at Decisions of the Bundesverfassungsgericht, *supra* note 25, at 147.

[46] The protection art receives in German law as discussed in Chapter 2.

[47] BVerfGE 54, 129, 1 BvR 103/77, May 13, 1980, available in translation at Decisions of the Bundesverfassungsgericht, *supra* note 25, at181.

> slip once to say that everything was Jew-ridden, or that the Freemasons were behind it, for that was the way the tone was ... a hatred nourished by the delusion of persecution that unsuccessful artists so often develop.[48]

The Court noted that the art critic had entered into the debate over art criticism and that, having offered his negative opinions, he would have to put up with sharp reactions, even if it diminished his reputation. "Even talks that were in basic tendency academic could give occasion for sharp, derisive criticism if they ... contained massive criticism of contemporary art criticism and thus also of the complainants' profession; all the more so since it contained personal attacks on known art critics and gallery owners, mentioned by name"[49] Thus, the protection of dignity may not override the protection of opinion, when that opinion is a response to strong opinion offered by the plaintiff.

Ronald Krotoszynski notes the difference in the German cases between *Strauss*, in which expression was not protected, and the cases involving attacks on those with Nazi ties or leanings.[50] He concludes: "Simply put, speech critical of Nazi collaborators or those who supported them is broadly protected, at least insofar as the government itself agrees with the speaker's characterization of the object of the accusation."[51] The *Lüth* opinion might well be read as supporting the conclusion that the Court's decisions were based on the interests of the government. Further support may be drawn from the fact that Strauss won his case involving the caricature, while his successor lost the case over Strauss as the model for the strong man cult.

But, comments regarding the continued specter of Nazism are also, perhaps, more inherently political then depicting an individual as a rutting pig. Professor Krotoszynski concludes that *Lüth* "represents the viewpoint-based jurisprudence of Article 5."[52] The only quarrel with that conclusion would be in the adjective. The free expression provisions of the German Basic Law, like those of most of the other democracies, involve balancing. Balancing certainly can involve the consideration of viewpoint, but it may or may not be the case that the balance is affected only by, or primarily by the interests of the government. The balance may instead be in how direct was the contribution the expression made to the political debate. While stating that Strauss had too

48 *Id.* at A(I)(1)(b); DECISIONS OF THE BUNDESVERFASSUNGSGERICHT, *supra* note 25, at 183.
49 *Id.* at A(II)(2)(b); DECISIONS OF THE BUNDESVERFASSUNGSGERICHT, *supra* note 25, at 187.
50 RONALD J. KROTOSZYNSKI, JR., THE FIRST AMENDMENT IN CROSS-CULTURAL PERSPECTIVE 123 (2006).
51 *Id.* 52 *Id.*

much influence over the judiciary would, presumably, have been protected as political expression, depicting him as a pig was more an attack on his honor.

Professor Whitman offers an interesting view on the German protection of honor. He notes a broad, even if sometimes less enforced, law of insult, under which certain gestures or even the use of the informal "du," in place of the formal "Sie," might lead to the filing of a complaint.[53] He finds the origins of this law of insult in a traditional social hierarchy. While the law of insult is generally applicable in modern Germany, it once applied only to those of high status and was tied into the tradition of dueling.[54] He argues that suppressing aristocratic duels became a major goal, and insulted aristocrats were encouraged to take legal action instead.[55] As the practice of dueling spread to the bourgeoisie, legal concerns over the insult also had to expand, eventually to include everyone.[56] Thus, the government concern would be over avoiding violent confrontation rather than the protection of its own political interests.

JAPAN

Some parallels to the law of Germany in protecting honor and dignity may be found in Japan. Indeed, if Professor Whitman's distinction between Germany and France on one hand, the United States on the other, is that the former are "honor cultures," while the United States is not, it might be expected the Japan would be more similar to France and Germany. The bushido code of the Samurai emphasized honor to the point of suicide to avoid shame (and the harsh treatment a captive might expect).[57] Face and honor for self and family continue to be important, and suicide may still be the route to preserve honor.[58]

The case that best matches the *Strauss* case is the *Hoppo Journal* case, *Ona v. Igarashi*.[59] That case involved an attack on Igarashi, the mayor of Asahikawa

[53] *See* Whitman, *supra* note 2, at 1296–97. He notes that actions involving the informal "du" sometimes, but not always, fail, "but the very fact that they are brought suggests that the popular conception of what counts as legally sanctionable lack of respect or disrespect goes far." *Id.* at 1299.

[54] *See id.* at 1314. [55] *See id.* at 1315. [56] *See id.* at 1319–22.

[57] *See, e.g.*, www.history.com/topics/samurai-and-bushido.

[58] *See, e.g.*, Erin Petrun, *Suicide in Japan*, CBS NEWS (Jul. 12, 2007), www.cbsnews.com/news/suicide-in-japan; Takako McCrann, *Shame, Honor, and Duty*, PBS (Sep. 27, 2007), www.pbs.org/mosthonorableson/shame.html.

[59] Supreme Court, Grand Bench, Jun. 11, 1986, 40 Minshū 4, 872, available in translation at LAWRENCE W. BEER & HIROSHI ITOH, THE CONSTITUTIONAL CASE LAW OF JAPAN, 1970–1990 606 (1996). Citations will be to the page numbers in the translation.

and a candidate for governor of Hokkaido, published in Ona's magazine. Igarashi obtained an injunction against publication, and Ona's appeal of the injunction reached the Supreme Court. The Court recognized that censorship is banned by Article 21 of the Japanese Constitution but said that prior restraint through court injunction is not censorship, because it is only imposed by a judicial court in a trial like proceeding.[60]

The Court also considered the injunction to be justified. The protection of one's reputation is protected by Article 13 of the Japanese Constitution, so injury to reputation must be reconciled with the freedom of expression. Even when the expression is on a public matter, the court says, in the following translation, that freedom is not unlimited.

> Expression which injures the reputation of another person is an abuse of freedom of expression and may be restricted. However, this should be so construed that when an act constituting civil or criminal defamation is found to relate to matters of public interest, and to have been done solely for the public benefit, and when the truth of the alleged facts is proved, such expression is not illegal. Even if the truth is not proved, when the perpetrator has sufficient grounds for mistakenly believing in the truth of the allegation, the action should not be construed as malicious or negligent.[61]

The article at issue argued that Igarashi lacked the wisdom, sense of responsibility, and clean and well-rounded character required to be Governor of Hokkaido, all of which would presumably be protected political criticism. It went on to say that he was "skillful at lying, bluffing and cheating," as a boy "cockroaches like Igarashi," that he is "a born liar," "an ugly character hiding behind a beautiful mask," "an opportunist without scruples who will do anything for his own selfish interests and success," and "a mayor like the rump of a bitch."[62] It added: "His true face is that of confidence man deceiving people by day and a bandit riding in darkness by night."[63] Turning to his private life, the article said: "He divorced his wife in a despicable manner, causing her to commit suicide, in order to get the new woman ... who had been a hostess in a club ..."[64] He was also said to have played on the favoritism of his father and young mother to displace older brothers by an earlier wife.[65] He was further described as always being concerned with his self-preservation and self-advancement, instead of serving the public, as excelling at graft and corruption and fattening his pockets, skillful in eluding the law, and running for governor because of the power it would bring.[66]

60 *See id.* at 607. 61 *Id.* at 608–9. 62 *Id.* at 610–11. 63 *Id.* at 611. 64 *Id.*
65 *Id.* 66 *See id.*

What was, perhaps, the most colorful language was to run between the title and the text. It said "A monster named Kozo is now wriggling on the earth of Hokkaido. It turns into a butterfly by day and a hairy caterpillar by night, carrying out that he wants to live in the red brick building. Its poisonous character bewilders the public. Now is the time to unmask the monster . . ."[67]

When the Court turned to balancing the interests involved, the Court recognized that the article was related to criticizing a candidate for public office and that, generally, under the circumstances, there should not be an injunction. But the Court said that in this instance of

> a considerable personal attack on the said appellee with extremely insulting and vulgar remarks, we cannot by any means find that it was written solely to promote the public interest . . . [T]he article's lack of credibility was obvious [and the] magazine issue . . . was capable of seriously and almost irreparably defaming the appellee.[68]

The Court unanimously concluded that the injunction was not a violation of the publisher's free expression rights.

There were a number of supplementary opinions. Justice Ito added that the content at issue was

> evidently untrue, not engaged in for public benefits, and able to inflict almost irreparable damage on a person's right to good reputation . . . [S]uch expression should naturally be regarded as inferior in value to the right to one's good name. It is not unconstitutional if such expression, injustice, is not made available in the free marketplace.[69]

Justice Nagashima's opinion is useful for its explanation of the differences between the crime of insult and the crime of defamation. The factor that distinguishes the two is that defamation asserts facts, but otherwise he saw them as similar.

> The protected interest in both cases is reputation, that is, the objective estimation of a person by society. The main legally protected interest could be the victim's sense of honor, as when one is cursed on public in a particular occasion; but insulting expressions recorded in documents, audio tapes or audio-visual tapes could extend the harm to another's objective reputation over time without an allegation of concrete facts.[70]

[67] *Id.* (insertions by the Court omitted). The "red brick building" referred to is the prefectural capitol of Hokkaido.

[68] *Id.* [69] *Id.* at 616 (opinion of Justice Ito). [70] *Id.* at 621 (opinion of Justice Nagashima).

The Justice recognized the right of fair comment but, again in translation, said:

> [N]ot included in fair comment are comments impermissible by generally accepted social ideas such as contemptuous defamation with content devoid of context and with no relationship to matters of public concern, or acts of expression intended mainly to insult, to slander, to condemn or deride another with allegations of fact, if any, used not to allege the truth of facts but to provide background information for personal attack. Such are not comments on behalf of the public and have nothing to do with public concerns.[71]

Applying those principles to the facts of the case, Justice Nagashima found that there was no public purpose behind the comments and said that the allegations were obviously untrue.[72]

The most interesting aspect of Justice Taniguchi's separate supplementary opinion may be his use of the "actual malice" standard used in defamation law in the United States, defined in the same manner as knowledge of falsity or reckless disregard for falsity.[73] Applying the standard, the Justice found it clear that Ona, the publisher, had acted with actual malice.[74] This position is similar to that of the United States Supreme Court in *Falwell*, even if the conclusion with regard to actual malice is different. There were, in the *Ona* case, statements that were more likely to be taken as assertions of fact, the statements with regard to Igarashi's treatment of his wife and brothers. However, Justice Taniguchi did not single out those statements, and it is possible that his conclusion with regard to the presence of actual malice applied throughout, even to those statements that might be better seen as opinion.

As with German law, Japanese law does not find every insult sanctionable and is willing to draw lines. *Kōchi v. Japan*[75] grew out of the publication of a series of articles titled "The Sins of the Vampire Tokuichiro Sakaguchi." "Vampire" would not seem all that different from "caterpillar." Furthermore, there was a more subtle insult in that one of the characters of the target's name, a character meaning "virtue," was replaced by a homonym that meant "gain" or "profit." The case was a criminal defamation action, based on false statements regarding corruption. The Court refused to let the conviction stand, despite the insult and the falsity. Because the defendant mistakenly

[71] *Id.* [72] *See id.* at 623. [73] *See id.* at 625 (opinion of Justice Taniguchi).

[74] *See id.* at 626.

[75] Supreme Court, Grant Bench, June 25, 1969, 23 Keoshū 7 at 259, available in translation at Hiroshi Itoh & Lawrence Beer, The Constitutional Case Law of Japan: Selected Supreme Court Decisions, 1961–70 175 (1979).

believed the statements to be true and had sufficient reason for his belief, he was not guilty. Thus, the protection of free expression may prevail even in the face of insult.

EXPLAINING THE DIFFERENCES

Professor Whitman suggests that the differences between the United States and Germany are the result of differences in how the two countries strive towards equality. There must be a sense of equality in a democracy; the value was implicit in providing everyone with an equal say in self-governance. But how is that sense of equality, in a manner more general than equal legal treatment, to be attained? Whitman suggests that the United States and Germany take diametrically opposed approaches. The United States employs a leveling down approach, while Germany levels up.[76]

The "leveling down" process in the United States can clearly be seen in the *Falwell* case. The examples, which the Court cited regarding the importance of caricature, including early depictions of George Washington, show the historical roots of this practice. It can also be seen in the regular use of character attacks in politics and the delight that the American public seems to feel in the exposure of any character flaws in politicians or celebrities.

Whitman offers an interesting analysis of the "leveling up" approach in Germany. He disagrees with suggestions that the origin is in reaction to the Nazi era, where the honor of at least a portion of the population was completely negated. He also rejects the position that this equality is the product of the work of Immanuel Kant and his assertion of the moral equality of all individuals. Instead, he argues that the decline in social hierarchy in insult law was not in reaction to the Nazis, but a product of their work.[77] Given the honor the Nazis saw in being of Aryan descent, honor must extend to all Germans. "Nazi doctrinal analysis . . . accepted the proposition that Germans of all social statuses participated in German honor, at least to some extent."[78]

While Whitman does not discuss Japan, he does discuss France.[79] He finds similarities with Germany, in that he says France, too, has an honor culture and a leveling up. There are similar origins in a dueling culture that eventually spread to the bourgeoisie and governmental concerns over the practice. The French Revolution, in his view, led to a change in the law in that

[76] *See* Whitman, *supra* note 2, at 1384–90. [77] *See id.* at 1322–32. [78] *Id.* at 1328.
[79] *See id.* at 1344–71.

aristocratic honor became of less concern.[80] That led to a body of law that he sees as more American than German, even though some defamatory utterances will end up in court.[81] He also sees this old law of insult as playing a role in French law of hate speech.[82]

While the honor culture is not found in French law, at least to the degree found in German law, Whitman finds it to be an aspect of French culture. "[E]nforcement of respect goes on in the world of education and everyday manners in ways rich in political meaning."[83] He finds parallels to Germany in the use of pronouns to address others and in opposition to the United States and the pervasiveness of American informality. The lack of actual law leads to the lack of inclusion of France in the analysis of this chapter, but Whitman's conclusions with regard to the culture are interesting.

What remains to be considered is why some cultures level up, while others level down. With regard to the countries discussed, the explanation may be in the origins of modern government in each. The birth of the United States was a process of leveling down. Denying the continued right of King George III to rule over the colonies, and insults directed at the monarch, can be seen as a form of leveling down. After the Revolution, there appears to have been a continued drive toward leveling, perhaps with the direction less clear. The Constitution prohibited the new country from granting titles of nobility, as well as banning any officer of the government from accepting a title from a foreign monarch or state.[84] Leaders were not to be so distinguished from the masses, and leveling down seems to have been the cultural means to that end.

Germany and Japan, in contrast, did not reject monarchies. The deposition of the monarch, in each case, was the result of losing a war. Transition that comes from without does not reflect internal culture. Germany and Japan could retain their honor cultures, while still transitioning, at least eventually, to democracy. France is more difficult to explain, in that there was a revolution in which the Royals were executed. This might lead to a culture that, as Whitman suggests, would be more similar to the United States. On the other hand, France did, rather quickly, become governed by an Emperor, so some

80 *See id.* at 1350. 81 *See id.* at 1352–56. 82 *See id.* at 1357. 83 *Id.* at 1361.

84 The United States Constitution, Article 1, § 9 , cl. 8 provides: "No Title of Nobility shall be granted by the United States: And no Person holding any Office of Profit or Trust under them, shall, without the Consent of the Congress, accept of any present, Emolument, Office, or Title, of any kind whatever, from any King, Prince, or foreign State."

degree of honor culture might have survived and might explain the cultural differences.

In any case, it would appear that democracies may choose to protect honor or may, as the United States does, side with even highly insulting expression. The protection of honor would become a problem for the maintenance of democracy, if it inhibited political debate. Lines must be carefully drawn so that serious political commentary remains protected. On the other hand, the experiences of some democracies would indicate that the debate can be required to proceed with some degree of civility and decorum.

11

Obscenity and Child Pornography

There is the potential for some confusion between pornography and obscenity. An explanation of how the words will be used here may help avoid any such confusion. Pornography consists of all materials with sexual content. "Pornography" is, then, a purely descriptive term. Obscenity has to do with a moral or, more importantly here, legal conclusion that material, in some way, goes beyond what is acceptable in a particular culture. Calling material "obscene" means that there are limitations placed on publication, distribution, or, perhaps, even possession.

The classes are clearly not coextensive. There is material with sexual content that a culture may consider acceptable. That material is pornographic but not obscene. Perhaps a more interesting issue is whether there may be material that is obscene but not pornographic. That is, does the concept of obscenity, the legal conclusion that the material is unacceptable, extend to material without sexual contact.

To provide some structure for the issues that are raised, it would be useful to consider the test set out in the United States for the regulation of obscenity. In *Miller v. California*,[1] the United States Supreme Court provided that test:

> The basic guidelines for the trier of fact must be: (a) whether "the average person, applying contemporary community standards" would find that the work, taken as a whole, appeals to the prurient interest; (b) whether the work depicts or describes, in a patently offensive way, sexual conduct specifically defined by the applicable state law; and (c) whether the work, taken as a whole, lacks serious literary, artistic, political, or scientific value.[2]

1 413 U.S. 15 (1973). The Court had already recognized, in Roth v. United States, 354 U.S. 476 (1957), that obscene material does not enjoy the protection of the First Amendment.

2 413 U.S. at 24 (citation omitted).

It became clear, in later cases, that the first two prongs of the test employ a community standards approach, while the serious value prong is a non-community-dependent reasonable person standard.[3]

Just to add to the confusion, a word should be said about child pornography, before discussing it later in the chapter. Child pornography is material with sexual content, where the actors pictured or portrayed are children. It is pornography, because it has sexual content. It also goes beyond what is acceptable in most cultures. In that regard, it would be thought to be obscene. While banned under United States law, child pornography need not meet the *Miller* definition of obscenity. In a society with a broader definition of obscenity, not tied to a definition like that in *Miller*, the label "obscene" would easily apply.

Having set out a few basics, the approach to the rest of this chapter will be to look at various issues raised by the *Miller* test. Differences in approach among a number of countries, with regard to those issues, will be examined.

THE SUBJECT MATTER OF OBSCENITY

The United States' View

From the test set forth in *Miller*, it would seem that the concept of obscenity in the United States focuses solely on sexual depiction. That is perhaps made even more obvious by the *Miller* Court's explanation of this sort of statute that would meet the second prong of the test. The Court's example was: "(a) Patently offensive representations or descriptions of ultimate sexual acts, normal or perverted, actual or simulated. (b) Patently offensive representations or descriptions of masturbation, excretory functions, and lewd exhibition of the genitals."[4] While willing to include elimination, the sexual focus is clear.

That focus is made still more clear in *Brown v. Entertainment Merchants Association*.[5] There, the Court considered a California statute that limited the access of minors to violent video games. The structure of the statute led the Court to describe it as "a State's attempt to shoehorn speech about violence into obscenity."[6] The Court rejected the contention that violence could be obscene. "[V]iolence is not part of the obscenity that the Constitution permits to be regulated."[7] The Court failed to recognize that the concept of obscenity, even for legal purposes, was broader in the time of the

[3] *See* Pope v. Illinois, 481 U.S. 497 (1987). [4] 413 U.S. at 25. [5] 131 S.Ct. 2729 (2011).
[6] *Id.* at 2734. [7] *Id.* at 2735.

framing of the Constitution.[8] It was not until the 1896 case *Swearingen v. United States*[9] that, according to scholars,[10] the Court limited obscenity to sexual depiction. Even if the Court's history is flawed, however, it is now clear that the concept in the United States is limited to sexual depiction.

This focus, and the test set forth in *Miller* and its predecessors, has required the Supreme Court to address some interesting issues. In *Mishkin v. New York*,[11] the Court had to consider a defense arising under the "average person" aspect of the appeal to the prurient interest. The material at issue involved bondage and sadomasochism, and the defense claimed this would not appeal to the prurient interest of the average person. The observation seems legitimate, and to avoid a loophole the Court concluded that, when material is marketed and distributed to a particular audience, the prurient interest of that target group is the relevant test.

This same variable obscenity standard also provided the basis for the decision in *Ginsberg v. New York*.[12] There, copies of a magazine containing pictures of provocatively posed nudes, magazines the Court called "girlie magazines," were sold to a sixteen-year-old boy. It was accepted that the magazines were not obscene for an adult audience, but the Court allowed the prurient interest of a sixteen-year-old, rather than that of an adult average person, to be the controlling factor. The conviction under a harmful-to-minors statute, mirroring the then test for obscenity but adjusting the focus of the test on minors, was held not to be unconstitutional.

The United Kingdom

The definition of obscenity in the United Kingdom is far less focused. The Obscene Publications Act of 1959, as amended by the Obscene Publications Act of 1964, provides

> an article shall be deemed to be obscene if its effect or (where an article comprises two or more distinct items) the effect of any one of its items is, if taken as a whole, such as to tend to deprave and corrupt persons who are likely, having regard to all relevant circumstances, to read, see or hear the matter contained or embodied in it.[13]

[8] For an argument that the concept was broader in the era of the Framing and that the concept of obscenity should extend to violence, *see* Kevin W. Saunders, Violence as Obscenity: Limiting the Media's First Amendment Protection (1996).

[9] 161 U.S. 446 (1896).

[10] *See, e.g.*, Frederick F. Schauer, The Law of Obscenity 19 (1976).

[11] 383 U.S. 502 (1966).

[12] 390 U.S. 629 (1968).

[13] Obscene Publications Act 1959, as amended by Obscene Publications Act 1964.

Deprivation and corruption can certainly result from materials containing other than sexual depiction.

An application of the act, showing this broader coverage, may be found in *Handyside v. The United Kingdom*,[14] a case from the European Court of Human Rights examining a prosecution under the act. The prosecution grew out of a publication titled *The Little Red Schoolbook*. The book was aimed at an audience of schoolchildren, aged twelve and older, with a 30 pence price that put it within their means. It was self-described as a reference book, meaning that it was not likely to be read straight through and that the impact of objectionable material in one section might not be ameliorated by other, unread, material in other sections.

Some of the material in the book had nothing to do with sex, with an introduction titled "All grown-ups are paper tigers" and chapters on Education, Learning, Teachers, Pupils, and The System.[15] The chapter entitled "Pupils" did contain a twenty-six-page section on sex, with subsections: "Masturbation, Orgasm, Intercourse and petting, Contraceptives, Wet dreams, Menstruation, Child-molesters or 'dirty old men', Pornography, Impotence, Homosexuality, Normal and abnormal, Find out more, Venereal diseases, Abortion, Legal and illegal abortion, Remember, Methods of abortion, Addresses for help and advice on sexual matters."[16] While the topics clearly touched on sexual matters, the concerns of British authorities were not with regard to any explicit depiction or description of sex but with the advice given.

The European Court described the objections found by the United Kingdom court. The United Kingdom court had found that the book was "a work of an extreme kind, unrelieved by any indication that there were any alternative views; this was something which detracted from the opportunity for children to form a balanced view on some of the very strong advice given therein."[17] Institutions such as marriage were largely ignored.[18] Other advice was seen as having a negative impact.

> Mixing a very one-sided opinion with fact and purporting to be a book of reference, it would tend to undermine, for a very considerable proportion of children, many of the influences, such as those of parents, the Churches and youth organisations, which might otherwise provide the restraint and sense of responsibility for oneself which found inadequate expression in the book ... [O]n the whole, and quite clearly through the mind of the child, the *Schoolbook* was inimical to good teacher/child relationships; in particular, there were numerous passages that [the UK courts] found to be subversive, not only

[14] App. No. 5493/72, 1 Eur. H.R. Rep. 737 (1976), http://hudoc.echr.coe.int/eng?i=001–57499.
[15] *Id.* at ¶ 20. [16] *Id.* at [17] *Id.* at ¶ 30. [18] *Id.* at ¶ 31.

> to the authority but to the influence of the trust between children and teachers … [T]he sense of some responsibility for the community as well as to oneself, if not wholly absent, was completely subordinated to the development of the expression of itself by the child.[19]

There were sections the United Kingdom courts found valuable. The treatment of homosexuality was said to be factual and compassionate; and the advice in the sections on venereal disease, contraception, and abortion also had value. "However, on the balance of probabilities, these matters could not outweigh what the court was convinced had a tendency to deprave and corrupt."[20]

Turning to more specific objections, the European Court said that in the discussion of sex in the "Be yourself" section in the chapter on pupils, there was material "that young people at a critical stage of their development could have interpreted as an encouragement to indulge in precocious activities harmful for them or even to commit certain criminal offenses."[21] The "Be yourself" section contained a passage that stated:

> Maybe you smoke pot or go to bed with your boyfriend or girlfriend – and don't tell your parents or teachers, either because you don't dare to or just because you want to keep it secret. Don't feel ashamed or guilty about doing things you really want to do and think are right just because your parents or teachers might disapprove. A lot of these things will be more important to you later in life than the things that are "approved of."[22]

The United Kingdom court had noted that there was no mention of the illegality of pot smoking or of underage sex.[23]

The section on pornography also drew criticism. The section did not contain any actual pornography but said:

> Porn is a harmless pleasure if it isn't taken seriously and believed to be real life. Anybody who mistakes it for reality will be greatly disappointed. But it's quite possible that you may get some good ideas from it and you may find something which looks interesting and that you haven't tried before.[24]

While the first two sentences were seen as "sane and sensible," the last sentence was seen as suggesting that children try new practices, which, coupled with a comment about people hurting each other, might lead to children harming each other.[25]

While prosecutions may occur in the United Kingdom over materials that would be obscene in the United States, the Obscenity Act clearly has broader

[19] *Id.* at ¶ 31–32. [20] *Id.* at ¶ 34. [21] *Id.* at ¶ 52. [22] *Id.* at ¶ 32. [23] *See id.*
[24] *See id.* [25] *See id.*

application. Strong sexual depictions may "deprave and corrupt," but clearly so may other material. There was no real sexual content to *The Little Red Schoolbook*. While there was discussion of issues related to sex, it was just that, discussion, rather than depiction or description. It is true the material was aimed at children, and while material with lesser appeal to the prurient interest may be barred for distribution to children in the United States, *The Little Red Schoolbook* should not be seen as appealing to that interest. It was the ideas presented that would "deprave and corrupt."

The European Union

The European Court of Human Rights found the conviction in *Handyside* to be consistent with the European Convention on Human Rights. That would indicate that the European Convention allows the suppression of material under at least as broad a definition as that contained in the United Kingdom's Obscenity Act. In fact, while the United States has an obscenity exception to the First Amendment and the United Kingdom has an act with "obscenity" in its title, the relevant European Convention article speaks in more general terms.

Article 10 (1) of the European Convention protects the freedom of expression. Article 10 (2), however, authorizes limitations on expression, providing "The exercise of these freedoms, since it carries with it duties and responsibilities, they be subject to such formalities, conditions, restrictions or penalties as are prescribed by law an unnecessary in a democratic society ... for the protection of health or morals, for the protection of the reputation or rights of others ..." That would seem to admit a broader class of material as subject to suppression. It is certainly broader than the obscenity exception to the First Amendment of the United States Constitution. While obscenity has a wider scope under the law of the United Kingdom, its application to the material in *Handyside* was clearly aimed at the protection of morals.

There are cases from the European Court of Human Rights having to do with explicit sexual depiction, material whose subject matter is comparable to that focused on by the obscenity exception to the First Amendment. As an example, *Müller v. Switzerland*[26] concerned three paintings that were held, by Swiss courts, to be in violation of Article 204 of the Swiss Criminal code. Under the code, "Anyone who makes or has in his possession any writings, pictures, films or other items which are obscene with a view toward trading in

[26] App. No. 10737/84, 13 Eur. H.R. Rep. 212 (1988).

them, distributing them or displaying them in public ... shall be imprisoned or fined."[27] Another provision of the same article provided that the court shall order that the items be destroyed.[28]

Müller, and a number of others, faced charges as a result of an exhibition of contemporary art. Müller created, as a part of the exhibition, three large paintings. The production and later display were open to the public. The Swiss appellate court described the paintings:

> These are not works which, in treating a particular subject or scene, allude to sexual activity more or less discreetly. They place it in the foreground, depicting it not in the embrace of man and woman but involving vulgar images of sodomy, fellatio between males, bestiality, erect penises and masturbation ... Sexual activity is crudely and vulgarly portrayed for its own sake and not as a consequence of any idea of informing the work.[29]

The defendants were convicted and fined. The paintings were confiscated, but because of the cultural significance of the paintings, they were placed in a museum to be made available only to serious specialists. Nearly eight years later, they were returned to the artist, seemingly under the assumption that he had learned his lesson and would not display them again publicly.

In affirming Müller's conviction, the Swiss Federal Court defined obscenity:

> [A]ny item is obscene which offends, in a manner that is difficult to accept, the sense of sexual propriety; the effect of the obscenity may be to arouse a normal person sexually or to disgust or repel him ... The test of obscenity to be applied by the court is whether the overall impression of the item or work causes moral offense to a person of ordinary sensitivity ...[30]

Interestingly, because of the focus on the sexual arousal of the normal person, the Swiss court had to address an issue similar to that faced by the United States, the prurient interest of the average person. The approach of the United States Supreme Court was to alter the standard to base it on the prurient interest of the target audience. The approach of the Swiss court was to change the focus from arousal to repugnance.

> Although Mr. Müller's three works are not sexually arousing to a person of ordinary sensitivity, they are undoubtedly repugnant at the very least. The overall impression is of persons giving free rein to licentiousness and even perversion. The subjects – sodomy, fellatio, bestiality, the erect penis – are obviously morally offensive to the vast majority of the population.[31]

[27] *Id.* at ¶ 20. [28] *See id.* [29] *Id.* at ¶ 16. [30] *Id.* at ¶ 18. [31] *Id.* at ¶ 14.

When the European Court heard the appeal, it had no difficulty in upholding the conviction. The law was sufficiently clear for the prohibition to be considered prescribed by law; there was no problem regarding vagueness or lack of foreseeability. The Court also found the aim being pursued by the government to be legitimate. It saw the code provision as designed to protect public morals and noted a connection between that protection and the protection of the rights of others not to be confronted and upset by the material.

> [T]he paintings in question depict in a crude manner sexual relations, particularly between men and animals ... [T]he general public had free access to them, as the organisers had not imposed any admission charges or age-limit. Indeed, the paintings were displayed in an exhibition which was unrestrictedly open to – and sought to attract – the public at large ... [T]he Court does not find unreasonable the view taken by the Swiss courts that those paintings, with their emphasis on sexuality in some of its crudest forms, were "liable grossly to offend the sense of sexual propriety of persons of ordinary sensitivity." ... [T]he Swiss courts were entitled to consider it "necessary" for the protection of morals to impose a fine on the applicants publishing obscene material.[32]

While the *Müller* case shows the reaction of both Switzerland and the European Court to material that was similar, setting aside the potential serious artistic value of the work, to material that might be considered obscene in the United States, it bears repeating that the focus in other countries may be more broad. The *Handyside* case did not involve sexual depiction, but it was said to deprave and corrupt. That was sufficient to be held obscene in the United Kingdom, a position that the European Court found justified by the protection of morals.

Canada

The Canadian Criminal Code contains a provision banning the publications or distribution of obscene materials.[33] The Canadian Supreme Court, in *Regina v. Butler*,[34] provided an understanding of what may be obscene under the statute. The Canadian definition shows a focus on sexual depiction. "In order for the work or material to qualify as 'obscene,' the exploitation of sex must not only be its dominant characteristic, but such exploitation must be 'undue.'"[35]

[32] *Id.* at ¶ 36. [33] *See* Criminal Code, R.S.C. 1985, c.C-46 § 159 (now § 163).
[34] [1992]1 S.C.R. 452. [35] *Id.* at ¶ 44.

While sex may be necessary, in Canada, to a finding of obscenity, it is not sufficient. The sexual depiction must constitute undue exploitation, and that depends on other factors. As the *Butler* Court explained it,

> the portrayal of sex coupled with violence will almost always constitute the undue exploitation of sex. Explicit sex which is degrading or dehumanizing may be undue if the risk of harm is substantial. Finally, explicit sex that is not violent and is neither degrading nor dehumanizing is generally tolerated in our society and will not qualify as the undue exploitation of sex unless it employs children in its production.[36]

Thus, while limiting the scope of the obscenity statute to material involving sex, matching the focus of the United States, violence and other degrading or dehumanizing factors play a role. While not reaching the breadth of the statute of the United Kingdom to address all influences that deprave or corrupt, the focus might be seen as centering on sexual imagery that has that impact. And, it is more than simply a depravation and corruption; it speaks to the prurient interest but one that addresses other concerns.[37]

COMMUNITY STANDARDS

In any large country or other large political entity, such as the European Union, there is likely to be some variation from locale to locale as to how tolerable sexual depiction, or other depraving or corrupting influences, may be. The United States Supreme Court, in *Miller*, used the phrase "contemporary community standards" in setting the standard for material's appeal to the prurient interest. It later became clear that the patent offensiveness in the second prong of the test also is based in contemporary community standards, while serious value is determined on a reasonable person basis.[38]

The *Miller* Court explained its reliance on community. The Court said that the size of the United States and variations among the states made a national standard unworkable.

> Under a National Constitution, fundamental First Amendment limitations on the powers of the States do not vary from community to community, but this does not mean that there are, or should or can be, fixed, uniform national

[36] *Id.* at ¶ 62.

[37] Regina v. Butler is also discussed *infra*, notes 75–84, and accompanying text. As will be seen, the decision to limit material may be based on factors other than how strong the appeal to the prurient interest may be.

[38] *See* Pope v. Illinois, 481 U.S. 497 (1987).

> standards of precisely what appeals to the "prurient interest" or is "patently offensive." These are essentially questions of fact, and our Nation is simply too big and too diverse for this Court to reasonably expect that such standards could be articulated for all 50 States in a single formulation, even assuming the prerequisite consensus exists.[39]

Further, the Court said that states should not have to live with the decisions made by other states.

> It is neither realistic nor constitutionally sound to read the First Amendment as requiring that the people of Maine or Mississippi accept public depiction of conduct found tolerable in Las Vegas, or New York City. People in different States vary in their tastes and attitudes, and this diversity is not to be strangled by the absolutism of imposed uniformity.[40]

In the Court's view, a national standard would require conservative communities to accept depictions based on their acceptability in more liberal communities.

The European Court of Human Rights has also used the idea of community in its obscenity jurisprudence. The communities are country based, but the idea and the rationale are the same. The reliance on country-based standards was set out in *Handyside*. The European Court of Human Rights examined the reliance of the United Kingdom on the Article 10(2) provision allowing restrictions on expression for the protection of health or morals. In doing so, the Court said:

> [I]t is not possible to find in the domestic law of the various Contracting States a uniform European conception of morals. The view taken by their respective laws of the requirements of morals varies from time to time and from place to place, especially in our era which is characterised by a rapid and far-reaching evolution of opinions on the subject. By reason of their direct and continuous contact with the vital forces of their countries, State authorities are in principle in a better position than the international judge to give an opinion on the exact content of these requirements as well as on the "necessity" of a "restriction" or "penalty" intended to meet them.[41]

Contracting States have a "margin of appreciation" given both to the legislature and to the national courts interpreting statutes.[42] While the European Court may review legislation and judicial decisions, deference is given to the standards of the member states.

[39] *Miller*, 413 U.S. at 30. [40] *Id.* at 32–33 (footnote omitted).
[41] App. No. 5493/72, 1 Eur. H.R. Rep. at ¶ 48. [42] *Id.*

Handyside did not involve explicit sexual imagery, but the European Court took a similar position with regard to the sexual material in *Müller*. The main issue for the Court was whether, under Article 10(2), the Swiss conviction and confiscation could be considered "necessary in a democratic society." In examining the issue, the Court discussed necessity and the "margin of appreciation."

> The Court has consistently held that in Article 10(2) the adjective "necessary" implies the existence of a "pressing social need." The Contracting States have a certain margin of appreciation in assessing whether such a need exists, but this goes hand in hand with a European supervision, embracing both the legislation and the decisions applying it, even those given by an independent court. The Court is therefore empowered to give the final ruling on whether a "restriction" or "penalty" is reconcilable with freedom of expression as protected by Article 10.[43]

The court saw its task to be determining whether or not the interference was proportionate to the legitimate aim and whether the Swiss court's reasoning was "relevant and sufficient."[44] The court repeated its "margin of appreciation" discussion from *Handyside* and went on to say:

> [H]aving inspected the original paintings, the Court does not find unreasonable the view taken by the Swiss courts that those paintings, with their emphasis on sexuality in some of its crudest forms, were "liable grossly to offend the sense of sexual propriety of persons of ordinary sensitivity." In the circumstances, having regard to the margin of appreciation left to them under Article 10(2), the Swiss courts were entitled to consider it "necessary" for the protection of morals to impose a fine on the applicants for publishing obscene material.[45]

It might be expected that community values would play a role in obscenity determinations in larger countries with a diversity of views corresponding to geographic regions. Thus, in the United States and in the European Union there would be a need for community values, while smaller countries might be expected to be more homogeneous. Canada, while smaller in population than the United States or the European Union, has the sort of diversity, with more conservative and more liberal provinces, that would indicate a role for community values.

At first blush, community does seem to play a role in obscenity determinations in Canada. In *Butler*, the Supreme Court of Canada noted that the

[43] App. No, 10737/84, 13 Eur. H.R. Rep. at ¶ 32 (footnotes omitted). [44] *Id.*
[45] *Id.* at ¶ 36 (footnote omitted).

Court had adopted a test based on the "community standard of tolerance."[46] The *Butler* Court said that the view was similar to that of Australia and New Zealand and quoted an explanation of the test.

> There does exist in any community at all times – however the standard may vary from time to time – a general instinctive sense of what is decent and what is indecent, of what is clean and what is dirty, and when the distinction has to be drawn. I do not know . . . that today there is any better tribunal than a jury to draw it . . . I am very far from attempting to lay down a model direction, but a Judge might perhaps, in the case of a novel, say something like this: 'It would not be true to say that any publication dealing with sexual relations is obscene. The relations of the sexes are, of course, legitimate matters for discussion everywhere . . . There are certain standards of decency which prevail in the community, and you are really called upon to try this case because you are regarded as representing, and capable of justly applying, those standards. What is obscene is something which offends against those standards.'[47]

The *Butler* Court goes on to explain that the issue is not a matter of taste but of tolerance.

> The cases all emphasize that it is a standard of tolerance, not taste, that is relevant. What matters is not what Canadians think is right for themselves to see. What matters is what Canadians would not abide other Canadians seeing because it would be beyond the contemporary Canadian standard of tolerance to allow them to see it.[48]

It may not be completely clear what counts as community. The Court does speak in terms of what Canadians will tolerate. There is also no suggestion that the Court is concerned about the people of Alberta having to tolerate what would be acceptable in Toronto. Yet, the acceptance of the jury as the best entity to decide what the community would tolerate may be seen as invoking the more local standard.

Turning to the case that *Butler* relied on for its obscenity test, *Towne Cinema Theatres v. Regina*,[49] some additional guidance may, perhaps, be found. The case overturned a conviction, where the trial judge based the decision on his own standards rather than the community standard of tolerance. The lead opinion discussed the need to follow the standards of the Canadian community, seemingly indicating a national standard. Perhaps

[46] [1992] 1 S.C.R. at ¶ 44. [47] *Id.* at ¶ 45 (quoting Regina v. Close, [1948] V.L.R. 445, 705–6).
[48] *Id.* at ¶ 47 (quoting Towne Cinema Theatres Ltd. v. Regina, [1985] 1 S.C.R. 494, 508–9).
[49] [1985] 1 S.C.R. 494.

better evidence for a national standard is seeming criticism of the trial judge, not only for imposing a subjective but a local standard rather than a national objective test.[50] Further, Justice Wilson, concurring in the result, said that in his view "a movie is either obscene under the Code based on a national community standard of tolerance or it is not."[51]

The Supreme Court of Canada seems to be using references to community in a way that differs from the invocation of community standards in United States or the margin of appreciation in Europe. The community is the Canadian community, and there is no suggestion that community value should vary from location to location. It may be questionable, however, whether a local fact finder is really capable of recognizing a national community standard in such a large and varied country.

Before leaving this discussion of *Butler*, it is worth noting that the Court seemed to see the potential relevance of a variable obscenity standard such as that in *Mishkin* and *Ginsberg*. The Court said:

> Since the standard is tolerance, I think the audience to which the allegedly obscene material is targeted must be relevant. The operative standards are those of the Canadian community as a whole, but since what matters is what other people may see, it is quite conceivable that the Canadian community would tolerate varying degrees of explicitness depending upon the audience and the circumstances.[52]

Note that this passage also speaks to the Canadian community as a whole, perhaps reinforcing the position that it is not a local standard.

The Japanese Supreme Court defined obscenity and the test to be applied in *The Lady Chatterley's Lover Decision*.[53] The Court said: "In essence, . . . in order for a writing to be obscene it is required that it cause the arousal and stimulation of sexual desire, or offend the sense of shame, or run counter to proper concepts of sexual morality."[54] The issue was seen as one of law rather than fact, although the standard set seems factual. The standard for the court when it makes such a decision is the good sense operating generally throughout society, that is, the prevailing ideas of society. These . . . "are not the sum of the understanding of separate individuals and are not a mean value of such understanding; they are a collective understanding that transcends both . . ."[55]

50 *Id*. at ¶ 47. 51 *Id*. at ¶ 76.

52 *Id*. at ¶ 42 (quoting the same passage from Towne Cinema)(emphasis originated in Towne Cinema).

53 Hanreishū, XI, No. 3, 997 (Criminal), available in translation at John M. Maki, *Court and Constitution in Japan: Selected Supreme Court Decisions* 3 (1964).

54 *Id*. at 7. 55 *Id*. at 9 (quoting the lower court).

It is clear that the Court sees the issue as one to be made by the judge. That would seem to lead to less reliance on local community standards, a result that seems reasonable in a geographically smaller, and seemingly more culturally homogeneous, country.

Reliance on community has raised an interesting problem in the age of the Internet. The *Miller* Court expressed concern that the people of Maine or Mississippi should not have to tolerate what was acceptable in New York or Las Vegas. But if the community standards of those more conservative communities apply to Internet publications accessed there, the people of Maine or Mississippi would be able to limit what those in New York or Las Vegas might see.

The United States Supreme Court seemed untroubled by these potential limits on the Internet. In *Ashcroft v. American Civil Liberties Union*[56] the Court refused to allow the lack of a geographic community to prohibit the imposition of obscenity standards on the Internet. It did take three separate opinions to reach that conclusion. A three-justice plurality said that publishers who did not wish to be judged by the standards of a particular community should not utilize a medium that reaches that community.[57] A second opinion suggested that there should be a national standard for judging Internet obscenity.[58] Still a third opinion agreed that a national standard was appropriate but expressed concern as to whether community standards could actually be avoided.[59] This reliance on differing rationales has, quite naturally, led to a split among the circuits of United States Court of Appeals.[60]

While there doesn't appear to be any law on this issue from the European Court of Human Rights, it seems an issue likely to arise. There is a United Kingdom case, *Perrin v. United Kingdom*,[61] that involved a French national who made available in the United Kingdom, through a globally available website, material that was obscene under United Kingdom law. The fact that the defendant was a resident of the United Kingdom may have made his conviction more reasonable, but this would seem likely to be an issue that will continue to raise problems in the future.[62]

[56] 535 U.S. 564 (2002). [57] *Id.* at 583 (citations omitted).

[58] *Id.* at 586 (O'Connor, J., concurring in part and concurring in the judgment).

[59] *Id.* at 597 (Kennedy, J., concurring in the judgment).

[60] *Compare, e.g.*, United States v. Kilbride, 584 F.3d 1240 (9th Cir. 2009), *and* United States v. Little, 365 Fed. App'x. 159 (11th Cir. 2010).

[61] Fourth Section Decision as to the Admissibility of Application no. 5446/03 by Perrin v. United Kingdom (2005), www.njcm.nl/site/uploads/download/160.

[62] For more on this issue, *see* Kevin W. Saunders, *Obscenity, Community, and the Internet* in FREE SPEECH IN AN INTERNET ERA 145 (Clive Walker & Russell Weaver, eds., 2013).

IDEAS VERSUS DEPICTIONS

Given the position of the United States Supreme Court that obscenity is limited to sex, certainly not just any idea could be considered obscene. But what about ideas about sex or sexual relations? The Supreme Court provided guidance on that issue in *Kingsley International Pictures v. Regents*.[63] The case was the result of the state of New York's refusal to grant a license required for the showing of the motion picture *Lady Chatterley's Lover*. The relevant state law provided that licenses shall be issued "unless such film or a part thereof is obscene, indecent, immoral, inhuman, sacrilegious, or is of such a character that its exhibition would tend to corrupt morals or incite to crime."[64] There was also New York law explaining what constituted immorality or character tending to corrupt morals or incite crime. Part of that definition brought within the scope of the statute a film "which portrays acts of sexual immorality, perversion, or lewdness, or which expressly or impliedly presents such acts as desirable, acceptable or proper patterns of behavior."[65]

Certainly, a version of *Lady Chatterley's Lover* could be produced containing sufficiently explicit sexual scenes as, perhaps, to be considered obscene, although the "serious value" prong of *Miller* might lead to the opposite result. That was not, however, the basis for the refusal to grant a license. The Regents concluded that "the whole theme of this motion picture is immoral under said law, for that theme is the presentation of adultery as a desirable, acceptable and proper pattern of behavior."[66] As the United States Supreme Court understood New York law, it "requires the denial of a license to any motion picture which approvingly portrays an adulterous relationship, quite without reference to the manner of its portrayal."[67] It was the idea that adultery may be acceptable, rather than any explicitness in the depiction of that adultery, that led to the denial.

The Supreme Court found the denial to be an infringement of the First Amendment.

> What New York has done ... is to prevent the exhibition of a motion picture because that picture advocates an idea– that adultery under certain circumstances may be proper behavior. Yet the First Amendment's basic guarantee is of freedom to advocate ideas. The State, quite simply, has thus struck at the very heart of constitutionally protected liberty ... [The First Amendment's]

[63] 360 U.S. 684 (1959).
[64] *Id.* at 685 (quoting McKinley's Consol. N.Y. Laws, c. 16, 1953, Education Law, s. 129.
[65] *Id.* (quoting McKinley's Consol. N.Y. Laws, 1953, Education Law, s. 122).
[66] *Id.*
[67] *Id.* at 688.

guarantee is not confined to the expression of ideas that are conventional or shared by a majority. It protects advocacy of the opinion that adultery may sometimes be proper, no less than advocacy of socialism ...[68]

So, for expression to be obscene under United States law, it must be explicitly sexual. Sexual commentary, or the expression of sexual opinion, even when contrary to morality, cannot be banned.

This seems clearly contrary to the position taken by the courts of the United Kingdom and the European Court of Human Rights in *Handyside*. The work at issue there did not contain explicit sexual depiction. The objection was that the positions advocated could corrupt and deprave those young people who read *The Little Red Schoolbook*. It is true, of course, that the intended audience in that case consisted of minors, but without an appeal to the prurient interest, that would not have sufficed in the United States. The real distinction is the United States' insistence that obscenity be tied to such explicit sexual depiction, in comparison to the United Kingdom's concern over any material that depraves or corrupts and the allowance in Article 10(2) of the European Convention on Human Rights for restrictions based on the general protection of morals.

The position, under United States law, that ideas cannot play a role in declaring a work obscene has led to a difference in outcomes in cases from the United States and from Canada on very similar ordinances.[69] The United States case, *American Booksellers Association v. Hudnut*,[70] arose in Indianapolis. An ordinance purported to address pornography, but since it included a ban, it might be seen as defining a form of obscenity. "Pornography" was defined as:

the graphic sexually explicit subordination of women, whether in pictures or in words, that also includes one or more of the following:

(1) Women are presented as sexual objects who enjoy pain or humiliation; or
(2) Women are presented as sexual objects who experience sexual pleasure in being raped; or
(3) Women are presented as sexual objects tied up or cut up or mutilated or bruised or physically hurt, or as dismembered or truncated or fragmented or severed into body parts; or
(4) Women are presented as being penetrated by objects or animals; or

68 *Id.* at 688–89.

69 For a discussion in more depth, see Kevin W. Saunders, *The United States and Canadian Responses to the Feminist Attack on Pornography: A Perspective from the History of Obscenity*, 9 Ind. Int'l & Comp. L. Rev. 1 (1998).

70 771 F.2d 323 (7th Cir. 1985), *aff'd*, 475 U.S. 1001 (1986).

(5) Women are presented in scenarios of degradation, injury, abasement, torture, shown as filthy or inferior, bleeding, bruised, or hurt in a context that makes these conditions sexual; or
(6) Women are presented as sexual objects for domination, conquest, violation, exploitation, possession, or use, or through postures or positions of servility or submission or display.[71]

The ordinance prohibited trafficking in pornography, coercing others to perform in such works, forcing pornography on others, and assaulting or injuring a person in a way directly caused by a specific pornographic work.[72] Note that the ordinance did not base liability on an appeal to the prurient interest, did not rest on community standards, and made no exception for works with serious value.

There were also potential civil actions. The ordinance provided a cause of action against the producer or distributor of any pornographic work, where a person who saw or read the work caused injury to the plaintiff.[73] Furthermore, any woman, and any man who could show injury similar to that suffered by women, could file an Indianapolis equal opportunity complaint acting against subordination.[74]

The Canadian case was one already discussed, *Regina v. Butler*. It was brought under Canada's general provision addressing obscenity, which defines the material as "any publication a dominant characteristic of which is the undue exploitation of sex, or of sex and any one or more of the following subjects, namely, crime, horror, cruelty and violence."[75] The similarity to the Indianapolis case was the result of the targeting of similar material in the *Butler* Court's conclusion that undue exploitation could be the result of "plac [ing] women (and sometimes men) in positions of subordination, servile submission or humiliation ... against the principles of equality and dignity of all human beings."[76] Thus, while the legislative enactments may have differed, the Indianapolis ordinance and the Canadian Court's application both addressed subordination and degradation.

Challenges to the two laws led to very different results. When the United States Court of Appeals for the Seventh Circuit addressed the Indianapolis ordinance, it concluded that it discriminated on the basis of the content of expression.

[71] Indianapolis, Ind., Code § 16–3(q) (1984). The ordinance originally had a definition of "sexually explicit," but a later amendment left the ordinance with no definition for the phrase. See 771 F.2d at 324.
[72] Indianapolis, Ind., Code § 16–3(g)(7) (1984). [73] *See* 771 F.2d at 325. [74] *Id.*
[75] Criminal Code, R.S.C., ch. C-46, § 163(8) (1985) (Can.). [76] [1992] 1 S.C.R. 452 at ¶ 51.

> Speech treating women in the approved way – in sexual encounters "premised on equality" ... is lawful no matter how sexually explicit. Speech treating women in the disapproved way – as submissive in matters sexual or as enjoying humiliation – is unlawful no matter how significant the literary, artistic, or political qualities of the work taken as a whole.[77]

That distinction, based in ideas, was held to be viewpoint discrimination. The ordinance differed in its treatment of sexually explicit materials based on the perspective presented. Material taking the disapproved of view could not use sexual imagery, while anything that managed to combine the approved view with sexually explicit imagery was not addressed. The court said: "This is thought control. It establishes an 'approved' view of women, of how they may react to sexual encounters, of how the sexes may relate to each other. Those who espouse the approved view may use sexual images; those who do not, may not."[78]

The Supreme Court of Canada, in contrast, found the similar infringement on expression to be justified by Section 1 of the Canadian Charter of Rights and Freedoms. The Court recognized that exploiting sex in a manner that degrades and dehumanizes falls outside community standards for the treatment of sex. A factor in community tolerance is the harm that may result from exposing the community to the expression at issue, particularly leading people toward antisocial behavior. Where explicit sexual depiction is degrading or dehumanizing and the risk of harm is substantial, the exploitation of sex will be undue.[79]

The Court engaged in its now familiar *Oakes* analysis to determine whether this infringement on expression was justified. While not ruling out the power of Parliament "to legislate on the basis of some fundamental conception of morality for the purposes of safeguarding the values which are integral to a free and democratic society,"[80] the Court instead identified the overriding objective of and justification for the statute as the avoidance of harm.

> The clear and unquestionable danger of this type of material is that it reinforces some unhealthy tendencies in Canadian society. The effect of this type of material is to reinforce male-female stereotypes to the detriment of both sexes. It attempts to make degradation, humiliation, victimization, and violence in human relationships appear normal and acceptable. A society which holds that egalitarianism, non-violence, consensualism, and mutuality are basic to any human interaction, whether sexual or other, is clearly

[77] 771 F.2d at 325 (citation omitted). [78] 771 F.2d at 328. [79] [1992] 1 S.C.R. 452 at ¶ 62.
[80] *See id.* ¶ 82.

> justified in controlling and prohibiting any medium of depiction, description or advocacy which violates these principles.[81]

This identification of a pressing and substantial concern was clearly based on the ideas conveyed rather than the level of explicitness of the sexual depiction.

Turning to the proportionality requirement, the Court found a rational connection between the objective and the application of the statute, concluding that it was rational to believe that exposure to such depictions could change attitudes and beliefs in a way that would be harmful to society. "Parliament was entitled to have a 'reasoned apprehension of harm' resulting from the desensitization of individuals exposed to materials which depict violence, cruelty, and dehumanization in sexual relations."[82] Minimal impairment was found in the fact that explicit sexual depiction that did not include violence or dehumanization was not prohibited, material with serious value was protected, and the statute did not reach private possession.[83] Finally, with regard to balancing, the Court said that the material at issue is "far from the core of the guarantee of freedom of expression … [and] appeals only to the most base aspect of individual fulfilment."[84] In contrast, the avoidance of harm and fostering of respect for all individuals were seen as of fundamental importance.[85]

SERIOUS VALUE

Serious value clearly plays a role, in fact the dispositive role, in determinations of obscenity in United States law. The third prong of the *Miller* test provides that material may be found obscene only when it, "taken as a whole, lacks serious literary, artistic, political, or scientific value."[86]

Under the law of the United Kingdom, there has been, since the original Obscene Publication Act of 1959, a provision protecting material with value. Section 4 (1) provided: "A person shall not be convicted …, if it is proved that publication of the article in question is justified as being for the public good on the ground that it is in the interests of science, literature, art or learning, or of other objects of general concern."[87]

[81] *Id.* at ¶ 85 (quoting Standing Comm. on Justice and Legal Affairs, *Report on Pornography* 18:4 (1978)).

[82] *Id.* at ¶ 112. [83] *See id.* ¶ 120. [84] *Id.* ¶ 125. [85] *See id.* a¶ 126 [86] 413 U.S. at 24.

[87] Obscene Publications Act 1959, § 4(1), www.legislation.gov.uk/ukpga/1959/66/pdfs/ukpga_19590066_en.pdf. *See also* Handyside v. United Kingdom, App. No. 5493/72, 1 Eur. H.R. Rep. 737 (1976) at ¶ 25.

Canadian obscenity law provides a defense to a charge based on the publication or distribution of obscene material, if the defendant establishes that the publication or distribution serves the public good.[88] In terms of artistic value, the *Butler* Court described the "internal necessities" or "artistic defence" as asking "whether the exploitation of sex has a justifiable role in advancing the plot or the theme, and in considering the work as a whole, does not merely represent 'dirt for dirt's sake' but has a legitimate role when measured by the internal necessities of the work itself."[89] This is not, however, an absolute test. Even when material passes the test, there is still the issue of whether or not it would be tolerated by the community, although doubt is to be resolved in favor of allowing the expression.[90]

The *Müller* case would seem to indicate that Switzerland does not protect material with serious artistic value. After all, the paintings that form the basis of that prosecution were by a recognized artist and were part of an organized exhibition of contemporary art. Given that the European Court of Human Rights found no violation of Article 10, it would seem that the Court does not grant automatic protection to works with serious artistic value. That is not to say that other forms of value would not provide greater attention. The Court required proportionality between the interference with expression and the legitimacy of the aim pursued.[91] Where a work has serious political value, even the legitimate end of protecting morality might not be sufficient to justify suppression.

The clearest statement that serious value does not provide protection of otherwise obscene material is found in Japan. Even there, however, the case law has been evolving to at least take such value into consideration. The first of these cases, at least among those available in English, is the *Lady Chatterley's Lover Decision*.[92] The case was an appeal of an obscenity conviction based on the 1950 sale of a Japanese translation of the novel. The High Court spent a good deal of time discussing the value of the D.H. Lawrence work. The Court noted that it was a well-known book in English literature and highly reputable from an artistic standpoint. "The author's artistic talents can be judged from the development of the plot, the analysis and depiction of nature, society, and the personality of the characters, and the dialogue, rich in humor and irony, which also reveals the breadth of the author's culture."[93] After briefly describing the novel's plot, the Court noted the political value of

[88] *See* Criminal Code, R.S.C. 1985, c.C-46 § 161 (3).

[89] [1992] 1 S.C.R. 452 at ¶ 57.

[90] *See id.* at ¶ 64.

[91] *See* Müller v. Switzerland, App. No. 10737/84, 13 Eur. H.R. Rep. 212 (1988) at ¶ 32.

[92] Hanreisbü, XI, No. 34, 997 (Criminal), *See supra* note 53.

[93] *Id.* at 5.

the work. "The ideas criticize the atmosphere of the aristocratic class, the destruction of the beauty of nature by industrialization, the influence on the lives of the people in farming villages, the tragic circumstances of workers in the coal mines, the desolation of men's minds, and the actualities of dehumanization."[94]

At the same time, the Court identified the most important theme as the "primacy of the complete satisfaction of sexual desire" and a philosophy that finds the perfection of humankind and the significance of human life in love.[95] This seems to be the Court's objection. "With this philosophy of life the author denies the traditional (or what he calls puritanical) code, morality, and concept of sex that are approved not only in his own country but all others as well, and affirms the freedom of extramarital sexual relations . . ."[96]

The issue for the Court, after having held that the novel fits the Japanese definition of obscenity, was whether the literary and political value of the novel keep it, nonetheless, from being held obscene. The Court answered that question in the negative:

> [T]he obscene character of the work cannot be denied on the grounds that it is an artistic composition and not pornography. The reason is that even though from the standpoint of art it is in outstanding composition, it is not impossible for it to be appraised as possessing obscenity from the legal and moral standpoints, which are of a different order. We cannot approve the principle of the supremacy of thought, which emphasizes only the artistic nature of a composition and rejects criticism from the standpoint of law and morality. Even though a composition may have high artistic merit, it does not necessarily follow that its obscene nature is thereby dissipated. Though it be art, it has no right to present obscene matters publicly. The artist, too, in the pursuit of his mission must respect both the sense of shame and moral law and he must not act contrary to the duties borne by the people at large.[97]

The Court does distinguish scientific works because of their objective and dispassionate presentation on matters of sex.[98] It seems not to be that science has more value, but a scientific description is less likely to appeal to what the Court considered shameful interests than an artistic depiction may.

[94] *Id.* at 5–6. [95] *See id.* at 6.

[96] *Id.* For a discussion of cultural and historic considerations behind the decision, *see* Ann Sherif, *Foreign Sex, Native Politics: Lady Chatterley's Lover in Post-Occupation Japan* in Representing the Other in Modern Japanese Literature: A Critical Approach 183 (Rachel Hutchinson & Mark Williams, eds. 2007).

[97] *Id.* at 11–12. [98] *See id.* at 12.

The evolution in the Court's views is explained in *Soto v. Japan*, otherwise known as the *Yojohan Obscenity Case*.[99] That case grew out of the 1972 publication of *Behind the Sliding Doors of a Small Room*. The Court did not find the material to be without value but said

> the portions portraying scenes of sexual intercourse between the sexes in a lascivious style – explicitly, in detail, and concretely – constitute the core of the work quantitatively and qualitatively; even if consideration is given to such things as its structure and development as well as its artistic and intellectual value, it is thus to be deemed to appeal primarily to the prurient interest of readers.[100]

The material was seen to have both artistic merit and to appeal to the prurient interest. Under these circumstances, a sort of balancing is required.

> In arriving at a judgment as to the obscenity of the literary work, it is necessary to examine all manner of points bearing on whether or not it is deemed to appeal primarily to the prurient interest of readers when the said work is taken as a whole, from these points of view: the extent, and its style, of explicit, detailed portrayal and depiction of sex in the said literary work; the relative weight given to that portrayal and depiction in the entire work; the correlation between the ideas and so forth expressed in the work and that portrayal and depiction; the structure and development of the work; and furthermore, the degree to which sexual stimulation is mitigated by artistry, intellectuality, and so forth.[101]

Under this more recent decision, a balancing is required. In the editor's notes to the English translation, it is said that the "judgment ... reversed previous court decisions that considered the 'artistry and intellectuality' of writing to be irrelevant in judging obscenity. Allowance for artistry and intellectuality may permit the courts to be more lenient in the determination of obscenity in future cases."[102] So, a work with serious value may still be held to be obscene, although value provides some weight against such a conclusion.

THEATERS AND PRIVATE POSSESSION

The clearest justification for limits on obscene material is when those materials confront unwilling recipients. But what about when explicitly sexual films

[99] 34 Keishū 6 at 433 (1980), available in translation at LAWRENCE W. BEER & HIROSHI ITOH, THE CONSTITUTIONAL CASE LAW OF JAPAN, 1970 THROUGH 1990. 468 (1996).
[100] *Id.* at 470. [101] *Id.* [102] *Id.* at 469.

are shown in a theater to an audience interested in the fare? Or, what about the private possession of obscene material in one's own home?

The United States Supreme Court addressed the first issue in a case decided the same day as *Miller*. In *Paris Adult Theatre v. Slaton*,[103] the Court took up the issue of whether the First Amendment protected the showing of obscene films in a theater in which admission was limited to adults. There were signs at the entrance indicating the nature of the material, as a warning to potential viewers, but with no exposure of erotic material to those passing by on the street. Hence, only those who were interested and willing to pay for admission were exposed to the sexually explicit material. The Court rejected the claim that these precautions resulted in the films being protected.

> [T]here are legitimate state interests at stake in stemming the tide of commercialized obscenity, even assuming it is feasible to enforce effective safeguards against exposure to juveniles and to passersby ... These include the interest of the public in the quality of life and the total community environment, the tone of commerce in the great city centers, and, possibly, the public safety itself.[104]

The Court went on to quote Chief Justice Warren for the proposition that "there is a 'right of the Nation and of the States to maintain a decent society.'"[105]

The Court may be seen as having limited its analysis to commercial exploitation of obscene material. It rejected the proposition that such conduct involving only consenting adults is beyond state regulation. "Commercial exploitation of depictions, descriptions, or exhibitions of obscene conduct on commercial premises open to the adult public falls within a State's broad power to regulate commerce and protect the public environment."[106] Further, the court said that the state was allowed to make the "morally neutral judgment" that such exhibitions tend to injure the community,[107] even though such limitations might well seldom be morally neutral.

The European Court of Human Rights has taken a different position. *Scherer v. Switzerland*[108] concerned a film shown in a "sex shop" specializing in materials for those with a same-sex orientation. As with the theater in the United States case, there were no erotic materials visible to passers-by. In fact, the Court said that even the nature of the establishment was not apparent and that customers were led to the shop only through advertisements in magazines

[103] 413 U.S. 49 (1973). [104] *Id.* at 57–58.
[105] *Id.* at 59 (quoting Jacobellis v. Ohio, 378 U.S. 184, 199 (1964) (Warren, C.J., dissenting)).
[106] *Id.* at 68–69. [107] *Id.* at 69. [108] App. No. 17116/90, 18 Eur. H.R. Rep. 276 (1994).

or at meeting places for those of same-sex orientation. Scherer was convicted of violating a criminal law barring the possession of obscene materials with a view toward distributing or displaying the materials to the public or so distributing or displaying materials. Interestingly, Swiss law was later changed to provide: "Anyone who, when exhibition or performance on closed premises is being held, warns those attending of the pornographic nature of the exhibition or performance shall not be liable to punishment."[109]

The European Court concluded that the conviction was a violation of Article 10. The criminal law was aimed at a legitimate goal, the protection of morals, but the Court said that the application of the law failed to comply with the requirement of a "pressing social need" and was not "necessary in a democratic society." The Court noted the opinion of the European Commission on Human Rights that

> the present case does not concern the protection of morals of adult persons in Swiss society in general, since no adult was confronted unintentionally or against his will with the film. Where this is so, there must be particularly compelling reasons justifying the interference at issue. In the present case, no such reasons have been provided by the Government.[110]

The Court agreed, concluding that the conviction was not justified by any "pressing social need" and the interference was disproportionate to the government's aims and was not "necessary in a democratic society."[111]

With regard to private possession, the United States Supreme Court has been more protective of obscene material. The *Paris Adult Theatre* Court had noted that it was addressing commercial use of the material. Private possession had, in fact, already come before the Court in *Stanley v. Georgia*.[112] That case grew out of the search of the appellant's home for evidence of gambling. Instead of such evidence, obscene material was discovered. The Court reversed the conviction for possession of obscene materials, concluding that private possession is protected by the First Amendment. "It is now well established that the Constitution protects the right to receive information and ideas ... This right to receive information and ideas, regardless of their social worth, is fundamental to our free society."[113] The Court also noted the "added dimension" provided by the fact that the possession was in the privacy of the individual's own home.[114]

> [A]ppellant is asserting ... the right to read or observe what he pleases – the right to satisfy his intellectual and emotional needs in the privacy of his own home. He is asserting the right to be free from state inquiry into the contents

[109] *Id.* at ¶ 24. [110] *See id.* at ¶ 65. [111] *See id.* at ¶ 66. [112] 394 U.S. 557 (1969).
[113] *Id.* at 564. [114] *See id.*

> of his library ... If the First Amendment means anything, it means that a State has no business telling a man, sitting alone in his own house, what books he may read or what films he may watch. Our whole constitutional heritage rebels at the thought of giving government the power to control men's minds ... Georgia asserts the right to protect the individual's mind from the effects of obscenity. We are not certain that this argument amounts to anything more than the assertion that the State has the right to control the moral content of a person's thoughts. To some, this may be a noble purpose, but it is wholly inconsistent with the philosophy of the First Amendment.[115]

The Canadian obscenity statute is aimed at distribution, publication, or public exposure; possession is only included if it is for such a purpose.[116] The Irish position appears similar to that of the United States. Films that are obscene or would harm public morality may be banned, while private possession appears to be allowed.[117] The United Kingdom bans even the possession of some pornographic material. The Criminal Justice and Immigration Act of 2008 bars the possession of "extreme pornographic images,"[118] while the Obscene Publications Act is aimed only at distribution and publication for distribution.[119] The Criminal Justice Act also defines extreme image as an image that is "grossly offensive, disgusting or otherwise of an obscene character" and which portrays, explicitly and realistically

> (a) an act which threatens a person's life, (b) an act which results, or is likely to result, in serious injury to a person's anus, breasts or genitals, (c) an act which involves sexual interference with a human corpse, or (d) a person performing an act of intercourse or oral sex with an animal (whether dead or alive) and a reasonable person looking at the image would think that any such person or animal was real.[120]

The statute does allow a defense, where a work has received a classification, where the possessor has a legitimate reason for the possession, does not know the content of an image in his or her position, or has received an unsolicited image and has not kept it for an unreasonable time.[121]

[115] *Id.* at 565–66. [116] *See* R.S.C. 1985, c.C-46 § 163.

[117] *See* Carol Daugherty Rasnie, *Pornographic Movies, Obscene Books, Fighting Words, and Pink Haired Students: Constitutional Freedom of Expression and Some Comparisons with Irish Constitutional Law*, 11 Seton Hall Constitutional L.J. 375, 424–25 (2001).

[118] *See* Criminal Justice and Immigration Act 2008 c.4 § 63, www.legislation.gov.uk/ukpga/2008/4/contents.

[119] *See* Obscene Publications Act 1964 § 2; *see also* William T. Goldberg, *Two Nations, One Web: Comparative Legal Approaches to Pornographic Obscenity by the United States and the United Kingdom*, 90 B.U. L Rev. 2121, 2140 (2010).

[120] Criminal Justice and Immigration Act at § 63(6) and § 63(7). [121] *See id.* at §§ 64–65.

CHILD PORNOGRAPHY

The United States Supreme Court recognized an exception to First Amendment protection, where child pornography is involved, in *New York v. Ferber*.[122] The defendant in the case ran a bookstore selling sexual material, and the charges were based on the sale of two films depicting young boys masturbating. He was convicted of promoting a sexual performance by a child under sixteen by distributing depictions of the performance.[123] Oddly, he was acquitted on charges of promoting an obscene sexual performance, even though *Mishkin*'s variable obscenity standard would seem to justify that conviction. The statute under which he was convicted does not, however, require that the depiction be obscene. Nor did it protect material with serious value.

The Supreme Court discussed the harm done to children through the production of child pornography. It recognized a compelling governmental interest in protecting the physical and psychological well-being of children, including the prevention of sexual and psychological abuse. The Court also concluded that a ban on distribution was required for the protection of children. "First, the materials produced are a permanent record of the children's participation and the harm to the child is exacerbated by their circulation. Second, the distribution network for child pornography must be closed if the production of material which requires the sexual exploitation of children is to be effectively controlled."[124] The Court's analysis seemed focused on establishing that limits on child photography can be justified under strict scrutiny, but the conclusion seemed to be that such material is exempted from First Amendment protection.

In a later decision, *Osborne v. Ohio*,[125] the Court extended its reasoning to include bans on possession of child pornography, based on the fact that it is possession that drives distribution that, in turn, motivates the abuse. The limits of this reasoning were set out by *Ashcroft v. Free Speech Coalition*,[126] where the Court struck down limits on sexually explicit material that appeared to depict children but was produced without using any actual child. With such material, there was no child harmed.

Bans on child pornography have become very widespread. As of 2012, Japan was said to be the only Organization for Economic Cooperation and

[122] 458 U.S. 747 (1982).
[123] *See id.* at 749; *see also* N.Y. Penal Law, Article 263 (McKinney 1980). [124] 458 U.S. at 759.
[125] 495 U.S. 103 (1990). [126] 535 U.S. 234 (2002).

Development (OECD) country without a ban on possession.[127] Production and distribution, and possession with intent to distribute were illegal, but possession was not.[128] There, too, it would appear that possession would soon be addressed, with controversy over such a ban focusing primarily on whether it should include animated works.[129]

The relevant statute in the United Kingdom would appear to go beyond the prohibitions approved in the United States, at least in one way. The Protection of Children Act of 1978 makes it an offense

(a) to take, or permit to be taken or to make, any indecent photograph or pseudo-photograph of a child; or
(b) to distribute or show such indecent photographs or pseudo-photographs; or
(c) to have in his possession such indecent photographs or pseudo-photographs, with a view to their being distributed or shown by himself or others; or
(d) to publish or cause to be published any advertisement likely to be understood as conveying that the advertiser distributes or shows such indecent photographs or pseudo-photographs or intends to do so.[130]

The statute defines a pseudo-photograph as an image that appears to be a photograph of a child, even if produced through graphics.[131] There is also a defense, if the individual has legitimate reason for such possession or did not know the nature of the images.[132]

The United Kingdom statute contradicts the position of the United States Supreme Court in that animated material may be the basis for a charge. The original act also failed to make possession illegal. That was addressed in the Criminal Justice Act of 1988.[133] The 1988 act made possession illegal, with defenses where the possessor had a legitimate reason for the possession, did not know the nature of the image or had received an unsolicited image which he or she deleted within a reasonable time.

[127] *See* Tomasz Jankowski & Teppei Kasai, *Pressure on Japan for Stronger Laws on Child Pornography*, REUTERS (Sep. 19, 2012), http://uk.reuters.com/article/2012/09/19/us-japan-pornography-idUKBRE88107H20120919.
[128] *Id.*
[129] *See Controversy Raging over Revisions to Child Pornography Law*, THE ASAHI SHIMBUN (Jul. 27, 2013), http://ajw.asahi.com/article/behind_news/social_affairs/AJ201307270063.
[130] Protection of Children Act 1978, ch. 37, § 1(1), www.legislation.gov.uk/ukpga/1978/37.
[131] *See id.* §§ 7–8. [132] *See id.* § 14.
[133] See Criminal Justice Act 1988, c. 33, Part XI, § 160, available at www.legislation.gov.uk/ukpga/1988/33/section/160.

Canada also has a statute, and the Canadian Supreme Court's decision on the acceptability of that statute under Sections 1 and 2 of the Charter provides an interesting analysis of a problem that has arisen under child photography laws in the United States. The problem involves sexting,[134] the transmission of a sexual image taken of oneself to another person, where the recipient is a sexual or romantic partner of the transmitter. While the United States Supreme Court has not addressed the issue, there has been concern. The practice violates child pornography laws, at least technically, since it is the distribution of the sexual image of a person under eighteen. Yet, if there is abuse in the initial transmission, it is a form of self-abuse; retransmission by the recipient adds abuse by another and should be treated more seriously.

In the Canadian child pornography case, *Regina v. Sharpe*,[135] the Court considered a statute banning the possession of material depicting a person who is or who is depicted as being under eighteen engaged in explicit sexual activity or with a dominant focus on the sexual organs of such a depicted person. It appears that the statute included material that did not involve any actual abuse of a child. The Canadian statute did provide a defense based on artistic merit or educational, scientific, or medical purpose or for material which would otherwise serve the public good. Presumably the material the defendant possessed, discs titles "Sam Paloc's Boyabuse – Flogging, Fun and Fortitude: A Collection of Kiddiekink Classics," did not have such value, and the defendant was left to rely on a claim that the limitations on such material violated his free expression rights.

The Court's Section 1 analysis easily found a pressing and substantial concern in the protection of children. The ban on child pornography was also found to be rationally connected to the objective, using analysis similar to that of the *Ferber* Court. The Court also found the infringement on speech to be minimal. That took the Court to the issue of proportionality between the infringement on expression and the protection. Generally, the Court held the statute to be proportional but with exceptions. It is the analysis of the exceptions where there is relevance to sexting.

> [T]he prohibition ... captures in its sweep materials that arguably pose little or no risk to children, and that deeply implicate the freedoms guaranteed under s. 2(b). The ban, for example, extends to a teenager's sexually explicit recordings of him or herself alone, or engaged in lawful sexual activity, held solely for personal use. It also reaches private materials, created by an

[134] *See, e.g.*, Julia Halloran McLaughlin, *Exploring the First Amendment Rights of Teens in Relationship to Sexting and Censorship*, 45 U. Mich. J.L. Reform 315 (2012).

[135] [2001] 1 S.C.R. 45.

> individually exclusively for him or herself, such as personal journals, writings, and drawings. It is in relation to these categories of materials that the costs of the prohibition are most pronounced. At the same time, it is here that the link between the proscribed materials and any risk of harm to children is most tenuous … Consequently, the law's application to these materials, while peripheral to its objective, poses the most significant problems at this final stage of the proportionality analysis.[136]

It may not be clear that the decision would protect the sexter, since sexting is not the possession of sexual images for one's own use; it involves transmission of those images. Nonetheless, there is recognition that the creation of the image may not have harmed the child, and the initial transmission to the child's intended recipient could plausibly be similarly treated. Further transmission would not come within the Court's exception and might, indeed, be harmful.

[136] *Id.* at ¶ 105.

12

Children and Expression

The issue of children and free expression, whether children have a right to access whatever material they might wish and whether media providers have a right to provide that material to children, is yet another issue on which the United States and most of the rest of the democratic world disagree. The position of the United States, in accord with its almost absolutist position regarding free expression, largely rejects limits on children's access. It is only where adult access may be limited that material of similar nature, even if less explicit, may be denied to children. In much of the rest of the world, types of material that would be available to adults are denied to children.

Failure to recognize this differences from country to country has led some in the United States to reject the views of psychologists regarding the impact of violent video games on children. There are a significant number of studies showing that playing violent video games increases aggression in the real world.[1] It has been argued in response that there must be a problem with the science, because the rest of the world also has violent video games without the same level of societal violence.[2] The assumption behind that response is

[1] *See infra* notes 17–26 and accompanying text.

[2] A blogger for *The Washington Post* posted, in December of 2012, a piece titled "Ten-Country Comparison Suggests There is Little or No Link Between Video Games and Gun Murders." Max Fisher, *Ten-Country Comparison Suggests There is Little or No Link Between Video Games and Gun Murders*, The Washington Post (Dec. 17, 2012), www.washingtonpost.com/blogs/worldviews/wp/2012/12/17/ten-country-comparison-suggests-theres-little-or-no-link-between-video-games-and-gun-murders. The study examined per capita video game consumption in ten countries and found no correlation with murder using firearms, concluding that it cannot then be video games that cause such violence. The problem with the analysis is that it assumes that the presence of violent video games in other countries means that, as in the United States, children have access to the games.
The argument was repeated in a *CQResearcher* article on media violence, saying: "Free-speech advocates ... point out that even though violent video games are played globally, few other

that the law in other countries mirrors that of the United States. In fact, those other countries relied on by the critics may have video games, but they restrict youth access.

This chapter will begin with an examination of law in the United States. The United States, in keeping with its willingness to restrict sexual material, does limit youth access to such material, even when similar material would be legal for adults. A Supreme Court case makes it clear, however, that other limits outside the sexual area may not be restricted; in particular, state attempts to limit access to violent video games are unconstitutional.

The examination will then demonstrate a contrast with law in Canada and in England. The Canadian Supreme Court has allowed restrictions on advertising aimed at children. In England, children's access was limited to the *Little Red Schoolbook*, even though the book's content was neither explicitly sexual nor violent. The objection was that the material contained in the book would corrupt the morals of children. The English restriction was held, by the European Court of Human Rights, not to be a violation of the European Convention on Human Rights, thereby demonstrating a wider acceptance of attempts to shield children from objectionable material. Both Canada and England also have restrictions on children's video game access.

After the discussion of the case law from the United States, Canada, and England, the analysis will turn specifically to restrictions on video games. This analysis allows a consideration of statutory limits, even where there is no case law growing out of those statutes. It also allows for an examination of the issue of children and expression in an area that is of particular current concern.

THE UNITED STATES

The one area in which the United States Supreme Court has allowed restrictions on the expression available to children has been where sexual material is involved. The Court, in *Ginsberg v. New York*,[3] found no constitutional violation in the application of a New York law to punish the sale of what it termed "girlie magazines" to a sixteen-year-old. The magazines at issue were not obscene for an adult audience, so sale to an adult would not have been in

countries match the United States in the rate of homicides." Christina L. Lyons, *Media Violence: Do Children Have Too Much Access to Violent Content?*, 24 CQ RESEARCHER 147, 150 (Feb. 14, 2014). The article quotes the Entertainment Software Association: "'The video games played in this country are played worldwide, and ours is the only country that sees our society's level of violence.'" *Id.* (quoting Dan Hewitt, Vice President of the Entertainment Software Association).

3 390 U.S. 629 (1968).

violation of law. There was, however, a New York statute prohibiting the knowing sale to a person under seventeen of material containing any representation of "a person or portion of the human body which depicts nudity, sexual conduct or sado-masochistic abuse and which is harmful to minors."[4] The statute also defined "harmful to minors" as

> that quality of any description or representation, in whatever form, of nudity, sexual conduct, sexual excitement, or sado-masochistic abuse, when it:
>
> (i) predominantly appeals to prurient, shameful or morbid interest of minors, and
> (ii) is patently offensive to prevailing standards in the adult community as a whole with respect to what is suitable material for minors, and
> (iii) is utterly without redeeming social importance for minors.[5]

That definition was based on the then current definition of obscene material with an added focus on minors.

The Court recognized that the provocatively posed nudes contained in the magazines, if they had been distributed to adults, would be protected expression. That is, the material was not obscene for an adult audience. However, restrictions on the same magazines, when they were distributed to children, did not violate the First Amendment. Thus, children could be shielded from material, at least of this type, that may be freely available to adults.

The key to this result was the fact that the Court had already recognized an exception to the First Amendment that left obscene material unprotected.[6] And, the Court had also recognized that, in determining what material is obscene, the audience for the material matters.[7] While only material that appeals to the prurient interest can be obscene, the prurient interest of a sixteen-year-old boy is easily provoked. While such provocatively posed nudes may not be obscene for adults, this more easily appealed to prurient interest of a sixteen-year-old left them unprotected as obscene, when distributed to children.

It was important, even when the case was first handed down, not to read it too broadly. It did not really allow restrictions to be placed on the distribution of material to children, just because the recipients were children. Rather, it required that similar material could be restricted for adults. It was because of

4 *Id.* at 647 (quoting N.Y. PENAL LAW § 484-h(2)(a)) (McKinney 1965)).
5 *Id.* at 646 (quoting N.Y. PENAL LAW § 484-k(1)(f)) (McKinney 1965)).
6 *See* Roth v. United States, 354 U.S. 476 (1957).
7 *See* Mishkin v. New York, 383 U.S. 502 (1966) (adopting the variable obscenity standard in allowing a conviction for the distribution of material that did not appeal to the prurient interest of the average person but did have such an appeal for an audience of sado-masochists).

the obscenity exception, allowing such adult restrictions, that this material could be barred for children. Even though the application of the obscenity exception may be broader when children are the recipients, the case did not provide a new exception for children. It did not address more general areas in which adult access was protected and whether children could, nonetheless, have their access restricted.

In 2011, that issue came back to the Court in *Brown v. Entertainment Merchants Association*.[8] The case grew out of a California statute prohibiting the sale or rental of certain video games to minors.[9] The affected games were those in which a virtual human being was killed, maimed, dismembered, or sexually assaulted in a way a reasonable person would see as appealing to a minor's "shameful or morbid interest" and that is "patently offensive to prevailing standards in the adult community as to what is suitable for minors," and taken as a whole "lack[s] serious literary, artistic, political, or scientific value for minors."

It seems clear that the state hoped to carry the result in *Ginsberg* over to violent material. It attempted to treat violent material in the same way that sexual material is treated, allowing greater adult access, while limiting the exposure of children. The Court rejected the use of, or analogy to, obscenity law. It noted that there had been a historical exemption for obscenity, while there has been no parallel exemption for violent material. That does seem true of Supreme Court cases from the late 1800s on, although in the era of the framing, the obscenity exception had a broader scope.[10] State attempts to limit the distribution of violent material continued into the twentieth century. While such an attempt was struck down by the Supreme Court, in *Winters v. New York*,[11] the Court did so on vagueness grounds and specifically warned against reading the case as holding that such material could not be limited under a properly drawn statute.

Because the Court did not find the material at issue to fit within an exception to the First Amendment, it required that the restriction meet strict scrutiny, that it be narrowly tailored to a compelling governmental interest. In the Court's view, the state could not meet that standard, because it failed to show "a direct causal link between violent video games and harm to minors."[12] The state had argued that it should be able to make a predictive judgment of harm based on what were described by the Court as "competing psychological

[8] 131 S.Ct. 2729 (2011). [9] CAL. CIV. CODE §§ 1746–1746.5 (West 2009).

[10] *See* KEVIN W. SAUNDERS, VIOLENCE AS OBSCENITY: LIMITING THE MEDIA'S FIRST AMENDMENT PROTECTION (1996).

[11] Winters v. New York, 333 U.S. 507 (1948). [12] 131 S.Ct. at 2738.

studies," but competing studies fell, in the Court's view, short of being compelling evidence. One of the problems the Court found was that it saw the science as demonstrating only correlation between violent video game play and aggression in the real world, rather than causation. But psychologists have, as Justice Breyer recognized in his dissent,[13] conducted studies that do demonstrate causation.

A second problem for the Court was that the measurement of real-world effects was based on feelings of aggression and acts such as the willingness to inflict a louder noise on another person. Such acts are certainly not as serious as the infliction of real violence, but experimental settings can only allow such mild impacts. Certainly, children cannot be allowed, in such a setting, to cause actual serious harm. Feelings of aggression and the infliction of loud noises must be used as a proxy for more serious behavior.

Only Justice Breyer seriously examined the science. His dissenting opinion provided two appendices, the first listing 115 studies demonstrating harm growing out of violent video games,[14] and the second listing thirty-four studies that failed to find harm.[15] In considering the latter thirty-four studies, it is important to recognize here that the failure to support a finding of harm is not the same as demonstrating that there is no harm. There may simply be no conclusion; the failure to establish a conclusion is not the same as establishing its negation.

After examining the science, Justice Breyer concluded that "there is substantial (though controverted) evidence supporting the expert associations of public health professionals that have concluded that violent video games can *cause* children psychological harm."[16] He admitted that he, like most judges, lacked the expertise to determine whether or not violent videogames cause harm to children. Given that lack, he was willing to let the scientific community answer the scientific question, citing to a 2000 joint statement by the American Academy of Pediatrics, the American Academy of Child & Adolescent Psychiatry, the American Psychological Association, the American Medical Association, the American Academy of Family Physicians, and the American Psychiatric Association asserting a causal connection between media violence and aggressiveness in children and suggesting that video games are of more concern than other media.[17] He also cited to a

[13] *See id.* at 2767–70 (Breyer, J., dissenting).
[14] *Id.* at 2771–78 (Breyer, J., dissenting).
[15] *Id.* at 2778–79 (Breyer, J., dissenting).
[16] *Id.* at 2772 (Breyer, J., dissenting)(emphasis in original).
[17] *Id.* at 2769 (Breyer, J., dissenting)(citing Joint Statement on the Impact of Entertainment Violence on Children (Jul. 26, 2000), www.aap.org/advocacy/releases/jstmevc.htm).

2005 resolution by the American Psychological Association and a 2009 statement by the American Academy of Pediatrics seconding this particular concern regarding violent video games.[18]

In contrast to Justice Breyer, the majority gave rather short shrift to the science, basing the rejection primarily on the claim that the science had been rejected by the lower courts, citing to cases from 2001 to 2009.[19] This, of course, failed to account for any further development in a rapidly developing area, a failure that was criticized in the opinion of Justice Alito, joined by Chief Justice Roberts, concurring in the result on the ground that the statute was too vague.[20]

Particularly telling was the failure to look at recently developed evidence from neuroscience. Neuroscience adds strength to the conclusions of the psychologists, a point recognized by Justice Breyer. He wrote: "Cutting-edge neuroscience has shown that 'virtual violence and videogame playing results in those neural patterns that are considered characteristic for aggressive cognition and behavior.'"[21] Perhaps the majority was again willing to rely on the lower courts, one of which had looked at neuroscience and rejected it on a very strange basis.

The federal district court, in *Entertainment Software Association v. Blagojevich*,[22] heard evidence that the region of the brain responsible for inhibition does not fully function in children exposed to media violence. However, the court's response was that lack of function in that region did not mean that judgment and inhibition were not being exercised elsewhere in the brain. But there is no indication that these functions ever occur elsewhere. This inability or unwillingness to understand or accept science was characteristic of the lower court opinions cited to by the *Brown* majority.

Another example is found in *Entertainment Software Association v. Hatch*.[23] A federal district judge in Minnesota examined the work of, perhaps, the leading psychologist in the field and said "Dr. Anderson's meta-analysis seems to suggest that one can take a number of studies, each of which he admits do not prove the proposition in question and 'stack them up' until a collective proof emerges."[24] That is the essence of meta-analysis, which is recognized as

[18] *Id.* at 2769–70 (Breyer, J., dissenting).
[19] *See id.* at 2739, n.6.
[20] *See id.* at 2742–43 (Alito, J., concurring).
[21] *Id.* at 2768 (Breyer, J., dissenting)(quoting René Weber et al., *Does Playing Violent Video Games Induce Aggression? Empirical Evidence of a Functional Magnetic Resonance Imaging Study*, 8 Media Psychology 39, 51 (2006)).
[22] 404 F.Supp.2d 1051 (N.D. Ill. 2005), *aff'd*, 469 F3d 641 (7th Cir, 2006).
[23] 443 F.Supp.2d 1065 (D.Minn. 2006).
[24] *Id.* at 1069 n.1.

a valid statistical method.[25] Its rejection could only be based on either statistical illiteracy or an unwillingness to allow science to suggest, contrary to accepted dogma, that expression can cause harm.[26]

The Court's rejection of the conclusions of the scientific community, as reflected in statements, as cited by Justice Breyer, by all of the major health organizations concerned with children's well-being seems to reflect the United States' approach to free expression generally. Free expression is so valued that limits can be justified only when there is seemingly absolute certainty that serious harm will unavoidably follow. Statistical analysis will always lack absolute certainty, so it will not be sufficient to justify limits on expression to children. This has certainly been true with regard to violent media, and it seems unlikely that any other limits on access by children, other than for sexual content, would meet with approval.

CANADA

The United States approach to examining limits on expression directed to children stands in stark contrast to the acceptance of psychological, statistical evidence in Canada. The Supreme Court of Canada, in *Irwin Toy v. Québec*,[27] considered provisions of Québec's Consumer Protection Act prohibiting television advertising directed toward children under thirteen.[28] The provisions were challenged by a company that wanted to advertise toys on a number of grounds, including that there was a violation of Section 2(b), the free expression provision of the Charter of Rights and Freedoms.

Since there was clearly an infringement of the company's expression, the issue became the Section 1 justification for the ban. That turned first on whether the limits were related to "concerns which are pressing and substantial in a free and democratic society."[29] The Court found the concern pressing and substantial and found great importance in the purpose of the statute.

[25] Although meta-analysis may be a complex statistical method, the theory is rather simple to understand on an intuitive level. Such an intuitive example may be found in baseball. If Player A gets more hits than Player B in any single baseball game, that does not prove him to be the better hitter. But "stacking up" these insignificant results over the course of a season, does demonstrate that he is the better hitter.

[26] This is not to say that there can be no objection to a meta-analytic study. There are any number of criticisms that may be offered, for example, criticism regarding the selection of the studies to include in the meta-analysis. That criticism from, in a sense, within the method differs from the wholesale rejection of this fully accepted analytic technique.

[27] [1989] 1 S.C.R. 927 (Can.). [28] R.S.Q., c. P-40.1, §§ 248–49. [29] 1 S.C.R. at ¶ 71.

> The concern is for the protection of a group which is particularly vulnerable to the techniques of seduction and manipulation abundant in advertising . . . [T]he concerns which have motivated both legislative and voluntary regulation in this area are the particular susceptibility of young children to media manipulation, their inability to differentiate between reality and fiction and to grasp the persuasive intention behind the message, and the secondary effects of exterior influences on the family and parental authority.[30]

The Court found a United States Federal Trade Commission report to be a sufficient basis for the province to conclude that

> the specific cognitive abilities of young children lead to the inability to fully understand child-oriented television advertising . . . The report thus provides a sound basis on which to conclude that television advertising directed at young children is *per se* manipulative. Such advertising aims to promote products by convincing those who will always believe.[31]

The Canadian Court was clearly more willing to accept the evidence of social science to justify limits on expression than has been the United States Supreme Court. What may be of even more interest is the fact that the Canadian Court was willing to allow the provincial legislature to go even beyond what was specifically justified by the Federal Trade Commission report relied on by the province. The report had concluded that it was children between two and six years of age who could not distinguish program from advertising, while the province had limited advertising directed at those under thirteen. That didn't bother the Court.

The province had submitted studies reaching different conclusions as to the age at which children become able to recognize the nature of advertising. While young children most clearly lacked the ability, it was less clear for older children. Nonetheless, the Court said "the legislature was not obliged to confine itself solely to protecting the most clearly vulnerable group. It was only required to exercise reasonable judgment in specifying the vulnerable group."[32]

> Where the Legislature mediates between the competing claims of different groups in the community, it will inevitably be called upon to draw the line marking where one set of claims legitimately begins and the other fades away without access to complete knowledge as to its precise location. If the

[30] *Id.* at ¶ 72.

[31] *Id.* at ¶ 73. The Court gave credence to Fed. Trade Comm'n, Final Staff Report and Recommendations, In the Matter of Children's Advertising (1981).

[32] [1989] 1 S.C.R. at ¶ 74.

> legislature has made a reasonable assessment as to where the line is most properly drawn, especially if that assessment involves weighing conflicting scientific evidence and allocating scarce resources on this basis, it is not for the court to second guess. That would only be to substitute one estimate for another.[33]

It is, of course, true that the Canadian case involved commercial speech which, even in the United States law, has less protection, but the Court's opinion does seem to reflect the more general acceptance of social science to justify limits. While a conflict among scientific studies may lead to the conclusion, in the United States, that a limit is not justified, the same was not true for the Canadian Court. Where there is a conflict, the Canadian Court takes the position that deference to the legislature is required.

> When striking a balance between the claims of competing groups, the choice of means, like the choice of ends, frequently will require an assessment of conflicting scientific evidence and differing justified demands on scarce resources. Democratic institutions are meant to let us all share the responsibility for these difficult choices. Thus, as courts review the results of the legislature's deliberations, particularly with respect to the protection of vulnerable groups, they must be mindful of the legislature's representative function.[34]

There is one more interesting aspect in the Canadian Court's discussion of the impact of the ban on free expression. The Court said that "[a]dvertisers are always free to direct the message to parents and other adults."[35] Thus, any deleterious effect was reduced. That fact, however, would not have swayed the United States Supreme Court. The California statute at issue in *Brown* did not bar parents from buying the games for their children.

Canada does, at the provincial and territorial level, limit youth access to certain video games, often as part of more general statutes addressing motion pictures and other forms of entertainment,[36] and these limitations have gone unchallenged.[37] As an example of a more general statute with application to video games, British Columbia allows a government official to place

[33] *Id.* at ¶ 75. [34] *Id.* at ¶ 80. [35] *Id.* at ¶ 90.

[36] For more depth in the discussion of statutes from the Canadian provinces and territories, *see* Kevin W. Saunders, *A Comparative Look at Children and Free Expression*, 22 TRANSNAT'L L. & CONTEMP. PROBS. 455 (2013).

[37] There was a challenge to in earlier version of Ontario's Theatres Act. In Regina v. Glad Day Bookshops, Inc., (2004) O.R. 3d 691 (Can. Ont. Sup. Ct. J.), the statute was struck down, but that was because of its effect on the ability to provide entertainment materials to adults, rather than children.

conditions, including the age of the audience, on the exhibition of motion pictures, and the statute makes clear that "motion picture" includes video games.[38] The statute applies to adult films, but such films include not only those with sexual content but also those involving brutality or torture.[39] In a statute aimed specifically at video games, New Brunswick requires that a government official view or play any video game distributed in the province and assign a classification or adopt the classification assigned by another jurisdiction, and distribution contrary to the classification is a violation of law.[40] While not all the provinces and territories impose restrictions, most do, and the restrictions do not seem to be seen as violating the free speech provision of the Canadian Charter of Rights and Freedoms.[41]

ENGLAND AND THE EUROPEAN UNION

An English case shows the breadth of scope of the material from which England will shield children. The most easily accessible report of the case comes from the European Court of Human Rights. *Handyside v. United Kingdom*[42] was an appeal from a publisher's conviction in English courts for a violation of the Obscene Publications Act of 1959[43] as amended by the Obscene Publications Act of 1964.[44] The relevant part of the amended act provided that

> an article shall be deemed to be obscene if its effect or (where the article comprises two or more distinct items) the effect of any one of its items is, if taken as a whole, such as to tend to deprave and corrupt persons who are likely, having regard to all relevant circumstances, to read, see or hear the matter contained or embodied in it.[45]

A violation of the Obscenity Act did not require sexually explicit depictions but could be based on anything with a tendency to deprave and corrupt.

The basis for the prosecution was the publication of a book titled *The Little Red Schoolbook*. The book was aimed at schoolchildren aged twelve years and older, and it sold at a price they could afford. The book's introduction was

[38] *See* Motion Picture Act, R.S.B.C. 1996, c. 314.

[39] *See id.* § 1.

[40] *See* R.S.N.B. 2011, c. 159.

[41] For statutes in other provinces, *see* Kevin W. Saunders, *supra* note 36, at 467–79.

[42] 1 Eur. Ct. H.R. (Ser. A) 737 (1976).

[43] Obscene Publications Act, 1959 c. 66. Certain aspects of the Act and the case in terms of defining obscenity may be found in Chapter 11.

[44] Obscene Publications Act, 1964 c. 74.

[45] 1 Eur. Ct. H.R. at ¶ 25 (quoting the amended act).

titled "All grown-ups are paper tigers." There were chapters on: Education, Learning, Teachers, Pupils, and The System. The chapter on pupils included a twenty-six-page long section on sex with subsections labeled "Masturbation, Orgasm, Intercourse and petting, Contraceptives, Wet dreams, Menstruation, Child-molesters or 'dirty old men', Pornography, Impotence, Homosexuality, Normal and abnormal, Find out more, Venereal diseases, Abortion, Legal and illegal abortion, Remember, Methods of abortion, Addresses for help and advice on sexual matters."[46]

The introduction said:

> This book is meant to be a reference book. The idea is not to read it straight through, but to use the list of contents to find and read about the things you're interested in and want to know more about. Even if you're in a particularly progressive school you should find a lot of ideas in the book for improving things.[47]

The English courts found this passage important, because children were likely to read only sections of the book. Even if what the courts saw as harm in one section might have been lessened by material in another section, the curative section might be left unread.

The European Court of Human Rights said that the English court could reasonably see the book as "a work of an extreme kind, unrelieved by any indication that there were any alternative views; this was something which detracted from the opportunity for children to form a balanced view on some of the very strong advice given therein."[48] The European Court went on to present the English court's examination of the book.

> For example, looking at the book as a whole, marriage is very largely ignored. Mixing a very one-sided opinion with fact and purporting to be a book of reference, it would tend to undermine, for a very considerable proportion of children, many of the influences, such as those of parents, the Churches and youth organisations, which might otherwise provide the restraint and sense of responsibility for oneself which found inadequate expression in the book.[49]

The English court had also concluded that the book was "inimical to good teacher/child relationships" and that a number of passages were "subversive, not only to the authority but to the influence of the trust between children and teachers."[50]

Turning to the tendency to deprave and corrupt, there was no sense of responsibility to the community or, if there was any sense of responsibility it

[46] *Id.* at ¶ 20. [47] *Id.* (quoting the introduction). [48] *Id.* at ¶ 30. [49] *Id.* at ¶ 31.
[50] *Id.*

was subordinate to the development of expression of self by the child. The English courts found particularly objectionable a passage titled "Be yourself."

> Maybe you smoke pot or go to bed with your boyfriend or girlfriend – and don't tell your parents or teachers, either because you don't dare or just because you want to keep it secret.
>
> Don't feel ashamed or guilty about doing things you really want to do and think are right just because your parents or teachers might disapprove. A lot of these things will be more important to you later in life than the things that are "approved of."[51]

The English court noted that the book failed to mention that smoking pot is illegal, except in an entirely different and perhaps unread section, and that there was no mention of the fact that sexual intercourse under the age of fourteen for boys and sixteen for girls was illegal.[52]

Another problem was raised by a section titled "Pornography." The English court noted a "sane and sensible" statement "'[p]orn is a harmless pleasure if it isn't taken seriously and believed to be real life. Anybody who mistakes it for reality will be greatly disappointed.'"[53] But, that statement was followed by another that the court did find objectionable: "'But it's quite possible that you may get some good ideas from it and you may find something which looks interesting and that you haven't tried before.'"[54] The concern over that statement was that it would raise the "real likelihood that a substantial number of children would feel it incumbent upon them to look for and practise such things."[55] An additional reference to "people hurting each other" also raised the possibility that children would try sexual acts that included engaging in cruelty.[56]

The English statute did provide a defense, "'if it is proved that the publication of the article in question is justified as being for the public good on the ground that it is in the interests of science, literature, art or learning, or other objects of general concern.'"[57] As to value that might provide a defense, the English court concluded that, while the book had its good points, any good was so intermixed with harmful points so as to detract from the good.

> [T]here were passages with regard to venereal diseases, contraception and abortion, containing dispassionately and sensibly, and on the whole completely accurately, a great deal of advice which ought not to be denied to young children. However, on the balance of probabilities, these matters

[51] *Id.* [52] *Id.* [53] *Id.* [54] *Id.* [55] *Id.* [56] *Id.*
[57] *Id.* at ¶ 25 (quoting Section 4 of the Obscene Publications Act).

> could not outweigh what the court was convinced had a tendency to deprave and corrupt.[58]

The case went before the European Court of Human Rights, when Handyside argued that the decision of the English court violated his free expression rights under Article 10 of the European Convention on Human Rights. The issue for the European Court was whether or not the infringement on expression could be justified under Article 10(2); was it prescribed by law and "necessary in a democratic society … for the protection of health or morals …"?

In determining whether the protection of morality required the suppression of the book in question, the European Court said that the member states of the European Union enjoy a "margin of appreciation" in applying their laws.

> [I]t is not possible to find in the domestic law of the various Contracting States a uniform European conception of morals. The view taken by their respective laws of the requirements of morals varies from time to time and from place to place, especially in our era which is characterised by a rapid and far-reaching evolution of opinions on the subject. By reason of their direct and continuous contact with the vital forces of their countries, State authorities are in principle in a better position than the international judge to give an opinion on the exact content of these requirements as well as on the "necessity" of a "restriction" or "penalty" intended to meet them.[59]

Given the margin of appreciation, the European Court said that it could not conclude that the English actions against the book violated the European Convention.

The decision of the English court, and its acceptance by the European Court, reflects a broader view as to what may be limited to protect morality, and in particular the protection of children, than United States courts would allow. *The Little Red Schoolbook* did not appeal to the prurient interest, even when that interest is examined in light of children. The objections were to the ideas to which the children were exposed. England took a position that favored shielding children that went far beyond what would have been allowed in the United States, and the European Court found that such limitation was not a violation of the free expression rights of the European Convention.

Given the English court's decisions in *Handyside*, as a reflection of that societal view, it is probably not surprising that the United Kingdom places limits on films and video games. The general regulatory scheme is found in

[58] *Id.* at ¶ 34. [59] *Id.* at ¶ 48.

the Video Recording Act of 1984,[60] as amended by the Video Recordings Act of 2010[61] and the Digital Economy Act of 2010.[62] The 2010 Digital Economy Act is important for having cleared up an issue in the 1984 Act with regard to regulatory exemptions for video games in that earlier statute.

Under the Digital Economy Act of 2010, a video game is exempt from regulation, " if – (a) it is, taken as a whole, designed to inform, educate or instruct; (b) it is, taken as a whole, concerned with sport, religion or music; or (c) it satisfies one of more the conditions in section 2A."[63] The act specifies the conditions that must be satisfied to fit within part (c).

(1) The conditions referred to ... are as follows.
(2) The first condition is that the videogame does not include any of the following—
   (a) depictions of violence toward human or animal characters, whether or not the violence looks realistic and whether or not the violence results in obvious harm,
   (b) depictions of violence towards other characters where the violence looks realistic,
   (c) depictions of criminal activity that are likely, to any extent, to stimulate or encourage the commission of offenses,
   (d) depictions of activities involving illegal drugs or the misuse of drugs,
   (e) words or images that are likely, to any extent, to stimulate or encourage the use of alcohol or tobacco,
   (f) words or images that are intended to convey a sexual message,
   (g) swearing, or
   (h) words or images that are intended or likely, to any extent to cause offence, whether on the grounds of race, gender, disability, religion or belief or sexual orientation or otherwise ...
(4) The second condition is that the designated authority, or a person nominated by the designated authority for the purposes of this section, has confirmed in writing that the videogame is suitable for viewing by persons under the age of 12.[64]

So, video games are exempt only if they avoid objectionable material or treat it in a sufficiently mild way, so as to be suitable for young children.

The 1984 Act had required classification certificates for nonexempt works, including age ratings.[65] That act also made it an offense to distribute

[60] Video Recordings Act 1984, c. 39. [61] Video Recordings Act 2010, c. 1.
[62] Digital Ecomony Act 2010, c. 24. [63] *Id.* at § 40(3). [64] *Id.* at § 40 (5).
[65] *See* Video Recordings Act 1984 c. 39 at § 9.

nonexempt video works that had not been issued a classification certificate, with penalties of up to two years' imprisonment.[66] If a work were knowingly distributed to someone who had not obtained the age required in the classification, there could be a penalty of up to six months' imprisonment.[67] The Digital Economy Act of 2010 made it clear that video games must also meet these distribution requirements.

There is a video game case from the United Kingdom that was decided under the 1984 act. The 2010 Digital Economy Act is more restrictive than the 1984 act, so the decision is still relevant. *Regina v. Video Appeals Committee of the British Board of Film Classification*[68] grew out of a decision by the British Board of Film Classification not to issue a classification to the game *Manhunt 2*. The impact of the refusal was to bar all distribution of the game; both children and adults would be unable to purchase it. The Board explained its determination in a way that made the game seem more uniquely objectionable than it would, at least now, be.

> 'Manhunt 2' is distinguishable from recent high-end video games by its unremitting bleakness and callousness of tone and overall game context which constantly encouraged visceral killing with exceptionally little alleviation or distancing. It is a game wholly devoted to stalking and killing human characters in a modern urban environment ... There is sustained and cumulative casual sadism in the way in which these killings are committed, and encouraged, in the game.
>
> Of particular concern to the board is the game's unrelenting focus on stalking and brutal slaying and the sheer lack of alternative pleasures on offer to the gamer. There is no significant objective other than killing and the only significant variety in the game play involves making use of the full range of weaponry ...[69]

Rockstar, the game's producer, appears not to have been concerned over the limits the Board had placed on distribution to children. But the complete denial of classification and its effective ban on distribution to adults was of concern and led to an appeal. The Video Appeals Committee of the British Board of Film Classification considered the original decision in light of a 1994 addition to the 1984 act. The 1994 addition provided:

> (1) The designated authority shall, in making any determination as to the suitability of a video work, have special regard (among the other relevant factors) to any harm that may be caused to potential viewers or, through their

[66] *See id.* [67] *See id.* [68] [2008] EWHC 203 (Admin).
[69] *Id.* at ¶ 6 (quoting a letter from the Board to Rockstar, the game's producer, dated Jun. 19, 2007).

> behavior, to society by the manner in which the work deals with–(a) criminal behaviour ... (c) violent behaviour or incidents; (d) horrific behaviour or incidents ...
>
> (2) For the purpose of this section– "potential viewer" means any person (including a child or young person) who is likely to view the video work in question if a classification certificate or a classification certificate of a particular description were issued ...[70]

The Appeals Committee said that the game could be refused classification only if its effects on society would be devastating, as demonstrated by actual harm being caused by similar games.[71] The Appeals Committee decided that the game should be classified so that it could be sold to those eighteen and older.[72]

When the Appeals Committee decision was taken to court by the government, the court concluded that the original decision should stand. The court said:

> Parliament clearly had in mind that a video work classified as suitable for viewing by adults might, in the home, nonetheless be readily viewed by children ... [E]ven in respect of video works classified as suitable only for adults the board and the appeals committee were required to have special regard to harm which may be caused to children as well as adults.[73]

The court also concluded that there was no requirement that actual harm had been caused by similar games: "The task of the designated authority is to have special regard to any harm that may in future be caused to potential viewers by the viewing of the video work under appeal."[74]

While the case was remanded for consideration in light of the court's explanation, it is clear that potential harm to children is sufficient for a refusal of classification. This is a far cry from the certainly demanded by the United States Supreme Court. Furthermore, the interest in shielding children is strong enough to ban the distribution to adults.[75]

[70] *Id.* at ¶ 4 (quoting Criminal Justice and Public Order Act of 1994 c. 33, s. 90(1).

[71] *See id.* at ¶¶ 13–15. [72] *See id.* at ¶ 8. [73] *Id.* at ¶ 13. [74] *See id.* at ¶ 20.

[75] This position is also in conflict with United States law. The United States Supreme Court, in Butler v. Michigan, 352 U.S. 380 (1957), struck down a statute that barred all distribution of material that would be harmful to children. The material at issue was sexual, but it had been sold to an adult. Distribution of the same material to children could clearly be barred, but the Court would not allow a limit on adult consumption based on harm to children. The Court said, "[t]he incidence of this enactment is to reduce the adult population of Michigan to reading only what is fit for children." *Id.* at 383. While that may not be acceptable in the United States, it is allowable in the United Kingdom.

GERMANY

Germany takes especially strong steps to protect children. In terms of video games, Germany is said to have "the strictest regulations in Europe."[76] In fact, the German Basic Law has a provision aimed directly at the protection of youth. After Article 5(1)'s recognition of the freedom of expression, the limits to that freedom found in Article 5(2) provide: "These rights shall find their limits in the provisions of general laws, in provisions for the protection of young persons, and in the right to personal honor." Even in the case of art, protected by Article 5(3) and not subject to the limits in article 5(2), the personal dignity provision of Article 5(1) may justify limits.[77]

The statutory source for the protection of minors from harmful influences is the Protection of Young Persons Act (the Act).[78] The Act addresses not only media but includes provisions regarding restaurants, gambling rooms, dances, and other places with a "undesirable impact" on minors, and it has provisions regarding alcohol and tobacco. As for films, the Act provides: "Presence of *Children* and *Adolescents* at public movie performances shall not be permissible unless the films shown have been cleared for them by the supreme state authority or an organization of voluntary self-control ..."[79] Another provision addresses "data media," a category that includes video games.

> Recorded video cassettes and other data media suitable for distribution and reproduction on a monitor or playing on a monitor, using data media with films or games, shall not be accessible in the public for *Children* and *Adolescents* unless they have been cleared and labelled for the respective age group by the supreme state authority or an organization of voluntary self-control ...[80]

[76] Laura Tate Kagel, *Balancing the First Amendment and Child Protection Goals in Legal Approach.es to Restricting Children's Access to Violent Video Games: A Comparison of Germany and the United States*, 34 GA. J. INTERN'L & COMP. L. 743, 747 (2006).

[77] Germany has used that provision in justifying limits on laser tag, even for adults, holding that the simulated shooting of others is an affront to human dignity. *See* Case C 36/02, Omega Spielhallen v. Oberbürgermeisterin der Bundesstadt Bonn, [2004] E.C.R. I-9641, eur-lex.europa.eu/LexUriServ/LexUriServ.do?uri=CELEX:62002J0036:EN:NOT. While it is true that the targets in laser tag are human beings, it seems likely that the result would carry over to minors engaged in virtual murders in video games.

[78] BUNDESGESETZBLATT (BGBL, I) at 2730 , 2003I, § 1. The statute may be found in translation at www.bmfsfj.de/RedaktionBMFSFJ/Abteilung5/Pdf-Anlagen/juSchGenglisch,property=pdf, bereich=,true.pdf.

[79] *Id.* at § 11. [80] *Id.* at § 12.

The Act also provides that there shall be a list of publications categorized as "harmful to young people" that must be unavailable to children and adolescents and provides for limits on how this material may be made available to adults, so that children remain protected.[81] Categories of media to be included as "harmful to young people" include

> Media carrying content glorifying war; . . .
>
> Media presenting in a disgraceful manner people who are dying or are exposed to severe physical or psychic suffering or violating human dignity by presenting actual facts and developments, although there is no justifiable public interest in such mode of reporting; . . .
>
> Extremely realistic, cruel and sensational presentations of violence for its own purpose and dominant of the given scene.
>
> Media which might have a severely damaging impact on the development and education of Children and Adolescents to responsible personalities in society.[82]

As for media that might have "a severely damaging impact," the statute includes "media and other publications with immoral and brutalising content or those instigating violence, crime and racism and media conveying the following message[]: 1. Presentation in details of acts of violence, murder and massacre for their own purpose . . ."[83] This language would clearly cover the video games that motivated the California statute but would also seem even broader in scope.

The provision for ratings by an organization for voluntary self-control requires some examination. There is such an organization in the United States, the Entertainment Software Review Board, an industry established board that rates video games. If the German government steps in to classify games, only if the industry fails to do so, that may seem to weaken the regulatory regime. That might seem to be the case, since ratings in Germany are provide by the Entertainment Software Self-Regulation Body, known as the USK from the abbreviation of its German name. The USK describes itself as "an organization which has been voluntarily established by the computer games industry. It is responsible for the classification of computer games in Germany."[84]

There are, however, major difference between the industry established boards in Germany and the United States. While compliance with the ratings

[81] *See id.* at § 15. [82] *Id.* at § 15(2). [83] *Id.* at § 18.
[84] *Welcome to the USK*, www.usk.de/en.

in the United States is voluntary,[85] that is not the case in Germany. As the USK explains, "[a]t the end of a joint classification procedure, age rating symbols are issued by the relevant state representatives. The system ensures that computer games are only sold to children and young persons if the contents of the game have been approved as suitable."[86] And, under the German statute, "the decision of the [USK] for computer-games as concerns age limits is no longer a mere suggestion but is accepted as having legally binding effect."[87] Penalties for violations are significant, with fines of up to 50,000 Euros for distributing materials, rated as beyond their ages, to minors.[88]

Another point to be made is that the German system is not an industry system in the sense that the United States system is. The USK does seem to claim to be an industry system, its policy statement saying: "The associations representing the computer games industry in Germany act in a self-regulatory manner in conducting a voluntary classification of computer and video games intended for publication in the Federal Republic of Germany."[89] But, given Germany's commitment to the protection of children, the industry must have recognized that non-regulation was not an option. It would have to participate, if it was to have any influence, a participation that may only technically be voluntary.

Furthermore, the makeup of the USK seems really to make it a government rating system in which industry representatives participate, in a rather minor way. The USK's Advisory Council has fourteen members; two from the computer games industry, two from the Supreme Youth Protection Authorities of the Federal States, one from the Supreme Federal Youth Protection Authorities, two representing independent groups providing social services to minors, one from the Department for Media Harmful to Young Persons, two from religious groups, a media education representative, an expert on youth protection, a representative from the Commission for the Protection of Minors in the Media, and a legal expert.[90] Any media influence would seem overwhelmed by other interests.

85 When the state of Michigan attempted to make the industry Entertainment Software Review Board (ESRB) ratings mandatory, the statute was challenged and was struck down in Entertainment Software Ass'n v. Granholm, 426 F. Supp. 2d 646 (E.D. Mich. 2006).

86 *Welcome to the USK, supra* note 84.

87 Marc Liesching & Christoph J. M. Safferling, *Protection of Juveniles in Germany-A Report on the New Legislation*, 4 GERMAN L.J. 541, 555 (2003).

88 *See* Laura Tate Kagel, *supra* note 76, at 756.

89 *General Policy Statement of the German Entertainment Software Self-Regulation Body*, Article 1(1) (2011), *available at* www.usk.de/fileadmin/documents/Publisher_Bereich/USK_General_Policy_Statement_2011.pdf.

90 *See id.* at Article 3(2).

The actual classifications are determined by "independent youth protection experts."[91] These experts also play a role in the appeals process for challenging a classification.[92] The industry does play a role in selecting experts, in conjunction with the Supreme Youth Protection Authorities of the Federal States.[93] But, there is a requirement that the experts have the occupational experience and training to assure that age classifications are "made on the basis of specialist knowledge and good judgment," and the experts cannot be employed by entities in the computer and video games industry.[94] This would all seem to minimize the influence of the industry.

In addition to reliance on non-industry experts, there are instructions for classifying games. The Policy Statement provides a list, similar to that in the Protection of Young Persons Act, of the sort of games that are to be classified as clearly harmful to minors. The Policy Statement also provides a standard for assessing games.

> The development of children and young people and their progress to becoming an autonomous and integrated member of society may be particularly impaired by the content of games which occasion nervous strain, which overexcite the imagination, which inhibit character, moral (including religious) and mental development, which cause disturbance or damage or which exert a disorienting effect in social ethics terms ... A game may only be passed as suitable for an age group if it cannot impair the development or progress of any cohort within said age group. This processes aligned toward those aged under 18 who are particularly susceptible to endangerment rather than to the average child or young person. Extreme cases are excluded.[95]

This may be what makes the German system so strict. Assessment is not based on the average child but on the susceptible child. Even eliminating the child who may be an "extreme case," this susceptible child assessment of impact will lead to stricter limitations on access.

VIDEO GAME LIMITS IN OTHER COUNTRIES

Turning to an examination of the limits placed by several other democratic countries on the access of children to violent video games shows those countries to be far more similar to England, Canada, and Germany than to

[91] *See id.* at Article 5(1). [92] *See id.* at Article 7. [93] *See id.* at Article 5(2).
[94] *See id.* at Article 5(3). [95] *Id.* at Article 19(3).

the United States. The brief survey will not include all the democracies, but the provisions are representative of the range of limits.[96]

A short discussion of Japan is warranted, because Japan has been seen as having a tradition of very violent media without the youth violence found in the United States. However, in the past decade, Japan has grown concerned over violent video games.[97] As is not uncommon, the concern was the result of a violent act in which a seventeen-year-old player of violent video games killed a teacher and injured two others.[98] The response was a call for limits on youth access to violent video games.[99]

In the Japanese Constitution, the provision protecting free expression is balanced by a provision that constitutional freedoms and rights should not be abused and that people should be responsible for using them in the public welfare.[100] This would seem to invite provisions to protect children from harmful media. In practice, prefectures have enacted youth protection ordinances directed at media, and by 1999, there were 23,685 items designated as harmful to minors.[101]

Given this earlier willingness to declare media harmful to minors, a rapid response to the 2005 killing was not a surprise. In that same year, Kanagawa Prefecture banned distributing *Grand Theft Auto III* to minors, with a fine of up to ¥300,000.[102] Tokyo also took action, requiring labeling by software manufacturers and requiring retailers to stock the material separately from non-harmful material and to request age identification from customers.[103] While the Tokyo approach was considered voluntary,[104] it would seem that the industry was willing to accept restrictions to avoid more stringent regulation.[105]

Looking to other countries in the European Union, the Union itself has been helpful in providing a summary of regulation by member states. The

[96] Kevin W. Saunders, *supra* note 36, presents a discussion of Australia, *id.* at 491–95, and New Zealand, *id.* at 501–3.

[97] For the development of the law in Japan, see Susan Minamizono, *Japanese Prefectural Scapegoats in the Constitutional Landscape: Protecting Children from Violent Video Games in the Name of "Public Welfare,"* 9 San Diego Int'l L.J. 135 (2007).

[98] *See id.* at 136. [99] *See id.* [100] *See id.* at 142–43.

[101] *Id.* at 150 (citing The Ministry of Foreign Affairs of Japan, Second Report of Japan under Article 44, Paragraph 1 of the Convention on the Rights of the Child, ¶ 159 (Nov. 2001), www.mofa.go.jp/policy/human/child/report2),

[102] *Id.* at 148. [103] *Id.* at 150. [104] *See id.*

[105] *See* Hirohiko Niizumi *Japanese Game Industry Moves to Restrict Sales to Minors: Voluntary Retailer Program to Separate Mature Games from All-Ages Games Hopes to Stem Government-Imposed Controls,* Gamespot (Jul. 19, 2005), www.gamespot.com/news/japanese-game-industry-moves-to-restrict-sales-to-minors-6129399.

Commission of the European Communities issued a 2008 report summarizing video game regulation in the European Union.

> Member states applying PEGI [Pan-European Games Information] and having specific legislation related to age classification in place or prepared are Finland, Greece, Italy, Latvia, Netherlands, Poland, Portugal, Slovakia and United Kingdom. The Netherlands and Poland also provide for criminal sanctions ...
>
> In France, PEGI is used to classify and label video games. Amendments to French Criminal Law in 2007 provide for age classification and labeling of video games according to age groups.
>
> Belgium, Bulgaria, Denmark, Estonia, Hungary, Ireland, Spain and Sweden apply PEGI, but have no specific legislation ...
>
> Germany and Lithuania have specific binding legislation ...
>
> In Austria, protection of minors falls under the competence of each Bundesland. Thus, there are big differences in the legislation on the protection of young people and how it is implemented.
>
> In Malta, where PEGI does not apply, video games fall under general legislation.
>
> Cyprus, Luxembourg, Romania and Slovenia were said to have reported that they have no age or content rating system.[106]

Turning from ratings to availability, the Commission provided an analysis of access to games among the Member States.

> Half of the Member States have specific legal provisions, in civil and criminal law, concerning the physical sale of video games with content harmful to minors, and there are various penalties to enforce these provisions.
>
> Member States aiming at or using a classification for distribution, circulation and advertising based on an age/content rating are Italy (a law is in the process of approval), the United Kingdom, Germany, Estonia, Greece, Latvia, Lithuania and Slovakia.
>
> France, Sweden and the Netherlands prohibit certain violent video games under criminal law (in Sweden also under the constitutional law) ...

[106] *Communication from the Commission to the European Parliament, the Council, the European Economic and Social Committee, and the Committee of the Regions on the Protection of Consumers, in Particular Mine Is, in Respect to the Use of Video Games* at intro., COM (2008) 207 final (Apr. 22, 2008), eur-lex.europa.eu/LexUriServ/LexUriServ.do?uri=CELEX:2008DC207:EN:NOT.

> In Belgium and Malta, there are a number of legal provisions governing the sale of video games, such as laws on racism and xenophobia, on commerce and consumer protection and public order.
>
> Bulgaria, the Czech Republic, Cyprus, Denmark, Hungary, Luxembourg, Poland and Romania have no specific legislation governing the sale of video games.[107]

In conclusion, the Commission called for, at least, a code of conduct for retailers but said that non-binding ratings may be ineffective. "In Belgium and Hungary, PEGI already applies, but it is not legally binding with the result that both countries see the protection of minors as inefficient. Belgium would favour legislation at European level."[108] The Commission did note that the United Kingdom, Ireland, Germany, and Italy have banned certain video games and said: "The commission is of the opinion that such bans should remain the exception, be proportionate and, therefore, be limited to serious breaches of human dignity."[109] But, the bans the Commission was speaking of were bans that prohibit all distribution, not age limitations. Overall, the flavor of the report is supportive of limiting children's access to harmful media.

BALANCING FREE EXPRESSION RIGHTS AND MINORITY

While this chapter's material would seem to indicate that a country may limit the access of children to free expression and still remain a democracy, there are some cautions to consider. Judge Richard Posner, in one of the early video games cases,[110] objected to an age limit set at eighteen. He noted that, by the time a child turned eighteen, the child must be a competent voter. In order to reach that level of competence, exposure to more material, before turning eighteen, may be required. Whether or not exposure to violent video games makes one a competent voter may well be questionable. If such media do contribute, it would seem that sexual media would as well, but the Supreme Court did allow limits, beyond those that could be imposed on adults, in *Ginsberg*. It is true that the age limit under the New York statute was seventeen, rather than eighteen. If violent material and sexual material are somehow important to the ability to cast an intelligent vote, perhaps limits should be removed not at the point of majority but sufficiently before that time to allow the child to gain media maturity.

[107] *Id.* at 4–5 (citations omitted). [108] *Id.* at 5. [109] *Id.* at 7.
[110] American Amusement Machine Ass'n v. Kendrick, 244 F.3d 572 (7th Cir. 2001).

A second caution has to do with the target of media restrictions. There is certainly media that is of value to children, well before they turn eighteen. A particularly important case may be made for material regarding sexual identity. A child struggling with his or her identity would find serious value in material addressing the issue. That is but one example suggesting a general approach that any limits not include material with serious value for minors.

With those caveats, other limitations might be allowed. The values behind free expression, discussed in Chapter 1, do not speak as strongly to children as to adults. In terms of political participation, children are excluded, and as long as they are allowed access sufficiently before the point at which they do become included, limits would not seem to have an impact on the value. In terms of autonomy or self-fulfillment, children are seen simply as not having as strong an interest as adults. Children are not allowed to smoke or drink, and there are limits on sexual activity. If these autonomy interests may be limited, it would seem that the autonomy interest in accessing media material might similarly be limited.

The threat of insurrection seems unlikely, and in any case that threat grows out of the inability to assert one's political positions, rather than the inability to purchase video games or material with sexual content. The fact that children should have the ability to assert a position does add another caution. Most of the material in this chapter has had to do with material being provided to children. It has not spoken to children as speakers. Even if there are limits on children as receivers, the voices of children may be important. Certainly, a child speaking out against abuse must be heard. Historically, it was the voice of young people, many under the then age of majority of twenty-one, that formed most of the dissent against the United States' actions in Vietnam. While not political participants, in the sense of voting, minors had political influence that deserved protection.

There is the contribution that free expression can make to the attainment of truth. Here, again, the speech of children may offer something of value. That is an argument for free expression by children. To make a contribution, children would also have to have some input, and that again argues for access to material with serious value for minors. It may be less an argument for more general access to minors by others seeking to further their views as to the truth. If one can convince only children, addressing them may be a subversion of the process of reaching the truth.

In addition to the decrease in the values that justify free expression, there are greater costs for expression to young people than to adults. Children are in their formative years, and material that may have no real negative impact on adults may harm children. That has been the claim of the social science examination of violent video games. It also seems to be accepted in the United States that exposure to graphic sexual material is harmful, although it would seem with less scientific evidence. There may also be concerns over advertising products that are illegal for consumption by children.

It would seem that these factors would call for careful consideration in setting limits on what is accessible to children. A position that children should have access to anything, or almost anything, available to adults is to ignore the harms that can be done to children and simply to assume that the benefits are the same for children as they are for adults. On the other hand, simply to accept any and all limitations on access by children ignores what may be important interests that they do have, as well as societal interests that may depend on access before the age of majority.[111]

[111] For further material on justifications for, and concerns raised by, limits on media access by children, *see* KEVIN W. SAUNDERS, SAVING OUR CHILDREN FROM THE FIRST AMENDMENT (2003).

13

Criminal Trials and Freedom of the Press

The criminal trial presents a freedom of expression issue in at least some democratic countries. The press has an interest in covering criminal investigations and the criminal trials that may ensue. On the other hand, press coverage may make it difficult for the criminal defendant to receive a fair trial in front of an impartial jury. Extensive coverage of the investigation and trial may make it difficult, if not impossible, to find a jury of individuals without knowledge of what has been reported or at least with an ability to set that knowledge aside.

It is particularly problematic where press reports have included what could be strongly probative evidence that may, for some reason, not be admissible at trial. If the defendant had confessed to the crime, but because of coercion or improper procedure the confession would not be admissible at trial, it may be especially difficult for a juror, believing that he or she knows the defendant to be guilty, to vote in favor of a not guilty verdict. If a prosecutor referred to a confession at trial, while the judge had ruled against admissibility, it would under United States law be grounds for a mistrial. But a press report should raise the same concerns. If the jury could not be thought to set aside the prosecutor's comments, it is unclear why it could be expected to set aside what it had learned from the press.

The scope of this problem is limited to only some democracies, those in which criminal cases are tried before a jury. "Juries are a priori more likely be prejudiced by damaging newspaper articles about the accused than are judges."[1] It is clear that juries are more likely to be prejudiced than at least some judges, but judges may also be influenced. In jurisdictions in which judges are elected, a judge may be concerned about his or her prospects, if a

[1] Eric Barendt, Freedom of Speech 322 (2d ed. 2005).

defendant damned in the press receives a judicial acquittal. This may have presented a problem in one of the important cases from the United States.[2] Furthermore, a lay judge, as opposed to a professional judge, may be more subject to influence.[3] Nonetheless, the quote is largely correct, and the conflict is found primarily in common law countries. In other countries in which guilt is determined by a panel consisting of a combination of lay jurors and professional judges, the interaction between the two may limit the impact of prejudicial publicity.[4]

This chapter will examine how the conflict between free expression and the rights of criminal defendants is handled in a number of these countries. After presenting the law, as it has developed in the United States, the law of press coverage of criminal trials in a number of common law countries, Canada, Australia, New Zealand, and the United Kingdom will be presented.

THE UNITED STATES

In United States law, there appears to be a true conflict between the freedom of press, as guaranteed by the First Amendment, and the sixth amendment right of a criminal defendant to a fair trial. Under the First Amendment, the press has the right to report whatever it takes to be in the public interest. Under the Sixth Amendment, the criminally accused has a right to a trial by jury, with a verdict based on the evidence presented at trial. The members of the jury cannot come into the trial with a bias against, or belief in the guilt of, the defendant. Extensive press coverage may contribute to negative attitudes toward the accused.

There are also evidentiary rules that protect the defendant. Evidence of prior crimes, or other bad acts, is not admissible as proof of the defendant's guilt on the charges at issue. Other evidence may be excluded from the trial, for a variety of reasons, such as the evidence being the product of an illegal search. Press coverage may make the jury aware of such evidence. Particularly

2 *See* Sheppard v. Maxwell, 384 U.S. 333 (1966). *Sheppard* is discussed *infra* notes 5–12 and accompanying text

3 *See* Worm v. Austria, 1996 Eur. Ct. H.R. 83. *Worm* is discussed *infra* notes 76–79 and accompanying text.

4 For discussions of recent adoptions of procedures involving lay jurors, *see*, *e.g.* Stephen C. Thaman, *Europe's New Jury Systems: The Cases of Spain and Russia*, 62 Law & Contemporary Problems 233 (1999); Matthew J. Wilson, *Japan's New Criminal Jury Trial System: In Need of More Transparency, More Access, and More Time*, 33 Fordham International L.J. 487 (2010).

when evidence is strongly indicative of guilt, the jury may have a difficult time ignoring this inadmissible evidence.

On the other hand, there are reasons favoring press coverage of trials, even beyond the freedom of the press and the general public's right to know. Coverage of criminal trials serves to let the public know that law breakers are being called to answer for their deeds. Furthermore, coverage of the criminal trial helps to assure that the process is not abused to inflict harm on an unpopular individual, without actually proving that individual's criminal violations. Coverage may also help the criminal defendant in that it may lead potential exculpatory witnesses to come forward.

This conflict in the United States is almost always resolved in favor of freedom of the press, but there are limits on the amount of damage that can be done to the criminal defendant. That limit is found in *Sheppard v. Maxwell*.[5] In that case, the defendant's pregnant wife had been bludgeoned to death in a bedroom of their home. The defendant claimed that he had fallen asleep on a couch, woke to hear his wife cry out, struggled with an unidentified person and had been rendered unconscious. When he came to, he found that his wife was dead. He chased the unidentified person but was attacked and again rendered unconscious.

Sheppard was considered a suspect by police and became the subject of intense media coverage. There was a front-page newspaper call for a coroner's inquest that led to an immediate proceeding. The inquest was moved to a school gymnasium and was heavily covered by the print and broadcast media. The newspapers reported, with emphasis, incriminating evidence. The papers also reported a relationship with a number of other women, although evidence at trial pointed to only one such relationship.

A later front page editorial asked: "Why Isn't Sam Sheppard in Jail?" later retitled "Quit Stalling-Bring Him In."[6] He was arrested that evening. Newspaper coverage continued with various claims about evidence having been found. In fact, the Court said publicity became even more intense, with five volumes of clippings regarding evidence from each of Cleveland's three newspapers and equally intense broadcast coverage.[7]

The Court also noted that the case was tried two weeks before an election in which the chief prosecutor was a candidate for judge, and the trial judge was standing for reelection. The newspapers published the names and addresses of the seventy-five prospective jurors, who then received letters and telephone calls, some of them anonymous. Furthermore, once the trial began, the judge allowed

[5] 384 U.S. 333 (1966). [6] *See id.* at 341. [7] *See id.* at 342.

a long temporary press table to be set up inside the bar, behind counsel table and reaching within 3 feet of the jury box.[8] While cameras were not allowed inside the courtroom, the sidewalks in front of, and the corridors within, the courthouse were filled with cameras, recording the comings and goings of witnesses, attorneys, and jurors. This coverage continued for the entire nine-week trial.

All this was too much for the Supreme Court.

> Sheppard was not granted a change of venue ... nor was his jury sequestered ... [T]he Sheppard jurors were subjected to newspaper, radio and television coverage of the trial while not taking part in the proceedings. They were allowed to go their separate ways outside of the courtroom, without adequate directions not to read or listen to anything concerning the case ... Moreover, the jurors were thrust into the role of celebrities by the judge's failure to insulate them from reporters and photographers ... [They were] exposed ... to expressions of opinion from both cranks and friends.[9]

The Court characterized the atmosphere at the courthouse as bedlam and said that the judge had lost his ability to control the situation.

The Court noted that the trial judge seemed to believe that he lacked power to control publicity and did not consider measures that might have reduced prejudicial material and protected the jury from outside influences. There was particular criticism over the failure to regulate the conduct of reporters inside the courtroom and the failure to protect witnesses. The prosecution also faced criticism. "The prosecution repeatedly made evidence available to the news media which was never offered in the trial. Much of the 'evidence' disseminated in this fashion was clearly inadmissible. The exclusion of such evidence in court is rendered meaningless, when news media make it available to the public."[10] The judge also shared the blame here, because of his failure to ban extrajudicial statements by trial participants.

In conclusion, the Court said:

> [U]nfair and prejudicial news comment on pending trials has become increasingly prevalent. Due process requires that the accused receives a trial by an impartial jury free from outside influences. Given the pervasiveness of modern communications and the difficulty of erasing prejudicial publicity from the minds of the jurors, the trial courts must take strong measures to ensure that the balance is never weighed against the accused ... Of course, there is nothing that proscribes the press from reporting events that transpire in the courtroom. But where there is a reasonable likelihood that prejudicial news prior to trial will prevent a fair trial, the judge should continue the case

[8] *See id.* at 342–43. [9] *Id.* at 352–53. [10] *Id.* at 360.

> until the threat abates, or transfer it to another county not so permeated with publicity. In addition, sequestration of the jury was something the judge should have raised sua sponte with counsel. If publicity during the proceedings threatens the fairness of the trial, a new trial should be ordered.[11]

The Court ordered that Sheppard be released. There was a retrial, but in the retrial Sheppard was acquitted.[12]

Sheppard may be seen as the high water mark for defendants' rights in this conflict between the First and Sixth Amendments. Supreme Court cases since then have involved judges who tried to protect defendants' rights but were seen by the Court as having inadequately protected the freedom of the press.

Ten years after *Sheppard* the tension between the First and Sixth Amendments was back before the United States Supreme Court in *Nebraska Press Association v. Stuart*.[13] There, a trial judge, and the Nebraska Supreme Court on appeal, seemed to take to heart the *Sheppard* mandate to protect the interests of criminal defendants.

The case involved the murder of six members of a family, and a sexual assault, in a small town of 850 people. A suspect was rapidly apprehended and arraigned. There was immediate, widespread news coverage at all levels from local to national and on all media. After three days, the prosecutor and defense counsel asked the County Court to restrict reporting, claiming that the likelihood of prejudicial news would make it difficult to impossible to find an impartial jury. The County Court issued an order prohibiting the release of any testimony given or evidence submitted and requiring the press to observe the Nebraska Bar-Press Guidelines. The Guidelines took the position that it was generally not appropriate to report confessions, provide opinions on guilt or innocence, make statements that might influence the outcome of a trial, or comment on evidence not put before the jury.[14]

A preliminary hearing was held, open to the public but subject to the order, and the defendant was bound over for trial. At that point, reporters and the Press Association asked that the restrictive order be vacated. The District Court hearing the motion entered a new order to apply until a jury was seated. The order barred reporting on five subjects:

> (1) the existence or contents of a confession ... to law enforcement offices, which had been introduced in open court at arraignment; (2) the fact or nature of statements [the defendant] had made to other persons; (3) the contents of a note he had written the night of the crime; (4) certain aspects

[11] *Id.* at 362–63. [12] *See* Nebraska Press Ass'n v. Stuart, 427 U.S. 539, 554 (1976).
[13] 427 U.S. 539 (1976). [14] *See id.* at 542 n.1.

> of the medical testimony at the preliminary hearing; and (5) the identity of the victims of the alleged sexual assault and the nature of the assault.[15]

The order also incorporated the Guidelines.

The Nebraska Supreme Court modified the order in an attempt to accommodate both fair trial rights and press interests. The modified order prohibited only reporting of three matters: "(a) the existence and nature of any confessions or admissions made by the defendant to law enforcement officers, (b) any confessions or admissions made to any third parties, except to members of the press, and (c) other facts 'strongly implicative' of the accused."[16]

When the case reached the United States Supreme Court, the Court recognized that "when the case is a 'sensational' one tensions develop between the right of the accused to trial by an impartial jury and the rights guaranteed others by the First Amendment."[17] But, the Court said that an unfair trial is not the inevitable result of even pervasive, adverse pretrial publicity.

> The capacity of the jury eventually impaneled to decide the case fairly is influenced by the tone and extent of the publicity, which is in part, and often in large part, shaped by what attorneys, police, and other officials do to precipitate news coverage. The trial judge has a major responsibility. What the judge says about a case ... is likely to appear in newspapers and broadcasts. More important, the measures the judge takes or fails to take to mitigate the effects of pretrial publicity the measures described in *Sheppard* may well determine whether the defendant receives a trial consistent with the requirements of due process.[18]

Here, the Court said the judge had acted responsibly and out of legitimate concern and that the attorneys also had also acted responsibly.

Turning to the First Amendment side of the equation, the Court noted "special protection against orders that prohibit the publication or broadcast of particular information or commentary orders that impose a 'previous' or 'prior' restraint on speech."[19]

> [P]rior restraints on speech and publication are the most serious and the least tolerable infringement on First Amendment rights ... If it can be said that the threat of criminal or civil sanctions after publication "chills" speech, prior restraint "freezes" it at least for the time ... Truthful reports of public judicial proceedings have been afforded special protection against subsequent punishment. For the same reasons the protection against prior restraint should have particular force as applied to reporting of criminal proceedings.[20]

[15] *Id.* at 543–44. [16] *Id.* at 545. [17] *Id.* at 551. [18] *Id.* at 554–55. [19] *Id.* at 556.
[20] *Id.* at 559 (citations omitted).

Applying the analysis to the case under consideration, the Court said that it had to examine the nature and extent of the news coverage, whether other measures could have mitigated any negative effects of that publicity, and whether the restraining order would have prevented that harm. The Court found no fault with the trial judge's conclusion that the pervasive publicity might impair the right to a fair trial. But the Court found little evidence as to whether other measures, inoffensive to the First Amendment, could have been employed to limit, or eliminate, that negative impact. The Court suggested as alternatives a change of venue, postponement to allow for a reduction in public attention, questioning of prospective jurors to determine who might already have a fixed opinion, and clear, emphatic instructions to decide the case only on the evidence presented.[21]

The Court also suggested sequestration but recognized that that insulates the jury only after it is sworn.[22] Sequestration is a commonly suggested remedy, but it has its impacts. It is certainly inconvenient for the jurors. It has also been suggested that sequestration may lead to a bias against the defendant: "[S]equestration has been thought to produce an anti-defendant bias in the jury, which would be too high a price to pay for the privacy given the jurors."[23] Alternatively, "jurors may also take out their anger on the prosecution. Since it is the state that initiates the entire trial process, it is the state who deserves to be punished."[24]

[21] *See id.* at 563–64. With regard to a change of venue, Nebraska law allowed only a change to an adjacent county, and those counties had been exposed to the same level of pretrial publicity. The Supreme Court said that state laws that restrict venue may need to yield to the constitutional requirement of a fair trial. *Id.* at 563 n.7.

[22] *See id.* at 564.

[23] Ryan Brett Bell & Paula Odysseos, *Sex, Drugs, and Court TV? How America's Increasing Interest in Trial Publicity Impacts Our Lawyers and the Legal System*, 15 GEORGETOWN J. LEGAL ETHICS 653, 667 (2002)(citing James P. Levine, *The Impact of Sequestration on Juries*, 79 JUDICATURE 266 (1996)). That article maintains

> Jurors who resent the experience of sequestration and are disturbed by it may vent their wrath on one of the trial adversaries. The physical and psychological discomfort of having one's life disrupted may be attributed to the accused who is blamed for having caused the entire unpleasant situation. To avenge the ordeal of sequestration, the juror comes down hard on the persons thought to have been responsible for triggering it—even if the defendants are in fact innocent.

Id. at 269. The Levine article cites a study that compared sequestered and nonsequestered New York juries and showed that sequestered juries returned 16 percent more convictions, although Levine suggests that the study was not adequately controlled. *Id.* (citing Bruce Winick & Alexander B. Smith, *Post-Trial Sequestered Juries Tilt Toward Guilty Verdicts*, N.Y.L.J., Dec. 12, 1986, at 1).

[24] Levine, *supra* note 23, at 269.

It was suggested that the sequestration of the jury in the Casey Anthony case, a case involving the death of a young girl and the highly publicized trial of her mother,[25] may have contributed to acquittal. Jean Casarez of *In Session* is quoted as suggesting that the *CSI* effect, the jury's unwillingness to sift through circumstantial evidence when crimes are so clearly solved using scientific evidence on such crime shows, combined with sequestration, played a role.

> The jury in the Casey Anthony case was sequestered for so many weeks . . . it is the opinion of some that the jurors were just tired when it got to the point of deliberations. They may have been motivated to get home, not motivated to look at every piece of detailed evidence. If they had meticulously gone through everything in the circumstantial case there could have been a conviction.[26]

So, while sequestration may cure some ills, it may have its own negative impact. Nonetheless, the *Nebraska Press* Court concluded that there is no showing that other measures would not have sufficed.

The Court also questioned the efficacy of the prior restraint order. There were difficulties regarding the territory over which the trial court had jurisdiction. It was also the case that the crime occurred in a community of only 850 people. Even without print or broadcast news, news would quickly have spread throughout the community. Furthermore, that news would have consisted of rumor, which might well have been inaccurate and might have done more damage to the defendant than the likely more accurate news provided by the media.[27]

There were additional problems. First, initially, the trial court had issued a very broad order and then held a preliminary hearing that was open to the public. At that hearing there was testimony regarding two incriminating statements by the defendant to third parties and a confession to the police. The second order, by the District Court, seemingly included a prohibition against reporting on those statements. Barring the reporting of evidence produced in an open hearing violated the principle that the press may report on events in the courtroom.[28] Secondly, the prohibition on "implicative" evidence was both too vague and too broad.

[25] For material on Nancy Grace, the Headline News cable channel personality who was central to the publicity, *see infra*, notes 100–4, and accompanying text.

[26] Graham Winch, *The Casey Anthony Effect* HLNtv (Jul. 5, 2012)(quoting Jean Casarez), www.hlntv.com/article/2012/07/03/casey-anthony-effect.

[27] *See* Nebraska Press Ass'n v. Stuart, 427 U.S. 539, 567 (1976).

[28] *Id.* at 568. The Court noted that the trial court would not have known that it could have closed the preliminary hearing, until the Nebraska Supreme Court so construed state law. The implication is that closing the hearing would have resolved this problem, since the statements would not have been made in an open hearing. The United States Supreme Court would later

In conclusion, the Court said it was not clear that, even with unchecked further publicity, twelve unbiased jurors could not be found. Nor could the Court conclude that any negative effect could not have been mitigated through other methods or that the order would have had the intended effect. The Court did say,

> we need not rule out the possibility of showing the kind of threat to fair trial rights that would possess the requisite degree of certainty to justify restraint. This Court has frequently denied that First Amendment rights are absolute and has consistently rejected the proposition that a prior restraint can never be employed.[29]

Despite this claim, it appears that the First Amendment rights are at least close to absolute, and it is highly unlikely, given the alternatives that the Court noted with approval, that a restraint on publication will stand up to First Amendment scrutiny.

After *Nebraska Press*, a series of cases opened other aspects of the criminal process to the public and the press. In *Richmond Newspapers, Inc. v. Virginia*,[30] a trial court ordered a trial closed to the public and the press. It was the fourth attempt at a trial, after three mistrials, the last of which resulted from a juror having read accounts of the earlier trials and passing on that information to the other jurors. It was presumably frustration over having continually to retry the case that led to the closure, in reliance on Virginia law that allowed a court to exclude from a trial anyone whose presence could impair the fairness of the trial.[31] Despite the series of failures, the Supreme Court concluded that criminal trials must be open, citing to a long history of public access. The Court relied not just on history but on the therapeutic value the trial may have to the community and the role of openness in preventing abuse of the criminal process. Here, too, the Court objected to the lack of findings of the unavailability of alternatives that would have ensured a fair trial, pointing again to sequestration not just of the jury but also of witnesses.[32]

This requirement of openness was extended in *Press-Enterprise Co. v. Superior Court*.[33] There, the Court held that California courts were limited in their right to deny access to preliminary hearings. Such hearings could not be closed without specific findings that showed the closure to be essential to

address the legitimacy of closing a preliminary hearing. *See infra* note 33, and accompanying text.

29 *Id.* at 569–70.

30 448 U.S. 555 (1980).

31 *See id.* at 560 (citing VA. CODE ANN. § 19.2 – 266 (Supp. 1980)).

32 *See id.* at 580–81.

33 478 U.S. 1 (1986).

preserving a right to a fair trial and that the California standard of "reasonable likelihood" of prejudice was less stringent than the First Amendment mandated test of "substantial probability."

Perhaps the most important issue, in terms of pretrial hearings, is the hearing to suppress evidence. The focus of a suppression hearing is whether or not the jury should be allowed to hear certain statements or see certain evidence. If it is closed to the public and the press, and the court suppresses the evidence, the existence of that evidence will not be known to potential jurors. If it is open to the press and public, whatever the ruling of the court, potential jurors who follow press reports will know of that statement or evidence. This may well be the most damaging sort of pretrial publicity. Sequestration does not keep it from jurors who have already seen the reports. While the judge may tell the jury that even inflammatory press reports may be inaccurate and irrelevant, and jurors may be able to disregard such publicity, excluded evidence may be another matter. It may be highly probative and may be excluded solely because of a violation of, for example, search and seizure rules. A juror may well be less able to exclude such extrajudicial evidence from consideration.

This issue came to the Court in *Gannett Co. v. DePasquale*.[34] There, the Court held that the Sixth Amendment right to a public trial did not provide the public or the press with a legally enforceable right of access to pretrial suppression hearings. The fair trial rights of the defendant, in this context overrode the public right to know. While the press may be able to report information it has, it does not have a right of access to this information.

Other than in the *Gannett* situation, it would seem that whenever there is a conflict between freedom of the press and concerns over the impact of publicity on a fair trial, under United States law, the freedom of press will win. This is not because there is a hierarchy of rights under the United States Constitution. It is simply that, despite the Court's insistence that the First Amendment is not absolute, the analysis will play out on the freedom of press side.

When there is an infringement of a right under the United States Constitution, the strict scrutiny test applies. The infringement can be justified only if there is a compelling governmental interest, and the infringement is necessary to, or narrowly tailored to, that interest. If a trial court orders a ban on publication, that is clearly an infringement. The right to a fair trial would be a compelling governmental interest, but it will be extremely difficult to show

[34] 443 U.S. 368 (1979).

the ban was necessary to, or narrowly tailored to, that interest. The ban will meet this second step, only if there is no other way to protect the fair trial rights of the defendant.

While the right to a fair trial is also constitutionally guaranteed, it is less clear that there has been an infringement, when there is not an order banning publication. Any claim of infringement is necessarily speculative, when other protective measures may suffice. It is only after the fact, after publicity has tainted the trial, that there can be any surety that there was an infringement. While that may lead to reversal on appeal, it will not reach back to order a ban. Even if the case is retried, the appellate admonition to the trial court will not be to order a publication ban but to implement additional measures that do not violate the freedom of the press.

This approach is consistent with a general unwillingness, under the First Amendment, to tolerate prior restraints. The elimination of such restraints was central to the concept of freedom of the press, and all such prior restraints must meet an exceedingly heavy burden.[35] Unless the press has acted unlawfully, publication bans are extremely unlikely to stand.[36]

CANADA

The Canadian Supreme Court's position with regard to the suppression of coverage of criminal proceedings, and the investigations leading up to those proceedings, sounds similar to that of the United States Supreme Court, but in practice, the situation in the two countries may differ significantly.

The Canadian Court considered the issue in *Dagenais v. Canadian Broadcasting Corp.*[37] Four members of the Catholic order the Christian Brothers were facing charges of physically and sexually abusing young boys at a school

[35] *See, e.g.*, Near v. Minnesota, 283 U.S. 697 (1931); New York Times v. United States, 403 U.S. 713 (1971).

[36] This is true even if there has been a violation of law or policy by non-press sources that led to the press's possession of the information. For example, in *Florida Star v. B.J.F.*, 491 U.S. 524 (1989), a newspaper published the name of a victim of a sex crime, contrary to state law that prohibited such publication. The newspaper obtained the name of the victim, because it was mistakenly posted on the wall of a police station in a room to which the press had access. The Court said that, while specific circumstances might sometimes justify a ban on the publication of the name of the victim, the blanket ban was a violation of the First Amendment. The availability of that information was due to a mistake, but even when the information was obtained through a violation of the law by a third-party, the result is still the same. In *Bartnicki v. Vopper*, 532 U.S. 514 (2001), information was obtained, by a third-party, in violation of laws protecting telephone conversations and was provided to the press. Even here, because the press itself had not broken the law, the publication was protected by the First Amendment.

[37] [1994] 3 S.C.R. 835 (Can.).

where they taught. In early December 1992, Dagenais' trial had already begun. The trial of the second defendant, Monette, was scheduled for February, with the judge already assigned. The other two defendants, Radford and Dugas, were scheduled for trial several months later, and the trial judges had not yet been assigned.

The Canadian Broadcasting Corporation advertised a miniseries titled "The Boys of St. Vincent." The miniseries, scheduled for two two-hour blocks on Sunday and Monday, December 6 and December 7, was a fictional account of sexual and physical abuse of children in a Catholic institution. The jury in the Dagenais trial was scheduled to be charged on December 7, and the defense, out of concern over the impact of the miniseries, asked the trial judge either to charge the jury on the Friday before the scheduled showing or to sequester the jury over the weekend. The trial judge denied both requests but did tell the jury not to watch the broadcast.

The defendants applied to another judge, Justice Gotlib, on the Ontario Court of Justice, seeking a restraining order directed to the Canadian Broadcasting Corporation, prohibiting the broadcast of "The Boys of St. Vincent" and the publication of any information relating to the broadcast, until the four trials were concluded. Justice Gotlib issued the order. The publication ban then went to the Court of Appeal for Ontario, where it was varied slightly. While the original order has simply restrained the broadcast, the appellate court limited the prohibition to broadcasting the program in the province of Ontario and by one English language television station in Montréal, until after the four trials but not through any appeals.

The CBC appealed to the Supreme Court of Canada. That court noted that under the common-law rule, a publication ban must be based on a real and substantial risk of interference with the defendant's right to a fair trial. The Court said that the rule did provide some protection for the freedom of expression, since it required some reason for the ban beyond speculative concern. But the common law rule developed before the adoption of the Canadian Charter of Rights and Freedoms, and the Court said that the question was whether the common-law rule provided sufficient protection under the Charter.

On that issue, Justice Lamer, writing for a majority of six justices, said:

> The pre-*Charter* common-law rule governing publication bans emphasized the right to a fair trial over the free expression interests of those affected by the ban. In my view, the balance this rule strikes is inconsistent with principles of the *Charter* . . . It would be inappropriate for the courts to continue to apply a common law rule that automatically favoured the rights protected by s. 11 (*d*) [fair trial rights of criminal defendants] over those protected by s. 2(*b*)

> [freedom of expression]. A hierarchical approach to rights, which places some over others must be avoided, both when interpreting the *Charter* and when developing the common law. When the protected rights of two individuals come into conflict, as can occur in the case of publication bans, *Charter* principles require a balance to be achieved that fully respects the importance of both sets of rights.[38]

Seeing the issue as one of balance would seem to be a different view than that of the United States courts. The Supreme Court of Canada specifically rejected the "clash model," saying that that model was more suited to United States law, because the United States Constitution has no equivalent to Section 1 of the Charter, which allows under certain circumstances infringement of Charter rights.[39]

The Court said that the common-law rule had to be adapted so as to consider the objective of the publication ban and the proportionality of the ban to its effect on the freedom of expression. The rule for publication bans could be restated as:

> A publication ban should only be ordered when: (a) Such a ban is necessary in order to prevent a real and substantial risk to the fairness of the trial, because reasonably available alternative measures will not prevent the risk; and (b) The salutary effects of the publication ban outweigh the deleterious effects to the free expression of those affected by the ban.[40]

The application of the rule to the case at hand proved easy. The Court said that there was no need to balance salutary effects against deleterious impact, because there were reasonable alternative measures that could have been taken. Those measures were similar to ones recognized by the United States Supreme Court.

> Possibilities that readily come to mind ... include adjourning trials, changing venues, sequestering jurors, allowing challenges for cause and voir dires during jury selection, and providing strong judicial direction to the jury. Sequestration and judicial direction were available for the Dagenais jury. Apart from sequestration, all of the other effective alternatives to bans are available for the other three accused.[41]

An interesting aspect of the Court's opinion was its conclusion that, as to proportionality under the *Oakes* test, more than a theoretical balancing between harm to Charter rights and the government objective must occur. The courts must consider the actual salutary effect of a ban.

[38] *Id.* at 877. [39] *See id.* at 882. [40] *Id.* at 878 (emphasis omitted). [41] *Id.* at 881.

> I would . . . rephrase the third part of the *Oakes* test as follows: there must be a proportionality between the deleterious effects of the measures which are responsible for limiting the rights or freedoms in question and the objective, *and there must be a proportionality between the deleterious and salutary effects of the measures.*[42]

That restated test requires consideration of the efficacy of a ban. In that regard, the Court said that technological advances, pointing to interprovincial and international television and radio, cable television, and information available on computers, make it difficult to enforce bans and speak to their efficacy.[43] Eric Easton suggests that Chief Justice Lamer may have had in mind a publication ban issued in a sensational Ontario murder trial, when he wrote the *Dagenais* opinion.[44] If so, that trial and ban provide the best evidence of the difficulties of enforcing publication limits in this technological era.[45]

The resolution of the modified *Oakes* balancing in this case may have been relatively easy. In addition to the availability of other measures, it is important to note that the broadcast in question involved purely fictional events. The broadcast may have led to greater public concern over abuse within Catholic institutions, but it did not speak to the guilt of the particular defendants. The Court said:

> More problematic is a situation in which there is a period of sustained pre-trial publicity concerning matters that will be the subject of the trial. In such circumstances, the effect of instructions is considerably lessened. Impressions may be created in the minds of the jury that cannot be consciously dispelled. The jury may at the end of the day be unable to separate the evidence in court from information that was implanted by a steady stream of publicity.[46]

A strong example of such a trial may be found in the prosecution of Paul Bernardo and Karla Homolka for the murder of two teenage girls in Ontario. The same trial provides an example of the difficulties that must be faced, in light of cross-border information, in enforcing a publication ban. Professor Easton provides a detailed discussion of the prosecution.[47] But, in brief, Homolka pleaded guilty to two charges of manslaughter. Bernardo faced two charges of first-degree murder, along with a significant number of other charges. Out of concern that the details of Homolka's plea would prevent Bernardo from receiving a fair trial, the judge barred the publication of most

[42] *Id.* at 889 (emphasis in original). The *Oakes* test is discussed in Chapter 1. [43] *Id.* at 886.

[44] *See* Eric B. Easton, *Sovereign Indignity? Values, Borders and the Internet: A Case Study*, 21 SEATTLE UNIV. L. REV. 441, 511 (1998).

[45] *See infra*, notes 47–55, and accompanying text. [46] *Dagenais*, 3 S.C.R. 835, 886.

[47] *See* Easton, *supra* note 44.

of the information growing out of her trial and closed that trial to all except accredited Canadian journalists.[48]

The frenzy of publicity over the details of the case is interesting in itself,[49] but perhaps of even more interest is the cross-border aspect of the enforcement of the order. When the British *Sunday Mirror* included a story that violated the ban, the paper's distributor, seemingly fearing a contempt charge, held back and eventually destroyed approximately 1000 copies.[50] When a United States television program planned to present details revealed at the trial, the province's attorney general threatened prosecution of Canadian cable systems carrying the program.[51] While Canadian owners of satellite dishes had access to the program, the owners of Toronto bars with dishes decided not to show the program.[52] When the *Detroit Sunday News and Free Press* ran a story, Canadian distributors either refused to sell the paper or removed the section with the story.[53] The *Buffalo News* printed a special Canadian edition that substituted another story for the coverage of the trial included in the United States edition; while Canadian police checked the trucks of distributors, individual Canadians were allowed to carry single copies of the United States edition back into the country.[54] While university computer systems blocked references,[55] that would have had only limited impact on Internet access generally. It is clear that cross-border enforcement was not a simple matter, but presumably, at least some of the publicity was lessened.

Returning to *Dagenais*, the greatest impact of the Supreme Court's decision may be with regard to its rulings on jurisdiction to obtain a ban on publication or to hear appeals from a trial judge's decision on a publication ban. If the Crown or the accused seeks a ban, the motion should be to the trial judge, if the judge has been appointed, or to a judge in the court at the same level as that in which the trial will occur, if the actual trial judge has not been appointed.[56] If the media want to challenge a publication ban issued by a

[48] *See id.* at 444. Notably, this was even over the objection of Bernardo's attorneys, who wanted it known that Homolka had been the beneficiary of a plea deal that might have impacted her testimony. *See id.* at 463–64. The Canadian media appealed the publication ban to the Ontario Court of Appeal, but that court deferred judgment until *Dagenais* resolved the jurisdictional issue that later deprived the Court of Appeal of jurisdiction. *See infra*, notes 56–75, and accompanying text.

[49] For a detailed description, *see id.* at 447–77. [50] *Id.* at 477–78. [51] *Id.* at 479–80.

[52] *Id.* at 480. [53] *Id.* at 482–83. [54] *Id.* at 483. [55] *See id.* at 485 & n.327.

[56] Dagenais v. Canadian Broadcasting Corp., [1994] 3 S.C.R. 835, 870 (Can.). The Court added that, if it is not clear at what level the case will be tried, the motion should be made before a Superior Court judge. The Court also recognized a potential problem under the collateral attack rule, when the application is ruled on by a judge other than the judge eventually named to conduct the trial. Any appeal over the outcome of the trial could not, under that rule,

provincial court, they should apply for certiorari to a Superior Court judge. Denial of certiorari is appealable to the Court of Appeal, and if the appeal is dismissed, the media should apply for leave to appeal to the Supreme Court of Canada.[57] If the publication ban is issued by a provincial Superior Court, the media should seek leave to appeal to the Supreme Court of Canada.[58]

What that meant for the case at hand was that Dagenais and Monette, the defendants in cases in which trial judges had been assigned, should have applied for a publication ban to those trial judges.[59] If the motions had been denied, there would have been no right to appeal, except to appeal the conviction at the end of the trial.[60] Justice Gotlib did not have jurisdiction to hear those motions.[61] The other two defendants, those for whom judges had not been assigned, correctly applied to a Superior Court judge, and Justice Gotlib did have jurisdiction to hear their motions.[62] Had their motions been denied, their appeal rights would also have been limited to the appeal of any conviction.[63] Since the publication bans were issued, the CBC had to apply directly to the Supreme Court of Canada for leave to appeal; the Court of Appeal had no jurisdiction.

The impact of all this would seem likely to leave the rulings of at least Superior Court judges largely intact. Where a publication ban is denied, there would be no appeal other than an appeal of a conviction. While that appeal could be based on the denial of fair trial, because of prejudicial publicity, it must be after-the-fact, rather than as an interlocutory appeal.

Where a publication ban is ordered, the only appellate route for the media is to the Supreme Court of Canada. While an order such as that in *Dagenais*, directed as it was at the CBC with, initially, a national impact, is likely to be seen as sufficiently important to lead the Supreme Court to grant the leave to appeal, that may not be so in more ordinary cases. The trial in a small, remote town, with an order directed only to local media, may not lead to a grant of leave. In fact, when the media appealed the gag order in the trial of Paul Bernardo, the Supreme Court refused to hear the challenge, possibly because the order would have expired before the Court could hear the case.[64]

So, while the *Dagenais* opinion makes the substantive Canadian law regarding publicity bans sound a lot like that of the United States, in practice it may prove less protective of press interests and, if so, more protective of trial rights. In many cases, a trial judge may rule in favor of the defendant's request,

include an attack on the ruling of the other judge. The Court said that in this situation the rule should be relaxed. *Id.* at 870–71.

[57] *Id.* at 872. [58] *Id.* [59] *Id.* at 873. [60] *Id.* [61] *Id.* [62] *Id.* at 873–74.
[63] *Id.* at 873. [64] *See* Easton, *supra* note 44, at 445.

and if the judge is at the Superior Court level, the media's only recourse is to the Supreme Court. That Court may not grant leave to appeal. In the United States, a ban on publication may be appealed to courts at a lower level and will be heard.

THE UNITED KINGDOM

In the United Kingdom, there is a statute addressing the conflict between free expression and fair trial. The Contempt of Court Act of 1981 provides for strict liability for interference with fair trials. The Act provides:

1 The strict liability rule.

In this Act "the strict liability rule" means the rule of law whereby conduct may be treated as a contempt of court as tending to interfere with the course of justice, in particular legal proceedings, regardless of intent to do so.

2 Limitation of scope of strict liability.

(1) The strict liability rule applies only in relation to publications, and for this purpose "publication" includes any speech, writing, programme included in a cable programme service or other communication in whatever form, which is addressed to the public at large or any section of the public.

(2) The strict liability rule applies only to a publication which creates a substantial risk that the course of justice in the proceedings in question will be seriously impeded or prejudiced.

(3) The strict liability rule applies to a publication only if the proceedings in question are active within the meaning of this section at the time of the publication.

(4) Schedule 1 applies for determining the times at which proceedings are to be treated as active within the meaning of this section.

3 Defence of innocent publication or distribution.

(1) A person is not guilty of contempt of court under the strict liability rule as the publisher of any matter to which that rule applies if at the time of publication (having taken all reasonable care) he does not know and has no reason to suspect that relevant proceedings are active.

(2) A person is not guilty of contempt of court under the strict liability rule as the distributor of a publication containing any such matter if at the time of distribution (having taken all reasonable care) he does not know that it contains such matter and has no reason to suspect that it is likely to do so.

(3) The burden of proof of any fact tending to establish a defence afforded by this section to any person lies upon that person ...

4 Contemporary reports of proceedings.

(1) Subject to this section a person is not guilty of contempt of court under the strict liability rule in respect of a fair and accurate report of legal proceedings held in public, published contemporaneously and in good faith.

(2) In any such proceedings the court may, where it appears to be necessary for avoiding a substantial risk of prejudice to the administration of justice in those proceedings, or in any other proceedings pending or imminent, order that the publication of any report of the proceedings, or any part of the proceedings, be postponed for such period as the court thinks necessary for that purpose ...

5 Discussion of public affairs.

A publication made as or as part of a discussion in good faith of public affairs or other matters of general public interest is not to be treated as a contempt of court under the strict liability rule if the risk of impediment or prejudice to particular legal proceedings is merely incidental to the discussion.

...

11 Publication of matters exempted from disclosure in court.

In any case where a court (having power to do so) allows a name or other matter to be withheld from the public in proceedings before the court, the court may give such directions prohibiting the publication of that name or matter in connection with the proceedings as appear to the court to be necessary for the purpose for which it was so withheld ...[65]

The Schedule 1, referred to in Section 2(4), provides that proceedings are active from their initial step to their conclusion. There are a variety of events that may comprise the initial step, including arrest or the issuance of a warrant or summons to appear.[66] Criminal proceedings are concluded by an acquittal or sentencing, or by another verdict, finding, order or decision ending the proceedings, or discontinuance by the operation of law.[67] There is also a provision defining appellate proceedings as being active, beginning at the time an application for leave to appeal or notice of appeal was filed. If the appellate

[65] Contempt of Court Act 1981 (c. 49), §§ 1–5, 11, (U.K.), as modified by Broadcasting Act, 1990, c. 42, § 203(1), sch. 20 (U.K.). The modified version is available at www.legislation.gov.uk/ukpga/1981/49.

[66] *See id.* at sch. 1, §4.

[67] *Id.*

court remits the case or orders a new trial, the proceedings are active from the conclusion of the appellate proceeding.[68]

So, the act provides for strict liability in that there does not have to be an intent to interfere with the administration of justice. But it does not impose strict liability with regard to whether or not there is an active proceeding or, for a distributor, whether the publication being distributed contains contemptible material. Not all mention of an ongoing criminal proceeding will constitute contempt. There does have to be a substantial risk the publication will impair the course of justice. Coverage of an actual trial is allowed, although the judge may limit the publication of certain material presented. And, not all comment that may have an impact on a trial is contemptible; a general discussion of public affairs will not constitute contempt, even if it has an incidental impact on the trial.

The Act is seen as a relaxation of a prior contempt law, although still far more restrictive of speech than in some other Commonwealth jurisdictions, and certainly in the United States.[69] Eric Barendt explains the assumptions behind the approach of the United Kingdom:

> English law assumes first, that certain types of publications may cause a serious prejudice to future legal proceedings, and secondly, that it is desirable to deter the press and other branches of the media from publishing material where that risk is particularly acute, despite the impact the law has on press freedom and freedom of speech.[70]

The relaxation followed a ruling by the European Court of Human Rights in the *Sunday Times* case.[71] That case involved a civil negligence action against the manufacturers of thalidomide over the infant deformities caused by the drug. The newspaper was critical of the manufacturer and could be seen as pressuring it to settle with those impacted by the drug. It seems, however, that the newspaper was unlikely to influence the judge hearing the case, so prejudice in the usual sense would not really be found. The European Court held the contempt ruling to be in violation of the free expression protections in Article 10(1) of the European Convention. While Article 10(2) does allow limits on expression in order to, among other things, protect the authority of the judiciary, that was not seen as really relevant to the case.

As Professor Barendt characterizes the situation in *Sunday Times*, it involved "an absolute contempt rule, applicable no matter how remote the risk of prejudice, for the purpose of preventing 'a gradual slide toward trial by

[68] *Id.* [69] *See* BARENDT, *supra* note 1, at 322. [70] *Id.* at 323.
[71] Sunday Times v. United Kingdom, 30 Eur. Ct. H.R. 1 (1979).

newspaper or television.'"[72] While he finds "no strong justification for treating as contempt of court a publication prejudging the issues in a forthcoming *civil* case, where there can be no suggestion the tribunal might be prejudiced by it . . . [,t]hese arguments do not apply with the same force to criminal cases, particularly those tried by a jury."[73] The new 1981 Contempt of Court Act was intended to bring English law in line with the requirements of Article 10.[74]

It appears that the European Court would accept the revision of the law, with its requirement of a substantial risk of serious impediment or prejudice to an ongoing criminal case. The European Court did uphold, in *Worm v. Austria*,[75] the conviction of a journalist for publishing an article highly critical of the defense tactics by a former Vice-Chancellor and Minister of Finance in his trial for tax evasion. The journalist had been found, by the Austrian courts, to be in violation of Section 23 of that nation's Media Act, which provides: "Anyone who discusses, subsequent to the indictment . . . [and] before the judgment at first instance in criminal proceedings, the probable outcome of those proceedings or the value of evidence in a way capable of influencing the outcome of the proceedings shall be punished by the court . . ."[76]

The European Court concluded that the interference with expression was justified under Article 10(2), as aimed at "maintaining the authority and impartiality of the judiciary."[77]

> The phrase "authority of the judiciary" includes, in particular, the notion that the courts are, and are accepted by the public at large as being, the proper forum for the settlement of legal disputes and for the determination of a person's guilt or innocence on criminal charge; further, that the public at large have respect for and confidence in the courts' capacity to fulfill that function.[78]

The Court recognized that reporting on trials is not inconsistent with fair trial rights also guaranteed under the Convention. The European Court said that the Austrian court had not restricted the right to inform the public in an

[72] BARENDT, *supra* note 1, at 327 (quoting Lord Cross in the House of Lord's consideration of the case, Att'y Gen. v. Times Newspapers Ltd,[1974] A.C. (H.L.) 273[323]).

[73] *Id.* at 327–28

[74] There was some movement toward change in the law prior to the decision by the European Court. Stephen J. Krause, *Punishing the Press: Using Contempt of Court to Secure the Right to a Fair Trial*, 76 B.U. L. REV. 537 (1996), describes efforts begun in 1974 to revise the Administration of Justice Act of 1960.

[75] Case of Worm v. Austria, 45 Eur. Ct. H.R. 1534 (1997).

[76] *Id.* at 1545 (more precisely at ¶ 23).

[77] *Id.* at 1548 (more precisely at ¶ 39).

[78] *Id.* at 1549 (more precisely at ¶ 40).

objective manner, but the article went beyond that. The views presented were "formulated in such absolute terms that the impression was conveyed to the reader that a criminal court could not possibly do otherwise than convict [the defendant]."[79]

Given the *Worm* decision, it does seem that the Contempt of Court Act of 1981 would be consistent with Article (10) of the European Convention. Professor Barendt notes that application of the act depends on the particular facts of the case and requires determining substantial risk and significant prejudice under the European Court's decision. He notes a case in which a news broadcast that reported an arrested suspect to be an escaped IRA terrorist was held not to be contempt, because the broadcast was nine months before the trial and was not later repeated.[80] He also notes the application of the defense in Section 5 of the act to an article implying that modern medicine had a tendency to end the lives of babies born with handicaps, published during an ongoing trial of a physician charged with murdering a handicapped boy.[81] The possible incidental impact, during this discussion of public affairs, was not contempt.

It is clear that Professor Barendt prefers the approach taken in the United Kingdom. He argues that moving the trial may not remove prejudice, where the newspaper broadcast has been national, that postponement interferes with the right to a speedy trial, and that sequestration both burdens jurors and does not remove the prejudice that may result from pretrial publicity.[82]

There is a criticism that the approach of the United Kingdom may be ineffective in the face of modern information technology and that England might do well to adopt controls on the seating the jurors.[83] This suggestion differs from the criticism of Canada's attempts to limit cross-border publicity. It is true that, in Canada or the United Kingdom, some publicity will be available from foreign sources, and those sources may include international broadcasts and newspapers or the Internet. Canada's treatment of the most available foreign newspapers and of cable carriers for foreign television at least limited the impacts of those sources. The Internet may prove more difficult, but if the law of the United Kingdom were to consider Internet service

79 *Id.* at 1553 (more precisely at ¶ 52).

80 *See* BARENDT, *supra* note 44, at 328 (citing Att'y Gen. v. Indep. Television News, Ltd., [1995] 1 Crim. App. 205 (Eng.).

81 *Id.* at 329 (citing Att'y Gen. v. English, [1983] 1 A.C. (H.L.) 116).

82 *Id.* at 331–32.

83 *See* Joanna Armstrong Brandwood, *You Say 'Fair Trial' and I Say 'Free Press': British and American Approaches to Protecting Defendants' Rights in High Profile Trials*, 75 N.Y.U. L. REV. 1412, 1443–44 (2000).

providers (ISPs) as distributors, notice to those ISPs that certain available websites constituted contemptible material might require their blocking.

The argument that international sources make the protection of fair trial rights impossible overstates the burden facing the courts. It is not necessary that no one in the jurisdiction have been affected. What is required is the ability to find the requisite number of jurors who have not been influenced. Those who are sufficiently interested and sophisticated in the use of the Internet may always be able to find information that would interfere with the right to a fair trial, but many will not be so interested and sophisticated. Similarly, most people don't read foreign newspapers. But it is necessary that the court be able to distinguish between those who do have access and those who either don't or were able to set that information aside. That may require the sort of voir dire employed in the United States.

NEW ZEALAND

The major New Zealand case on the conflict between fair trials and free expression is *Gisborne Herald Co. v. Solicitor-General.*[84] In that case, the New Zealand Court of Appeal considered a conflict growing out of publicity regarding a case in which a police constable was seriously wounded in the course of his duties. The constable had to be sent to a special hospital unit 500 miles away from Gisborne. His wife gave birth that night, and she and their new baby were also sent to that hospital to visit the constable. There was extensive media coverage, including news that the suspect, who had previous convictions for violent crimes and was on bail, had been arrested and charged.

The *Gisborne Herald* ran a story on the constable and his family, but the main focus of the article was on the defendant, the charges he faced in other courts, his previous convictions, and the fact that he was on bail despite police opposition to the grant of bail. While the issue of prisoners being released on bail might well be a matter of public concern, it was not currently being debated in the area media, so the Court concluded that the article could not be viewed as incidental to a current continuing discussion.[85]

Contempt proceedings were brought based on interference with the fair administration of justice in the trial concerning the constable, as well as with regard to a trial in Napier on the other charges he was facing. With regard to the trial in Napier, the Court found, given the distance between the two

[84] [1995] 3 NZLR 563. [85] *Id.* at 566.

locations and the lack of circulation of the *Herald* in Napier, that there was no real risk of interference. The court did say:

> In the absence of empirical New Zealand data tending to minimize the risk of jury prejudice through knowledge of previous convictions for violence and bail histories, we prefer to follow what the Chief Justice described as the orthodox view: to publish the criminal record of an accused or comment on the previous bad character of any case before trial is a prime example of interference with due administration of justice and, subject to considerations such as time and place, almost invariably is regarded as a serious contempt.[86]

That was a strong statement setting out a category of information the release of which would normally be contempt, even if distance kept it from being such in this case.

Turning to a consideration of the trial to occur in Gisborne, the Court recognized that sometimes the time between the article and the trial may be relevant. Early statements about a crime and the defendant may fade in the public mind, as minds turn to other news. Later statements may, however, reinforce the impact of earlier publicity. But some stories are assumed to have lasting impact.

> [T]he content of an early, or late, publication containing prejudicial material about a person charged may ensure that it remains in the public memory and that recollection of the prejudicial material is triggered by later news stories about the victims and the coming trial. Again, the sheer lapse of time may dim memory. But in some cases mud may stick.[87]

The Court seemed to leave a great deal of discretion to the trial judge, noting the difficulty of making an assessment of prejudicial impact without adequate empirical data.

> In the absence of any statutory prescription or reliable empirical data concerning the dissipation of the prejudicial impact of publication in the New Zealand media to assist decision making, Judges have to rely on their professional expertize and life experience in determining where to draw the line . . . [T]he common law of contempt requires the Courts of New Zealand . . . to make those judgments as best they can.[88]

Applying those general principles to the case at hand, the Court could not conclude that the lower courts had erred in concluding that there was a real risk that the article would be sufficiently prejudicial to preclude a fair trial.

[86] *Id.* at 568. [87] *Id.* at 569. [88] *Id.* at 570.

The Court also went on to discuss the tension between fair trial and free expression more generally. It specifically rejected the approach taken by the Supreme Court of Canada in *Dagenais*. With regard to the alternative measures suggested in *Dagenais*, the Court said that they were not common in New Zealand: Change of venue is infrequent, inconvenient for witnesses and expensive; challenging jurors for cause is rare, an examination of prospective jurors regarding their views is undesirable; and sequestration is not an ordinary practice and would affect the lives of jurors; an adjournment may violate the right to be tried without delay.[89]

The Court also seemed to express a lack of surety with regard to any benefits that might grow out of the Canadian Supreme Court's rejection of the common law in favor of the rule expressed in *Dagenais*.

> [T]he absence of current empirical data to support a long-standing assumption embedded in public policy is not, in our view, adequate justification for shifting policy ground in favour of another approach which is also deficient in supporting policy data and analysis. The present rule is that, where on the conventional analysis freedom of expression and fair trial rights cannot both be fully assured, it is appropriate in a free and democratic society to temporarily curtail freedom of media expression so as to guarantee a fair trial.[90]

This last statement is a clear endorsement of the greater importance of a fair trial right in comparison to, at least immediate, free expression. The Court seems to take the position that trial rights must be protected from the outset. Free expression may be delayed. While the press has the right to cover a story and a trial, the right to fair trial may require postponement of at least some of that coverage.

AUSTRALIA

Paul Marcus and Vicki Waye find some similarity between the United States and Australia in their commitment, inherited from England, to open criminal trials as a check on abuse, but they note differences in the handling of trial publicity.[91] As they explain the difference between the two countries,

> Australian courts are inclined to approach the danger of unbridled media power on the basis that prevention is better than cure. The remedial techniques preferred by U.S. courts to redress the actual dangers that may arise

[89] *Id.* at 575. [90] *Id.*

[91] Paul Marcus & Mickey Waye, *Australia and the United States: Two Common Criminal Justice Systems Uncommonly at Odds*, 12 Tul. J. Int'l & Comp. L. 27 (2004).

> when media coverage undermines a defendant's due process rights, such as sequestration and questioning of jurors on the effect of pre-trial publicity, are not generally practiced in Australia where they are seen as an impediment to the efficiency of the trial process.[92]

The Australian approach is clearly more akin to that in New Zealand and the United Kingdom than in the United States and Canada. Professors Marcus and Waye note that, under the decision of the Australian High Court in *Hinch v. Attorney General (Victoria)*,[93] it is contempt to publish material that may tend to prejudice a legal proceeding, with no need to show actual prejudice.[94] Among the content that would constitute contempt, when a trial is pending or underway, is the publication of past convictions or confessions, material that is clearly prejudicial and that may be excluded at trial.[95]

Marcus and Waye also note that where the potential for prejudice is outweighed by the public interest in discussion of the issues raised by the case, there will be no contempt.[96] This was actually the issue in *Hinch*, and the case is interesting in illustrating the process of balancing fair trial rights and free speech rights. *Hinch* involved three radio broadcasts, by Hinch, relating to Michael Glennon, an individual facing charges of child molestation. Glennon was a Catholic priest who directed a foundation that ran children's camps and conducted other activities for children.

Hinch had a history of concern over child molestation, preceding the charges against Glennon. Once the charges were filed, Hinch specifically included comments on Glennon in his broadcasts. He pointed to earlier charges and convictions against Father Glennon for sexual assault and questioned how Glennon could be allowed to continue to run the foundation in which he was involved. The comments were certainly prejudicial to Glennon's right to a fair trial. On the other hand, child sexual abuse and the need to take steps for its prevention, including removing abusers from positions of authority, are matters of public concern, and discussion of such matters should not be stifled.

The High Court noted law regarding this balance in a civil context, citing *Ex Parte Bread Manufacturer's Ltd.* for the proposition that the administration of justice is not the only matter of public interest and that other public interests may be superior.

> The discussion of public affairs in the denunciation of public abuses, actual or supposed, cannot be required to be suspended merely because the

[92] *Id.* at 83.
[93] (1987) 164 C.L.R. 15. (Austl.), www.austlii.edu.au/au/cases/cth/HCA/1987/56.html.
[94] Marcus & Waye, *supra* note 91, at 83. [95] *See id.* at 84. [96] *See id.*

> discussion of the denunciation may, as an incidental but not intended by-product, cause some likelihood of prejudice to a person who happens at the time to be a litigant ...[97]

The first issue for the Court was whether the same rules should apply to criminal cases. The risks involved in prejudice in a criminal case are greater and may merit more protection, but the interest in the discussion of public affairs remains the same. The Court concluded that the same balance should be drawn in reconciling the two concerns.

The issue then became the application of the rule. Certainly, the public interest was strong, and there was no reason to suspend all discussion of concerns regarding the abuse of children. But the rule requires that the prejudice resulting from the comments be "an incidental but not intended by-product." In the view of the Court, the comments were focused on Father Glennon, so any impact was not incidental. If Hinch had continued to express his general concerns, the fact that the trial was current would not have made his comments contempt. But directing those comments specifically at the defendant did constitute contempt.

This willingness to find content, again, places Australia in camp with United Kingdom and New Zealand. While in the United States there could be no contempt in a similar situation, and the trial court would have tried to control the impact through voir dire, jury instructions and, perhaps, sequestration, Australia tends not to use those measures. The practice of Australia is to ask potential jurors questions only regarding their relationship to a party and whether they know of a reason why they cannot render a verdict based only on the evidence, and it is rare to challenge jurors for cause.[98] And, more generally, Australian courts have a "lack of faith in the efficacy of remedial measures employed by U.S. courts."[99]

BALANCING CONCERNS

As with most differences regarding the treatment of free expression issues among democracies, there are arguments on both sides of the issue. There is a public right to know about the administration of justice. Secret trials are anathema to democracy, and the press must be allowed to report on the criminal process. While this most clearly speaks to open-ended bans on reporting, bans limited to the period between arrest or the filing of charges

[97] 164 C.L.R. at ¶ 2 (quoting Ex parte Bread Manufacturers Ltd., (1937) 37 SR (NSW) 242, 249–50).

[98] Paul Marcus & Vicki Waye, *supra* note 91, at 94–95.

[99] *Id.* at 85.

and the end of the trial also raise difficulties. Publicity might have brought forth additional witnesses, and some of these witnesses might even benefit the defense. It may also be important to public confidence in the justice system to know how a trial is progressing.

On the other hand, there are aspects of the unbridled freedom of the press that characterizes the approach in the United States that make it less than attractive. Nancy Grace is, depending on one's tastes in entertainment and views on the rights of criminal defendants to a fair trial, either an icon of, a phenomenon in, or a scourge on American television. Her nightly program on HLN, a cable television news outlet, has made a specialty of coverage of criminal cases, leading up to and during their trials. While she has been on the air longer, she may be best known for her roughly three years of daily coverage of the death of Caylee Anthony, a young Florida girl, and the investigation and later trial of her mother Casey Anthony.

When the jury returned not guilty verdicts on charges of murder, manslaughter and child abuse, she strongly expressed her disagreement. She is quoted as saying

> I absolutely cannot believe Caylee's death has gone unavenged ... Now I know, it is our duty as American citizens to respect the jury system ... But I know one thing, as the defense sits by and has their champagne toast after the not guilty verdict, somewhere out there the devil is dancing tonight.[100]

Casey Anthony may or may not have, in fact, killed her daughter, but clearly the verdict did not fit the script. Nancy Grace, despite her purported respect for the jury system, seemed to find it hard to accept a conclusion that didn't comport with early episodes in what has been described as "her act."[101] And, the unwillingness to accept the jury's verdict, in anything but the legal sense, was shared widely, at least among her viewers. Writing about the focus

[100] Mary Elizabeth Williams, *Nancy Grace Knows More than a "Kooky Jury,"* SALON (Jul. 6, 2011), www.salon.com/2011/07/06/nancy_grace_caylee_anthony_verdict/. Casey Anthony was not Nancy Grace's first target. She had, five years before the Anthony verdict, interviewed the mother of a missing child and interrogated her on the air; the next day the mother shot herself to death, and a wrongful death suit based on the program was reportedly settled for $200,000. *See id.* She also expressed strong views on a rape case involving Duke University lacrosse players, reportedly saying "I'm so glad they didn't miss a lacrosse game over a little thing like gang rape," *id.*, a case that ended up with acquittals and the prosecutor being disbarred.

[101] *See* David Zurawik, *Are Nancy-Grace-Led Media as Vile as Casey Anthony Lawyer Claims?*, THE BALTIMORE SUN (Jul. 5, 2011) ("Grace has been a one-woman, all-supreme, TV, judge-and-jury for a long time now. It's her act, and it seems as if she couldn't care less where the facts lie or how her judgments of guilt affect suspects' lives."), http://articles.baltimoresun.com/2011-07-05/news/bal-casey-anthony-defense-attorney-nancy-grace-blasts-tv-talking-heads-in-verdict-wake-20110705_1_hin-casey-anthony-nancy-grace.

on the death of Caylee Anthony, while so many similar deaths have gone ignored, a journalist concluded:

> Millions of people woke up Wednesday morning as convinced as they had been the morning before that Casey Anthony is guilty of murder. For them, the poor jury's work means nothing and never will. But, for some of the rest of us, with the shadow of the Anthony case finally gone from daily view, the sun now shines on a day when other victims of crime may finally get their due. And that's about the best thing I can say about a case, and a trial, that will leave no lasting mark upon the law despite the fury generated and the rubble it leaves in its wake.[102]

As the same journalist pointed out, Caylee Anthony was one of over 16,000 persons murdered in the year she died; hundreds of other parents have been accused of murdering their children since Caylee went missing.[103] So, why the media spotlight on this one case?

> Anthony is a white, middle-class woman ... who had a darling, photogenic little girl. On many levels, her story connected with the vast swath of Americans who are themselves white, middle-class and child-rearing ... The fascination with her case ... was most vibrant within a demographic that is particularly attuned to investing in this sort of story ... [P]ut another way, the Casey Anthony story was made for Nancy Grace and Nancy Grace was made for the Casey Anthony story.[104]

So, Nancy Grace cannot be made to stand alone in facing criticism over this sort of coverage. She has obviously struck a chord with the American public. While this may not really exonerate her, it implicates a significant portion of the American public.

This sort of coverage may well have a negative impact on a criminal defendant's right to a fair trial. And, even if the individual is acquitted, there is the likelihood, as seems to have occurred in the Casey Anthony case, that this extrajudicial evidence will make it difficult for the public to accept the validity of the acquittal. This raises the concern, recognized by the European Court, that the public may lose its belief in the judicial process as the way to resolve disputes.

[102] Andrew Cohen, *Why Casey Anthony Made Prime Time*, The Atlantic (Jul. 6, 2011), www.theatlantic.com/national/archive/2011/07/why-casey-anthony-made-prime-time/241425/.
[103] *Id.* [104] *Id.*

14

Government Secrecy

It is important in a democratic government that the people know what the government is doing. If at least a part of the role of free speech in the preservation of democracy is to protect the public's ability to criticize governmental abuse, the public cannot play that role effectively if it has limited ability to learn of that abuse. Thus, openness is important to democracy. On the other hand, governments, even democratic governments, have some need for secrecy. Clearly, information regarding the military that would help an enemy must be protected. Sensitive negotiations with other governments might need to be secret, at least until they are concluded. On the other hand, information that is important to public participation in decision-making must be made available to the public. And, there is little to no reason to protect information that is simply embarrassing or makes known government abuse.

There are several important areas that might be addressed regarding secrecy or openness. Three will be addressed here.[1] The first is the ability of the government to prevent its members or agents from revealing information, especially classified information. The second is, if such information is released, whether or not a government can suppress publication by a media outlet in receipt of the information. The third, which will be discussed only briefly and is only tangentially related to free expression, is the positive requirement placed on a government to make information available, typically through a statute providing for the freedom of information.

[1] There are other topics involving secrecy that could be addressed in a more complete exposition. There are, for example, trade secret laws that raise their own legal issues. Since the protection of such secrets seems aimed more at the protection of the businesses that own the information, rather than the shielding of the government from public scrutiny, that topic will not be considered here. There may also be restrictions on information regarding criminal trials in an effort to preserve the fair trial rights of defendants. Criminal trial issues are discussed in Chapter 13.

GOVERNMENT AGENTS AND THE RELEASE OF INFORMATION

There are a number of cases involving the release of information classified under a secrecy law or a release of which would cause damage to the state. There are also statutes addressing such leaks of information. Furthermore, there may be limits on the release of even non-classified and non-damaging information, where the employment relationship between the agent and the government bans such a release.

Criminal Penalties

The United States

The Espionage Act of 1917 contains provisions providing criminal penalties for obtaining and disclosing national defense materials. Section 793 provides:

(a) Whoever, for the purpose of obtaining information respecting the national defense with intent or reason to believe that the information is to be used to the injury of the United States, or to the advantage of any foreign nation, goes upon, enters, flies over, or otherwise obtains information concerning any [military installation or equipment]; or

(b) Whoever, for the purpose aforesaid, and with like intent or reason to believe, copies, takes, makes, or obtains, or attempts to copy, take, make, or obtain [certain forms of information] connected with the national defense; or

(c) Whoever, for the purpose aforesaid, receives or obtains or agrees or attempts to receive or obtain from any person, or from any source whatever, [similar documents and materials] knowing or having reason to believe ... that it has been or will be obtained, taken, made, or disposed of by any person contrary to the provisions of this chapter; or

(d) Whoever, lawfully having possession of, access to, control over, or being entrusted with [similar materials] which information the possessor has reason to believe could be used to the injury of the United States or to the advantage of any foreign nation, willfully communicates, delivers, transmits or causes [or attempts to do so] to any person not entitled to receive it, or willfully retains the same and fails to deliver it on demand to the officer or employee of the United States entitled to receive it; or

(e) [Mirroring subsection (d) with regard to persons having unauthorized possession, etc.]

(f) [Addressing loss of such materials through gross negligence and the failure to report the loss of such materials]

> Shall be fined under this title or imprisoned not more than ten years, or both …[2]

Section 794 further provides:

> (a) Whoever, with intent or reason to believe that it is to be used to the injury of the United States or to the advantage of a foreign nation, communicates, delivers, or transmits, or attempts to communicate, deliver, or transmit, to any foreign government … information relating to the national defense, shall be punished by death or by imprisonment for any term of years or for life, except that the sentence of death shall not be imposed unless … the offense resulted in the identification by a foreign power … of an individual acting as an agent of the United States and consequently in the death of that individual, or directly concerned nuclear weaponry, military spacecraft or satellites, early warning systems, or other means of defense or retaliation against large-scale attack; war plans; communications intelligence or cryptographic information; or any other major weapons system or major element of defense strategy.
>
> (b) Whoever, in time of war, with intent that the same shall be communicated to the enemy, collects, records, publishes, or communicates, or attempts to elicit any information with respect to the movement, numbers, description, condition, or disposition of any of the Armed Forces, ships, aircraft, or war materials of the United States, or with respect to the plans or conduct, or supposed plans or conduct of any naval or military operations, or with respect to any works or measures undertaken for or connected with, or intended for the fortification or defense of any place, or any other information relating to the public defense, which might be useful to the enemy, shall be punished by death or by imprisonment for any term of years or for life.[3]

The two sections, taken together, would seem to cover the activities that comprise classical spying or intelligence work, the gathering of information, and the transmission of that information to those who would damage the United States. The application of the sections in such circumstances of classical spying should not raise any free expression concerns. Certainly, communication is expression, but communication of secret information between two spies would seem reasonably unprotected for the same reasons as ordinary criminal conspiracy.

[2] 18 U.S.C. § 793 (West 2012).
[3] *Id.* at § 794.

What is, perhaps, more difficult is the communication of defense information not to a foreign power but to the press. There are not a great number of cases on this issue. It appears that prior to the administration of George W. Bush, there was only one successful prosecution, with another occurring during that administration and others in succeeding administrations.[4] Even if the prosecutions have a short history, there are cases worth examining. *United States v. Morison*[5] provides an example of charges being brought against a government employee growing out of the release of classified information to the press. The charges alleged a violation of two provisions of the Espionage Act, Section 793(d) regarding the disclosure of information lawfully possessed and 793(e) addressing material that is not lawfully possessed. Morison was employed by the Naval Intelligence Support Center with a "Top Secret-Sensitive Compartmented Information" security clearance. He had also been moonlighting, with the Navy's approval, for *Jane's Fighting Ships*. The agreement with the Navy limited the materials that could be passed on. The defendant, however, passed on to *Jane's* information regarding explosions at Soviet bases and photographs of a Soviet aircraft carrier under construction. The photos were taken from the desk of a coworker.

The defense argued that, because the material was leaked to the press rather than sent to a foreign government, his conduct was not prohibited by the statute. The court refused to accept the position that the statute was limited to classical spying and concluded that it applied to transmittal, as the language indicated, to anyone. The court further concluded that the First Amendment did not protect the transmittal to the press, saying:

> Nor do we find any authority for the proposition that Congress could not validly prohibit a government employee having possession of secret military intelligence material from transmitting that material to "one not entitled to receive it," whether that recipient was the press or not, without infringing the employee's rights under the First Amendment.[6]

While the court may have found the case easier, because it saw the defendant's actions as "motivated not by patriotism and the public interest but by self-interest"[7] in seeking employment with *Jane's*, its rejection of a First Amendment defense did not rest on that factor.

4 *See* Heidi Kitrosser, *Free Speech Aboard the Leakey Ship of State: Calibrating First Amendment Protections for Leakers of Classified Information*, 6 J. Nat'l Security L. & Pol'y 409, 409 (2013).

5 844 F.2d 1057 (4th Cir. 1988). For an example of the case involving the provision of classified information to a foreign government, see United States v. Rosen, 557 F. 3d 192 (4th Cir. 2009).

6 844 F.2d at 1070. 7 *Id.* at 1077.

In a more recent case, *United States v. Kiriakou*,[8] the defendant was charged with having passed national defense information to journalists regarding operations in Abu Zubaydah and the involvement of certain covert operatives in the Rendition, Detention, and Interrogation Program. The defense argued that the charges, brought under Section 793(d), required the intent to injure the United States, as required by other subsections. The court concluded that, consistent with the language of the subsection, only a reason to believe that the material could be used to injure the United States was required. For that reason, a claim of good faith in making the material known to the public was irrelevant.

An even more difficult issue is raised by the possibility of any criminal charges against a media entity for publishing such material. Professor Mary-Rose Papandrea says that the principal case disallowing prior restraints on the publication of government information leaves open that possibility.

> Prior restraints are historically disfavored, and a careful reading of the various opinions in the *Pentagon Papers* case indicates that a majority of Justices might have ruled in the government's favor had it not sought a prior restraint but rather prosecuted the newspapers after publication. It is ... certainly possible that a court confronted with a criminal prosecution against a government outsider based on the unauthorized dissemination of national security information would decide that balancing the harm to national security against the value to the public debate is an appropriate method of resolving the First Amendment concerns at stake.[9]

The United Kingdom

The United Kingdom's Official Secrets Act of 1989[10] contains broad prohibitions on the release of certain information by both government agents and others. Section 1 of the Act provides:

(1) A person who is or has been—
  (a) a member of the security and intelligence services; or
  (b) a person notified that he is subject to the provisions of this subsection,
  is guilty of an offence if without lawful authority he discloses any information, document or other article relating to security or intelligence

[8] 898 F. Supp. 2d 921 (E.D. Virginia 2012).

[9] Mary-Rose Papandrea, *Balancing and the Unauthorized Disclosure of National Security Information*, 97 Iowa L. Rev. Bull. 94, 106 (2012). *See also* the *Pentagon Papers* cases discussed *infra* notes 49–54 and accompanying text.

[10] Official Secrets Act, 1989 c. 6.

which is or has been in his possession by virtue of his position as a member of any of those services or in the course of his work while the notification is or was in force.

. . .

(3) A person who is or has been a Crown servant or government contractor is guilty of an offence if without lawful authority he makes a damaging disclosure of any information, document or other article relating to security or intelligence which is or has been in his possession by virtue of his position as such but otherwise than as mentioned in subsection (1) above.

(4) For the purposes of subsection (3) above a disclosure is damaging if –

  (a) it causes damage to the work of, or of any part of, the security and intelligence services; or

  (b) it is of information or a document or other article which is such that its unauthorised disclosure would be likely to cause such damage or which falls within a class or description of information, documents or articles the unauthorised disclosure of which would be likely to have that effect.

(5) It is a defence for a person charged with an offence under this section to prove that at the time of the alleged offence he did not know, and had no reasonable cause to believe, that the information, document or article in question related to security or intelligence or, in the case of an offence under subsection (3), that the disclosure would be damaging within the meaning of that subsection.

(6) Notification that a person is subject to subsection (1) above shall be effected by a notice in writing served on him by a Minister of the Crown; and such a notice may be served if, in the Minister's opinion, the work undertaken by the person in question is or includes work connected with the security and intelligence services and its nature is such that the interests of national security require that he should be subject to the provisions of that subsection.[11]

Section 2 addresses defense information, providing:

(1) A person who is or has been a Crown servant or government contractor is guilty of an offence if without lawful authority he makes a damaging disclosure of any information, document or other article relating to defence which is or has been in his possession by virtue of his position as such.

[11] *Id.* at § 1.

(2) For the purposes of subsection (1) above a disclosure is damaging if—
(a) it damages the capability of, or of any part of, the armed forces of the Crown to carry out their tasks or leads to loss of life or injury to members of those forces or serious damage to the equipment or installations of those forces; or
(b) otherwise ... endangers the interests of the United Kingdom abroad, seriously obstructs the promotion or protection by the United Kingdom of those interests or endangers the safety of British citizens abroad; or
(c) it is of information or of a document or article which is such that its unauthorised disclosure would be likely to have any of those effects.[12]

Other sections address Crown servants and government contractors and information regarding international relations and criminal and special investigations.[13]

Other Jurisdictions

Canada's Security of Information Act[14] provides criminal penalties for the release of certain information. Section 4(1) provides:

> Every person is guilty of an offence under this Act who, having in his possession or control any ... information ... by any person holding office under Her Majesty, or that he has obtained or to which he has had access while subject to the Code of Service Discipline within the meaning of the *National Defence Act* or owing to his position as a person who holds or has held office under Her Majesty, or as a person who holds or has held a contract made on behalf of Her Majesty, or a contract the performance of which in whole or in part is carried out in a prohibited place, or as a person who is or has been employed under a person who holds or has held such an office or contract,
>
> (a) communicates the ... information to any person, other than a person to whom he is authorized to communicate with, or a person to whom it is in the interest of the State his duty to communicate it ...

The Act applies not only to government agents who release information; it also applies to those who receive information covered by the Act. Section 4(3) provides:

[12] *Id.* at § 2.

[13] *See id.* at §§ 3–4. *See also infra* notes 62–78 and accompanying test for provisions addressing those in receipt of information.

[14] R.S.C., 1985, c. O-5.

> Every person who receives any secret official ... information, knowing, or having reasonable ground to believe, at the time he receives it, that the ... information is communicated to him in contravention of this Act, is guilty of an offence under this Act, unless he proves that the communication to him of the code word, password, sketch, plan, model, article, note, document or information was contrary to his desire.

There is a Canadian case contesting the application of the Security of Information Act to a journalist. In *O'Neill v. Canada*,[15] the Ontario Superior Court of Justice took up the case of a journalist for the *Ottawa Citizen* who had written an article regarding a Syrian-born Canadian citizen who had been arrested by the United States and deported to Syria. The article appeared to have been based, at least in part, on material covered by the Act. Based on the claim that the journalist was in violation of the Act, warrants were issued to search the journalist's office and home. The court case addressed the journalist's contention that the warrant and certain portions of the act were an unconstitutional violation of her rights under Section 2(b) of the Canadian Charter.

The journalist argued that the Act was overly broad, and the court agreed. In the view of the court, the sections were "standardless" giving the government the ability to arbitrarily protect any information it chose to classify as "secret official" or "official." While overbreadth might also apply to other applications of the Act, the court suggested that it was a particular problem for those outside the government.

> This is particularly difficult and dangerous from the perspective of those outside of government who are in receipt of government information, whether occasionally or frequently, deliberately or inadvertently and who are not bound by governmental policies or guidelines regarding the classification of government information.[16]

So, while the statute may have been overly broad under the circumstances, its application to a government agent may not raise a problem. The court took a similar approach to the claim that the statute was vague, concluding that it left too much discretion to government officials.

While the conclusion that the statute was overly broad and vague would have been sufficient to declare the application of the Act and the warrants unconstitutional, the court went on to consider Section 2(b). The court did conclude that there was a "pressing and substantial" purpose in government being able to deter the release of certain types of information relevant to

[15] (2006) 82 O.R. 3d 241 (Ont. Sup. Ct.). [16] *Id.* at ¶ 39.

national security. The court, however, concluded that the provisions were not proportional to the purpose. This conclusion also turned on lack of specificity in the statute. Because the provisions could be applied to a wide range of material, even in the court's view material that did not cause harm to the national interest, the provisions were not sufficiently tailored to the purpose to be proportional.[17] The extent of the application of this reasoning to government agents may be questioned, given the court's earlier seemingly limiting language.

The Swiss criminal code contains a provision addressing the release of "secret official deliberations." Section 293 provides:

> Anyone who, without being entitled to do so, makes public all or part of the proceedings of an investigation or of the deliberations of any authority which is secret by law or by virtue of a decision taken by such authority acting within its powers shall be punished with imprisonment or a fine.[18]

Other provisions of the same section address complicity and provide that a court may decide not to impose a penalty if the secret involved is only of minor importance. Application of the prohibition to a public official involved in such an investigation or working for such an authority is obvious. The statute has, however, also been applied to those receiving and then publishing such information. This application has not always been well received by European authorities.

In *Weber v. Switzerland*,[19] the European Court of Human Rights considered the case of a journalist who had been fined for revealing the existence of a confidential judicial investigation. Weber had himself been a party in the judicial investigation, alleging that he had been defamed in a letter published, by another party, in the letters column of a newspaper. The letter alleged that Weber had been unscrupulous in certain fundraising activities. It said that if Weber had the courage to release his tax returns, he would be revealed to be sponging off decent people. The letter writer admitted the virulence of the accusations to the investigating judge and attributed it to a nervous breakdown. Weber was not satisfied with the progress of the investigation and, at a press conference, revealed the existence of the defamation proceedings.

Weber argued, before the European Court, that the fine was a violation of his rights under Article 10. The Court concluded easily that there had been an interference and that the penalty was prescribed by law. The Court also had no difficulty in concluding that the infringement was in the pursuit of a

[17] *See id.* at ¶¶ 99–103.
[18] Schweizisches Strafgesetzbuch [Criminal Code] Dec. 21, 1937, SR 311.0, Article 293.
[19] App. No. 11034/84, 12 Eur. H.R. Rep. 508 (1990).

legitimate aim. It was "intended to ensure the proper conduct of the investigation and was therefore designed to protect the authority and impartiality of the judiciary."[20] It was necessity in a democratic society that gave the Court pause, although the court did not pause long. It concluded rather quickly that because the investigation had been practically complete, it was not necessary to impose the penalty.[21]

This case may not be all that interesting from the point of view of freedom of the press. While Weber was a journalist, it was not really his journalistic activities that led to his conviction. He was a litigant unhappy with the procedure in his case, and it was in that role that he released information. Perhaps his status as a journalist led to attendance at his press conference, but that does not make his activity journalistic. Perhaps the Court decision is better seen as finding insufficient harm in a revelation by an ordinary citizen, who is also a litigant, to justify a penalty.

A second case from Switzerland does raise the issue of the application of Section 293 to a journalist. In *Stoll v. Switzerland*,[22] the European Court of Human Rights took up the case of a journalist who had obtained a copy of a paper with details of the negotiations between Swiss banks and the World Jewish Congress regarding compensation for Holocaust victims. The paper was marked "confidential." Its source was not clear, but it seemed the journalist's possession must have been the result of a breach of confidence. The journalist used the document in publishing a series of articles that were critical of the Swiss ambassador to the United States, who was involved in the negotiations. The articles included extracts indicating a lack of sensitivity for the victims of the Swiss banks' activities. The publications led to the journalist's conviction, under Section 293, and the imposition of a fine.

The case before the European Court alleged a violation of Article 10 of the European Convention. The Court accepted that the fine was prescribed by law and accepted as a legitimate aim the prevention of the disclosure of information that has been received in confidence. The issue for the Court again came down to whether or not the infringement represented by the fine was necessary in a democratic society. In that regard, the Court recognized the importance of protecting the press.

> [T]here is little scope under Art. 10(2) of the Convention for restrictions on political speech or on debate of questions of public interest. The most careful scrutiny on the part of the Court is called for when, as in the present case, the measures taken or sanctions imposed by the national authority are capable of

20 *Id.* at ¶ 45. 21 *See id.* at ¶ 51. 22 App. No. 69698/01, 44 Eur. H.R. Rep. 53 (2007).

> discouraging the participation of the press in debates over matters of legitimate public concern.[23]

The Court accepted that protecting the confidentiality of diplomatic reports is justified in principle but also said that the media's role as a watchdog applies even to foreign policy.[24]

Turning to a consideration of the articles at issue, the Court noted that they raised matters of public interest. The issue of compensating Holocaust victims for the assets that remained in Swiss banks had been widely discussed in the media and deeply divided public opinion. They touched more generally on the role of Switzerland in World War II. "[T]he public had a legitimate interest in receiving information about the officials dealing with such a sensitive matter and their negotiating style and strategy."[25] The Court also questioned whether the revelations caused any real injury. It distinguished between the admittedly important interest in protecting the diplomatic corps from outside interference but indicated that that was of lesser importance than the protection of national security or the public safety.[26]

While the penalty was said to have been relatively light in that the journalist had not been prevented from publishing his article, the Court still found a lack of proportionality. In doing so it reflected the concerns often expressed by United States courts over the chilling of free expression.

> While the penalty did not prevent the applicant from expressing himself, his conviction nonetheless amounted to a kind of censorship which was likely to discourage him from making criticisms of that kind again in the future. In the context of a political debate such a conviction is likely to deter journalists from contributing to public discussion of issues affecting the life of the community. By the same token, it is liable to hamper the press in the performance of its task of purveyor of information and public watchdog.[27]

There is also a French criminal case that reached the European Court of Human Rights, but the charges were not brought under a statute addressing the disclosure of secret or confidential information. Instead, the charge was a violation of a provision prohibiting knowingly handling goods that have been taken, misappropriated or obtained through serious crime. The defendants in *Fressoz and Roire v. France*[28] had handled photocopies of tax returns that had been provided by a tax official in breach of confidence. They were journalists, and the tax returns were those of the chairman of Peugeot. There was some industrial unrest at the time, and the article for which the returns provided information had to do with large raises and the comparison of the Chairman's

[23] *Id.* at ¶ 46. [24] *See id.* at ¶ 48. [25] *Id.* at ¶ 49. [26] *See id.* at ¶ 52. [27] *Id.* at ¶ 58.
[28] App. No. 29183/95, 31 Eur. H.R. Rep. 2 (2001).

salary to that of workers. Thus, the receipt of the materials was in furtherance of informing the public, and the European Court entertained an Article 10 challenge to the convictions.

The Court accepted the legitimate aim of protecting reputational rights and preventing the disclosure of confidential information but concluded that the conviction was not proportionate to that interest. The Court again stressed the importance of the press and its contributions to public debate and noted that the article had been not so much about the chairman as about the company. Furthermore, the Court said that the defendants did not know the source of the photocopies, which could have come from someone other than the tax official. Perhaps most importantly, under French law, it seems that individuals have a right to consult a list of individual taxpayers disclosing their taxable income and liability. There could have been no charge for receiving misappropriated goods had the authors simply examined that list. The Court saw an illicit motive in the prosecution. Noting that the chairman's complaint was over having had his income disclosed, the Court said: "The fact that applicants had been convicted of the purely technical offense of handling photocopies disguised what was really a desire to penalise them for publishing the information, although publication in itself was quite lawful."[29] The impact of such a conviction on the press was simply unacceptable.

These are not the only countries with official secrets acts, and they are not the only ones to address not only agents of the government but publishers of information. For example, the Irish Official Secrets Act of 1963 addresses holders of public office, providing:

> A person shall not communicate any official information to any other person unless he is duly authorised to do so or does so in the course of and in accordance with his duties as the holder of a public office or when it is his duty in the interest of the State to communicate it.[30]

The Act also addresses government contractors, providing that a person who has been a party to a contract, or employed by such party, may not communicate to third parties any information relating to the contract.[31]

There is also a provision that would seem to address journalists and publishers. The Act provides:

> A person shall not, in any manner prejudicial to the safety or preservation of the State—

[29] *Id.* at ¶ 46.

[30] Official Secrets Act, 1963 at § 4(1) (Act No. 1/1963), www.irishstatutebook.ie/1963/en/act/pub/0001/print.html.

[31] *See id.* at § 5(1).

(a) obtain, record, communicate to any other person or publish, or
(b) have in his possession or under his control any document containing, or other record whatsoever of,[certain information regarding the national defence or the Garda, but also including] any other matter whatsoever information as to which would or might be prejudicial to the safety or preservation of the State.[32]

While another section provides that communication with foreign agents or unlawful organizations is evidence of being communication in a manner prejudicial to the state, that would not seem to limit the application of the Act to others, providing there was evidence of prejudicial impact.[33]

The Australian equivalent of an official secrets act is found in Section 79 of the Crimes Act of 1914.[34] The Act addresses certain information a person has in his possession or control, where it is obtained in violation of the law, has been entrusted to the person by a government officer, or is a government employee or contractor, and where it was his or her duty to treat it as secret. The Act clearly addresses leaks. Subsection 2 provides:

If a person with the intention of prejudicing the security or defence of the Commonwealth or a part of the Queen's dominions:

(a) communicates a prescribed sketch, plan, photograph, model, cipher, note, document or article, or prescribed information, to a person, other than:
  (i) a person to whom he or she is authorized to communicate it; or
  (ii a person to whom it is, in the interest of the Commonwealth or a part of the Queen's dominions, his or her duty to communicate it;

or permits a person, other than a person referred to in subparagraph (i) or (ii), to have access to it; . . .

he or she shall be guilty of an indictable offence.

Three other subsections might be seen to address journalists and publishers. Subsection (3) provides:

If a person communicates a prescribed sketch, plan, photograph, model, cipher, note, document or article, or prescribed information, to a person, other than:

(a) a person to whom he or she is authorized to communicate it; or
(b) a person to whom it is, in the interest of the Commonwealth or a part of the Queen's dominions, his or her duty to communicate it;

or permits a person, other than a person referred to in paragraph (a) or (b), to have access to it, he or she shall be guilty of an offence.

[32] *Id.* at § 9(1). [33] *See id.* at § 10(1).
[34] *Crimes Act 1914* § 79, www.austlii.edu.au/au/legis/cth/consol_act/ca191482/s79.html.

While not specifically addressing publications, that would seem to be the communication of information to persons other than those authorized.

Additionally, subsection (5) provides:

> If a person receives any sketch, plan, photograph, model, cipher, note, document, article or information, knowing or having reasonable ground to believe, at the time when he or she receives it, that it is communicated to him or her in contravention of section 91.1 of the Criminal Code or subsection (2) of this section, he or she shall be guilty of an indictable offence unless he or she proves that the communication was contrary to his or her desire.

And, subsection (6) further addresses the receipt of protected information.

> If a person receives any sketch, plan, photograph, model, cipher, note, document, article or information, knowing, or having reasonable ground to believe, at the time when he or she receives it, that it is communicated to him or her in contravention of subsection (3), he or she shall be guilty of an offence unless he or she proves that the communication was contrary to his or her desire.

Neither subsection explicitly exempts journalists.

Civil Sanctions Against Leakers

The United States

Frank Snepp had been an employee of the Central Intelligence Agency (CIA). When he accepted his position he signed an agreement promising that he would not publish anything relating to the Agency or its activities or intelligence activities more generally without prior approval by the Agency. He was barred from disclosing any classified information, but he could not publish *any* information without such approval. Snepp, however, published a book about CIA activities in South Vietnam and did so without such prepublication approval. The government, at least for purposes of litigation, conceded that the book did not disclose any classified information. But the government sought a remedy for Snepp's violation of his employment contract.

In *Snepp v. United States*,[35] the United States Supreme Court held that a constructive trust could be established in favor of the government over the profits from the publication. The government had an interest not only in protecting the secrecy of classified information but also in assuring confidentiality for those who might provide information. "When a former agent relies on his own judgment about what information is detrimental, he may reveal

[35] 444 U.S. 507 (1980).

information that the CIA – with its broader understanding of what may expose classified information and confidential sources – could have identified as harmful."[36]

The Court said that a constructive trust protects both the government and the former agent and is a customary remedy for breach of trust.

> It deals fairly with both parties ... If the agent secures prepublication clearance, he can publish with no fear of liability. If the agent publishes unreviewed material in violation of his fiduciary and contractual obligation, the trust remedy simply requires him to disgorge the benefits of his faithlessness.[37]

Disgorgement simply removes the financial incentive to violate the terms of the contract.

There was a dissent, written by Justice Stevens, joined by Justices Brennan and Marshall, that saw greater first amendment concerns.

> [T]he Court seems unaware of the fact that its drastic new remedy has been fashioned to enforce a species of prior restraint on a citizen's right to criticize his government. Inherent in this prior restraint is the risk that the reviewing agency will misuse its authority to delay the publication of a critical work or to persuade an author to modify the contents of his work beyond the demands of secrecy.[38]

The United Kingdom

The *Spycatcher* case grew out of the publication of a book of that title by Peter Wright, a former member of the British Security Service or MI5.[39] The book discussed the agency's organization, methods, and personnel. It also alleged illegal activities, including an attempt to undermine the Labour Government, and claimed that the director was a Soviet agent. Some of the same claims had already been published in other books and discussed in television interviews.

The publication raised a number of issues. It would appear that criminal charges might have been brought against the author, under the Official Secrets Act. However, at the time of publication, the author was living in

[36] *Id.* at 512. [37] *Id.* at 515. [38] *Id.* at 526 (Stevens, J., dissenting) (footnote omitted).

[39] The saga that comprises the *Spycatcher* case is recounted in a number of places. Earlier litigation in Australia and the United Kingdom is discussed in the decision by the European Court Human Rights in Observer and Guardian v. United Kingdom, App. No. 13585/88, 14 Eur. H.R. Rep. 153 (1991). The litigation is also discussed in a later decision by the European Commission of Human Rights, Times Newspapers v. United Kingdom, App. No. 18897/91,15 Eur. H.R. Rep. CD 49 (1993). Further insight may be found in ERIC BARENDT, FREEDOM OF SPEECH 139–41 (2d ed. 2005).

Australia, which was also where the book was to be published. There were also attempts to enjoin publication of the book in Australia and of newspaper excerpts in the United Kingdom, attempts that will be discussed below. The basis was similar to that in *Snepp*, that the disclosure of the information was a breach of the duty of confidentiality under Wright's employment contract. Adding to the similarity, the United Kingdom had sought an accounting of profits against the newspaper that published excerpts from the book, an attempt that the European Court of Human Rights suggested was acceptable as an alternative to any continuing injunction.[40] Other than jurisdictional problems with regard to Mr. Wright, presumably the same remedy might have been imposed against him.

There is a case decided by the European Court of Human Rights that speaks to accounting for profits by an author. *Blake v. United Kingdom*[41] involved an individual who had served in the Secret Intelligence Service, while also spying for the Soviet Union. That spying led to a sentence of forty-two years' imprisonment, but he escaped to the Soviet Union. In 1989, he wrote an autobiography based in substantial part on information he had acquired while in the Service. The government sought, in 1991, to prevent him from receiving any financial benefits from the book and eventually, in 1997, received an injunction against him receiving any payment of benefits. The House of Lords, in 1998, allowed an appeal.

When the case went to the European Court, the Court found a violation of the European Convention, but the decision was not based on Article 10. Instead, the Court found a violation of the Article 6 right to a hearing within a reasonable time on matters of civil rights and obligations. Clearly, United Kingdom courts did not see the accounting for profits as violative of any right of free expression. The fact that the European Court did not even consider Article 10 may also be taken to indicate that that court also saw no violation of expression rights.

Other Jurisdictions

A case from the European Court Human Rights from Moldova, not a fully functioning democracy, provides an indication of the limits of the Court's tolerance for civil penalties. *Guja v. Moldova*[42] involved a dismissal from the Prosecutor General's Office for leaking two documents. The leaker believed

[40] *See* App. No. 13585/88, 14 Eur. H.R. Rep, at ¶¶ 39, 69 (1992).
[41] App. No. 68890/01, 44 Eur. H.R. Rep. 29 (2007).
[42] App. No. 14277/04, 53 Eur. H.R. Rep. 16 (2008).

the documents disclosed that high-ranking politicians had interfered in a criminal proceeding. The leak was in response to a call by a journalist for those with knowledge of corruption to release that information, and the documents were used in an article regarding corruption.

The Court said that there has been an interference with Guja's Article 10 rights, even though he had not been the author of the article and despite the fact that the leak could be seen as workplace misconduct. The Court accepted the legitimate aim of preventing the disclosure of confidential information but concluded that the dismissal was not necessary in a democratic society.

> The signalling by a civil servant or an employee in the public sector of illegal conduct or wrongdoing in the workplace should, in certain circumstances, enjoy protection. This may be called for where the employee or civil servant concerned is the only person, or part of a small category of persons, aware of what is happening at work and is thus best placed to act in the public interest by alerting the employer or the public at large.[43]

While the employee should first disclose the wrongdoing to a superior or competent authority, where that is not an available option, public disclosure may be justified.

> In a democratic system, the acts or omissions of government must be subject to the close scrutiny not only of the legislative and judicial authorities but also of the media and public opinion. The interest which the public may have in particular information can sometimes be so strong as to override even a legally imposed duty of confidence.[44]

Given the public interest, dismissal, which the Court considered a harsh measure, was not justified. The court did say that less significant penalties might have been imposed.

It is also important to note that the Court found no indication of bad faith on the part of Guja. "The Court does not find any reason to believe that the applicant was motivated by a desire for personal advantage, held any personal grievance ... or that there was any other ulterior motive for his actions."[45] The indication is that, had there been a profit motive, the result might have been different. Thus, the case does not call into question the European Court's willingness to accept the sort of accounting for profit imposed in *Snepp* and that might have been imposed in the *Spycatcher* case.

[43] *Id.* at ¶ 72. [44] *Id.* at ¶ 74. [45] *Id.* at ¶ 93.

BANS ON PUBLICATION

Once information has been released but is not generally known to the public, the issue becomes whether a government may prohibit the media from making that information more widely available. The general trend here seems to be one in which governments, at least sometimes seemingly overreaching, asserted the need to limit dissemination, with courts sometimes expressing skepticism.

The United States

There are provisions of the Espionage Act that address publication, but they are rather specific in the materials covered by the bans. Section 794(b) bans the publication, in time of war, of movements, numbers, and disposition of the Armed Forces, naval vessels, aircraft, and war materials, military plans, or other public defense information useful to the enemy.[46] Section 797 prohibits the publication of photos or other representations of vital, as designated by the President, military or naval installations or equipment, without obtaining permission.[47] Section 798 prohibits the publication of classified information regarding government codes, ciphers, cryptographic systems, communication intelligence activities, or material the publisher knows to have been obtained through communications intelligence activities.[48] There are, however, cases in which the government has sought to prevent the publication of materials not in those categories.

The *Pentagon Papers Case*

The best-known United States case involving an attempt by the government to restrain publication by newspapers is the *Pentagon Papers Case, New York Times v. United States*.[49] The *New York Times* and the *Washington Post* had both obtained copies of a classified study titled "History of U.S. Decision-Making Process on Vietnam Policy." The United States asked the federal district courts for the Southern District of New York and the District of the District of Columbia to enjoin publication, and both courts rejected the request. The cases proceeded quickly to the appellate level, with the District of Columbia Circuit affirming, while the Second Circuit remanded and continued a stay on publication. The speed with which the cases then made it through the Supreme Court was incredible. The Courts of Appeal had

[46] 18 U.S.C. § 794 (West 2012). [47] *Id*. at § 797. [48] *Id*, at § 798.
[49] 403 U.S. 713 (1971).

rendered their judgments on June 23, 1971. The *New York Times'* petition for certiorari, in the Second Circuit case, and the government's application for interim relief, in the DC circuit case, were both filed on June 24. A Supreme Court hearing was scheduled for June 26, with the parties' briefs received only two hours before argument. The Court's decision was delivered on June 30.

The Court handed down an extremely short *per curiam* decision. The only reasoning presented was a statement that: "'Any system of prior restraints of expression comes to this Court bearing a heavy presumption against its constitutional validity.' The Government 'thus carries a heavy burden of showing justification for the imposition of such a restraint.'"[50] The Court said that the government had not met that burden and vacated the stays.

While the Court's opinion was extremely short, each of the nine justices added an opinion in concurrence or dissent. Justice Black, joined by Justice Douglas, in a concurring opinion, said the stays should have been vacated even before oral argument, saying "every moment's continuance of the injunctions against these newspapers amounts to a flagrant, indefensible, and continuing violation of the First Amendment."[51] He particularly objected to the claim of an "inherent power" on the part of the President, even without the grant of authority by Congress, to stop publication by resort to the courts.

Justice Douglas, also in concurrence and joined by Justice Black, noted that the material at issue was all historical, none more recent than 1968 and none providing current information useful to an enemy. Concern over the information was more a matter of embarrassment than of strategic or tactical importance. As he saw it, that flew in the face of the First Amendment. "The dominant purpose of the First Amendment was to prohibit the widespread practice of governmental suppression of embarrassing information ... Secrecy in government is fundamentally anti-democratic, perpetuating bureaucratic errors. Open debate and discussion of public issues are vital to our national health."[52]

Even those in concurrence recognized that in some circumstances restraints may be proper. As Justice Brennan noted:

> [O]ur cases ... have indicated that there is a single, extremely narrow class of cases in which the First Amendment's ban on prior judicial restraint may be overridden. Our cases have thus far indicated that such cases may arise only when the Nation "is at war," during which times "(n)o one would question but that a government might prevent actual obstruction to its recruiting

[50] *Id.* at 714 (citations omitted). [51] *Id.* at 715 (Black, J., concurring).
[52] *Id.* at 723–24 (Douglas, J., concurring).

> service or the publication of the sailing dates of transports or the number and location of troops."[53]

There were three justices in dissent: Chief Justice Burger and Justices Harlan and Blackmun. Their objections focused on the speed of the litigation and the failure to seek the answers to important questions. Among the questions seen as needing an answer were whether or not the disclosure of the documents in question would in fact seriously impair national security and how much weight should be given to the Executive Branch's views on that issue.[54]

The Progressive

The Progressive, a Madison, Wisconsin magazine, planned to publish an article titled "The H-Bomb Secret: How We Got It, Why We're Telling It." *United States v. The Progressive*[55] was an attempt by the United States government to enjoin the publication. There was some contention over how available to the public the information contained in the article already was. The magazine and author said that the material was already publicly available and that, though some of the information may have at one time been classified, it had been declassified and was available both to the public and foreign nations.[56] The government countered that not all the information had been made public and that, in any case, the setting out of core concepts in conjunction with one another posed a danger. The court seemed convinced by the government's contentions.

> Does the article provide a "do-it yourself" guide for the hydrogen bomb? Probably not. A number of affidavits make quite clear that a *sine qua non* to thermonuclear capability is a large sophisticated industrial capability coupled with a coterie of imaginative, resourceful scientists and technicians. One does not build a hydrogen bomb in the basement. However, the article could possibly provide sufficient information to allow a medium size nation to move faster in developing a hydrogen weapon. It could provide a ticket to by-pass blind alleys.[57]

53 *Id.* at 726 (Brennan, J., concurring) (citations omitted).

54 *See id.* at 754 (Harlan, J., dissenting).

55 467 F. Supp. 990 (W.D. Wisc. 1979). The case was later dismissed, when the issue became moot. *See* 610 F.2d 819 (7th Cir. 1979).

56 In a motion for rehearing, the court concluded that the earlier declassification did not stop the government from seeking to suppress publication. *See* Untied States v. The Progressive, 486 F. Supp. 5 (W.D. Wisc. 1979).

57 467 F. Supp. at 993.

There was, then, the danger not that the average reader of *The Progressive* could use the article to build a bomb but that it might provide assistance to the development of such a weapon by a foreign government.

The court recognized the very heavy burden the government must bear in seeking a prior restraint, but it also recognized the propriety of restraining strategic and tactical military information in time of war. On the side of free expression, the defendants argued that the article would alert people to what it described as a false illusion of security created by government secrecy in this area. They saw the article as providing people with the information they would need to make an informed decision on an issue of great public concern.[58] The court, even accepting the contention, said that there was no reason why the public had to know the technical details of how to construct such a weapon in order to debate the issue.[59] The defendants also argued that they were protected by the *Pentagon Papers* case, but the court saw differences between the two cases. Rather than the old information that might simply have caused embarrassment in the earlier case, the information here was potentially dangerous. Furthermore, while the government had not claimed authorization under any statute in the earlier case, it argued that it was justified under the Atomic Energy Act in the later case.[60]

The court concluded that not all of the information was in the public domain and that publication would injure the United States.

> What is involved here is information dealing with the most destructive weapon in the history of mankind, information of sufficient destructive potential to nullify the right to free speech and to endanger the right to life itself . . . Faced with a stark choice between upholding the right to continued life and the right to freedom of the press, most jurists would have no difficulty in opting for the chance to continue to breathe and function as they work to achieve perfect freedom of expression . . . A mistake in ruling against *The Progressive* will seriously infringe cherished First Amendment rights. If a preliminary injunction is issued, it will constitute the first instance of prior restraint against a publication in this fashion in the history of this country, to this court's knowledge . . . It will infringe upon our right to know and to be informed as well . . . A mistake in ruling against the United States could pave the way for thermonuclear annihilation for us all. In that event, our right to life is extinguished and the right to publish becomes moot.[61]

58 *See id.* at 994. 59 *See id.*

60 Section 2274 of the Atomic Energy Act prohibits communicating restricted data to anyone, where there is reason to believe the data can be used to injure the United States or secure an advantage on the part of a foreign nation. *See* 42 U.S.C. § 2274 (West 2012).

61 467 F. Supp. at 995–96.

Faced with that "stark choice," the court issued the injunction.

The United Kingdom

The Official Secrets Act includes a provision that applies to those in receipt of information from those directly covered by the Act. Section 5 provides:

(1) Subsection (2) below applies where—
   (a) any information, document or other article protected against disclosure by the foregoing provisions of this Act has come into a person's possession as a result of having been—
      (i) disclosed (whether to him or another) by a Crown servant or government contractor without lawful authority; or
      (ii) entrusted to him by a Crown servant or government contractor on terms requiring it to be held in confidence or in circumstances in which the Crown servant or government contractor could reasonably expect that it would be so held; or
      (iii) disclosed (whether to him or another) without lawful authority by a person to whom it was entrusted as mentioned in sub-paragraph (ii) above ...

(2) Subject to [certain exceptions], the person into whose possession the information, document or article has come is guilty of an offence if he discloses it without lawful authority knowing, or having reasonable cause to believe, that it is protected against disclosure by the foregoing provisions of this Act and that it has come into his possession as mentioned in subsection (1) above.[62]

It would appear that any publisher of a newspaper within the criminal jurisdiction of the United Kingdom could face criminal charges for the publication of *Spycatcher* or excerpts from the book. Section 1 of the Official Secrets Act applies to those who are or who have been members of the intelligence service, a category that Wright fit, so his disclosure was unlawful. The second level disclosure through the publication of the newspaper would appear to be covered by Section 5, and such a violation would, under Section 10, subject a person to imprisonment for up to two years. Yet, the government brought only civil actions seeking to bar publications.[63]

[62] Official Secrets Act 1989 c. 6 § 5.

[63] With regard to criminal action, an Australian publisher would be beyond the criminal jurisdiction of the United Kingdom and, for that matter, would seem not to be a proper subject for an injunction issued directly by a court of the United Kingdom. With regard to British

The civil actions growing out of the publication of *Spycatcher* present a long and convoluted history of publication in a number of countries and litigation in a number of jurisdictions. Fortunately, the history is recounted in a European Court of Human Rights case, *Observer and Guardian v. United Kingdom*,[64] considering a complaint by those newspapers with regard to interlocutory injunctions on the publication of details of the book and of information obtained from the author. It is that history that will be recounted, more briefly, here.

In September 1985, despite not having acted against other books or Mr. Wright's television interview, the United Kingdom sought an injunction in Australia restraining publication of the book, based not on official secrecy but instead on a violation of the duty of confidentiality under which he had worked. While these proceedings were under way, in June 1986, the *Observer* and *Guardian* published stories about the Australian litigation and gave some details regarding the contents of the book manuscript. While the newspaper reporters had engaged in their own investigations, it seemed likely that some of their sources had come from the offices of the publishers of the book.

The Attorney General of England and Wales filed suit in the High Court of Justice of England and Wales alleging breach of confidence and asking for a permanent injunction restraining publication. Interim injunctions were granted

newspapers, there may have been an issue, after the publication of the book elsewhere, whether or not the newspaper publication was, and was recognized as being, damaging. Included in the exceptions noted in Section 5(2) of the Official Secrets Act is one contained in Section 5(3):

> In the case of information or a document or article protected against disclosure by Sections 1 to 3 above, a person does not commit an offence under subsection (2) above unless –
> (a) the disclosure by him is damaging; and
> (b) he makes it knowing, or having reasonable cause to believe, that it would be damaging . . .

On the other hand, a report published in the European Human Rights Reporter said that there need not be any harm under the Act.

> The Committee remains concerned that powers under the Official Secrets Act 1989 have been exercised to frustrate former employees of the Crown from bringing into the public domain issues of genuine public interest, and can be exercised to prevent the media from publishing such matters. It notes that disclosures of information are penalised even where they are not harmful to national security.

U.N. Hum. Rts. Committee, Consideration of Reports Submitted by States Parties under Article 40 of the Covenabt Concluding Observations of the Human Rights Committee United Kingdom of Great Britain and Northern Ireland, U.N. Doc. CCPR/C/GBR/CO/6 at ¶ 24.

64 App. No. 13585/88, 14 Eur. H.R. Rep. 153 (1992).

on June 27, 1986 by Justice Millett with some modification in July. Later that month the Court of Appeal upheld the injunctions, with slight modifications.

The action returned to Australia, with a trial in November and December 1986 and a judgment on March 13, 1987 in which Justice Powell rejected the United Kingdom's claim, concluding that much of the information in the book was no longer confidential and that what remained would not be harmful to the British government. The United Kingdom appealed to the New South Wales Court of Appeal, where judgment was reserved and the defendants gave "undertakings not to publish whilst the appeal was pending."[65]

On April 27, 1987 three more newspapers in the United Kingdom became involved. *The Independent* published a summary allegedly based on the manuscript, with reports on the summary also published in *The London Evening Standard* and the *London Daily News*. The Attorney General then applied to the Queen's Bench for leave to file contempt charges against the newspapers. This action was based not on breach of confidence but on "the public interest in the due administration of justice."[66] Over the next week, similar reports were reprinted in newspapers in Australia and the United States. Perhaps more importantly, on May 14, the publisher Viking Penguin announced that it had purchased the United States publication rights to the book.

On July 12, *The Sunday Times*, another United Kingdom newspaper that had purchased serialization rights, published its first installment. The next day the Attorney General began contempt proceedings against that newspaper. Back in the United States, Viking Penguin published on July 14, and the book became a bestseller there and in Canada, where the British Government took no legal action. A number of copies then made their way back into the United Kingdom.

The Sunday Times indicated that it intended to publish the second installment on July 19, unless it was enjoined from doing so. The Attorney General obtained a temporary injunction, but the same court that granted that stay three days later discharged the injunctions against *The Observer* and *The Guardian* and dismissed the claim for the injunction against *The Sunday Times*. The Attorney General appealed the judgment with regard to *The Observer* and *The Guardian*, but not *The Sunday Times*.

On July 24, the Court of Appeal concluded that, given the publication of the book in the United States, the injunctions against *The Observer* and *The Guardian* were no longer appropriate in their original form but would have to be varied to bar only publication of any part of the book itself and statements by Mr. Wright on security matters but not summaries of his allegations.[67] Despite the now

[65] *Id*. at ¶ 21. [66] *Id*. at ¶ 22. [67] *See id*. at ¶ 34.

general availability of the information, the various members of the court said the continuation of the injunctions could restore confidence in the Security Service, by assuring the material could not be published without prior authorization, could protect the government's interest until trial, or could deter future breaches of confidence.[68] On July 30, the Appellate Committee of the House of Lords agreed that those injunctions should remain in force.

At this point, on September 24, 1987, the action returned to Australia, where the New South Wales Court of Appeal held that the Attorney General's claim was not justiciable in an Australian court, because it was either an attempt to enforce the law of a foreign country or to determine a question regarding the public interest of that country. The Attorney General then appealed to the High Court of Australia, but that court refused to restrain publication, because of the publication of the book in the United States, and eventually agreed with the lower court that the claim did not assert an interest enforceable in Australia. The book was then published in Australia, as well as in Canada and Ireland, and copies became widely available elsewhere.

Back in the United Kingdom, the Attorney General brought proceedings against *The Sunday Times* for breach of confidence, seeking an injunction and accounting of profits. That trial, along with the trial of his actions against *The Observer* and *The Guardian*, took place in October 1987, with the judgment on December 21. The European Court describes the result in the United Kingdom High Court, in a judgment by Justice Scott:

(a) The ground for the Attorney General's claim for permanent injunctions was no longer the preservation of the secrecy of certain information but the promotion of the efficiency and reputation of the Security Service.

...

(e) [*The Observer* and *The Guardian*] were not in breach of their duty of confidentiality, created by being recipients of Mr. Wright's unauthorised disclosures, in publishing their respective articles ...; the articles were a fair report in general terms of the forthcoming trial in Australia and, furthermore, disclosure of two of Mr. Wright's allegations was justified on an additional grounds relating to disclosure of "iniquity".

(f) [*The Sunday Times*], on the other hand, had been in breach of the duty of confidentiality in publishing the first installment of extracts ..., since those extracts contained certain material which did not raise questions of public interest outweighing those of national security.

[68] *See id.*

(g) [*The Sunday Times*] were liable to account for the profits accruing to them as a result of the publication of that installment.
(h) The Attorney General's claims for permanent injunctions failed because the publication and worldwide dissemination of *Spycatcher* ... had had the result that there was no longer any duty of confidence lying on newspapers or other third parties ...[69]

The Attorney General and *The Sunday Times* both appealed and the Court of Appeal affirmed. The case then went to the Appellate Committee of the House of Lords which also affirmed, saying a duty of confidentiality does arise in a third party possessing information known to be confidential, but that duty may be extinguished by the information becoming generally available; thus, the injunctions should be discharged.[70] The publication by *The Sunday Times* did breach the duty of confidence and wasn't protected by prior disclosure, publication in the United States, or the disclosure of iniquity, and *The Sunday Times* was liable to account for its profits.[71] The Lords also made it clear that members of the Security Service owe a lifetime duty of confidence to the Crown.[72]

Returning to the contempt case involving *The Independent*, *The London Evening Standard*, and the *London Daily News*, the trial took place in April 1989. The Court concluded that *The Independent* and *The Sunday Times* had been in contempt, and the decision was upheld on appeal.

That was the historical context in which the case *Observer and Guardian v. United Kingdom* reached the European Court of Human Rights. The two newspapers alleged that the interrogatory injunctions to which they had been subjected from July 11, 1986 to October 13, 1988 violated their rights under Article 10. The European Court had no difficulty finding that the interference was prescribed by law and turned to whether or not the government's aims were legitimate under Article 10(2). With regard to permissible aims, the Court said that it was undisputed that the aim was to maintain the authority of the judiciary and protect that the litigants' rights would not be prejudiced during a trial, with a further legitimate aim being the protection of national security.[73]

With regard to whether the interference was "necessary in a democratic society," the Court split the inquiry into two different periods: one from July 11, 1986, when the injunctions were originally imposed, to July 30, 1987, when the injunctions were continued by the House of Lords, and the second running from July 30, 1987 to October 13, 1988, the date of the final decision. With regard to the first period, the Court concluded that the United Kingdom

[69] *Id.* at ¶ 40. [70] *Id.* at ¶ 42. [71] *See id.* [72] *See id* [73] *See id.* at ¶ 56.

was entitled to think that the injunctions were necessary in a democratic society and were proportionate.

> [T]he injunctions did not erect a blanket prohibition. Whilst they forbade the publication of information derived from or attributed to Mr Wright in his capacity as a member of the Security Service, they did not prevent [*The Observer* and *The Guardian*] from pursuing their campaign for an independent inquiry into the operation of that service ... Moreover, they contained provisos excluding certain material from their scope, notably that which had been previously published ...[74]

The second period presented a different situation. *Spycatcher* had been published in the United States in July, 1987. The book was available in other countries, and the United Kingdom did not attempt to stop importation. The confidentiality of the information had been destroyed. The government still claimed a legitimate aim.

> [T]he purpose of the injunctions had ... become confined to the promotion of the efficiency and reputation of the Security Service, notably by: preserving confidence in that Service on the part of third parties; making it clear that the unauthorised publication of memoirs by its former members would not be countenanced; and deterring others who might be tempted to follow in Mr Wright's footsteps.[75]

The Court saw that aim as insufficient to justify the continued injunctions, particularly given the actions already taken against Mr. Wright himself and the availability of an action against him to account for profits.

The *Sunday Times* case also went to the European Court of Human Rights. *The Sunday Times v. The United Kingdom (No. 2)*[76] also found the continuation of the injunctions past the date of publication in the United States to be a violation of Article 10. Here too, with confidentiality destroyed and no continuing threat to national security, the metamorphosis of purpose to the efficiency and reputation of the service was insufficient.

The *Sunday Times* also filed a European action claiming that the contempt charges that it faced for its publication of the initial excerpts violated its rights under Article 10. That claim was rejected by the European Commission on Human Rights in *Times Newspapers v. United Kingdom*.[77] The publication of the excerpts had occurred two days prior to publication of the book in the United States, so confidentiality had not

[74] *Id.* at ¶ 64. [75] *Id.* at ¶ 69. [76] App. No. 13166/87, 14 Eur. H.R. Rep. 229 (1991).
[77] App. No. 18897/91, 15 Eur. H.R. Rep. CD 49 (1993).

then been destroyed. The Commission said that the contempt citation was aimed at the permissible goal of protecting the authority of the judiciary and the rights of parties. The Commission also found the contempt to be proportionate, noting that there was no prior restraint and that contempt liability was a minor penalty.

After discussing the *Spycatcher* cases, Professor Barendt summarizes the view of the European Court with regard to injunctions. "While it held that prior restraints were not as such incompatible with the Convention, it added that 'the dangers inherent in prior restraints are such that they call for the most careful scrutiny on the part of the Court.'"[78] That might seem similar to the position expressed by the United States Supreme Court, but given the analyses in the cases in the two courts, it would seem that an injunction might be more likely to stand up in the European Court.

Other Jurisdictions

There is also a case arising in the Netherlands that was heard by the European Court of Human Rights. *Vereniging Weekblad Bluf! v. The Netherlands*[79] grew out of the publication of a confidential report by the internal security service, the BVD. The first print run was seized before it was released, but a second run was released and distributed, until an order was issued withdrawing it from circulation. The report showed the BVD's interest in the Communist Party and the anti-nuclear movement and discussed the Arab League and the Polish, Czechoslovakian and Romanian security services. The director of the BVD said that, while none of the individual statements contained any information that was still a state secret, taken together they could present a picture of the sort of information generally available to the security service.

The law of the Netherlands allowed for the withdrawal from circulation of materials the unsupervised possession of which was contrary to law or public interest.[80] There was also a criminal law provision:

> Anyone who deliberately communicates or puts at the disposal of a person or organisation not authorised to have knowledge of it any information whose secrecy is necessary in the interests of the State or its allies, or any item from which it is possible to extract such information, shall, if he knows or should reasonably suspect that the information is of this kind, be liable to imprisonment for a period not exceeding six years or a fine ...[81]

[78] Eric Barendt, *supra* note 39, at 141. [79] App. No. 16616/90, 20 Eur. H.R. Rep. 189 (1995).
[80] *See id.* at ¶ 20. [81] *Id.* (quoting the Criminal Code of the Netherlands).

In the government's view the information fit that category, and its withdrawal and seizure were authorized.

The European Court found the two interferences, seizure and withdrawal, to be prescribed by law. The Court also accepted that "the proper functioning of a democratic society based on the rule of law may call for institutions like the BVD which, in order to be effective, must operate in secret ..."[82] The interferences were aimed at this protection of national security and were legitimate under Article 10(2).

When it came to necessity in a democratic society, the Court's analysis had some similarity to that of the United States Supreme Court in *The Pentagon Papers* case. As in the United States case, the European Court noted that the information involved was old. The document itself was six years old. The Court questioned the importance of the information and noted that marking the report "Confidential" indicated only a low degree of secrecy. The Court did not consider whether the initial seizure would have been considered necessary but concentrated on the withdrawal of the second press run. At the time of the withdrawal, the information had been widely circulated. The protection of the information was no longer justified, since it was no longer a state secret. The withdrawal order was, thus, a violation of Article 10.

There is also a European Court case out of Switzerland that raised an interesting mix of issues. *Monnat v. Switzerland*[83] was a case brought by a journalist for the Swiss Radio and Television Company. He was responsible for a current affairs program in which he reported on the history of Switzerland in World War II, suggesting an affinity between Swiss leaders and the far right, money laundering for the Nazis and the involvement of the banking and insurance industry in the retention of unclaimed Jewish assets. When the program was aired, there were a number of complaints to the Independent Complaints Authority. The Radio and Television Company, in response, said that it had put an embargo on the program, so that copies would not be available.

When the case went to the European Court, the Court said that if the applicant had intended to complain about the supervision of broadcasting under the Federal Radio and Television Act, that complaint was inappropriate. But the embargo placed on copies of the program was another matter. With regard to that issue, the Court found a legitimate aim in "protect[ing] the right of viewers to receive objective and transparent information."[84] The Company's requirement that one-sided presentations be plainly labeled as subjective served that purpose.

82 *Id.* at ¶ 35. 83 App. No. 73604/01, 51 Eur. H.R. Rep. 34 (2010). 84 *Id.* at ¶ 41.

Here too, the difficulty was over whether the embargo was necessary in a democratic society and, particularly, whether the embargo was proportional to the interests. In that regard, the Court noted the political nature of the material presented and the public concern over the issue. It also noted that the criticism was directed not at the Swiss people but at Swiss leaders during the war, and there is a lesser margin of appreciation for governments in limiting political criticism. The Court concluded, with regard to the Article 10 complaint:

> [T]he Court considers that, having regard in particular to the interest of a democratic society in ensuring and maintaining freedom of expression, to the limited margin of appreciation regarding information of public concern, to the fact that the criticism in the instant case concerned the actions of senior government officials and politicians, and to the serious nature of the report in question and the research on which it was based, the Swiss authorities' upholding of the complaints was not a measure that was reasonably proportionate to the legitimate aim pursued.[85]

Thus, the embargo in response to the complaint was a violation of Article 10.

FREEDOM OF INFORMATION

The material thus far discussed in this chapter has concerned government attempts to limit the dissemination of material that it sees as better kept secret. But that is only one side of the story with regard to the role of information in a participatory democracy. Judge Wilkinson, in his concurring opinion in *Morison*, stressed the importance of access and drew support from the views of James Madison. "Public debate ... is diminished without access to unfiltered facts. As James Madison put it in 1822: 'A popular Government, without popular information, or a means of acquiring it, is but a Prologue to a Farce or a Tragedy; or, perhaps both.'"[86] A country could be said to allow free expression, without having a Freedom of Information (FOI) law, as long as it does not, at least excessively, limit the publication of information that a newspaper may come to possess. Yet, there would be less expression without access to information. Since, while important, the issue is somewhat tangential to the subject matter of this work, it will only be discussed very briefly.[87]

[85] *Id.* at ¶ 71. [86] *Morison*, 844 F.2d at 1081 (Wilkinson, J., concurring).

[87] For more insight on the freedom of information, in a comparative context, see John M. Ackerman & Irma E. Sandoval-Ballesteros, *The Global Explosion of Freedom of Information Laws*, 58 ADMIN. L. REV. 85 (2006); Katharine Larsen & Julia C. Atcherley, *Freedom of Expression Based Restrictions on the Prosecution of Journalists under State Secrets Laws: A Comparative Analysis*, 5 J. INT'L MEDIA & ENT. L. 49, 51–57 (2013–2014).

In addition to the policy argument regarding the importance of freedom of information or FOI laws, evidence of growth in democratic countries and in other countries presumably striving toward democracy indicates a recognition of that importance. FOI acts are not a new phenomenon. The earliest dates to Sweden in 1766, but the period of greatest growth is in the latter part of the twentieth century into the twenty-first century.[88] A 2006 article counts sixty-six nations with FOI acts.[89] Another article, published six years later in 2012 finds the number to have grown to ninety-three.[90]

While some of this growth might be seen naturally to follow the integration of Eastern European countries into the democratic world, it has also been suggested that FOI laws have become more necessary with the development of the administrative state.

> With the rise of the administrative state, the link between freedom of expression, citizen participation in government, and freedom of access to government information becomes more important. Citizens can only be considered to be fully informed and able to participate as democratic citizens if they are able to access the information held about them and on their behalf by the government. In the age of the administrative state, expression and participation become meaningless if the polity is ignorant of the internal workings of government.[91]

The work of bureaucrats is, perhaps, less likely to come to light, without legal provisions allowing citizens to demand access.

While there now seems to be a general recognition of the importance of FOI laws, there is a good bit of variation among those laws. They vary as to what is covered, what exemptions to disclosure exist, who makes the final determination when a governmental entity refuses to disclose, and how cumbersome and expensive access proves to be. It is the examination of those differences that is beyond the scope of this work.[92]

88 *See* Ackerman & Sandoval-Ballesteros, *supra* note 87, at 96–98.

89 *Id.*

90 *See* Larsen & Atcherley, *supra* note 87, at 53.

91 Ackerman & Sandoval-Ballesteros, *supra* note 87, at 93.

92 For a fairly detailed examination, *see id.*

15

A Matter of Choices

When someone complains about some form of offensive expression such as hate speech or cartoons of the Prophet Mohammed, the response may well be: "That's what free speech is all about." But the lesson of this volume should be that it is less than clear just what free speech is all about. Different countries, all of them democracies, take a variety of approaches to any number of issues involving expression.

It is true that a country with fewer restrictions on expression may be seen as having more free expression than a more restrictive country. A country that allows unrestricted hate speech or unrestricted campaign contributions may be seen as more free in terms of expression. Much the same could be said with regard to liberty. A country that allows free access to marijuana, commercial sex, and physician-assisted suicide may be seen as having more liberty than a country that restricts these activities. But the more restrictive country should not be seen as lacking liberty, just as the country that limits some forms of speech should not necessarily be seen as lacking free expression. In both areas, there are additional interests to be balanced against liberty or expression.

Some justices of the United States Supreme Court, when willing to look beyond only history and tradition, have analyzed the nature of liberty. Justice Harlan, in his concurring opinion in *Griswold v. Connecticut*, said that the Due Process Clause of the Fourteenth Amendment protected whatever was "inherent in the concept of ordered liberty."[1] Much earlier, Justice Washington considered the privileges and immunities of citizens of the United States. He said that the privileges and immunities were rights that were "in their nature, fundamental; which belong of right to the citizens of all free governments."[2]

[1] 381 U.S. 479, 500 (1965)(Harlan, J., concurring in the judgment).
[2] Corfield v. Coryell, 6 F.Cas. 546, 562 (C.C.E.D. Pa 1825).

Perhaps the best way to analyze what is inherent in the concept of ordered liberty or what constitutes the body of liberties to be found in all countries deserving to be called free is an examination of just what occurs in those countries. The Court has looked to other countries in its analysis of liberty. In *Lawrence v. Texas*, striking down Texas's homosexual sodomy statute, the majority looked to the conclusions of a United Kingdom Parliamentary commission and to a decision by the European Court of Human Rights.[3] In another area, that of the juvenile death penalty, the Court also looked to other free countries in disallowing such executions.[4] While this is slender authority for any conclusion that guidance is to be drawn from other free countries, it may be a start in that direction.

Just as an examination of other free countries may help in determining what constitutes core liberties, an examination of the treatment of expression in other democratic countries may provide guidance in terms of how much freedom of expression is essential. That examination shows clearly that restrictions that would not be allowed in the United States can be imposed, without a country devolving into a totalitarian, or even not fully democratic, country.

The result of this analysis shows that there are a number of choices a country may make with regard to expression. Commonly, a country's legislature makes one choice, and the country's courts, or in the case of European countries, the European Court of Human Rights, may make another. As has been seen, the free-speech provisions of a number of constitutions and of the European Convention, provide for balancing of free expression and other values. With that invitation, courts may be more willing to allow the legislative choice to stand, although certainly with some limits.

The United States Constitution does not invite such balancing, but there are still choices to be made. Here, too, the legislature makes a choice, and the choice is tested in the courts. United States courts may see themselves not as making their own conflicting choice but as, instead, enforcing the limits the Framers placed on attempts to limit expression. But there is more than deference to the Framers at work, and the strength of the First Amendment's protections of expression is largely due to the work of the United States Supreme Court.

It is true that there is the rather absolute sounding language of the First Amendment, providing that Congress shall make "no law" inhibiting the freedom of speech or the press, but that cannot be taken literally. It has never been seen to bar prosecution for the speech acts that may make up an ordinary

[3] 539 U.S. 558, 572–73 (2003). [4] *See* Roper v. Simmons, 543 U.S. 551, 575–77 (2005).

criminal conspiracy. The Supreme Court has also recognized exceptions to the protection of expression. On what would have to be recognized as shaky historical grounds, the Court, in *Roth v. United States*, concluded that obscene materials were unprotected.[5] In later cases, the Court recognized an exception for child pornography.[6] It still later allowed a conviction for pandering, as child pornography, material that did not involve children and would have been protected.[7] On the other hand, the Court has rejected exceptions for depictions of animal abuse,[8] the distribution of violent video games to children,[9] and lying about the receipt of military honors.[10]

History might have been able to provide an explanation for the decisions to deny or extend protection, but there is little evidence to be gleaned here. There is historical debate over exactly what the Framers meant by the free expression provisions of the First Amendment. But the historical debate justifies nothing as broad as the current dimensions of protection. On one side of the debate, there are arguments that the First Amendment was intended only to bar limits on publication, while allowing post-publication punishment.[11] On the other hand, it has been argued that the amendment was intended to go beyond allowing publication to include protection for speech that was critical of government abuse.[12]

There is certainly no historical evidence that the Framers had in mind the protection of hate speech, corporate contributions to campaigns, deliberate lies, or any of a number of other areas of harmful speech. In fact, in the case of children and expression, the protection seems inconsistent with the views of the Framers. Justice Thomas, in his dissent in *Entertainment Merchants Association v. Brown*, demonstrated that the decision of the majority to allow access by children to violent video games could not be squared with the views of the Framers.[13]

[5] 354 U.S. 476 (1957). The Court cited to statutes at the time of the framing that it took as indicating that not all speech was protected, *see id.* at 482 n.10, although none of them were directed at obscene materials. The Court also looked to cases and statutes in the era shortly after the First Amendment and found evidence that obscene materials or also unprotected, *see id.* at 483 n.13, although, here too, the evidence with regard to obscenity was weak.

[6] *See* Ferber v. New York, 458 U.S. 747 (1982).

[7] *See* United States v. Williams, 553 U.S. 285 (2008).

[8] *See* United States v. Stevens, 559 U.S. 460 (2010).

[9] *See* Entertainment Merchants Ass'n v. Brown, 131 S.Ct. 2729 (2011).

[10] *See* Alvarez v. United States, 132 S.Ct. 2537 (2012).

[11] *See* LEONARD W LEVY, EMERGENCE OF A FREE PRESS (1985).

[12] *See* Vincent Blasi, *The Checking Value in First Amendment Theory*, 2 AMER. BAR FOUND. RES. J. 521 (1977).

[13] 131 S.Ct. 2729, 2752–59 (2011)(Thomas, J., dissenting). *See also* Kevin W Saunders, *The Framers, Children and Free Expression*, 25 NOTRE DAME J. L., ETHICS & PUB. POL'Y 187 (2011).

While this indicates that choice is also at work in United States law, the conclusion should not be that the choices made by United States courts are wrong or unwise, even when in conflict with most of the rest of the democratic world. They are, however, choices. And, as the comparative analysis contained herein shows, other choices could have been made without damaging the democratic nature of the United States. Even given the necessity of free speech to democracy, there is room for disagreement as to the dimensions of the protection of expression. There is room for limits on expression, without destroying the democratic nature of a country.

Index